LONGMANS' LINGUISTICS LIBRARY

TOWARDS A SEMANTIC DESCRIPTION OF ENGLISH

Towards a Semantic Description of English

Geoffrey N. Leech

Senior Lecturer in English
University of Lancaster

LONGMANS

LONGMANS, GREEN AND CO LTD
London and Harlow
Associated companies, branches and representatives
throughout the world

© Longmans, Green and Co Ltd 1969
First published 1969

Made and printed in Great Britain by
William Clowes and Sons, Limited, London and Beccles

SBN 582 52401 6

Preface

Students of language have long been used to contemplating the feasibility of a comprehensive account of the grammar or phonology of a language; but that one should attempt to write a "semantics of English" in the same way as one might write a "grammar of English" has seemed a far-fetched dream. It is not surprising that semantics should lag behind other branches of linguistic study in this way, in view of the many theoretical issues which confront the investigator before he can devote himself to the actual task of describing meaning in a language such as English. Yet if such an aim were not even contemplated, the study of meaning would remain for ever fragmented and provisional. This is my justification for trying, in this present work, to bring that far-fetched dream, "a semantics of English", closer to reality, and for putting aside the cautionary wisdom of "Fools rush in . . ." in favour of the less prudent motto "Nothing venture, nothing gain".

Before a satisfactory attempt at a "semantics of English" can be made, each particular descriptive problem (such as that of the meaning of the present tense in English) must be integrated, in three separate ways, within a general plan of linguistic analysis. First of all, it must be related to a general semantic theory which specifies the method of analysis as one applicable equally to all problems of semantic description. Secondly, it must be related to other "semantic fields" within the same language, so that features of meaning may be generalised to the language as a whole. Thirdly, it must be related systematically to the relevant lexico-grammatical structures, so as to form part of an integrated total description of the language. Without these three requirements, any serious discussion of the superiority of one solution to another is premature.

Of the three, the last requirement has been least considered in this study. In general, I have related semantic and grammatical structures only informally, making no attempt to unite the present semantic description with any specific grammatical description of English. In this, however, my practice is no worse than that generally accepted in contemporary work on grammar, whereby investigators support a particular grammatical analysis on informal semantic grounds; for example, by pointing out that a sentence is ambiguous, or that two sentences have the same meaning. Ultimately, however, a more detailed and rigorous integration of semantic description with lexico-grammatical description is called for.

The other two requirements underlie the whole design of this book. The principle that semantic theory and semantic description cannot progress independently of one another is embodied in the division of the book into a theoretical part (Part 1, "An Outline of a Semantic Theory") and a descriptive part (Part 2, "On the Semantics of English"), in which the theory is applied. The artificiality of the separation of "semantic fields" within the same language is proclaimed in the many cross-references between Chapters 7–9 on "Time", "Place", and "Modality". These descriptive chapters are brought together not only by their partaking in the same general technique of analysis, but by their sharing of common features of meaning with a wide range of application in the English language.

Both the theoretical and the descriptive parts of the investigation are, unavoidably, compromises, in which it has been necessary to sacrifice, often drastically, the competing ideals of comprehensiveness, mathematical explicitness of formulation, and detail of treatment. Without such sacrifices, the synthesis aimed at could not have been attempted.

In its penultimate form, this book was submitted as a Ph D thesis to the University of London, and I am very grateful to my supervisor, Randolph Quirk, and to my external examiner, Ronald Waldron, for their sympathetic and helpful criticism. Part 1 had passed through many different versions in the preceding six years, and at every stage had benefited from the advice and criticism of colleagues and other experts. I particularly want to thank John Lyons for generously giving his time in reading and commenting abundantly on the final version, as well as on earlier versions. Michael Halliday and Roger Fowler have also earned my gratitude for detailed comments; others whose help has been much appreciated are Sidney Greenbaum and John Thompson. I am indebted to my fellow-teachers of English language at University College London for taking over my teaching responsibilities for a term's leave of absence in 1968: thanks to their kindness, I was able to finish this study much earlier than would otherwise have been possible. Finally, I would like to thank Peggy Drinkwater of Longmans for her publishing skill and her patience.

University College London   G N L
May, 1969

Contents

3 Formators   44

4 Some extensions of the theory   60

8 Place

9 Modality

Part 1
An outline of a semantic theory

Chapter 1

First principles

1.1 Preliminary remarks

It is salutary to begin a study in theoretical semantics, as Uriel Weinreich did in his memorandum to the Conference on Language Universals in 1961 (see Weinreich 1963, 115–16),[1] with a confession of "the state of our ignorance". Amongst Weinreich's complaints on the lack of knowledge of, and of enlightened inquiry into, the general semantic properties of language, were the following: "The most important works on semantics . . . are on the whole preoccupied with the one semiotic process of naming, *ie* with the use of designators in theoretical isolation; they pay relatively little attention to the combinatory semiotics of connected discourse. Linguistic facts are cited as anecdotal illustrations of this or that segment of the theory, but no attempt is made to sample a whole language representatively. . . . There exists a fatal abyss between semantic theory and semantic description . . . , an abyss which dooms the former to emptiness and the latter to atomization." Weinreich ended this pessimistic survey, before beginning a penetrating discussion of theoretical and descriptive issues, with a modest hope "that a critical discussion . . . may help to put certain questions into researchable form. Considering the state of semantic studies so far, even this would be a memorable achievement for our Conference."

Since 1961, in some measure at least, Weinreich's hope has been fulfilled, and questions have been put "into researchable form". Yet his complaint about the fragmentary nature of semantic knowledge, not surprisingly, remains valid. Theoretical questions still tend to be pursued in isolation from descriptive ends, and vice versa. The relation between lexical meanings and the meanings of whole sentences and discourses has only been tentatively explored. The ability of any theory to account for more than a selection of the semantic facts of natural languages has yet to be established.[2]

One of the positive achievements of recent work in semantics has been a movement towards agreement on what its aims are. Thus Katz and Fodor (1963), Lyons (1963), Lamb (1964a, 1964b, etc), and Weinreich (1963, 1966) all seem to be in agreement, implicitly or explicitly, that semantics has to explain "meaning" in the sense involved in such notions as "meaningfulness", "paraphrase", "antonymy", "definition", "negation", "implication"; and that it is feasible to separate this task from the study of "meaning" in the sense in which that term applies to stylistic effects, emotive associations, etc.[3] They are, in other words, interested in studying and describing natural languages at the level which has preoccupied philosophers in their construction and investigation of artificial languages.

The vast problems philosophers have foreseen in the explication of the logical-semantic structure of natural languages[4] should intensify the sense of ignorance felt by anyone who has seriously applied himself to this field of almost unimagined complexity, and should caution a reader not to expect too much from exploratory studies such as the present one. It must be clear, however, that the goals and methods of linguistics and of linguistic philosophy are not really comparable. Whereas the philosopher's overriding interest in language is that of discovering how it conveys or may be made to convey knowledge of the real world, the linguist approaches language as an object, not as a means of knowledge – ie as a part of the real world which it is his business to study. A language, so considered, is a social and psychological phenomenon: a capability shared by the members of a linguistic community. This difference of focus naturally leads to differences in the interpretation of basic concepts. A criterion of "meaningfulness", for a philosopher, will tend to revolve around the evaluation of sentences for truth and falsehood. For a linguist, on the other hand, "meaningfulness" must be dealt with by reference to what utterances make good sense, or fail to make good sense, to the people whose linguistic knowledge and behaviour he is studying.

In this investigation, I have drawn on the work of all the recent writers just mentioned, and on that of many others, as footnotes will make clear. It would be strange indeed if there were not many points of contact with previous treatments of the same subject matter. None the less, the approach I take is in many ways a fresh one. I hope it will be considered sufficient justification of this new approach that it (a) explains certain aspects of semantic competence which to my present knowledge have not been formulated within other semantic theories of natural language,[5] (b) gives satisfactory answers to a varied range of problems in the semantic description of English, as I have attempted to show here in both Part 1 and Part 2, and (c) goes some of the way towards providing a comprehensive "semantics" of a natural language. It would be premature to attempt to compare this with other models, except in a very impressionistic way, with respect to the simplicity of its explanations.

A semantic theory, in so far as it is completely general, claims to be unbiased towards the facts of particular languages. I have here concentrated on the problems of the English language only: nevertheless I hope that with a greater or lesser amount of modification, this approach will prove applicable to other languages.

1.2 What semantics is about

What kinds of fact does a semantic theory have to explain? This question, asked of a theory on any subject, provokes a self-evident reply, for there is no satisfactory way of charting in advance the territory which is the concern of a particular discipline.[6] The only recourse is to an informal statement, in ordinary, non-technical language. "The aim of semantics is to explain and describe meaning in natural languages." To make our starting-point in ordinary usage more explicit, we may even say that the goal of semantics is to explain what underlies the use of the word *means* and related terms (*sense, nonsense, signify, ambiguous, antonym, synonym,* etc) in English and other languages. The word *means* is by no means so hopelessly vague and confusing as some philosophers, linguists, and literary critics have sought to show.[7] Much of its assumed vagueness stems from its use not only for cognitive meaning, but for the factors of tone, attitude, emotion, etc, evoked by a particular form of language. The distinction between these senses is admittedly difficult to draw, as, indeed, are most of the demarcation lines in linguistics.[8] However, I shall now assume, and later (in §5.3) defend the assumption, that such a line can and ought to be drawn – otherwise most of the basic concepts of semantics are worthless.

For example, I shall use the term "synonymous" to mean "equivalent" as regards cognitive meaning only. The further requirement of equivalence as to context of use is so strong as to make the notion of synonymy virtually useless in linguistics. Yet this additional requirement has often been imposed in the past, leading to the triumphantly negative conclusion "there is no such thing as a synonym".[9] Similarly, I shall interpret "ambiguity" as referring to the condition of one formal item having more than one cognitive meaning.[10] If it was maintained that an expression had a "different meaning" for every difference in tone, evocative effect, etc, the notion of ambiguity would be as indeterminate as the notions of tone, evocative effect, etc, and no precise way of determining whether a formal item was ambiguous would be available.

1.3 Basic semantic concepts

With regard to the concepts of a theory two important questions arise: (a) whether they can be empirically justified, and (b) whether one or more of them can be considered more "basic" or "primitive" than the others. Question (a) seems more of a stumbling block in semantics than in any other field of study. The "abyss between semantic theory and semantic description" deplored by Weinreich (see §1.1) might indeed be attributed partly to the unfortunate inability of semanticists to take fundamentals for granted, as these, at least in the past thirty or forty years, have been continually under attack. Above all, the notions of cognitive synonymy and analytic truth have been challenged by linguistic philosophers, notably W. V. Quine,[11] although this challenge has not prevented other philosophers from considering them fundamental to serious logical study.[12] For reasons stated in §1.1 I do not consider objections to the philosophical use of concepts necessarily relevant to their use in linguistics. In fact, the concepts of synonymy and analyticity as employed in linguistic semantics are not directly vulnerable to Quine's criticisms: their validity as theoretical constructs is to be judged not on their individual relation to observables, but on their position within a total semantic theory, which in its turn is answerable to the evidence of empirical observation.[13] We shall return to this topic in §§1.4–8.

Question (b) above concerns possible relations of priority between the different concepts of the theory. Here it is instructive to examine the proposals of Katz and Fodor (1963: 172–81), whose assignment of priority to certain concepts forms a natural starting-point for discussion.[14] Katz and Fodor in fact delimit the domain of a semantic theory by the process not recommended at the start of this section – by staking out the territory in advance. They arrive at the subject of semantics by a method of elimination informally paraphrased below:

1 The aim of linguistics is to give an account of a person's mastery of his native tongue.

2 Semantics has to account for those aspects of this mastery not accounted for in grammar ("grammar" is used here in the sense current in earlier transformational literature:="syntax and phonology").

3 The following skills fall into the category mentioned in (2), and are therefore the concern of semantics:

[a] the ability to perceive ambiguities in sentences (apart from ambiguities explained by syntactical rules).

[b] the ability to detect semantic anomalies (*eg* in the sentence *The paint is silent*, which is nonsensical rather than ungrammatical).

[c] the ability to match sentences of like meaning: *ie* to recognise and produce paraphrases.

(This argument determines the "lower bound" of semantics; Katz and Fodor similarly apply logic to the determination of the "upper bound", a subject which will not concern us in detail until §§5.2–4.) They concede that a semantic theory, whilst accounting for the way in which people interpret sentences under headings [a] to [c], would also mark "every other semantic property or relation that plays a role in this ability" (p.176).

There is no point in commenting here on the disadvantages of this procedure of determining the boundaries of a subject negatively, by reference to external factors, especially that of characterising semantics as what is left over after grammatical analysis is exhausted. This position seems to have been superseded in the thinking of Katz and the transformational school generally, along with some other significant aspects of transformational theory as formulated up to the time of Katz and Fodor's article (see, for example, the quotations from Chomsky (1965: 159) at the opening of Chapter 5 below). The important thing to notice is that Katz and Fodor design their theory primarily for the explication of only three concepts: ambiguity, semantic deviance, and paraphrase. Other concepts, such as antonymy, implication, and analyticity are to be explained only incidentally, if they are to be explicated at all.[15] These three concepts are apparently crucial to Katz and Fodor because they view semantics simply as an "interpretative" component, having as its input phrase markers generated by syntactic rules, and as its output interpretations or readings assigned to these phrase markers. Ambiguity, literal meaninglessness, and paraphrase come into prominence in this interpretative conception of semantics, because they can be associated directly with particular output conditions: an ambiguity is associated with a multiple semantic output for a single phrase marker; an anomalous or meaningless sentence with a null output; and paraphrase with the condition of more than one sentence having identical outputs.[16] As Katz and Fodor's interpretative view of semantics is not going to be adopted here (see §2.6), we need not, unless shown some independent reason, follow them in their assignment of priorities.

One semantic notion may be considered more "basic" than others on one of two separate grounds. It may enter into the definition of a second term, and thus be considered "formally prior". If *ambiguous* is defined as "having more than one meaning", then the notion of "meaning" formally precedes, *ie* is more primitive than, that of "ambiguity". Secondly, it may be considered "empirically prior" in that it forms a link in the chain relating other theoretical concepts to observable evidence. The notion of "well-formedness" would be empirically prior to all others if the only kind of semantic evidence accepted consisted of judgements of well-formedness.

Although they do not discuss their proposal in these terms, it is clear that Katz and Fodor's three concepts are not formally basic: on the

contrary, their place in the theory presupposes the notion of a "reading"
or "interpretation", and this in turn is defined by reference to "dictionary entry", "projection rule", etc (pp. 181–96). On the other hand, it
is by no means clear that they are empirically fundamental. Why, for example, should it be easier to confirm the ambiguity of a particular sentence rather than (say) the fact that it implies, or is implied by, another
given sentence? It is tempting to conclude that the three aspects singled
out by Katz and Fodor are not particularly fundamental in any sense,
except in that they provide a convenient informal starting-point for their
theory, reflecting an *a priori* assumption about what is most important
in semantics. At least, there appears to be no positive reason why anyone
else should follow their priorities in constructing a semantic theory.

1.4 The empirical ground of semantics

The preceding rather negative argument has been necessary in order to
disassociate the present inquiry from Katz and Fodor's assumptions in
their article, which has been the most widely discussed of modern contributions to semantic literature. But we still have to attempt an answer
to the question "What theoretical categories are most basic?" The
matter of formal priority in the structure of the theory can be put on one
side, as it only arises at the sophisticated level of formalising a theory in
the most elegant and economical way – *ie* of deciding which statements
within the theory are to be axioms, and which are to be theorems de-
duced from the axioms. The question of empirical priority is, however,
important, because it is crucial to the justification of semantic analyses,
and hence to the grounds of argument to be employed in this book.

It has been common, in linguistics, to consider the nature of empirical
evidence in black-and-white terms. The choice has been presented between relying entirely on corpus evidence at one extreme, and relying
heavily, if not exclusively, on introspective evidence at the other.[17] In
this debate, not enough justice has been done to intermediate positions;
for example, one whereby the introspections of the linguist, as his own
informant, are accorded a provisional measure of evidential validity, but
are held answerable ultimately to more objective confirmation, provided
by corpus evidence and informant tests. The analyst's intuition, as the
source of the most readily available form of evidence, has of course a
validity *pro tem* if in any particular argument, linguists are agreed as to
the "facts" of the case. But before a descriptive statement can be applied
to whole speech communities, it must be referable to data beyond the
classroom; hence the significance of native informant tests, and the importance of devising tests which will reliably furnish the kind of information which can be used in support of or against a given semantic
description.

As work on such tests has so far been only sporadic, we cannot decide at this stage what aspects of semantic competence are most amenable to objective testing. Our present task is therefore to pick out those semantic concepts which seem more "fundamental" in that (a) they are matters on which people's intuitions tend to agree; and (b) they are likely to prove more easily testable. Among the notions I take to be more fundamental than others in this sense are IMPLICATION, PARAPHRASE, and MEANINGLESSNESS.[18]

The first two of these three concepts have been assumed elsewhere to be the most easily submissible to objective test.[19] Implication, a relation between two assertions, is reducible to judgements of truth value, in many respects the "safest" of all starting-points for semantic investigation. One assertion X implies another assertion Y within a given language L, if the speakers of L are agreed that if X is true, Y cannot be false.[20] Paraphrase, as a relation between the truth values of assertions, has been styled "cognitive synonymy", and may be defined in terms of implication: assertions X and Y are paraphrases of one another if X implies Y and vice versa. Yet it would be unwise to consider cognitive synonymy empirically less fundamental than implication simply because it is formally derivable from it. Paraphrase elicitation tests may prove more reliable or more convenient sources of data than implication tests.[21] We may also suppose that synonymy of assertions (understood as equivalence of truth value) is on the whole a more testable concept than synonymy of lexical items, understood in terms of designative equivalence. Whereas people might quarrel on whether *boy* "means the same as" *lad*, put in the appropriate frame of mind (*eg* that of a detective reconstructing the circumstances of a crime), they would most likely agree that the reports 'A boy came into the room at five past eight' and 'A lad came into the room at five past eight' were factually equivalent – *ie* that one of them could not be true whilst the other one was false.

The third concept, that of meaninglessness, corresponds partially to Katz and Fodor's semantic anomaly or deviation. But I shall apply the term "meaningless" not only to assertions like 'The paint is silent', but also to contradictions (necessarily false assertions) and to tautologies (necessarily true statements, which convey no information except about the language in which they are expressed).[22] The notion of meaninglessness is parallel to that of ungrammaticality. Meaningless utterances are not meaningless to varying degrees, however,[23] but rather in different ways – being variously classifiable as tautologies, contradictions, etc. Tautologies are not absurd in the same sense as contradictions. Indeed, in contexts of metalinguistic discussion and instruction they are often perfectly acceptable. It is therefore advisable to make a terminological distinction between meaningless utterances (which include both tautologies and contradictions) and absurd or nonsensical utterances (which include contradictions, but exclude communicatively vacuous utterances such as tautologies).

The complaint may be made that in concentrating on the negative aspect of the meaningful/meaningless dichotomy, I am committing myself to talking about far-fetched linguistic examples which one would be unlikely to hear uttered; and that I am thereby avoiding discussion of the everyday English language. Such a charge, familiar in theoretical linguistics, is one to which a semanticist is particularly vulnerable, since it is so frequently convenient for him to describe a language by appeal to the evidence of what it does not, rather than what it does permit. In justification of this approach, I plead firstly that people's reactions to deviant utterances are generally more dramatic and linguistically relevant than their reactions to normal ones; and secondly, that our purpose, in so far as it is to define the set of meaningful utterances of a language, is best served by studying the boundaries of the set, since in this way we ensure that the definition is neither too limited nor too extensive. No suggestion is intended that utterances allowed by the theory to be "meaningful" are necessarily either readily acceptable or of frequent occurrence (see §§1.6–8).

I have introduced the three basic notions of implication, paraphrase, and meaninglessness, with reference only to assertions, with which this study will be mainly concerned. All the same, it is easy enough to see how they can be extended also to questions, commands, and exclamations. The paraphrase relation, conceived as equivalence with respect to truth value, may be said to hold between two *yes/no* questions, for example, if their affirmations and denials are congnitively synonymous (see §4.1.3).

(Although no use will be made in this study of the results of informant tests, insistence on the empirical priority of certain concepts is not mere hair-splitting. One material result of adhering to this principle is that we restrict the claims of introspection to the elicitation of *particular* facts of *specified* kinds. This restriction seems to be implicit in the methodology of all linguists, even those who profess the all-sufficiency of the appeal to intuition. Thus if a linguistically trained speaker of English claimed "My intuition tells me that every sentence in English has an indirect object", we might take it upon ourselves to argue him out of his "intuition", which could be better described as an analytic or scientific insight (however bad) into the structure of his own language. If, on the other hand, he claimed "My intuition tells me that *Everybody knows their own minds* is ungrammatical", we would most likely accept this statement as irrefutable, since not to do so would be to challenge the speaker's ability to act as an informant. An indiscriminate appeal to intuition creates confusion between different planes of abstraction at which people make observations about language, and does not clearly indicate where the operational knowledge of the linguist *qua* native speaker gives way to the analytic knowledge of the linguist *qua* scientist.[24])

1.5 Basic statements

Since implication, paraphrase, and meaninglessness are considered empirically fundamental notions for the purpose of this study, we may define a class of BASIC STATEMENTS as particular statements formed with a vocabulary of predicates consisting of "implies", "paraphrases", "is meaningless", and other predicates which entail "is meaningless" (*eg* "is a tautology"). Any statement in this class (*ie* statements of the general form "X implies Y", "X paraphrases Y", "X is a tautology", etc) will be taken on trust as requiring no confirmation, as the assumed basis of common agreement between writer and reader. Generally, however, a statement of one form can be used in support of another. If the statement

'John is an abbot' implies 'John is a man'

is accepted, this should guarantee also the acceptance of

'If John is an abbot, John is a man' is a tautology

and

'John, who is an abbot, is not a man' is a contradiction.

In other words, any semantic description of English would have to show that these statements, and any trio of statements following a similar pattern, are either all true or all false. But there is no evident reason why the truth of one type of basic statement should be easier to determine than that of another. We consider them to be mutually corroborating.

A semantic description may be provisionally characterised as a system of statements and rules (augmented by the ordinary laws of logic) from which it is possible to deduce a set of basic statements (defined as above) whose validity is not questioned.[25] I need scarcely add that the aim of this study is not to construct such a description of English, but merely to sketch the general lines on which one may be constructed.

In accepting, within the framework of this study, intuitive evidence as requiring no further support, I am merely following widely accepted practice in present-day linguistics. It must be stressed, however, that introspection is considered here to have limited validity, and to require ultimate objective confirmation through informant tests. To anyone who disagrees with the facts of English to be presented here, I can only reply "Then we must agree to disagree."

A more deep-rooted objection would come from someone who rejects not so much the actual basic statements, as the empirical meaningfulness of the predicates "implies", "is a tautology", etc they contain. A brief attempt to answer this objection follows.

1.6 Competence and performance

An important assumption in Katz and Fodor's approach, and one which we follow here, is that a person's linguistic COMPETENCE, or general underlying knowledge of his language, is the subject of semantic study, and not his linguistic PERFORMANCE – *ie* the particular detail of how he uses or interprets this or that sentence in a given context.[26] As an illustration of the importance of this distinction, we might take the utterance *That girl is a boy*, said in reply to a person who had mistaken the sex of a baby. This sentence, which expresses a contradiction, belongs to a class of facetious stock responses which point out a wrong assumption on the part of the addressee: *The undergraduate you were talking to is a lecturer, actually; Didn't you know those wallflowers are geraniums?* etc. The effective message in all these cases is: 'What you referred to as an "*x*" is in reality a *y*.' Anyone interested in studying language as a communicative medium has firstly to explain the fact that such sentences are nonsensical on a literal plane of interpretation, and secondly to explain how they are nevertheless construed, in practice, with no difficulty at all. The former of these explanations is a matter of competence, and the latter of performance.

In reply to those who would like semantics to be purely a matter of performance, I would contend that the simplest way to explain uses and interpretative reactions in given contexts is by prior analysis in terms of competence. In the quoted instance, we are able to account for the jocularity of *That girl is a boy* (which scarcely any addressee would greet with a straight face) by pointing to its underlying absurdity. Such a remark can be ruled out from occurrence in contexts where facetiousness or the fanciful use of language is out of place. Furthermore, generalisations on the plane of competence link this sentence to others which are generally far less acceptable, because they fall outside the class of stock responses of which it is a member: *The girls who were boys stayed behind; She had six girls including three boys;* etc. In this I am merely emphasising at the semantic level the distinction Chomsky has drawn (1965: 11) between GRAMMATICALITY (a property belonging to competence) and ACCEPTABILITY (a property identified in performance). Identifying an assertion as a contradiction enables one to predict, with some accuracy, its communicative effect (bafflement, amusement, etc) in given situations. Contradictions as a class have very restricted acceptability, and in certain registers are completely unacceptable – *ie* do not occur at all except in error. Similarly, tautologies, although acceptable in metalinguistic discourse, occur vacuously in discourses on non-linguistic subjects, and are rare in everday language situations. Again, the very vacuousness of a tautology enables it to be used, like the contradiction, for special communicative purposes in certain contexts. For example, the appeal to self-evident truth in *Well, either you did it or you didn't* carries an ironic message of peevish impatience: "You are so evasive or stupid that I have to point out to you what cannot but be true." *I know what I know* conveys, by its lack of cognitive content, the speaker's intention to withhold what information he possesses.

1.7 Acceptability and meaningfulness

We see from the foregoing that acceptability and meaningfulness are distinct, but related concepts. Since informant tests will register what is acceptable rather than what is meaningful, their use in the checking of basic statements like "*X* is a tautology" would seem to depend on our ability to determine what factors intervene to make (a) certain meaningless utterances acceptable, and (b) certain meaningful utterances unacceptable, at least to the point where we know enough about these factors to stop them interfering with the confirmation of semantic analyses. As they are open to systematic study, the task of relating meaningfulness or grammaticality to acceptability should not be so difficult as Chomsky and others have assumed.[27]

Utterances which are meaningless but acceptable have already been exemplified. The opposite category – meaningful but unacceptable – includes innumerable assertions invariably false for factual rather than semantic reasons. Examples are 'Pigs can fly'; 'He sat on his own head'; 'They sentenced the driver to two hundred years in a holiday camp'. To demonstrate the ludicrous character of these sentences, one would give a lesson in zoology, anatomy, criminal law, etc, rather than point to inherent incompatibilities of meaning. However, their incongruity in actual discourse resembles that of contradictions, and evokes a similar response from the addressee. These can probably not, therefore, be distinguished from contradictions on grounds of acceptability.[28]

The problem is not confined to the distinction between contradictions and factual absurdities: it applies also to other basic predicates. The uncontradictable remark 'He didn't sit on his own head' is just as implausible in a narrative as a tautology like 'The hat on his head was being worn'. To an informant, 'He jumped from the fiftieth floor' may imply 'He committed suicide' as surely as it implies 'He jumped from a building', although only the latter inference could be brought within the scope of semantic rules. Here we confront the familiar philosophical problem of how to defend the division between analytic and synthetic-but-invariably-true statements; between factual and logical implication; and more generally, the problem of another dualism more easy to work with than to justify – that between meaning and reference (see Lyons, 1963: 51; 1968: 424–8). Looking at these categories in the light of the competence/performance dichotomy, we may say that the competence whereby we recognise them is different – in the one case, linguistic (semantic) knowledge, and in the other, general knowledge of the world – but in performance, the two may well be indistinguishable.

1.8 Analyticity/syntheticity and related distinctions

The common objection to the analytic/synthetic distinction is twofold: (a) it is without empirical foundation, and (b) it is consequently impossible to draw, except in an arbitrary manner.[29] To answer the first point, we make sure that the empirical requirement is not a particularly strong one. We do not demand that a group of informants should be able to distinguish uniformly between analytic and synthetic assertions. Rather we claim that (a) it is possible to identify, on grounds of performance, a set of assertions (let us call them "informatively vacuous") including both 'This pig can't fly' and 'This pig is an animal', and (b) that the set of tautologies derived from a semantic description is a subset of this. In other words, we predict performance from competence, not competence from performance. The semantic description is challenged by the discovery of a tautology which is not informatively vacuous, but not by a synthetic assertion which *is* informatively vacuous. Interpreted in this way, the analytic/synthetic distinction becomes the limit of a theory's accountability: synthetically necessary truths are defined simply as those which it is beyond the semantic theory's power to explain.

The second difficulty, that of deciding whether a given assertion is analytic or synthetic, has not been answered, but has been reformulated in a clearer way: it is the problem of deciding whether the scope of a theory should be extended to explain a certain observation or not. The same problem arises also for contradiction, implication, and paraphrase. This decision can be made only by standards internal to the theory: I shall later (in §5.3) put forward a strategy (though not a formal criterion) for making it.

There is a latent inconsistency in the preceding discussion, in that I have on the one hand treated "X is a tautology" as a basic statement requiring, for the purposes of argument, no confirmation; and have on the other hand admitted the lack of means to determine whether an informatively vacuous assertion is tautologous (analytic) or simply factually uncontradictable. How can the class of tautologies be considered at the same time indeterminable and determined beyond controversy? The way out of this contradiction is to modify our previous position as follows. Basic statements are not in themselves regarded as incontrovertible, but as implying statements (about performance) which are incontrovertible. "X is a tautology", for instance, implies the statement that X is informatively vacuous, which is taken to be directly referable to observations. This means that it is possible to quarrel over whether an assertion is analytic or synthetic without bringing into question the empirical correctness of the description. A basic statement "X is a tautology" can only be challenged by a statement "X is synthetic", and the reply to this challenge is "In that case, X does not fall into the category of meaningless assertions, and can be ignored by our description." This dispute, and the disputes over similar distinctions, are thus rendered innocuous, although all other things considered one would like a description to account for as many observations as possible.

To avoid falling into other inconsistencies of this kind, it is best to revise our terminology (so far used somewhat loosely) in such a way as to make it clear whether the class of utterances or utterance pairs denoted by a certain term is identified in competence or performance. In each case the "competence class" is a subclass of the "performance class", so it is also useful to have a term for the complementary subclass, which is considered beyond the scope of semantic description. For this purpose, the epithet "factual" will be used in contrast to "logical". It will help to tabulate the various categories, with examples intended to reflect people's usual judgements of the distinctions involved:

1 UNCONTRADICTABLE ASSERTIONS
    [a] LOGICALLY UNCONTRADICTABLE (TAUTOLOGIES):
       'I like what I like.'
    [b] FACTUALLY UNCONTRADICTABLE:
       'Tomatoes are red when ripe.'
    [c] (Borderline case: 'Everyone is born before he dies.')

2 NONSENSICAL ASSERTIONS
    [a] LOGICALLY NONSENSICAL (CONTRADICTIONS):
       'That boy is a girl.'
    [b] FACTUALLY NONSENSICAL:
       'A friend of mine has just eaten the British Museum.'
    [c] (Borderline case: 'He climbed up the surface of the lake.')

3 IMPLICATION
    [a] LOGICAL IMPLICATION:
       'She has at least three sons' implies 'She has at least three children'.
    [b] FACTUAL IMPLICATION:
       'John can play the violin' implies 'John is human'.
    [c] (Borderline case: 'He committed bigamy' implies 'He committed a crime'.)

4 PARAPHRASE

[a] LOGICAL SYNONYMY:
'Henry is married to Pam' is a paraphrase of 'Pam is married to Henry'.

[b] FACTUAL SYNONYMY:
'Human beings are often irrational' is a paraphrase of 'Featherless bipeds are often irrational'.

[c] (Borderline case: 'Jane is my friend' is a paraphrase of 'I am Jane's friend'.)

Impressionistically, the difference between [a] and [b] under each heading is that in case [a] membership of the general category is determined simply by the meanings of the component parts of the assertion, whereas in case [b] it is determined by reference to our knowledge of the world. It seems impossible to deny the law exemplified in case [b] in the factual universe, but not impossible within some fictitious universe of the imagination. Freaks or miracles or future developments might make assertions like 'Tomatoes are red when ripe' contestable. 'A friend of mine has eaten the British Museum' would be credible in a conversation between monsters, and so on. On the other hand, the falsity of 'That boy is a girl' cannot be challenged unless the meaning of *boy* or *girl* is altered in such a way to abolish the incompatibility of meaning between these two words.

The difference between "logical law" and "natural law" in these examples relates them to the philosophical distinction between meaning and reference. What is at issue is whether a particular property is essential to the meaning of an expression, or is merely a non-criterial or "accidental" concomitant of what it refers to. Returning to the examples under the heading "3 IMPLICATION" above, we note that 'She has at least three sons' implies 'She has at least three children' because a definition of *son* has to include the feature 'child' (in the sense in which 'child' is converse of 'parent'). But it is intuitively difficult to accept that the definition of 'able to play the violin' has to involve a feature 'human'. The assignment of the "borderline" case to category [a] or [b] hinges on whether the notion of 'bigamy' in the expression *committed bigamy* is considered inseparable from the notion of 'crime' – or whether, for example, in some hypothetical society committing bigamy merely amounts to committing an indiscretion. The other "borderline" examples give rise to a similar dilemma. It is for cases like these, where individual intuition is not clear, that informant tests prove most useful.

Not that I am recommending faith in impressionistic decisions in dealing with these problems. Rather, I repeat, my claim is that the seeming vagueness of these demarcation disputes can be reduced, within a linguistic framework, to the clearer and more practical question of determining (on internal grounds) the limits of what a semantic theory has to explain.

1.9 Summary

To prepare the ground for what is to follow, it has been necessary to discuss at some length (though hardly at sufficient length for a thorough justification) some questions of semantic metatheory. To clarify the position adopted, I shall briefly enumerate the most important points emerging from the chapter, emending terminology where appropriate in the light of §1.8.

[a] The *a priori* assignment of superior importance to certain semantic skills or concepts has been avoided, together with the determination of the boundaries of semantics by external criteria.

[b] Nevertheless certain concepts may be considered empirically prior to others, in that statements about them are more easily given empirical support.

[c] We therefore treat certain predicates as basic, and particular statements containing these predicates and no others are regarded as basic statements, which for the purpose of discussion are undisputed.

[d] Predicates taken to be "basic" in this sense are: (X) IS MEANING-LESS, (X) IS A TAUTOLOGY, (X) IS A CONTRADICTION (these last two entail the first), (X) LOGICALLY IMPLIES (Y), (X) IS LOGIC-ALLY SYNONYMOUS TO (Y). We do not preclude the addition of further basic predicates, *eg* ones referring to contradictory and vacuous questions ('Is your wife married?' etc).

[e] These basic predicates are selected provisionally only, as those apparently giving rise to the least disagreement and the fewest difficulties of confirmation. Ultimate choice of basic predicates must await further research on semantic performance. (It is plausible that "presupposition" (see §4.1.3) and "inconsistency" (see §2.8.3) should be placed in the "basic" category.)

[f] A semantic description of a language accounts for all basic statements asserted of that language, by reducing them as far as possible to general rule.

[g] The confirmation of a semantic description consists in the checking of basic statements against the observed facts of linguistic behaviour.

[h] However, this relationship between basic statements and observations is not direct, since the former belong to linguistic competence and the latter to linguistic performance.

[i] The distinction between competence and performance, or (to use older terminology) between langue and parole, is accepted as central to linguistic study, and leads to a natural incorporation into the meta-

theory of semantics of the philosophical distinctions between meaning and reference, analyticity and syntheticity, logical and factual implication, etc.

[j] Since linguistics is centrally concerned with the explanation of competence, semantics (as a branch of linguistics) is concerned with meaning rather than reference, analytic rather than synthetic truth, etc.

[k] The question of distinguishing between meaning and reference, analytic and synthetic truth, etc, becomes, in the context of linguistic semantics, the problem of determining a reasonable bound to the set of data a semantic description has to explain.

Chapter 2

The semantics of system and structure

2.1 System-and-structure theory

The words "system" and "structure", which are key technical terms in Halliday's article "Categories of the Theory of Grammar" (1961), may be used as familiar labels for the type of linguistics expounded in that article, and since developed in many studies by Halliday and others. These terms have become even more prominent in recent work on English grammar (Halliday, 1966, 1967–8; Huddleston *et al* 1968), in which grammatical description has been viewed (to oversimplify) as consisting of [a] a set of systems interrelated in networks and constituting the "deep grammar" of a language, [b] a set of structures constituting the "surface grammar", and [c] a set of realisation rules relating [a] to [b]. By a SYSTEM is understood a set of features in contrast with one another, so that the possession of one by a relevant linguistic unit precludes its possessing any of the others. By a grammatical STRUCTURE is understood an immediate constituent structure of the familiar kind: a set of constituents partially ordered by the one–many relation of rank-inclusion or "domination", such that the members of each subset of immediate constituents are linearly ordered in sequence. Grammatical systems are generally specified as having a finite number of terms or members (generally but not necessarily two); however, this limitation does not exist in semantics, where certain types of system (those described as "hierarchic" systems in §2.2) have an infinite number of terms. A further difference is that whilst selection from a grammatical system has to be made wherever the choice becomes available, in semantics such choices are normally optional.

To see the value of the concepts of system and structure for semantics, it is best to examine two methods of semantic analysis, that of systemic analysis and that of structural analysis, independently before considering their relation to one another.

2.2 Systemic analysis (componential analysis)

Systemic analysis in semantics is perhaps better introduced under the title COMPONENTIAL ANALYSIS by which it has been known in fruitful applications in the study of kinship systems, colour terminology, and other fairly restricted domains of meaning.[1] Componential analysis is founded on the notion of semantic contrast: expressions are assumed to contrast simultaneously on different dimensions of meaning, or (to use the present terminological preference) within different semantic systems. Components (or semantic features) are the factors, or contrastive elements, which it is necessary to posit in order to account for all significant meaning relations. In the example [A] below, the semantic relationships between prominent senses of nine English words are represented through three binary systems:[2]

$$[A]\ Systems \begin{cases} +\text{HUM 'human'} \\ -\text{HUM 'brute'} \\ \text{('animal')} \end{cases} \begin{cases} +\text{MALE 'male'} \\ -\text{MALE 'female'} \end{cases} \begin{cases} +\text{MAT 'mature'} \\ -\text{MAT 'immature'} \end{cases}$$

Semantic specifications (definitions) of words:

+HUM	*human, man*	+HUM +MAT	*adult, grown-up*
−HUM	*animal*	+HUM −MAT	*child*
+HUM +MALE +MAT	*man*	+HUM −MALE +MAT	*woman*
+HUM +MALE −MAT	*boy*	+HUM −MALE −MAT	*girl*

A convenient way to represent components on paper is to assign some distinctive sequence of capital letters to each system, and a different prefix to each term within the system. The sequence of letters representing the system may be chosen for mnemonic value. The prefixes + and − are generally used when the system has two terms; otherwise 1, 2, 3, etc.

A combination of components is represented simply by the conjoining or listing of their symbols, and it should be observed that the order in which the symbols are placed, in this notational system, is not significant: −MALE +HUM +MAT or +HUM +MAT −MALE would be alternative symbolisations for *woman*. (The words in single quotation marks in example [A] and elsewhere are merely explanatory labels for the purpose of presentation.)

This componential notation provides a simple characterisation of certain semantic relationships:[3]

[a] LOGICAL INCLUSION

   x logically includes *y* if all the components of *x* are also components of *y* (*eg* +HUM +MAT 'adult' logically includes +HUM +MALE +MAT 'man').

[b] LOGICAL EXCLUSION

   x logically excludes *y*, and vice versa, if *x* contains a component systemically contrasting with a component in *y* (*eg* +MAT and −MAT in +HUM +MALE +MAT 'man' and +HUM −MAT 'child').

[c] COMPONENTIAL SYNONYMY

Two expressions (see §2.6) are componentially synonymous if they have the same semantic representation (*eg: adult, grown-up:* +HUM +MAT.)

The relation of componential synonymy, like that of cognitive synonymy (equivalence of truth value) discussed in §1.4, is independent of variations of register, emotive association, etc. For example, *adult* is clearly a formal term and *grown-up* a colloquial one: this does not prevent us from regarding them as synonymous.

Much of the task of semantic description, in the view presented here, consists in devising a notation which will accurately and unambiguously reflect the semantic properties of any expression in the language. It is, then, a sufficient condition of semantic equivalence (synonymy) that two expressions are assigned the same notational specification. (Why this is not also a *necessary* condition of synonymy is explained in §4.3 and §4.4.) To show that an expression has a deviant or anomalous meaning, on the other hand, one has to show that its specification violates some rule which applies to all meaningful specifications. For example, the expression *male woman* is marked for a semantic oddity (oxymoron), on the grounds that the semantic specification of *male* (+MALE) logically excludes that of *woman* (+HUM −MALE +MAT). *Female woman* represents a different kind of irregularity (pleonasm): the meaning of *woman* (+HUM −MALE +MAT) logically *includes* that of *female* (−MALE).

The three systems introduced above belong to a class of systems called BINARY TAXONOMIC SYSTEMS. This is a particularly important class; however, to avoid any suggestion that it is the only type of system allowed by the theory, other types are exemplified in [B] below. The categories are mutually exclusive. (In these examples, note that the systems only represent the respect in which the words listed *contrast* in meaning. The *whole* meaning may be unstatable without reference to other systems.)

[B]

1 MULTIPLE TAXONOMIC SYSTEMS: 'bedroom'/'hall'/'kitchen'..., etc (a taxonomic system having more than two members).

2 POLAR SYSTEMS: 'rich'/'poor'; 'strong'/'weak'; etc. (Polar systems accept modifications of degree: '*quite* strong'; '*very* weak'; etc).

3 HIERARCHIC SYSTEMS: 'one'/'two'/'three'/...; 'inch'/'foot'/ 'yard'/...; etc (the terms of a hierarchy are systematically orderable, and can be likened to positions on a scale).

4 RELATIVE SYSTEMS: 'parent'/'child'; 'above'/'below'; etc (the terms of a relative system are roughly equivalent to logical "converses").

Systems need to be classified in this way because of differing logical implications; for example, hierarchic systems are distinguished by their relation to special classes of tautologies ('A yard is longer than a foot', 'Three is more than two', etc) and special classes of contradictions ('A yard is shorter than a foot', etc). Particular logical properties of polar and relative systems will be pointed out in §§2.8.2–3 and §§4.1.1–2.

2.3 Structural analysis

Now we turn to the second notion of semantic analysis, for which a partial model may be seen in the predicate calculus of formal logic. The basic element for this type of analysis may be entitled the PREDICATION – this being a cover term for assertions (propositions) and assertion-like units, such as questions and commands. Let us take as a prototype of the predication a formula $a \cdot r \cdot b$, which may be read "a bears (bore, bearing, etc) the relation r to b". It is significant that a large number of sentences in English and, presumably, in all languages, are matched with other sentences which, one may claim, express the same predication in a reverse order.[4]

Some examples are:

[a] *John hit Bill*   *Bill was hit by John*
[b] *The will benefits John*   *John benefits from the will*
[c] *His conduct shocked me*   *I was shocked at his conduct*
[d] *John is the parent of Bill*   *Bill is the child of John*
[e] *John is Bill's teacher*   *Bill is John's pupil*
[f] *John owns this house*   *This house belongs to John*
[g] *The bus is behind the car*   *The car is in front of the bus*
[h] *The money is inside this box*   *This box contains the money*
[i] *You left before I arrived*   *I arrived after you left*
[j] *John gave a book to Bill*   *Bill received a book from John*
[k] *John lent a book to Bill*   *Bill borrowed a book from John*
[l] *John sold a book to Bill*   *Bill bought a book from John*
[m] *John told the news to Bill*   *Bill heard the news from John*

Each sentence in this list, I take it, is synonymous with the sentence with which it is paired. Of course, there are differences of emphasis, but these do not involve differences of cognitive meaning. This perhaps is seen more convincingly if we conjoin one assertion with the negation of its fellow, thereby arriving at a contradiction: 'The bus is behind the car, but the car isn't in front of the bus'; 'The car is in front of the bus, but the bus isn't behind the car'.

The descriptive problem here is to explain the synonymy of each pair, whilst accounting for apparent semantic contrasts, such as that of 'is parent of' and 'is child of'. The solution is partly anticipated by the principle that identical meanings, wherever possible, should receive identical specifications. In paraphrase pair [g] above, for example, it is clear that 'is behind' and 'is in front of' contrast in meaning (in fact they are converses), and must therefore have different symbolisations, say r^1 and r^2. Using the symbols a and b respectively for 'the bus' and 'the car', we arrive at two specifications which, far from being the same, differ as to both the order and the identity of the symbols they contain: $a \cdot r^1 \cdot b$ and $b \cdot r^2 \cdot a$. To reconcile this with the requirement of identical specifications, two conventions of notation are adopted:

I The opposition exemplified by 'is behind' and 'is in front of' is indicated by different marks of directionality, conveniently by arrows, as in $\rightarrow r$ and $\leftarrow r$; I shall later (in §2.4) explain the obvious connection between this and the class of relative systems mentioned in §2.2.

II The difference between left-to-right and right-to-left order is not distinctive; *ie* formulae which are mirror-images of each other count as notational variants of the same specification.

According to convention (I), the formulae above are rewritten $a \cdot \rightarrow r \cdot b$ and $b \cdot \leftarrow r \cdot a$; and according to convention (II), these two formulae are regarded as equivalent. These two conventions formalise the insight that order of elements in semantic structure is independent of order in grammatical or phonological realisations (cf Lamb, 1964b: 70).[5]

The concept of structure elucidated here is of extreme simplicity: a predication (P) has three constituents, of which one, the medial element (M), separates two terminal elements (T). This, in terms of a tree diagram, is:

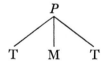

Two factors only have to be added to this rudimentary "tree" to give a complete account of semantic constituent structure: they are the principles of recursive embedding or rank-shift (§2.5.1) and of optional constituency (§4.2.1). Semantics is far simpler than grammar in this respect.

2.4 The marriage of systemic and structural analysis

The question now to be asked is: how are systemic analysis and structural analysis to be synthesised? It is evident that both are necessary parts of a total semantic theory.[6] It is also evident that systemic analysis applies to the constituent elements of a predication (T and M), rather than to the predication as a whole (P). If it applied to the predication as a whole, an assertion such as 'The woman loves the child', which makes perfectly good sense, would be marked as an absurdity, through the co-occurrence of the opposed components +MAT and −MAT ('mature' and 'immature') in 'woman' and 'child' respectively. On the other hand, there is no difficulty in seeing each of the meanings of the *woman, loves*, and *the child* (the logical constituents of this assertion) as specifiable in componential terms.

Hence we have a clear and elementary scheme for a semantics of system and structure, in which the two basic terms "component" and "predication" are brought together through the mediation of a third term, which will be called (following Weinreich, 1966: 38–9) the CLUS-TER.[7] The cluster is a "complex symbol" in Chomsky's sense (1965: 82); it is a constituent of a predication, consisting of a combination of components or semantic features, *eg* +HUM +MALE −MAT 'boy'. A predication consists of three constituents T, M, T (two terminal clusters separated by a medial cluster), and these in turn consist of a number of components (varying from nil upwards). But note that "consists of" is used in two different senses in the foregoing sentence: the constituents of a predication are ordered, whereas the components of a cluster are not.

The assertion 'The woman loves the child' can now be represented by a more complete specification, incorporating the componential "content" of each cluster:

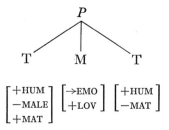

Even this is incomplete, giving no account of "logical words" like *the* and *is*, nor of factors like tense and number. It introduces two new systems, a relative and a polar system:

$(a) \cdot \rightarrow$ EMO $\cdot (b)$	'(a) has an emotional disposition towards (b)'
$(a) \cdot \leftarrow$ EMO $\cdot (b)$	'(b) has an emotional disposition towards (a)'
+LOV	'favourable emotional disposition'
−LOV	'unfavourable emotional disposition'

The first system, ⇄EMO, distinguishes between 'loves' and 'is loved by'; the other system ±LOV, distinguishes 'loves' from 'hates'.

The connection between relative systems and the medial element of every predication can now be elucidated. The relative system is the category of system carrying the directional contrast implied in the use of an arrow in $a \cdot {\rightarrow} r \cdot b$, etc. This connection is exactly expressed in the provision that *every medial cluster contains a relative component* (in the above case, ${\rightarrow}$EMO), and that the arrow of this relative component can be regarded as a property of the cluster as a whole, thus determining the order of elements in the predication. The other elements of the predication, the terminal clusters, contain no relative components (except indirectly, through downgrading, which is to be explained in §2.5.2).

At this stage, we have two notations for symbolising clusters. The symbols T and M are function symbols, denoting terminal and medial clusters respectively; the symbols in the formula $a \cdot r \cdot b$, on the other hand, are "content variables", denoting any arbitrary combination (not excluding the null combination) of features; *ie* any componential formula, whether or not this constitutes a total cluster. r, s, and t represent combinations including a relative component (*eg* ${\rightarrow}$EMO), whereas a, b, c, and d represent other combinations. An arrow is added to r, s, or t if the ordering of the elements needs to be specified, but is otherwise omitted. These variable symbols will from now on be preferred to the function symbols M and T, since all necessary functional information can in fact be inferred from them.

Observe that the same predication may still be represented in three distinct ways: (a) by a single variable symbol, an italic capital letter (P, X, Y, etc); (b) by "content" variables (*eg:* $a \cdot r \cdot b$); and (c) more specifically, in terms of components:

$$+\text{HUM} -\text{MALE} +\text{MAT} \cdot {\rightarrow}\text{EMO} +\text{LOV} \cdot +\text{HUM} -\text{MAT}$$

This formula is just as explicit as the previous tree specification of 'The woman loves the child', for every aspect of immediate constituent structure, even the factor of order, is predictable from the componential content. The formula above contrasts with $+\text{HUM} -\text{MALE} +\text{MAT} \cdot {\leftarrow}\text{EMO} +\text{LOV} \cdot +\text{HUM} -\text{MAT}$ ('the child loves the woman') in exactly the same way as $a \cdot {\rightarrow} r \cdot b$ contrasts with $a \cdot {\leftarrow} r \cdot b$. A dot, in both these kinds of formula, represents a boundary between clusters.

2.5 Rank-shift and downgrading

The structural apparatus outlined so far suffices for the semantic description of a finite number of extremely simple utterances. However, the only elaboration of this needed for even the most semantically complex of sentences is the introduction of two mechanisms, RANK-SHIFT and DOWNGRADING,[8] whereby a predication is assigned a subordinate role within another predication. In their consequences for the complexity of semantic structure, rank-shift and downgrading may be likened to the embedding principle of the phrase structure component of a transformational grammar (see Chomsky, 1957: 21–5), by which one sentence is given the status of a constituent within another.

2.5.1 *Rank-shift*

The term "rank-shift", familiar in systemic grammar (see Halliday, 1961: 251), applies to the circumstance of one unit containing as a constituent some other unit of higher or equal rank. On the maximally simple semantic rank-scale there are only two units: the "highest" unit (predication), and the "lowest" unit (cluster), which has no constituent structure. Rank-shift is therefore limited to the case of a predication which is a constituent of another predication. This is exemplified by the following (the rank-shifted portions are italicised):

> 'Observers were shocked at *the management's sacking of two hundred employees.*'
> 'I saw *him cross the street.*'
> '*Two peaches for sixpence* is good value.'

It is not difficult to see how these examples can be fitted to the following tree structure:

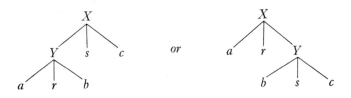

(Apart from the arbitrary choice of variable symbols, the alternative diagrams are mirror-images of each other, and are therefore equivalent.) In the linear representation of tree structure, rank-shifted predications are enclosed in round brackets; $(a \cdot r \cdot b) \cdot s \cdot c$ and $a \cdot r \cdot (b \cdot s \cdot c)$ are respectively linear versions of the above two diagrams. There is no defined limit of tolerance to the depth of constituent structure produced by rank-shifting one predication inside another.

2.5.2 *Downgrading*

"Downgrading" is the term I attach to the assignment of a component-like status to a predication. This component-like status is most clearly recognisable in predications expressed by a relative clause: in 'the woman whom I love', for example, it is clear that (a) 'whom I love' has the internal composition of a predication, and that (b) it has the external role of a single component, equivalent to 'good' in 'the good woman', etc. Slightly less obviously, downgrading occurs in the semantic specifications of lexical items and constructions such as the following, for which an expression containing or consisting of a relative clause is an obvious paraphrase: *blind* (*man*) ('that cannot see'); *forgivable* (*mistake*) ('that can be forgiven'); *meteorologist* ('person who studies the weather'); *a disgrace* ('something one ought to be ashamed of'); *dog-lover* ('person who loves dogs'); *brick wall* ('wall which is made of bricks'); *bachelor* ('man who has not yet married'). Downgrading might be informally described as the transfer of the predication from the sphere of structural analysis to that of systemic analysis.[9]

It is a general condition of downgrading that one of the terminal constituents of the downgraded predication should have a cross-referential function, which can be represented by the letter θ. This feature θ, expressed in the relative pronoun of a relative clause, must for the present be taken as an unexplained primitive, but its place in the theory (as the "definite formator") will be explained in §3.3.[10] In the notation, a downgraded predication will be enclosed in angle brackets, so that a general formula for a cluster containing one may be written $a \langle \theta\, b \cdot r \cdot c \rangle$. As left-to-right order is not significant in the writing of either componential or predicational formulae, it is mere convention (reinforced by the syntactical placing of the relative pronoun and relative clause in English) which causes the above symbolisation to be preferred to the equivalent ones $\langle \theta\, b \cdot r \cdot c \rangle\, a$; $\langle c \cdot r \cdot b\ \theta \rangle\, a$; $a \langle b\ \theta \cdot r \cdot c \rangle$; etc. Recall that the content variables *a*, *b*, etc, stand for any componential formula (*ie* set of components, not excluding the zero set) which does not include a relative component. At this stage, however, a broader definition of "componential formula" is required: this expression will be applied to any combination or set of DESIGNATIVES, where a designative is defined as either a component such as +HUM, −MALE, or a downgraded predication. In other words, a variable such as *a* can range over combinations of which downgraded predications such as $\langle \theta\, a \cdot r \cdot b \rangle$ are members.

Downgrading also occurs in medial clusters, where it is the key to the semantics of adverbial modification, tense, aspect, and modality. The pluperfect meaning of *had worked* for instance, might be represented $r \langle \theta\, a \cdot s \cdot b\ \langle \theta\, c \cdot t \cdot d \rangle \rangle$. A quasi-paraphrase which brings out the underlying semantic structure is: 'which happened before *b*, which happened before now.' As we see in this example, the principle of recursive depth is applicable to downgrading, as well as to rank-shift. These two types of subordination in different combinations largely account for both variety and complexity in semantic structure.

There is the theoretical possibility of a second type of downgrading: the downgrading of a cluster, instead of a predication. Although we shall have no cause to make use of this kind of downgrading in the rest of this study, it may well prove the best means of analysing clusters containing such modifying elements as 'good', 'very'; *ie* elements expressed by descriptive adjectives and adverbs of degree. An analysis of 'very high heels' on this pattern would be written $\langle\langle a\rangle\ b\rangle\ c$, where a ('very') is downgraded within the cluster containing b ('high'), which is in turn downgraded within the cluster containing c ('heels'). A possible motive for an analysis of this kind is provided by the ambiguity of 'dark yellow flower', noted by Weinreich (1963: 131).[11] On one reading, 'dark' modifies 'yellow', and on another reading, both 'dark' and 'yellow' are equally modifiers of 'flower'. These could be distinguished as $\langle\langle a\rangle\ b\rangle\ c$ and as $\langle ab\rangle\ c$ respectively. (Note here that ab stands for the union of a and b.) Further, in a later section (§2.8.2) we shall see that the terms of polar systems, generally expressed by adjectives such as 'good' and 'bad', do not conform to rules of logical inclusion when combined with other kinds of component in the same clusters, thus providing an exception to generalisations of componential analysis. This may be a good reason for analysing them as belonging to a cluster separate from that expressed by the following noun.

2.6 Autonomy of levels

It is now time to consider the relationship between semantics and the formal (grammatical and lexical) level of linguistic description.[12]

In the preceding section I have implicitly taken sides on an important question. Modern theoretical approaches to semantics can be divided into those in which semantic statements are made about units or elements identified in grammar (in the narrower and more traditional sense of "grammar"), and those in which semantic statements are made about semantic units specially set up for that purpose. The first approach is the more conventional one, and has been adopted by linguists working within transformational grammar. Since semantics according to this approach is dependent upon an input from another component of the theory, its role may be described as "interpretative".[13] The second approach has been adopted by Sydney Lamb (1964a, etc) and is indeed the natural one to adopt within a general theory dividing language into strata or levels. We may take it to be a fundamental principle of this approach that each level (phonology, form, orthography, semantics) is an autonomous subtheory in the sense that descriptive statements within the level make no reference to units or properties defined at other levels. The principle of AUTONOMY OF LEVELS, as it may be called, naturally presupposes, within the total theory, a component which specifies the interrelations between the separate levels: this will take the form of a set of grammatical-phonological, semantical-grammatical rules, etc. This principle must be distinguished from the principle of "separation of levels" common in structural linguistics of the 1950s.[14] There is no suggestion that the description at one level should be made without taking note of descriptive facts at other levels; indeed, one of the major considerations in evaluating alternative analyses is the relative simplicity of the level-to-level rules they call for. Therefore, although terms employed in grammatical description are not mentioned in semantic description, the analyst continually has to take account of what is known about other levels of analysis.

The maximal simplification, other things being equal, of level-to-level rules is the only motive which leads one to refer to one level in the course of constructing a description of another level. This relative compartmentalisation of different aspects of linguistic study is one practical advantage of working within a stratum-type theory. As my major task is to explain an approach to semantics, I shall not find it necessary to refer to given grammatical analyses of English. To take account of the factor of level-to-level simplicity, it will be sufficient to refer to the grammatical level in more general terms. Of course, there must eventually be a stage at which descriptions of different levels are synthesised, and then is the time for weighing up carefully the relative claims for simplicity of the components of the total description: *eg* for deciding whether the level-to-level rules should be made more complicated in order to effect an economy in the semantic level. But such a synthesis cannot be anticipated at this stage of inquiry.

It may well be asked what descriptive advantage, if any, has the "autonomy of levels" approach to semantics over the more traditional approach, in which statements of meaning are linked to grammatical units such as morpheme, word, and sentence.

First, it may be noted that by treating formal (*ie* grammatical and lexical) and semantic descriptions as logically independent, we have a means of characterising certain concepts important for semantics. SYNONYMY, whether logical or componential synonymy, is the condition by which one semantic description satisfies more than one formal item. AMBIGUITY, as traditionally understood, is the opposite condition of one formal item satisfying more than one semantic description.[15] The terms "polysemy" and "multiple meaning" are also used for this latter condition, but are generally applied to individual words or lexical items, rather than to whole sentences.

A second reason for preferring the autonomy principle can be appreciated only after a brief consideration of what is involved in the alternative form of theory. An interpretative semantics essentially consists of two components: a dictionary, which gives the meanings of individual morphemes (or lexemes), and a combinatorial component, which derives the meaning of a complex expression, and ultimately of a whole sentence, from the meanings of the morphemes of which it is composed.[16] One trouble with this approach is that every idiom constitutes a violation of combinatorial rules: unlike the meaning of *green paint*, that of *green fingers* (in its idiomatic sense) cannot be regularly derived from the meanings of its constituent parts. The whole phrase, it appears, has to be assigned a separate dictionary entry. This, however, is only part of the difficulty: many idioms, like *get away with, catch sight of, not cricket*, etc, do not correspond to any grammatical constituent, and many also are formally discontinuous, at least in surface grammar: *give . . . reason to, make amends to . . . for*, etc. It is obviously better, in dealing with numerous cases of this kind, to have a theory which does not tie semantic statements to particular grammatical units, or even to grammatical units at all.[17]

Thirdly, one difficulty which has been noted (Weinreich, 1963: 120, 125) in an interpretative approach is that many morphemes combine within themselves two very different semantic functions: the logical function of formators (see §3.1) found in words like *the, is, some, all, not*, and the referential function of designators – *ie* the kind of meaning expressed by most words of lexical content. For example, *come* and *go* express the designative meaning of 'motion', together with the formative meaning conveyed by *hither* and *thither* respectively. *Bring* and *take* are parallel examples; *never* combines the designative meaning 'time' with the formative meaning 'no' – and there are many more instances. This is clearly a matter in which it is inappropriate to regard the morpheme as the minimal unit of semantic statement, and for which indeed the notion of the morpheme as a meaning-bearing element is best replaced by the conception of two or more distinct meaning-bearing elements underlying a single morpheme.

Perhaps a more weighty reason for abandoning the interpretative model is that the two types of semantic analysis exemplified in §2.2 and §2.3 – systemic and structural analysis – are not directly relatable to any particular grammatical unit. Componential analysis is not restricted to morphemes or lexemes: the semantic contrast ±MALE between *man* and *woman, ram* and *ewe*, etc, is paralleled by that between the phrases *male frog* and *female frog*. Conversely, structural analysis is not restricted to sentences or clauses. Words such as *blind* (= 'that cannot see', *omniscient* (= 'who knows everything'), and *laudable* (= 'which ought to be praised') can be semantically equated with relative clauses, and taken to express a downgraded predication. The meaning of such words can clearly not be described in purely componential terms: how, otherwise, would we be able to explain the analyticity of the assertion expressed by a sentence like *Blind animals cannot see?* For both systemic and structural analysis, then, greater generalisation is obtained if semantic statements are not made in terms of grammatical units.

We are now better able to see why in semantic statements discussed in §1.4 (*eg* "*X* is a tautology"), the "*X*" in question is a semantically, not grammatically defined term: in the given case, an assertion (one class of predication) rather than a sentence (a grammatical unit).[18] We can also see the point of adhering to a convention, already surreptitiously established, of representing formally (*ie* lexico-grammatically) identified and semantically identified examples differently – the former by italics, and the latter by single quotation marks. This means that because of the interfering factors of synonymy and ambiguity, *my favourite dance* identifies a different linguistic abstraction from 'my favourite dance'. The latter represents only one of a number of possible meanings *my favourite dance* (*eg* 'my favourite kind of dance' or 'my favourite occasion for dancing' – whichever is determined, implicitly or overtly, by the context of discussion). Moreover, 'my favourite dance' is not distinct from 'the dance I like best', in that both represent a single meaning. Because of the unavoidable indeterminacy of the practice of identifying a meaning by one of its formal realisations, a citation within single quotation marks is best regarded as a rough and ready device of exposition: an approximate identification of something which can only be exactly represented in a special notation.

As there is only a partial correspondence between grammatical and semantic categories, it is convenient to use the neutral term EXPRESSION for any lexico-grammatically identified stretch of language whose exact grammatical constituency is irrelevant to the discussion.

2.7 Rules of expression

Since my intention is to avoid, as far as is reasonable, reference to other components of a total linguistic theory, I shall content myself with a very brief and speculative sketch of what the rules of expression or realisation linking semantic to formal (lexico-grammatical) description must be like. The function of these level-to-level rules may be thought of as that of associating a set of well-formed formal specifications with each well-formed semantic specification. If this "synonymic set" is empty, the semantic specification is said to be "blocked", and no formal expression of it within the language is possible.[19] At present, I see no reason why the association should not be made in the opposite direction: *ie* why rules of expression should not also be used to supply appropriate semantic interpretations for given formal specifications. No directional dependence is assumed between levels. However, for the limited purpose of the present discussion, it will be easier to adopt a "generative" role for the semantic level, and to regard semantic specifications as an input (not the total input, since grammatical and lexical choices are also conditioned by stylistic, thematic, and dialectal factors) to the formal level of analysis.

One set of expression rules (the "dictionary") pairs lexical items with semantic specifications which constitute their "definitions". The term "lexical item" applies here not only to individual lexical nouns, verbs, adjectives, etc, but to idiomatic expressions, which, as we observed in §2.6, cut across grammatical constituent boundaries. In general, however, the extent of a lexical item may be delimited semantically rather than grammatically, as not exceeding that of a cluster in an independent predication.[20] This means that any dictionary definition can be rendered as a "feature formula"; ie that componential analysis, augmented by formators (see Ch. 3) and by the apparatus of downgrading, is adequate for the statement of lexical meanings.

The precise form of grammatical expression rules has not been determined. It seems, however, that two types of rule in this class would be particularly prominent: one type would match semantic and grammatical features, and another would match semantic and grammatical segments.

Examples of FEATURE EXPRESSION RULES are those which match semantic features (whether components or downgraded predications) with such grammatical features as "countable" and "uncountable" (of nouns), "present" and "past" (of verbs), and "time", "place", "manner", etc (of adverbials). Only in a few limiting cases is this to be considered a matter of one-to-one correspondence.

SEGMENTAL EXPRESSION RULES map structural constituents (clusters or predications), or units which result from the addition and subtraction of such constituents, on to grammatical units; and more particularly, they establish relations between clusters and grammatical units of "group" rank (see Halliday, 1961: 253), ie noun phrases, verbal phrases, adverbial phrases, etc. The following rules of this kind are no more than first approximations; it must not be assumed that they are completely general in their application. For example, noun phrases containing *all*, *some*, and other quantifying words, are exceptions to the rule that a noun phrase expresses a single terminal cluster or rank-shifted predication (see §3.5). Nevertheless, a sufficient idea will be conveyed of the relation between semantics and grammar to provide a rough grammatical check on semantic analyses.

Semantic segment	*Matching grammatical segment*
1 Independent predication	Sentence
2 Terminal cluster	*a* Noun phrase
	b Adjectival phrase (see, however, modifications in §§4.2.1, 6.1)
3 Medial cluster	*a* Transitive or equative verbal phrase (+adverbial phrase(s)/ clause(s))
	b Preposition

Semantic segment	Matching grammatical segment
4 Medial cluster + terminal cluster	*a* Adverbial phrase/clause *b* "True" intransitive verb (see, however, §4.2.1)
5 Rank-shifted predication	*a* Noun clause *b* Gerund clause *c* Infinitival clause *d* Noun phrase "nominalisation"[21]
6 Downgraded predication	*a* Prepositional phrase *b* (In terminal clusters) defining relative clause *c* (In medial clusters) adverbial phrase/clause

As long as grammar and semantics are understood to have independent standards of well-formedness, many of the complications one might expect in rules of expression (on the analogy of transformational rules in generative grammar) can be avoided. For example, from the point of view of expression rules, the following utterances may be regarded as in free variation:

I realise that he is ill.
*I realise him to be ill.

The latter is ruled out solely on grammatical grounds; *ie* on the grounds that *realise* (unlike, for example, *believe*) does not belong to the class of verbs allowing complementation by an infinitival clause.

As the order of elements in a semantic specification is independent of left-to-right sequence, one of the tasks of the expression rules must be to determine the sequential relation of constituents in the correponding formal analysis. This can be done indirectly, by associating terminal clusters with grammatical functions (*eg* Subject, Complement, Prepositional Complement) whose sequential relation is eventually to be determined by grammatical realisation rules. Take the case of a predication $a \cdot \rightarrow r \cdot b$, which can be expressed either by *Bill owns this book* or *This book belongs to Bill*. If the lexical item *owns* is chosen, the terminal cluster *a* expressed by *Bill* has to be mapped onto the subject of *owns*, and *b* on to its object. If the item *belongs to* is selected, the relations are reversed, the *a* cluster this time being expressed by a prepositional complement.[22]

As a sentence generally corresponds in extent to an independent predication (*ie* a predication which is neither rank-shifted nor downgraded), the role of expression rules, for practical purposes, may be regarded as that of matching independent predications with sentences. (Perhaps in

2 + T.S.D.E.

this we see some justification for the traditional definition of a sentence as a piece of language "expressing a complete thought".)

It seems preferable to consider the rules of expression ordered so that a "dictionary search" precedes the segmental rules of grammatical expression; *ie* to let lexical choices determine some grammatical choices, rather than vice versa. This problem is evident in cases such as the choice between *She put up with his behaviour* and *She tolerated his behaviour*: according to whether *put up with* or *tolerate* is picked out by a dictionary search, the constituent structure, and hence the grammatical specification of the sentence, will vary. Or, to use a similar example, *continue* may be followed by an infinitive clause (*eg: to work*) whereas the synonymous verb *carry on* may not. In both cases, grammatical selections are implicated in the selection of a lexical item. The alternative of regarding lexical choices as conditional upon grammatical ones, apart from being instinctively wrong, would be extremely wasteful, because it would lead to the generation of a large number of grammatical representations for which no lexical items expressing the required meaning would be available. The kind of task required of a dictionary search would be "Find a lexical item which fits into the frame *He——ed the hedge* such that the meaning of the sentence is 'He looked through the hedge'." In far too many cases (perhaps the vast majority), the generation would be blocked by a failure to find a lexical item within the language meeting the required conditions.

It should be noted that in the dictionary search, a choice would be provided, where applicable, between an expression consisting of one or of more than one lexical item (*eg* between +HUM +MALE −MAT: *boy* and +HUM +MALE −MAT: *male child*); also between a single lexical item and a grammatical construction (*eg* between *blind* and *that cannot see*).

2.8 Semantic categories and relations

We now go on to examine what special categories and relations, apart from those applied in other levels of linguistic study, are required for a semantic theory. In the course of this discussion, the notions of analyticity, contradiction, and implication will be reintroduced, and their relationship to systemic and structural analysis explained. We shall thus have a means of following through the empirical consequences of systemic-structural descriptions, by seeing what basic statements (see §§1.5–1.9) can be derived from them.[23]

2.8.1 *Logical inclusion and exclusion*
The relations of logical inclusion and logical exclusion mentioned earlier (§2.2) can now be associated with a particular semantic unit, the cluster. Note that they can apply to a medial cluster *r* just as well as to a terminal

cluster *a*. For instance, it can be said that the medial cluster 'went' of 'John went home' logically includes 'crawled' in 'John crawled home', 'ran' in 'John ran home', 'went slowly' in 'John went slowly home', etc. This means that the set of designatives (components or downgraded predications) defining 'went' is a subset of the set defining 'crawled', etc. In a revised definition of logical inclusion, the term "component" must be replaced by that of "designative", so as to include predications downgraded to component status (§2.5.2).

Another point is that semantic components can in many cases be ordered hierarchically in dependence, such that a selection from one system is dependent upon a particular choice from another system. Thus the presence in a cluster of a member of the ±HUM ('human'/'brute') system presupposes the presence of the term +ANIM from the system ±ANIM ('animate'/'inanimate'), this selection in its turn being dependent on that of +CONC from ±CONC ('concrete'/'abstract'). This hierarchical ordering of systems and components has been most evident in the work of anthropological linguists on FOLK-TAXONOMIES (native classifications) of diseases, plants, etc.[24] The character of this classificatory aspect of linguistic organisation outside semantics has been thoroughly explored both within transformational grammar ("redundancy rules", Chomsky 1965: 168–70) and within system-and-structure grammar (Huddleston *et al*, 1968). Semantic redundancy rules have been proposed by Katz and Postal (1964: 16–18).

2.8.2 *Logical implication*

A general condition for the relation "logically implies" (which we shall henceforth abbreviate to "implies") is the following:

[C] An assertion $a \cdot r \cdot b$ implies an assertion $c \cdot r \cdot b$ if (the specifications being otherwise identical)
(i) *a* logically includes *c*.
(ii) the clusters *a* and *c* are construed as if universally quantified.[25]

Examples are:

'Children love apples' implies 'Boys love apples'.
'Men are mortal' implies 'Postmen are mortal'.
'I love fruit' implies 'I love apples'.

(The third example looks different from the first two in that it is the final part of each assertion that is different, instead of the initial part. However, since the convention of mirror-image notation set up in §2.3 still applies, the difference is only apparent: all three assertions satisfy the conditions named in the definition [C]. This increase in the generality of rules of implication and similar rules discussed in §§2.8.3–5 is an additional point in favour of the mirror-image convention.)

The second condition included in the definition needs explanation. It is well known that in English a noun X without a preceding article or determiner can be construed either as 'all X' (or perhaps 'X in general'), or as 'some X', although the circumstances which lead to one interpretation rather than another are not absolutely clear. Notice this contrast in the interpretation of *water* in *Give me water* against *Water consists of hydrogen and oxygen,* and of *children* in *Children ran down the street* as opposed to *He was fond of children.* A noun preceded by an indefinite article is similarly capable of dual interpretation as 'one/a certain X' or as 'any X'. For the above rule of implication, then, we stipulate that the nouns *children, men, apples,* etc, should be construed *all children,* etc. A proper investigation of this question of quantification, both implicit and explicit, must wait until §3.5.

The kind of implication defined above might be described as DEDUC-TIVE IMPLICATION, since it is a mode of inferring a more specific assertion from a more general one. There is, on the other hand, an INDUCTIVE type of implication, in which the reverse holds. To define it, we make slight, but extremely significant changes in definition [C], reversing the direction of the logical inclusion, and altering the quantification:

[D]
(i) a is logically included in c.
(ii) a and c are construed as if existentially quantified (*ie*: X is read as 'some X').

Examples of inductive implication are:

'John is eating peanuts' implies 'John is eating nuts'.
'Crowns are made of silver' implies 'Crowns are made of metal'.
'Boys ran down the street' implies 'Children ran down the street'.

Only the rule of inductive implication appears to apply if the elements which differ in the two assertions are medial, rather than terminal clusters:

'John is madly in love with Susan' implies 'John is in love with Susan'.
'Children ran down the street' implies 'Children went down the street'.

The rule of implication which accounts for cases such as these is this:

[E] An assertion $a \cdot r \cdot b$ implies an assertion $a \cdot s \cdot b$ if (the specifications being otherwise identical) r is logically included in s.

This and the preceding rules of implication have applied to assertions differing, if at all, in only one element. But we need merely add that implication is a *transitive* relation (*ie* that if X implies Y and Y implies Z, then X implies Z), to extend the definitions to innumerable cases so far unaccounted for. Hence to explain that 'Boys ran down the street' implies 'Children went down the street', we show that the former assertion implies (by rule [D]) 'Children ran down the street', which in turn (by rule [E]) implies the latter.

Further rules are needed to explain implication in cases where the implying and implied assertions contain rank-shift:

(i) 'I saw ten men hurriedly cross the street' implies 'I saw ten men cross the street'

(ii) 'Disrespect of old people by young people is unpardonable' implies 'Disrespect of old women by young men is unpardonable'.

The condition here is that (the assertions being otherwise identical) the rank-shifted predication in the former should imply that in the latter. (Example (i) illustrates inductive implication, and example (ii) deductive.) A similar condition is required to deal with examples containing downgrading:

'People who bet on horses are immoral' implies 'People who bet on piebald horses are immoral' (deductive implication).

'A man wearing a red waistcoat entered the room' implies 'a man in a waistcoat entered the room' (inductive implication).

Certain exceptions to the rules as so far stated cause us to reconsider the scope of the relations of implication and logical inclusion:

'Small animals need protection' does *not* imply 'Small elephants need protection'.[26]

'A tall four-year-old child lives next door' does *not* imply 'A tall person lives next door'.

'*Paradise Regained* is a short epic' does *not* imply '*Paradise Regained* is a short poem'.

If 'small' were deleted from both assertions in the first example, the relation of implication would hold. This would also be the result if 'tall' and 'short' were deleted from the second and third pairs of assertions respectively. The component which has to be deleted is a term of a polar system which is factually biased towards the object being described: *ie* it is a general factual truth that elephants are large, that four-year-old children are short, and that an epic poem is long. The attribution of the contrasting quality to these objects, however, does not result in an absurdity, because we understand it in a relative sense: 'a small elephant' = 'an elephant small for an elephant', etc. It is this relative aspect of the meaning of a polar system which causes the relation of implication to break down in such cases.

We have a choice between redefining implication so that it does not apply to *all* cases of logical inclusion, and redefining logical inclusion so as to exclude its application to a pair of clusters which both contain the same term of a polar system. The latter course is preferable, for as we shall see, it will enable us to use the relation of logical inclusion in other rules to which the same exceptions occur: for example, 'Elephants are animals' is a tautology, whereas 'Small elephants are small animals' is not.

It may be wondered whether the omission of all pairs containing the same term of a polar system is too severe a restriction on the relation of logical inclusion. Do we need to exclude from this relationship such pairs as 'large animals' and 'large elephants'; 'a beautiful epic' and 'a beautiful poem'? This might be avoided if we could classify 'Elephants are large animals' etc as analytic truths – *ie* if elephants could be made large "by definition". The trouble is, as we shall see in §5.3, that once having admitted such an assertion to the set of analytic truths, we should have to admit innumerable other assertions referring to other elephantine attributes; the componential definition of *elephant* would become of indefinite length, and the full determinacy of semantic statements would have to be abandoned. We must regretfully conclude that to save the whole conception of a systemic semantics, the size of elephants has to be considered a matter of factual, not linguistic knowledge.

2.8.3 *Logical inconsistency*[27]

In terms of truth value, the relation of (logical) inconsistency obtains between statements which cannot both be true at the same time. Its close connection with the relation of logical exclusion between clusters is very roughly parallel to that between implication and logical inclusion. The following is a general rule of inconsistency:

[F] $a \cdot r \cdot b$ is logically inconsistent with $a \cdot s \cdot b$ if (the assertions being otherwise identical)

(i) r and s logically exclude one another,

(ii) the difference between r and s does not include a difference of time reference.

Examples:

'I am taller than Peter' is inconsistent with 'Peter is taller than I'.

'I like parlour games' is inconsistent with 'I heartily detest parlour games'.

The second condition of rule [F] is necessary to account for the compatibility of pairs such as 'I am taller than Peter' and 'Peter used to be taller than I'.

To the above rule we add a supplementary rule as follows:

[G] If assertions X and Y are inconsistent and Y deductively implies Z, then X and Z are inconsistent.

This explains, for example, why:

'Men dislike women' is inconsistent with 'Men like beautiful women' where the intermediate statement X is 'Men like women'.

One limitation of these rules has to be accounted for. There is often no logical contrast between opposite terms of a relative system (expressed either by contrasting lexical items or contrasting order of elements). Although so far the relation of logical exclusion has applied tacitly to converses such as:

$(a)\cdot\rightarrow$EMO $+$LOV$\cdot(b)$ '(a) loves (b)'   and
$(a)\cdot\leftarrow$EMO $+$LOV$\cdot(b)$ '(b) loves (a)'

it is clear that the one does not contradict the other: 'John loves Susan' and 'Susan loves John' could both be true statements. There are even converses which are logically equivalent as to truth value: 'John is a colleague of Peter's' and 'Peter is a colleague of John's'. As the logical properties of relative systems will be examined more closely in §4.1.1, it will be sufficient to observe here that contrasting terms in a relative system $\rightleftarrows$R are the basis of a relation of logical exclusion only when the relative system is classified as asymmetric; *ie* when it is a condition that $a\cdot\rightarrow$R $b\cdot c$ is inconsistent with $a\cdot\leftarrow$R $b\cdot c$ (examples are 'is taller than'/ 'is shorter than'; 'is parent of'/'is child of').

2.8.4 *Tautologies*

One major type of tautology, or analytically true statement, may be characterised loosely as an assertion which is implied by another assertion downgraded inside it. A more careful definition is as follows:

[H] An assertion of the form $a\ \langle\theta\ b\cdot r\cdot c\rangle\cdot s\cdot d$ is a tautology if
(i) the assertion $a\cdot r\cdot c$ (*sic*) implies the assertion $a\cdot s\cdot d$.
(ii) a is construed as if universally quantified (see §2.8.2 and §3.5).

Let us take two assertions sharing a universally construed cluster, one of which implies the other:

'Boys run to school' implies 'Boys go to school'.

From these we construct a tautology by downgrading the former in the latter, replacing the one occurrence of 'boys' (a) by a cluster $(\theta\ b)$ representing the semantic function of the relative pronoun (the actual rule governing this replacement, the "rule of co-reference", is stated in §4.3.1):

'Boys who run to school go to school.'

Condition (ii) above is possibly redundant, since it is difficult to construe assertions of this kind existentially. 'A boy running to school is going to school' is interpreted as 'Any boy ...' rather than 'Some ...'. Particular assertions ('The boy ...') on the other hand obey the general rule of tautology [H]:

'The man eating peanuts is eating nuts.'

The following specimen tautologies are marked according to whether the two assertions (downgraded and independent) are identical, or whether deductive implication, inductive implication, or a combination of both is involved:

'People who are lucky are lucky'	(identical)
'Owners of cars possess vehicles'	(inductive)
'Ideas profitable to men benefit scientists'	(deductive)
'Apples are liked by children who passionately love fruit'	
	(inductive and deductive)
'Philatelists collect stamps'	(identical)
'Edible fungus can be consumed'	(inductive)

As numerous words like *edible* and *philatelist* have definitions incorporating downgraded assertions, the underlying semantic structure of such tautologies need not be evident in their syntactic structure.[28] This is illustrated by the last two examples.

2.8.5 *Contradictions*

Contradictions, or logically false assertions, can be formed by downgrading one assertion within another with which it is inconsistent, after the fashion of the preceding rule for tautology:

'I detest any man I like.'
'John's older brother is younger than John.'
'Men who disagree with women agree with beautiful women.'
'Anglophiles dislike the English.'[29]

Other classes of tautology and contradiction will be defined in Chapter 3.

2.9 The null symbol ($\varnothing$)

The zero symbol $\varnothing$ in systemic analysis represents the empty set of components. From the definition of logical inclusion in §2.2 it may be seen that all other componential formulae are logically included in $\varnothing$, which may be thought of as the unit of maximum designative generalisation, capable of being roughly expressed as 'Something/one or other' or 'Anyone/thing whatever', according to whether it is construed existentially or universally.

Strictly speaking, however, the empty formula $\varnothing$ always has zero expression, and its presence explains the effect of "ellipsis" in sentences such as:

You've been fighting again. ('You've been fighting SOMEONE or SOMETHING again')
Is she in love? ('Is she in love WITH ANYBODY?')
I'm thinking. (I'm thinking ABOUT SOMETHING')
Those animals bite. ('Those animals bite PEOPLE')

The gloss on the right contains an added expression, written in capitals, of very general meaning. These sentences all express predications exemplifying the general formula $a \cdot r \cdot \varnothing$.

Because of the already studied connection between logical inclusion and implication, we are able to include within the class of logical implications cases where the implied statement contains an empty cluster, but is otherwise identical to the implying statement. Just as 'John is eating peanuts' inductively implies 'John is eating nuts', so

'John is eating peanuts' implies 'John is eating'.
'He smokes cigarettes' implies 'He smokes'.

Inductive implication, in turn, accounts for the analyticity of assertions like

'A cigarette smoker smokes.'
'The man who is eating peanuts is eating.'

Empty clusters are especially important in the analysis of rank-shifted predications, where both terminal clusters may be empty:

Robbery of the old by the young is a vicious crime.
Robbery of the old is a vicious crime.
Robbery is a vicious crime.

The three contrasting subjects of these sentences express respectively predications of the form $(a \cdot r \cdot b)$, $(a \cdot r \cdot \varnothing)$, and $(\varnothing \cdot r \cdot \varnothing)$. Just as the last of these (universally construed) implies the second, which implies the first, so the whole independent predications in which they are rank-shifted are equivalently related by implication, as predicted in §2.8.2. Other familiar grammatical constructions whose meaning cannot be readily analysed without the postulation of empty clusters are:

[a] Passive clauses without agents:
   The letter has been posted, ('by SOMEONE OR OTHER' is understood)
[b] Clauses with modal auxiliaries:
   You have to apply in advance. (meaning approximately 'You are obliged by SOMEONE OR OTHER to apply in advance')
[c] Agent nouns: *teacher, leader, smoker, driver,* etc (meaning 'someone who teaches SOMEONE OR OTHER, etc).

2.10 Justifying semantic analyses: an example

In the course of this chapter I have tried to move step by step from two relatively clear notions of semantic analysis, "systemic" and "structural" analysis, to a comprehensive notation within which the basic notions of logical synonymy, implication, tautology, and contradiction can be defined. The rules of §2.8 are the means to an empirical justification of particular semantic analyses. By following them through, we can

2*

arrive at basic statements whose validity can be checked by an informant.

We may wish, for example, to check the componential analysis of the words *man, woman*, etc in §2.3 and *love* and *hate* in §2.4. According to the componential definitions and the rules of logical inclusion and exclusion, the following specimen statements can be made:

+HUM +MAT 'adult' logically includes +HUM −MALE +MAT 'woman'.

+MALE 'male' logically includes +HUM +MALE −MAT 'boy'.

→EMO +LOV 'love' logically *ex*cludes →EMO −LOVE 'hate'.

From these, with the help of the rules of deductive implication and inconsistency, the following additional statements (among others) can be derived:

+HUM +MAT·→EMO −LOV· +HUM +MALE− MAT
'Adults hate boys'.

implies:

+HUM −MALE +MAT·→EMO −LOV· +HUM +MALE −MAT
'Women hate boys'.

+HUM −MALE +MAT·→EMO +LOV· +MALE
'Women love males'.

implies:

+HUM −MALE +MAT·→EMO +LOV· +HUM +MALE −MAT
'Women love boys'.

+HUM +MAT·→EMO −LOV· +HUM +MALE −MAT
'Adults hate boys'.

is inconsistent with:

+HUM −MALE +MAT·→EMO +LOV· +HUM +MALE −MAT
'Women love boys'.

(As before, these are skeletal specifications, from which factors of number and tense are omitted.) Now we can derive the following tautologies, bearing in mind that each cluster is universally construed:

+HUM −MALE +MAT·→EMO −LOV· +HUM +MALE −MAT
$\langle \theta \cdot \leftarrow$EMO −LOV· +HUM +MAT$\rangle$
'Women hate boys hated by adults'.

+HUM −MALE +MAT $\langle \theta \cdot \rightarrow$EMO +LOV· +MALE$\rangle \cdot \rightarrow$EMO
+LOV· +HUM +MALE −MAT
'Women that love males love boys'.

and the following contradiction:

+HUM +MAT·→EMO −LOV· +HUM +MALE −MAT
$\langle \theta \cdot \leftarrow$EMO +LOV· +HUM −MALE +MAT$\rangle$

'Adults hate boys beloved by women'.

This is obviously a rudimentary and much simplified example of what is involved in the confirmation of a semantic analysis. I have illustrated only a small number of all possible basic statements which follow from this analysis; moreover, the rules provided up to now define only subsets of the sets of tautologies, implications, etc, which a comprehensive theory has to account for. The main function of the next chapter will be to provide further criteria for membership of these sets, and thus to extend the scope of the theory.

Chapter 3

Formators

The features of which clusters are composed are divided into three categories: (a) DESIGNATORS, (b) FORMATORS, and (c) DOWNGRADED PREDICATIONS (see §2.5.2).[1] The distinction between (a) and (b) is far from new in philosophy, where it is generally applied to words, and is at the root of the division between so-called "logical words" (*all*, *not*, *is*, *the*, etc), and words which have a referential function (*book*, *hit*, *tall*, etc). In the present context, the term "formator" has the following interpretation. Formators are those features whose meaning is wholly determined by the theory, in this sense: they are explicated by special conditions under which assertions in which they occur are classed as tautologous or contradictory, or by special relationships of implication and incompatibility into which they enter. Designators correspond to what we have so far called "components". Formators will be represented, in the notation, by Greek letters, or else by conventional logical symbols.

3.1 Some formators

In formulating the rules governing tautologies which contain formators, we often establish a link between a formator and a theoretical class or relation. Correspondences of this kind can be made between the negative formator 'not' and the class of contradictions; between the conditional formator 'if' and the relation of implication; between the affirmative formator 'true' and the class of tautologies; between the attributive formator 'be' and the relation of logical inclusion. As an exhaustive statement of rules of meaning for formators would be too ambitious an aim for the present purpose, I shall merely give by way of illustration some rules applying to the negative and conditional formators.

3.1.1 *The negative formator 'not'* ($\sim$)

If and only if the statement $a \cdot r \cdot b$ is a contradiction, then the statement $a \cdot \sim r \cdot b$ (*ie* the statement which can be formed from $a \cdot r \cdot b$ by the addition of the negative formator) is a tautology.

Examples:

'John's older brother is not younger than John.'
'These boys are not adults.'

Two additional and equally obvious rules are that an assertion $a \cdot r \cdot b$ is logically inconsistent with its negation $a \cdot \sim r \cdot b$; and that the negation of a tautology is a contradiction:

'Philatelists do not collect stamps.'
'These boys are not children.'

The negative formator only occurs in the medial cluster of a predication.

3.1.2 *The conditional formator 'if'* ($\rightarrow \supset$)

The formator $\rightarrow \supset$ always constitutes a medial cluster linking two rank-shifted assertions. Like some other formators, it has the value of a relative component such as $\rightarrow$EMO, in that it occurs only within the medial element of a predication, and determines the factor of directionality: there is a significant contrast between 'If X, then Y' and 'If Y, then X'. $(X) \rightarrow \supset (Y)$ is a tautology if and only if the assertion X implies the assertion Y; for example:

'If children love apples, boys love apples.'

Likewise, if X and Y are logically inconsistent, $(X) \rightarrow \supset (Y)$ is a contradiction:

'If children love apples, boys hate apples.'[2]
'If the car is behind the bus, the bus is not in front of the car.'

3.1.3 *Other formators*

Among other formators are the antonymous features 'true' and 'false', whose explanation presupposes the concept of a "metasemantic cluster" introduced in §3.4; also the conjunctive and disjunctive formators 'and' and 'or', whose meaning has been made clear in propositional logic. The phenomenon of co-ordination complicates semantic structure in a manner yet to be formulated in the present theory.

3.1.4 *How many formators are there?*

Formators can be regarded as semantic features with idiosyncratic logical properties – with properties, that is, which cannot be subsumed under the general rules applying to the various classes of designative system described in §2.2. It is necessary, therefore, for the semantic theory to contain an enumeration of the formators and of the special rules which apply to them. As a general principle, obviously, the smaller the number of formators, the greater the simplicity of the theory. However, even if this theory were developed to the stage of detail at which all logical properties of all semantic features were known and stated, it would still not be an easy matter to draw up a list of formators. This is because the distinction between formators and designators is by no means so clear-cut as it appears at first glance. There is both a positive and negative aspect of the distinction: on the one hand formators are features requiring special statements of meaning, and on the other they can be seen as features lacking a property of designators – *viz* their systemic contrastiveness. These two criteria do not always coincide. The negative formator $\sim$ is a formator in both these senses, whereas the formator 'true' is in systemic contrast to 'false', just as (for example) the designator 'male' is in opposition to 'female'. 'True' and 'false', that is, are terms of a binary taxonomic system. Similarly, $\rightarrow\supset$ is not a single, non-contrastive feature, but rather part of a relative system $\rightleftarrows\supset$, in which the factor of order is contrastive just as it is in a designative system such as $\rightleftarrows$EMO. A typology of semantic features must therefore recognise a difference between "partial formators" and "full formators"; and moreover in the "partial" categories, degrees of "formativeness" must be recognised, according to the number of special statements that have to be made. Whether a given feature is counted as a formator for the purposes of this notation, is to some extent an arbitrary decision; nevertheless, it simplifies presentation if formators and designators are treated as distinct categories.

We now turn our attention to some formators requiring extra detailed consideration.

3.2 Attribution: the formator system $\leftrightarrows\beta$

The attributive formator system is set up here to account for the principal use of the verb *to be*. Like $\rightleftarrows\supset$, it has the value of a relative system, and only occurs in medial clusters.

The class of tautologies relating to attribution is defined by the following rule:

An assertion $a \cdot \rightarrow\beta\, b \cdot c$ (*ie* an assertion containing $\rightarrow\beta$ without intervening rank-shift) is a tautology if and only if:

(i) a is logically included in c.
(ii) a is either definite (*eg* 'the man') or is universally construed.[3]

Here are some examples:

'Women are female.'   'These boys are children.'
'Fresh water is water.'   'Prehistoric man was human.'

If *a* logically excludes, instead of logically includes, *b*, the attributive formator $\rightarrow\beta$ defines a corresponding set of contradictions:

'Women are male.'   'These boys are adults.'
'A house is a vegetable.'   'Wise people are foolish.'

There are, however, exceptions to this generalisation. Sentences such as *The valley was a lake in Miocene times*[4] and *All adults have been children* are not contradictory according to an interpretation under which they refer to two different periods of time. Perhaps, to preserve the general principle of contradiction, these should be semantically analysed as metonymic variants of 'What is (now) a valley was a lake in Miocene times', etc.

A question to be asked is: "Is it necessary to have an attributive formator, or can the theory be so modified as to account for the above tautologies and contradictions in another way?" Later (in §4.2.1) we shall find the means to eliminate this formator, which has been introduced here as a necessary stage in the presentation, not as a necessary construct of the theory.

3.3 The definite formator 'the' (θ)

The definite formator θ, expressed by the definite article, is also a factor in the meaning of personal pronouns, demonstratives, present and past tense, the adverbs *here, there, now, then*, and all proper names. Its semantic status may be explained as follows:

Any terminal cluster consisting of the features θ, X^1, X^2, ..., X^n is logically included in a cluster X^1, X^2, ..., X^n; whereas no cluster whatever apart from itself is logically included in a cluster containing θ.

This means that θ resembles a designative component except that no other cluster can be logically included within the cluster which contains it; in other words, it signals maximum specification or particularity of meaning. From the description above, we see why assertions like 'The house is a house', 'Those peaches are peaches', 'This philatelist collects stamps', etc, are tautologous, whereas no assertion of the form '*a* is the house', '*a* is John' is a tautology, except in the trivial case where the two sides of the predication are equivalent: 'The house is the house', 'John is John'. Since 'this man' is logically included in 'man/men', 'This man is mortal' inductively implies 'A man is mortal' (= 'There is at least one mortal man') and is deductively implied by 'Men are mortal' (where 'men' is taken as if universally construed).[5] We have already noted (§2.8.4) the construction of tautologies such as 'The man who is eating peanuts is eating nuts' on this basis.

One of the major functions of the definite formator is that of indicating textual CO-REFERENCE or textual "cross-reference"; *ie* of marking the cluster to which it belongs as having identical reference to that of a cluster or componential formula in its linguistic environment. In the notation, this can be shown by an arrow joining the two units related by co-reference:

'John reached the door.'   'He opened it.'

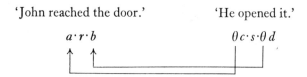

$$a \cdot r \cdot b \qquad\qquad \theta c \cdot s \cdot \theta\, d$$

An alternative, more economical notational device, is to mark the definite formator and the cluster or formula to which it co-refers by the same prime marking as follows:

'John reached the door.'   'He opened it.'
$$a' \cdot r \cdot b'' \qquad\qquad \theta' \, c \cdot s \cdot \theta'' \, d$$

Many cases traditionally described as ellipsis can be explained by postulating that in certain grammatically determined conditions a cluster consisting of the definite formator alone has "zero expression", *ie* has no formal or phonological manifestation, like the empty cluster (see §2.9).[6] We interpret the sentences below, for example, as if some expression of definite meaning, such as the one added in capitals on the right-hand side of the page, is to be "understood" from context:

He's arrived.   *He's arrived* HERE (or THERE).
I object.   *I object* TO THAT (*viz* TO THAT REMARK).
He's winning.   *He's winning* IT (*viz* THE RACE, *etc*).
He came home later. *He came home later* THAN THAT.
Are you sure?   *Are you sure* OF THAT?
No, I haven't.   *No, I haven't* DONE IT.

These pairs of sentences are practically, if not completely synonymous. Each sentence on the left exemplifies the general semantic structure $a \cdot r \cdot \theta$. In the sentences on the right, the "pro-words" *here, that, it,* etc, convey certain information not conveyed in the sentences on the left (for example, *it*, in opposition to *him* and *her*, expresses the feature 'non-personal'); nevertheless, as we shall see in §4.3.1, this does not affect the synonymy of the matched sentences, provided they are assumed to have identical co-reference.

Zero expression in conjunction with textual co-reference is an extremely important factor in semantic analysis. It is, for example, basic to the semantics of co-ordination and comparison in English and other languages. The formal difference between the synonymous sentences *He knows more than I do* and *He knows more than I* is explicable as the difference between expressing a definite formator co-referring to 'knows' in the former case by the "substitute verb" *do*, and in the latter by zero. Without the concepts of co-reference and zero expression, we could not account for the semantic equivalence of the following sets of expressions:[7]

> *He knows more than I know.*
> *He knows more than I do.*
> *He knows more than I.*

> *I can't open this window. Can you open this window?*
> *I can't open this window. Can you do it?*
> *I can't open this window. Can you?*

> *I read the book and my friend read the book.*
> *I read the book and so did my friend.*
> *I and my friend read the book.*

The correct description of these sets as synonymous depends on a general rule to the effect that a definite cluster is assigned by "transference" the meaning of any cluster or componential formula to which it co-refers. This rule will be formulated in §4.3.1.

The definite formator was introduced earlier in §2.5.2, in the initial account of downgrading. We are now able to restate the condition of downgrading in the following form: every downgraded predication within a terminal cluster has as one of its terminal elements a cluster containing the definite formator; and this formator co-refers to the remaining componential content of the cluster in which the downgrading occurs. More succinctly, the following formula represents a general condition of well-formedness on all terminal clusters containing downgraded predications: $a'\langle\theta'\ b\cdot r\cdot c\rangle$. (The corresponding rule for medial clusters is explained in §3.5.) This analysis brings out the essentially deictic and connective character of relative pronouns, and accounts for their semantic affinity to co-referential personal pronouns: an affinity which appears, for example, in the possibility of paraphrasing the relative pronoun in a non-restrictive relative clause by a personal pronoun in an independent clause:

'This is my friend John, who works at the Home Office.'
'This is my friend John – he works at the Home Office.'

There is a choice here, as in many other cases of co-referential deixis, between zero expression and expression by a *th*-form (*that*): *A show I like* and *A show that I like*.

3.4 Metalinguistic clusters

Reference, as distinct for co-reference, to linguistic forms cited in the text is another special function of the definite formator θ. In this capacity, it contributes to the solution of problems of "metalinguistic" use which manifest themselves in many apparent anomalies of both grammatical and semantic analysis.[8]

The relation of reference is on the outskirts of linguistics, in that the Y of any statement "X refers to Y" is usually taken to stand for some non-linguistic entity or class of entities. The "metalinguistic" problem arises in just those cases which the linguist cannot ignore: the cases of language referring to language. In the present context, the relation of reference will be understood in the following way. The cluster is the only linguistic unit which refers or denotes. A cluster is termed META-LINGUISTIC if it has linguistic denotata. One might, however, classify metalinguistic clusters more exactly by specifying the linguistic levels at which their referents are identified:

"Metaphonological" cluster: 'vowel', 'syllable', etc.
"Metagrammatical" cluster: 'verb', 'sentence', etc.
"Metasemantic" cluster: 'name', 'statement', etc.

The "naming" relation, as in 'X is the name of Y', is a referential relation in which X is a definite cluster (*ie* one containing the definite formator) and Y is an individual entity, rather than a class of entities. As examples of metalinguistic naming, we may take citations of words, as in 'The definite article in English is *the*', or quotations, as in 'He said "All is ready"'. The latter may be transcribed

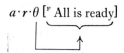

$$a \cdot r \cdot \theta \, [^{\text{F}} \text{All is ready}]$$

where it is understood that square brackets enclose what θ refers to. The superscript 'F' indicates that the sentence referred to is formally, rather than phonologically or semantically construed.

A corresponding metasemantic reading would contain the same statement translated into reported speech: 'He said that all was ready.' Note that this does not have the same truth value as 'He said "All is ready"', as the narrator does not commit himself to reproducing the actual form of words used: 'He said that all was ready' is synonymous with 'He said everything was ready.' Here again, there is a choice between zero expression and expression by the *th-* form *that*. It is obviously the metasemantic, rather than metaformal rendering, which occurs in assertions about truth value, as in 'That I saw him is true.'

The use of inverted commas in writing is generally a sign of the meta-formal use of language, whether in direct quotation or in some other mode of reference. The extent to which we rely on these graphic symbols for interpretation can be judged from the examples below, from which inverted commas and initial capitals (in proper names) have been omitted:

(a) *I prefer mary to joan.* (in a discussion of girls' names).
(b) *John smith's name is john smith.*
(c) *Cabbages refers to cabbages.*
(d) *The show is called stop the world I want to get off.*
(e) *Be is a verb but but and and are conjunctions.*

These examples are chosen to illustrate the need for some account of reference for a semantic theory, and indeed, for an adequate grammatical analysis as well. Without an account of reference, we would be at a loss to explain the ambiguity of sentence (a). We would also be unable to explain why (b) and (c) are tautologous, and why (c), (d), (e), which appear to a greater or lesser extent to be ungrammatical, are nevertheless both semantically and grammatically well-formed utterances. Here is a clear case where semantic information is necessary for a satisfactory account of grammar.

3.5 Quantification

The universal quantifier (1α) and the existential quantifier (2α) are two formators required to explain the meaning of such words as *all, every, everyone, anywhere* on the one hand, and *some, somebody, somewhere,* etc on the other. Once the meaning of *some,* etc, has been established, it is also easy enough to account systemically for a fair number of other items: *many/few, much/little, often/seldom,* etc, are distinguished in each case by the same polar system; *one/two/three/* . . . by a hierarchic system; *more/less* by a relative system.

It is as well to make clear from the start that the logical term "quantifier" is a misnomer in so far as it suggests a restriction of reference to countable objects. The rules of quantification apply indifferently to countable expressions like *all people, some friends,* and to mass expressions like *all food, some paper.*

The complications of analysing quantification in natural languages are considerable. It has been assumed, for example, that an active sentence expressing a combination of universal and existential quantification has a different meaning from its passive counterpart: that *Everybody in the room speaks (some) two languages* is not synonymous with *(Some) two languages are spoken by everybody in the room.*[9] Such an assumption, if justified, would weaken the case for considering the ordering of semantic structure to be independent of sequential order in grammatical structure, and hence for adopting the "mirror-image" convention in the present notation. I shall naturally want to show that it is false.

Certainly, two distinct interpretations are involved in the example above. In the one interpretation, it is merely asserted that everyone in the room is bilingual; in the other, that it is possible to name two particular languages L_1 and L_2 (say French and Russian) such that everybody in the room speaks both L_1 and L_2. However, it is not true (at least according to the intuitions of myself and those I have consulted) that these two readings are each restricted to either active or passive: on the contrary, both of them are possible for both the active and the passive sentences.[10] In support of this, we may consider a sentence for which one of the two interpretations is ruled out because of its factual absurdity: *Everybody in the room has drunk some water.* The idea which seems to be dominant in the passive sentence above cannot be seriously considered in this case: it would be ludicrous to suppose that the very same mass of water has been consumed by a number of different people. Therefore we interpret *Some water has been drunk by everybody in the room* in a way which makes it synonymous with the active sentence. A similar example would show that if the sense most readily associated with the active sentence cannot be reasonably entertained, the other reading is still available. In other words, even though the choice of active or passive appears to predispose the interpreter to one meaning rather than another, active and passive sentences under mixed quantification, as elsewhere, have the same choice of meaning. We might add that other factors, such as stress and intonation, seem to influence the selection of an interpretation more significantly than does the choice between active and passive.

An analysis which simply attaches a quantifier as an extra feature to a cluster to which it is grammatically related (*eg* 1α +HUM +MALE +MAT 'all men') is inadequate for two reasons. Firstly, it fails to account for the ambiguity just discussed; and secondly, it is incompatible with the observation that quantified assertions, unlike most others, can undergo the operation of negation in two different ways. Thus one negative assertion corresponding to 'Everybody in the room speaks two languages' is 'Everybody in the room does not speak two languages', and another is 'Not everybody in the room speaks two languages'.[11] Since the negative formator as so far defined occurs only in medial clusters, and since only one medial cluster occurs in a predication, we are led to suppose that any predication containing a quantifier must contain at least one additional predication, either through rank-shift or downgrading. This assumption also solves the problem of the above ambiguity: rank-shift or downgrading, as forms of subordination, introduce an extra factor of order into semantic structure, so that by reversing the relation of dependence between two predications, one may account for a difference of meaning. By this means, one is able to deal with the complexities of quantification without adding to the structural apparatus already in use.

The solution proposed here may at first seem needlessly complex, but will be shown later to be what is required to meet the facts of quantification. It is to set up two separate formator systems: (a) a system of quantification which represents the distinction between 'all' and 'some' (symbolised 1α and 2α respectively); and (b) a relative system $\rightleftarrows o$ which, as it were, 'carries' the quantifier as part of a medial cluster, and which is expressed (when it is expressed at all) by *of* (as in *some of the cars*). The two systems are interdependent; *ie* a term of one cannot occur without a term of the other. A statement containing a quantifier can then be expressed by a main QUANTIFICATIONAL PREDICATION within which is rank-shifted a PRINCIPAL PREDICATION, as in these two examples:

(1) $\theta' \cdot 1\alpha \rightarrow o \cdot (c' \cdot \rightarrow l \cdot f)$ 'All cats like fish'
(2) $\theta' \cdot 2\alpha \rightarrow o \cdot (c' \cdot \rightarrow l \cdot f)$ 'Some cats like fish'

The arrow of the feature $\rightarrow o$, in such formulae, always points towards the rank-shifted predication. (Here $c=$'cats', $\rightarrow l=$'like', $f=$'fish'; we abandon the convention of restricting content variables to particular letters a, b, etc). There are now two sets of negative forms: those resulting from the negation of the main predication

(3) $\theta' \cdot {\sim}1\alpha \rightarrow o \cdot (c' \cdot \rightarrow l \cdot f)$ 'Not all cats like fish'
(4) $\theta' \cdot {\sim}2\alpha \rightarrow o \cdot (c' \cdot \rightarrow l \cdot f)$ 'Not any ($=$no) cat likes fish'

and those resulting from the negation of the principal predication

(5) $\theta' \cdot 1\alpha \rightarrow o \cdot (c' \cdot {\sim}\rightarrow l \cdot f)$ 'All cats do not like fish' ($=$'No cat likes fish')
(6) $\theta' \cdot 2\alpha \rightarrow o \cdot (c' \cdot {\sim}\rightarrow l \cdot f)$ 'Some cats do not like fish' ($=$'Not all cats like fish').

The semantic equivalence of (5) to (4) and of (6) to (3) will be studied below. For the moment, we may note that these specifications correctly show examples (3) and (4), rather than (5) and (6), to be logically inconsistent with (1) and (2) respectively, in that they represent negations of the main predication.

The presence of the definite formator on the left of all these formulae can best be explained through a comparison with the quantificational formulae of predicate logic, in which quantifiers are placed in front of the propositions they govern as follows:

$(x)Mx$ 'For every x, x is mutable' (*ie* 'Everything is mutable').

$(\exists x)Gx$ & Dx 'There is at least one x, such that x is a game
                                    and x is dangerous' (*ie* 'There are dangerous
                                    games', or 'Some games are dangerous').

Just as in the conventional predicate calculus, use of variables such as x
and y establishes a denotative connection between the quantifier and the
quantified expression, so in the notation of this study, the co-reference
of the definite formator provides a link between the quantificational
predication and one cluster of the main predication. Without this co-
referential connection, there would be no way in the notation of
distinguishing between 'all cats like fish' and 'cats like all fish'. Co-
reference can therefore be seen as the equivalent in natural languages of
the use of variables in algebraic languages.

Echoing the conventional "natural language translation" of formulae
of predicate calculus, one may read the formula $\theta' \cdot 1\alpha \rightarrow o \cdot (c' \cdot \rightarrow l \cdot f)$ as
'For all of them, cat like fish', where by 'them' is understood, by co-
reference, as any member of the class denoted by c. This type of rendering, however, tends to make the formula seem rather remote from
everyday English, whereas in fact the specification of expression rules
for it would not be difficult. Let us first of all examine the corresponding
definite expression:

> *All of the cats like fish*
> $\theta' \cdot 1\alpha \rightarrow o \quad (\theta \quad c' \quad . \quad \rightarrow l \cdot f)$

Apart from the initial definite formator, which as usual when standing
alone in a cluster, has zero expression, there is an exact sequential correspondence here between the grammatical and semantic elements of
the sentence. (This example, it is true, makes things look slightly simpler
than they are: the order of *all* and *of* are semantically undetermined,
since 1α and $\rightarrow o$ are unordered features of the same cluster. In the notation, I have for ease of reading used the notational variant $1\alpha \rightarrow o$ which
reflects the syntactic ordering.) There is only one further complication
in the relation between the indefinite sentence *All cats like fish* and its
semantic structure: this is the obligatory dropping of the preposition *of*,
which will have to be handled by the rules of expression or by deep
grammatical structure.

If a predication contains two quantifiers, the second quantifier may be
represented as downgraded inside the medial cluster of the principal
predication, which is itself rank-shifted inside the main predication. We
thus distinguish the two meanings of *All cats like some fish* by two formulae differing virtually in nothing more than the order in which one predication is subordinated inside another:

(a) $\theta' \cdot 1\alpha \rightarrow o \cdot (c' \cdot \rightarrow l \langle \theta'' \cdot 2\alpha \leftarrow o \cdot \theta''' \rangle \cdot f'')''$
(b) $\theta' \cdot 2\alpha \rightarrow o \cdot (f' \cdot \leftarrow l \langle \theta'' \cdot 1\alpha \leftarrow o \cdot \theta''' \rangle \cdot c'')''$

Perhaps the import of these formulae can be more securely grasped if they are "translated" into our semi-formalised "Pidgin English" as follows:

(a) 'For all of them, cat like fish (for some of them)'.

(b) 'For some of them, fish is liked by cat (for all of them).'

Co-reference is here shown by arrows. Every occurrence of the definite formator θ in these formulae has zero expression.

(One aspect of the symbolisations above must be explained without delay: *viz* the co-reference of θ'' in the downgraded cluster to the whole of the remainder of the predication in which the downgraded predication occurs. When downgrading occurs within a *terminal* cluster, as we have seen, the definite formator θ within the downgraded predication co-refers to the remainder of the cluster: $a'\langle\theta'\ b\cdot r\cdot c\rangle$. This condition cannot apply to a medial cluster, however, for if the rule of co-occurrence is followed through (§4.3.1), the terminal cluster $\theta'\ b$ is then assigned a relative component, in violation of the condition of well-formedness stated in §2.4. When downgrading occurs in a *medial* cluster, therefore, the definite formator co-refers to the whole of the main predication. In pictorial terms, this may be represented (for any formula $a\cdot r\ \langle\theta\ b\cdot s\cdot c\rangle\cdot d$) as follows:

$$a\cdot r\cdot d \qquad\qquad \langle\theta\ b\cdot s\cdot c\rangle$$

or, adapting the convention of distinguishing marks already established, as $(a\cdot r\ \langle\theta'\ b\cdot s\cdot c\rangle\cdot d)'$. The round brackets for this purpose mark the extent of the unit to which co-reference is made, it being understood that the downgraded predication itself is excluded from it. This rule helps to explain the synonymy in many cases (see §4.3.3) of the above formula with one in which $a\cdot r\cdot d$ is rank-shifted inside the predication containing s and c: *viz* $c\cdot s\cdot(a\cdot r\cdot d)$. By the rule of co-reference (§4.3.1), in fact, the complete equivalence of these formulae, apart from downgrading and the content of b, which is generally nil, can be shown.)

There are two rather arbitrary-seeming aspects of this treatment of quantification. The first is the manner of downgrading the second quantifier within the principal predication, which will be shown to be less arbitrary in §4.3.3. The second is the introduction of two formator systems, the system of quantification $1\alpha/2\alpha$ and the relative system $\rightleftarrows o$. To show the necessity of both systems, one need only observe that two semantic contrasts are involved: the contrast between 'all' and 'some', and the contrast of order signalled by $\rightleftarrows o$. This point can be made more conclusive if it is pointed out that the nature of the opposition between 'all' and 'some' is paralleled elsewhere in the language, so that it is feasible to set up a special class of systems (let them be called INVERSION systems) which explains not only the contrast between 'all' and 'some', but also the contrast between 'compel' and 'allow', between 'necessary' and 'possible', etc (see §9.2.3). The special property of these oppositions is illustrated in the synonymy of the statements (5), (4) and (6), (3) transcribed towards the beginning of this section:

'All cats do not like fish.' = 'No cat likes fish'
'Some cats don't like fish.' = 'Not all cats like fish'

The rule illustrated here could be summed up in ordinary language "A quantificational formula containing a negative is equivalent to the formula which results from CHANGING THE QUANTIFIER AND CHANGING THE POSITION OF THE NEGATIVE SIGN". Parallel examples from the field of modality are these:

'He compelled me not to shut the door' = 'He did not allow me to shut the door.'
'He allowed me not to shut the door' = 'He did not compel me to shut the door.'

Such equivalences will be treated in more detail in Chapter 9. For the present, we need only note that they add support to the present analysis by showing that it is possible to treat the contrast between 'all' and 'some' not as unique, but as an instance of a general type illustrated elsewhere in the language.

An extra advantage of the present analysis lies in its ability to represent a considerable range of quantificational expressions. We have already seen, in passing, that it is possible to represent the contrast between definite and indefinite meaning, in quantificational expressions, by the presence or absence of the definite formator in the quantified cluster:

$$\theta' \cdot 1\alpha \to o \cdot (c' \cdot \to l \cdot f) \qquad \text{'All cats like fish'}$$

contrasts with

$$\theta' \cdot 1\alpha \to o \cdot (\theta \, c' \cdot \to l \cdot f) \qquad \text{'All the cats like fish'}$$

likewise 'Some cats ...' with 'Some of the cats ...', etc. In addition, expressions containing *many*, *not many*, *a few*, *not a few*, etc, fall easily into place if we represent the contrast between 'many' and 'a few' by a polar system dependent on 2α:

$$\theta' \cdot 2\alpha + \text{MANY} \to o \cdot (c' \cdot \to l \cdot f) \qquad \text{'Many cats like fish'}$$
$$\theta' \cdot 2\alpha - \text{MANY} \to o \cdot (c' \cdot \to l \cdot f) \qquad \text{'A few cats like fish'}$$

This means that both statements are correctly shown as implying 'Some cats like fish', by rule [E], §2.8.2. The negation of the quantification cluster in these two cases produces 'Not many' (='few') and 'Not a few' respectively.

As the discussion of quantification up to this point has centred on the problems of obtaining correct analyses, we have yet to "define" quantifiers by rules of use, as in the case of other formators. However, this is not a difficult task. The original rules for implication, inconsistency, tautology, and contradiction in §§2.8.1–5 incorporated the concepts of universal and existential quantification, although at that stage we had to be content with the rather vague indication that clusters were to be universally or existentially "construed". To determine the status of quantifiers by rule, we need merely return to the rules of §§2.8.2–5, and replace formulae like $a \cdot r \cdot b$ (where a is to be "universally construed") by $a' \cdot 1\alpha \rightarrow o \cdot (\theta' \cdot r \cdot b)$, etc. Thus to illustrate the rule of deductive implication (rule [C] of §2.8.2) as modified for explicit quantification, we amend the three examples given previously as follows:

'All children love apples' implies 'All boys love apples'.
'All men are mortal' implies 'All postmen are mortal'.
'I love all fruit' implies 'I love all apples'.

These and similar changes will produce rules and examples for tautologies and contradictions containing quantifiers.

The more precise characterisation of quantification in this section will, in turn, retrospectively clarify the rules of §2.8.1–5. But there still remains the puzzle of what difference of meaning there is, if any, between a quantified predication, and an equivalent predication in which quantification is implicit rather than overtly expressed. Is there any difference in meaning between, for example, *Children love toys* and *All children love toys*, if it is presumed that the existential interpretation 'Some children love toys' is ruled out in the former sentence? Perhaps, even allowing for the theoretical ambiguity, the former is vague in a way that the latter is not. 'All children love toys' is uncompromising enough in its assertiveness for us to be sure it is inconsistent with 'Some child doesn't like toys': but with 'Children love toys', one is not so sure. Even if it should be decided that such pairs are synonymous, this does not commit us to giving them the same formal specification, as the theory allows such relationships to be accounted for by special rules of synonymy (see §4.3–4).

3.6 The concept of "becoming"[12]

The concept of "becoming", common to such verbs as *get* ('come into possession of'), *lose* ('come to be without'), *arrive* ('become present'), *leave* ('become absent'), *learn* ('come to know'), is represented in the theory by the INCEPTIVE formator system $\rightleftarrows \iota$. As this system is bound up with factors of time and tense which cannot be anticipated here, I shall do no more than point out one or two of the special statements of meaning it is required to account for.

A special relation of implication depends on the connection between the "inceptive" and "perfective" aspects (see §7.6.4):

> 'My mother has become (fallen) ill' implies 'My mother is ill'.
> 'Jacob has learnt to swim' implies 'Jacob knows how to swim'.

Hence there are such tautologies as 'Someone who has learned to swim knows how to swim'. There are also special tautologies involving time, in that an event of "becoming" inevitably precedes the state in which it results, and follows the negative state which it terminates:

> 'Having learned how to swim, Jacob knew how to swim.'
> 'Before learning how to swim, Jacob didn't know how to swim.'

As with the quantifiers, we may use the observation that there are two possible negative forms of an inceptive assertion to argue that at least two predications, one main and one subordinate, must be postulated here as well. To see this, notice that 'The door is not open' is synonymous with 'The door is shut', and, furthermore, that there is a difference of meaning between 'The door became not-open' (= 'The door became shut') and 'The door did not become open'. This difference may be represented by the contrast between $a' \cdot \rightarrow \iota \cdot (\theta' \cdot \sim r \cdot b)$ and $a' \cdot \sim \rightarrow \iota \cdot (\theta' \cdot r \cdot b)$, where the positive form $a' \cdot \rightarrow \iota \cdot (\theta' \cdot r \cdot b)$ would stand for 'the door became open' (*ie* 'the door opened') and the simple predication $a \cdot r \cdot b$ for the 'door was open'. Perhaps a still clearer example is the contrast between

$a' \cdot \rightarrow \iota \cdot (\theta' \cdot \sim r \cdot b)$ 'My brother lost the job.'
                                 ('My brother came to not-have the job.')

and

$a' \cdot \sim \rightarrow \iota \cdot (\theta' \cdot r \cdot b)$ 'My brother didn't get the job.'
                                 ('My brother didn't come to have the job.')

Here the simple predication $a \cdot r \cdot b$ would be 'My brother had the job'.

The above formulae have an additional resemblance to quantificational formulae, in that the rank-shifted predication is linked to the main predication by co-reference. A similar argument may be used to justify this. If one spells out an inceptive statement in "Pidgin English" it is something like:

> 'My brother· become· he· have· job'
> a' · $\rightarrow \iota$ ·$(\theta' \cdot$ r · $b)$

By such an analysis, we have a means to account for the difference in meaning between 'John is getting to behave like his young sister' and 'His young sister is getting to behave like John':

'John · become · he · behave like · young sister'

$$a' \quad \cdot \quad \to_\iota \quad \cdot (\theta' \cdot \quad r \qquad \cdot \qquad b)$$

'Young sister · become · she · behave like · John'

$$b' \qquad \cdot \quad \to_\iota \quad \cdot (\theta' \cdot \qquad r \qquad \cdot \quad a)$$

The difference corresponds precisely to the choice of co-reference with one terminal cluster of the simple predication rather than with another. It is true that in many cases – perhaps most – there is no difference of meaning to be represented in this difference of formula. However, our aim is not to construct a notation which represents all cases of synonymy, but to construct one which distinguishes all cases of non-synonymy. The occurrence of just one case like the 'young sister' example above should be sufficient argument for an account such as has been allowed for.

Chapter 4

Some extensions of the theory

4.1 Semantic well-formedness

In Chapters 2 and 3, I have, in passing, given one or two positive conditions of well-formedness. There is, for instance, the rule (see §2.5.2 and §3.3) that a downgraded predication must contain a definite cluster co-referring to the remaining designative content of the cluster within which the cluster is downgraded.[1] There are also various rules governing the occurrence of formators: the negative formator occurs only in medial clusters, the definite formator only in terminal clusters, etc. Generally, however, it seems that the question of semantic well-formedness is best approached negatively, by identifying and eliminating classes of semantic violation.

To this end in §2.2 we were given a criterion for identifying irregularly formed componential formulae: clusters containing systemically contrasting components are excluded as cases of "oxymoron". The range of formulae excluded by the definition of oxymoron is extended by rules of dependence (§2.8.1). Not only are clusters such as 'male aunt' shown to be intrinsically absurd (because of the presence of both +MALE 'male' and −MALE 'female'), but also 'male house', since 'male' entails 'animate', and 'house' includes the contrasting feature 'inanimate'. That is to say, the combination +MALE −ANIM is indirectly an oxymoron, because +ANIM is implicit in it. Rules of dependence do not always take the form "X depends on Y", where X is a system and Y is a semantic feature. It is conceivable to have rules stating

(a) the dependence of one system on another system
(b) the dependence of a feature on a system
(c) the dependence of one feature on another feature.

Moreover, conjunctions and disjunctions of features may also form dependence conditions. A rule of form (a) is elucidated as follows: a formula containing a feature from a system X is well-formed only if some feature from a system Y can be inserted without a violation occurring. Which of these conceivable kinds of rule are necessary to a satisfactory account of language is a question to which no definite answer will be attempted here. It appears, however, that dependence relations of type (b) do not occur, and that those of types (a) and (c) are always matched by a reciprocal relation, such that if X depends on Y, Y also depends on X. A theory is clearly more powerful to the extent that it imposes restrictions on the form of dependence rules; and a semantic description of a language is simpler to the extent that it avoids the more complicated forms of dependence rule, *ie* those involving the conjunction and disjunction of features. Each dependence rule imposes its own condition of well-formedness.

In addition we have been furnished with various criteria for membership of the class of contradictions and related kinds of semantic violation. But the determination of this class is by no means complete. In the following sections I shall suggest what further sorts of rule have to be constructed, to give a more exhaustive account of the notion of "contradiction", and more generally, the notion of "semantic violation".

4.1.1 *Logical properties of relative systems*

We have observed (§2.8.2) that the idea of systemic contrast, on which that of logical exclusion is founded, and hence, indirectly, also that of contradiction, is not necessarily applicable to relative systems. For instance $(a)\cdot\rightarrow$EMO $+$LOV$\cdot(b)$ ('(a) loves (b)') does not logically exclude $(a)\cdot\leftarrow$EMO $+$LOV$\cdot(b)$ ('(a) is loved by (b)'); nor is 'I love anyone who loves me' a contradiction – indeed, it is quite a plausible statement. The logical properties of relative systems cannot be generalised, but have to be stated individually for each system. For this purpose categories familiar in relational logic, such as transitivity, symmetricity, and reflexivity, can be used. Examples of assertions which such logical conditions would rule out as violations are:

> 'He sat in front of himself' ('in front of' is irreflexive).
> 'The two events happened after each other' ('after' is asymmetric).
> 'I have two fathers' ('father of' is one-many).
> 'John is engaged to Rachel, who is engaged to Peter' ('is engaged to' is one-one and symmetric).

Two important classes of relative system worthy of brief mention are the following.

[a] *Ordering systems* ('above'/'below'; 'to the right of'/'to the left of'; 'in front of'/'behind'; 'better than'/'worse than'; etc) are transitive, irreflexive, and asymmetric. The condition of asymmetricity ensures

that the rules of logical exclusion, inconsistency, and contradiction (see §§2.8.1, 2.8.3, 2.8.5) apply to these cases: 'The man in front of John is behind him' (where 'him' is co-referent with 'John') is a contradiction.

[b] *Reciprocal systems* ('level with', 'married to', 'cousin of', 'different from', 'opposite', 'near to', etc) have the property of symmetricity; *ie*: $a \cdot \to r \cdot b$, if $\to r$ includes a term of a reciprocal system, implies $b \cdot \to r \cdot a$. Here the regular contrast between terms of a system is fully neutralised, so that converses are logically synonymous. Perhaps the best way to formulate this condition of symmetricity is by means of a dependence rule which writes $\to$R for every occurrence of $\leftarrow$R, if $\rightleftarrows$R is a reciprocal system. Thus $a \cdot \to$R $b \cdot c$ (*eg* '*a* is next to *c*') and $c \cdot \to$R $b \cdot a$ ('*c* is next to *a*') would both end up as $a \cdot \leftarrow$R $\to$R $b \cdot c$ after the application of the dependence rule. In accordance with the condition of symmetricity and the rules of negation (§3.1.1), assertions such as 'I am married to a woman who is not my wife' (*ie* '. . . who is not married to me') are marked as contradictions.

4.1.2 *Contextual properties of relative systems*
A different kind of condition on the occurrence of relative components is one imposed by the content of the adjacent terminal clusters. This aspect of well-formedness is often discussed with reference to grammatical structures under the heading of "co-occurrence restrictions" or "selection restrictions".[2] None the less, it appears that not all conditions of this kind can be satisfactorily explained in syntax; no one, for instance, has suggested setting up features of nouns {+LION}, {+PARTRIDGE} to account for the occurrence of *a pride of lions* and *a covey of partridges* and the non-occurrence of **a covey of lions* and **a pride of partridges*. In any case, as Weinreich points out with another example and in another connection,[3] the exclusion of *pride* (in the operative sense) from any grammatical context except ——*of* [+LION] would rule out acceptable expressions like *a pride of such beautiful animals, a pride of beasts*, etc, and would moreover fail to convey the information, evident to any speaker of English who knows his collective nouns, that the animals referred to in these two expressions are in fact lions.

It is possible to make use of the lack of co-extensiveness between semantic and formal units by actually writing in, as part of the definition of 'pride', the definition of 'lion'. The meaning of *pride* as a countable noun is in outline as follows: $g' \langle \theta' \cdot c \cdot l \rangle$ (to be read 'a (social) group consisting of lions'). We assume that *lion* is defined by reference to a multiple taxonomic system 1, 2, 3, . . . , *n*SPE enumerating species of animal so that 'lion' logically excludes 'tiger', 'rabbit', 'hedgehog', etc (see §5.3). The phrase *of lions* can be added to *a pride* without any change in the semantic specification, since the meaning 'of lions' is already present in the meaning of *pride*. Thus *of lions* is correctly shown to be semantically redundant in this context. In contrast, phrases such as *of rabbits* require the addition of a contrasting term *i*SPE to the cluster 'lions', so that this cluster, now 'lion-rabbits', is shown to be an oxymoron, and the whole expression *a pride of rabbits* (correctly again) to constitute a semantic violation. Selection restrictions between noun and verb, etc, can also be handled in this way: the requirement that both the subject-noun and object-noun of *marry* have to be human can be represented in a partial definition of the form $+$HUM$\cdot \rightarrow$MAR$\cdot +$HUM. By this method, violations of selection restrictions are neatly accounted for, by being subsumed in a type of absurdity already recognised and described: that of oxymoron.[4]

One difficulty about this way of dealing with selection restrictions is that it appears to destroy the hope, expressed in §2.7, that lexical definitions may be limited in extent to an independent cluster. However, the contextual feature $\{+$HUM$\}$ does not really belong to the definition of *marry*, but to the whole concept of 'marriage' as a relationship, whether that is expressed through the verb *marry* or by other means, such as through the nouns *nuptials, wedlock, wife, husband, spouse.* In other words, $\{+$HUM$\}$ has to be generalised to all environments of the system $\rightleftarrows$MAR, and we may therefore consider its specification the function of a special kind of redundancy rule, which attributes a feature to the terminal cluster adjacent to the cluster in which $\rightarrow$MAR occurs. The notation for stating this rule is as follows:

$\rightarrow$MAR $\{+$HUM$\}$

to be read:

'Any terminal cluster following the medial cluster containing $\rightarrow$MAR contains the feature $+$HUM.'

(Contextual redundancy rules attribute features either to the INITIAL cluster or the FINAL cluster of the predication; that is, to the terminal cluster BEFORE or AFTER the medial cluster in question. "Initial" and "final", "before" and "after", are here to be interpreted with reference to the direction of the arrow, not to left-to-right ordering on the printed page.) As $\rightleftarrows$MAR is a reciprocal system (see §4.1.1), the operation of this rule, together with the dependence rule which adds $\leftarrow$MAR, will ensure that any formula containing the feature $\rightarrow$MAR must ultimately contain the configuration $+$HUM$\cdot \leftarrow$MAR$\rightarrow$MAR$\cdot +$HUM. If, however, we regard lexical definitions, as in transformational grammar, as *minimal* specifications (containing only those features which cannot be supplied by redundancy rules), then the principle that lexical definitions do not exceed the bounds of an independent cluster can still be upheld.

Like dependence rules, contextual redundancy rules are not always limited to the addition of a single feature. At least the following alternative types of contextual property have to be allowed for:

(a) attribution of a single feature, or a conjunction or a disjunction of features.
(b) attribution of a metalinguistic cluster (see §3.4).
(c) attribution of a rank-shifted predication of a given class (statement, question, command) and/or with a given designative content in its medial cluster.
(d) attribution of a rank-shifted predication with a terminal cluster bound by co-reference to the terminal cluster of the main predication.

As is evident from this list, what precedes or follows a medial cluster may be specified not only in terms of designative content, but in terms of other conditions, such as that the terminal element is not a cluster at all but a rank-shifted predication. For example, it is a condition of using the relative components 'think', 'know', 'hope', etc, that the final element of the predication must be rank-shifted assertion: *eg* 'that you are wrong'. (An exception to this is the permissibility of a cluster consisting of $\emptyset$ or θ.) 'Promise' is an example of a relative component which not only demands a following rank-shifted assertion, but a rank-shifted assertion with a given designative content in its medial cluster, namely a semantic specification of future time.

Again as in the case of dependence rules, one would like to be able to restrict the range of theoretically possible contextual properties as much as possible. Notice, for example, that the above list allows for specification of designative features within the medial cluster, but not the terminal clusters of a rank-shifted predication (except for the case of co-referential θ allowed for in (d) above). But there are powerful restrictions inherent in this whole method of stating selection conditions. It is assumed, in particular, that the content of a, in a predication $a \cdot r \cdot b$, is irrelevant to the semantic determination of what can occur in b. This means that the theory cannot explain the absurdity of

(1) 'A man has been eating this book' $(a \cdot r \cdot b)$

in contrast to the acceptability of

(2) 'A worm has been eating this book' $(c \cdot r \cdot b)$
(3) 'A man has been eating this food' $(a \cdot r \cdot d)$

since if $a \cdot r$ and $r \cdot b$ are individually acceptable combinations, the predication $a \cdot r \cdot b$ as a whole cannot contain any violation of selection restrictions. In any case, however, this is the sort of absurdity one would regard as factual rather than linguistic. (One case in which this limitation on the form of contextual conditions does not seem to work is in the case of predications $a \cdot \rightarrow \beta \, b \cdot c$ containing the attributive formator. This difficulty will be dealt with in §4.2.1.)

If it is accepted, as proposed here, that a violation of selection restrictions is simply a special case of oxymoron, there still remains the need for a weaker category of semantic incongruity to account for certain problems of co-occurrence in the fields of spatial and temporal relations.

English locative prepositions are divisible into groups according to the "dimensionality" they attribute to the reference of the following nominal. *At, to, from* indicate an absence or irrelevance of spatial dimension (*at the bus-stop, to the door*); *on, on to, off* suggest a line or a surface (*on the road, the frontier, the ceiling* – but note that *on* can also mean 'on top of'); *in, into, out of* suggest an area or a volume (*in the field, the room,* etc).[5] The choice of preposition does not reflect the actual dimensional properties of the object of orientation, but rather the way in which it is imagined by the speaker. *At London* would be appropriate to a conversation in which inter-continental distances were under discussion (*eg: I stopped at London on my way to New York*), and London was envisaged just as a point on the map. Otherwise the preposition *in*, making London into an area, would be used. If we analysed the meaning of these prepositions by the method applied to *pride* and *marry* above, we would distinguish *at, on,* and *in*, etc, by the occurrence in the terminal cluster of contrasting components IDIME ('no dimension relevant'), 2DIME ('line or surface'), and 3DIME ('area or volume'). However, the 'London' of *at London* would now logically exclude that of *in London*, and this would lead to false analyses: for example, the unobjectionable assertion 'The town you were in was the town I was at' would be classified as a contradiction.

A rather similar problem confronts us in the semantic analysis of verbal aspect (see §7.5 below). The difference between 'He spoke for five hours' and 'He was speaking for five hours' (to over-simplify) is that in the first case the speech is psychologically comprehended as an event in its entirety, and in the second case as a continuing activity. However, it would be patently wrong to regard these two assertions as logically inconsistent – a conclusion which would be forced upon us if we construed this as a systemic contrast in the meaning of the verb.

Yet there are cases of complete incompatibility even in these fields of "weakened" semantic contrast. They occur for example with items whose meaning expressly includes some notion of dimensionality, such as *point* and *line*. We would presumably want to class as violations phrases such as *in this point on the map* (instead of *at this point on the map*), or *in the finishing line* (rather than *on the finishing line*). The case is clearer for temporal relations: *in six o'clock* and *at the year 1904* are equally unacceptable, the one assigning duration to a point in time, the other assigning lack of duration, or instantaneity, to a period.

A solution to this problem of "weakened" selection restrictions is to state them by means of ASCRIPTION FEATURES which do not actually form part of the componential content of the adjacent terminal cluster, but are rather matched against its content, such that co-occurrence with a systemically contrasting component is marked as a violation.[6] The locative use of the preposition *in* for example, would be associated with the ascription feature [3DIME] which in the phrase *in this point of the map* conflicts with the component IDIME inherent in the meaning of *point*. As the meaning of *London*, however, would contain no inherent feature of dimensionality, the preference of *in London* to *at London* would be a matter of psychological and factual plausibility, not semantic incompatibility. Systems of ascription features are attributed *as a whole* to the terminal cluster. A particular definition, however, may select a particular feature from the system; *eg* [IDIME] for *at*, [2DIME] for *on* and [3DIME] for *in*. (For further exemplification see §§7.1, 7.5, and 8.1.)

4.1.3 *Nonsensical questions and commands*
A slightly less problematic task is that of extending the class of absurd predications beyond assertions to questions and commands. Corresponding to tautologies and contradictions are questions which logically require the answer "Yes" and the answer "No" respectively: 'Is your wife married?'; 'Did you see the invisible man?' Other questions are nonsensical because they rest on absurd presuppositions[7]; 'How many people in this street own cars which don't belong to them?' presupposes the contradiction 'Some people in this street own cars which don't belong to them'. There are also logically impossible commands like 'Please eat up this delicious inedible fish'. Such categories of absurdity seem to be derivable in fairly straightforward ways from contradictions. Selection restrictions apply as much to questions and commands (*eg* 'Do you eat happiness?', 'Meet me under six o'clock') as to assertions.

4.2 One-place and many-place predicates

The method of description given so far differs from the orthodox analysis of predicate logic in that it restricts predicates (or, in the present terminology, predications) to those having two places. In predicate logic, in contrast, there are one-place predicates such as Wx ('x is white'), two-place predicates such as Lxy ('x loves y'), three-place predicates such as $Gxyz$ ('x gives y to z'), and indeed n-place predicates for any positive integer n. Through rank-shift and downgrading, however, it is possible to reduce all these various types to one: the two-place predicate.[8]

The advantages of this reduction are great. Not only is the theoretical apparatus of description greatly simplified, but the many unexplored problems of analysing the logical structure of many-place predicates are brought within range of solution. Certain problems arise, however, with the one-place predicate, and it is to these that attention will first be given.

4.2.1 *One-place predicates*

As we saw in §3.2, it is quite easy to treat a one-place or "simple" predicate as a special kind of (two-place) predication, in which the linking or medial element is the attributive formator $\rightarrow\beta$. This is an advantage for the rules of expression, for it allows a direct correspondence to be made between a semantic structure $a \cdot \rightarrow\beta\ b \cdot c$ and the grammatical structure Subject-*be*-Complement. But the structural parallel between assertions like 'I am hungry' and assertions like 'I know Harry' is not so close as this analysis suggests.

First, the final element of $a \cdot \rightarrow\beta\ b \cdot c$ 'I am hungry' cannot be quantified in the same way as the initial element a. 'I am all hungry' or 'I am some hungry' are not sensible statements, unless 'all' is taken as quantifying the initial element a, so that the total meaning is 'all of me is hungry'. (Adverbs like *somewhat* and *entirely* are not relevant, as applied to *hungry* they would be interpreted 'to some degree', 'to the entire extent', etc.)

Second, a prominent class of semantic components occurring at c, *viz*, those expressed by descriptive adjectives *hungry*, *rich*, *bright*, etc, cannot occur at a except in combination with other components. For instance, whereas it is possible to say *John is hungry*, it is not possible to say *Rich is hungry or **Hungry knows Harry*.[9]

Third, the converse interpretations associated with the direction of the arrow in a relative system do not materialise in the case of $\rightleftarrows\beta$. There is no contrast in meaning between $a \cdot \rightarrow\beta\ b \cdot c$ 'I am hungry' and $a \cdot \leftarrow\beta\ b \cdot c$ 'Hungry is me', since in fact the second ordering is nonsensical. In the few cases where both orderings do result in an acceptable statement, for example, 'John is the manager' and 'The manager is John', there is no need for distinct semantic specifications, as the two versions appear to be cognitively synonymous.

A different method of analysis, dispensing with the attributive system $\rightleftarrows\beta$, may therefore be proposed. It is suggested that one of the terminal elements of a predication should be considered optional, thus making provision for a predication of the simpler "one-place" structure $a: m$. (The colon (:), marking the boundary between terminal and attributive elements, serves as a symbolic means of discriminating two-place and one-place predicates.) With the absence of a second terminal element, there is no need for the relative system's role of ordering the terminal elements with respect to one another. Thus the element m otherwise corresponding to the medial cluster of a two-place predication (we may call it the ATTRIBUTIVE CLUSTER) does not contain a relative component. From this it follows, also, that there is no possibility of converse interpretations arising from opposite orderings: $a:m$ and $m:a$, according to the mirror-image convention, are merely interchangeable notational variants. The range of features capable of occurring at m overlaps with that capable of occurring at a, but the content of each cluster is generally distinguishable, in that m is the cluster which contains features of tense and aspect, being in this respect equivalent to the medial cluster of a two-place predication. The terminal cluster a can, as in a two-place predication, be replaced by a rank-shifted predication, symbolised (X) in the formula $(X):m$ or $m:(X)$. The variables m, n, p, and q will be reserved for feature combinations, such as that representing 'hungry', which can constitute attributive clusters, so that they may be kept distinct, in the notation, from both terminal and medial clusters.

Allowing optional elements in the structure of a predication has this additional advantage: it gives us the means to assign semantic structure to sentences such as *It is raining*, which could not otherwise be satisfactorily dealt with. Since the subject *it* in such sentences is without content, they can best be treated as expressing "zero-place predicates", that is, in the present system, predications from which both terminal elements are omitted.

In the light of the modifications of this section, it is necessary to revise the notation of the earlier definitions of implication, tautology, etc (§§2.8.2 to 2.8.5), which were framed for two-place predicates only. Thus rule, [C] of §2.8.2, may be restated:

An assertion $a \cdot r \cdot c$ implies an assertion $b \cdot r \cdot c$ or an assertion $a:m$ implies an assertion $b:m$ if (the specifications being otherwise identical)

(i) a logically includes b

(ii) the clusters a and b are construed as if universally quantified.

So extended, the rule will apply both to two-place and one-place predicates. It would be preferable, however, for a concise statement of this and other rules, to have a cover symbol (say u) applying indifferently to medial and attributive clusters. The alternative structures $a \cdot r \cdot b$ and $a:m$ could then be subsumed in a single formula $a \cdot u \cdot (b)$, the bracket round b indicating that that element is optional in the formula. Nevertheless, to avoid introducing further notational complications, I shall continue the practice of restricting formulaic exemplification, wherever possible, to two-place predicates, letting it be understood that with simple emendations any formula could be normally applied equally well to one-place predicates.

One point that can still be raised in defence of the analysis using the system $\rightleftarrows\beta$ is that it maintains a correspondence between grammatical structure (Subject-*be*-Complement) and semantic structure $(a \cdot r \cdot b)$; whereas in the present analysis, the verb *be* has to be supplied, as an element without content, to "carry" the features of tense, etc, which are normally assigned to the verbal group in clause structure. However, this argument is weakened, with reference to language in general, by observation that in some languages, including Russian, sentences analogous to *He is tall* have no verbal element. Moreover, with reference to English in particular, many grammatical constructions expressing attribution do not contain the verb *be*: *They called him a traitor* for **They called him be a traitor; with his hat crooked* for **with his hat being crooked;* etc. The one-place predicate structure also underlies, it is assumed, "true intransitive verbs" like *sleep, die, bark*, and *laugh*.

4.2.2 *Many-place predicates*
No more than the barest and most tentative sketch of this forbidding subject can be given here.

Three-place predicates can be readily reduced to two-place or one-place predicates through the subordination of one predication inside another, either by rank-shift or downgrading. The indirect object construction of *a gives/sells/lends b to d* and the object-complement construction of *a makes b m* (*eg: She makes me angry*), for instance, can be semantically analysed as follows:

$$a \cdot \to c \cdot (b \cdot \to h \cdot d) \quad \text{'}a \text{ causes } b \text{ to have } d\text{'}$$
$$a \cdot \to c \cdot (b : m) \quad \text{'}a \text{ causes } b \text{ to be } m\text{'}$$

To represent a four-place predicate R*abcd*, three predications may be ordered in dependence in several different ways; some possibilities are:

(i) $a \cdot r \cdot (b \cdot s \cdot (c \cdot t \cdot d))$
(ii) $(a \cdot r \cdot b) \cdot s \cdot (c \cdot t \cdot d)$
(iii) $a \cdot r \cdot (b \cdot s \cdot \langle \theta' \cdot t \cdot c \rangle \cdot d)'$

Which is the correct analysis has, of course, to be determined on empirical grounds: *ie* what consequences each analysis has in terms of basic statements.

In these formulae I have omitted the factor of quantification, which would clearly add to the complexity of the structure, by introducing extra rank-shift and downgrading. Quantification, in fact, provides support for the analysis of many-place predicates into predications on the lines proposed here. (Exemplification will be limited, as usual, to binary predications.) It seems that a maximum of four different quantificational readings can be given to a three-place predicate. To see this, let us examine as an illustration the predicate 'Person *a* commits crime *b* on day *c*'. As in the case of the two-place predicates considered in §3.5, the different interpretations can be displayed by associating them with the order of syntactic expression which favours them; *ie* the linear order which corresponds to semantic ordering in dependence:

    (i) 'Every crime was committed by somebody on some day.'
   (ii) 'Somebody committed every crime on some day.'
  (iii) 'On some day, every crime was committed by somebody.'
  (iv) 'On some day, somebody committed every crime.'

My first task here is to convince any sceptical reader that four separate interpretations, corresponding to these four renderings, are possible. For this purpose, I shall construct a "model", *ie* an imaginary world against which the truth of each of the four assertions may be measured under specified conditions. My model contains just three people, John, Jim, and Jane; three crimes, larceny, burglary, and bigamy; and three days, Monday, Tuesday, and Wednesday. Thus for the purpose of the model, 'Everybody' means simply 'John, Jim, and Jane', and so on. Each possible state of affairs within the model is described by a conjunction of particular assertions, *eg* 'John committed larceny on Monday, and Jim committed bigamy on Wednesday'. It is usually possible to compress the expression of each set of conjoined statements unambiguously within a single sentence. A set of statements is said to "satisfy" one of the quantified assertions (i) to (iv) if its truth, given the limitations of the model, is sufficient to guarantee the truth of the latter.[10] We can now demonstrate the difference between any two readings by presenting a set of particular statements which satisfy one, but not the other:

[a] 'John committed larceny on Monday, Jim committed burglary on Tuesday, and Jane committed bigamy on Wednesday.' This satisfies (i), but not (ii), (iii), or (iv).

[b] 'John committed larceny on Monday, burglary on Tuesday, and bigamy on Wednesday.' This satisfies (i) and (ii), but not (iii) or (iv).

[c] 'John committed larceny on Monday, Jim committed burglary on Monday, and Jane committed bigamy on Monday. This satisfies (i) and (iii), but not (ii) or (iv).

[d] 'John committed larceny, burglary, and bigamy on Monday.'

   This satisfies all four statements.

   The differing truth conditions in [a], [b], and [c] above are sufficient to show that four interpretations are possible. What is less easy to show is that *no more than* four interpretations are possible, either for this example, or for any other predication containing three quantifiers. So far, it appears that the maximum number of interpretations for one-, two-, and three-place predicates are as follows:

1-PLACE: 1 – *a.*
2-PLACE: 2 – *a b, b a.*
3-PLACE: 4 – *a b c, b a c, c a b, c b a.*

Two further orderings of the terms of the three-predicate are apparently not semantically significant, in that syntactic orderings with which they would naturally be associated do not yield further interpretations: *Every crime was committed on some day by somebody* and *Somebody on some day committed every crime* suggest interpretations (i) and (iv) respectively. It appears, then, that the number of interpretations measured against the number of predicates follows the series 2^{n-1} (1, 2, 4, 8, . . .), rather than the series of factorial numbers $n!$ (1, 2, 6, 24, . . .), which would be correct if every term were given equal weight with the others, as in orthodox predicate calculus. The two missing orderings, *a c b* and *b c a*, are those in which *c* occurs between *a* and *b*, and are precisely those which would be discounted if *a* and *b* were bracketed together in constituent structure. The series 2^{n-1} (*ie* the doubling of the number of interpretations for each additional place) is what is predicted if terms are considered to be related through binary bracketing, as in the system proposed here. The analysis of many-place predicates into nested binary predicates follows naturally, therefore, from the study of what interpretations are possible under mixed quantification.

Another reason for favouring this reduction is that it simplifies the statement of co-occurrence conditions and of logical conditions such as symmetry and transitivity. If, for example, '*a* showed *b c*' is analysed '*a* let *b* see *c*' (formulaically, $a \cdot \rightarrow l \cdot (b \cdot \rightarrow s \cdot c)$), then the selection restrictions which apply to 'see' will apply automatically to the *b* and *c* of '*a* showed *b c*': the same rule which excludes 'The cupboard saw an interesting photograph' will exclude 'He showed the cupboard an interesting photograph', and no special statement of selection restrictions for 'show' will be necessary. Similarly, if '*a* married *b* to *c*' is analysed as '*a* (ceremonially) caused *b* to be married to *c* (*ie:* $a \cdot \rightarrow c \cdot (b \cdot \rightarrow m \cdot c)$), then the statement of the condition of symmetricity on the relationship 'is married to' can be extended at no further cost to the relationship expressed by the transitive verb. This condition will account for the analyticity not only of 'Anyone John is married to is married to John', but also of 'Anyone who married John to Susan married Susan to John'.

4.3 Formal rules of synonymy

One of the principles on which this approach to semantics has been founded is that linguistic occurrences having equivalent meaning should be represented by the same descriptive formula (§2.3). If this convention were followed consistently, no extra rules for establishing synonymy would be required. However, the plain fact is that this principle cannot account for all relations of synonymy, or at least cannot do so without inordinate complication of the rules of expression and semantic structure. We might therefore look upon the various rules of synonymy to be given in this and the following sections as acknowledgements of the limited efficacy of the convention of "one meaning – one specification".

Rules of synonymy are divided into FORMAL and SUBSTANTIVE rules: those general rules which apply without respect to designative content, and those which operate on particular designatives.[11] The following are among the most important rules of the former kind (" = " represents the relation of synonymy).

4.3.1 *Rule of co-reference*

$$a' \ldots \theta' \, b = ab$$

This equation simply expresses in a formal way what has already been explained in §3.3: a cluster containing θ co-referring to a is semantically equivalent to the same cluster with a substituted for θ. "a" and "b" in this equation (as elsewhere) stand for arbitrary sets of features, and ab for the union of a and b. For example, 'My friend . . . she's an artist' is synonymous with 'My (female) friend is an artist'; here b includes the meaning 'female' not present in a, so that ab contains more features than a alone. Note that 'The house in whom I live' is rejected as a violation, because ab in this case is an oxymoron, containing the opposed terms 'animate' and 'inanimate', 'animate' being entailed by the 'human' feature of 'whom'.

4.3.2 *Rule of negated negation*
This rule can be paraphrased "Two negatives make a positive":

$$a \cdot {\sim} {\sim} r \cdot b = a \cdot r \cdot b$$

The severe constraints on the occurrence of negated negation, demonstrated, for example, by the oddity of sentences like 'I didn't not like her', may be regarded as grammatical rather than semantic.

4.3.3 *Rule of subordination*
In the analysis of mixed quantification in §3.5, we distinguished between the two meanings of *All cats like some fish* by a different order of subordination: the one quantifying predication contained the principal predication, whereas the other was downgraded inside its medial cluster, and these functions could be exchanged, to supply contrasting specifications:

(1) $\theta' \cdot 1\alpha \rightarrow o \cdot (c' \cdot \rightarrow l \, \langle \theta'' \cdot 2\alpha \leftarrow o \cdot \theta''' \rangle \cdot f''')''$
(2) $\theta' \cdot 2\alpha \rightarrow o \cdot (f' \cdot \leftarrow l \, \langle \theta'' \cdot 1\alpha \leftarrow o \cdot \theta''' \rangle \cdot c''')''$

However, it is only in a case of *mixed* quantification (*ie* of an assertion containing both 1α and 2α) that such an ambiguity arises. Consequently, a sentence like *All cats like all fish* (where the quantifiers are identical) or

All cats like this fish (where there is only one quantifier) is given two specifications on the lines of (1) and (2) above for only a single meaning. This calls for a rule of synonymy (subject to certain conditions) which shows the equivalence of the alternative specifications:

$$a \cdot \rightleftarrows r \, (b \cdot s \cdot c) = (b \cdot s \, \langle \theta' \cdot \rightleftarrows r \cdot a \rangle \cdot c)'$$

(The two sets of arrows preceding *r* indicate that the direction of the arrow on the right-hand side must be the opposite of that of the left-hand arrow, which may, however, point in either direction.) Such a rule is, indeed, required for other reasons. Consider the ambiguity of the following examples:

He doesn't listen on purpose.
He didn't do it to annoy his daughter.
He hasn't been staying here for a long time.
I don't feel particularly upset because of what he said.

In each case there is an interpretation in which the adjunct (*on purpose*, etc) is included within the scope of the negation, and one in which it is not.[12] The latter interpretation is the one that comes to the fore if the adjunct is placed before the subject: *Because of what he said, I don't feel particularly upset*, although even here the former meaning, given special intonation, seems possible. The situation here is a close parallel of that of mixed quantification, and is fittingly handled by the same distinction of subordinating order. The one specification $(b \cdot \sim s \, \langle \theta' \cdot r \cdot a \rangle \cdot c)'$ shows the adjunct (represented by $a \cdot r$) to be included within the scope of the negation (*ie* within the negated predication), whereas the other $a \cdot r$ $(b \cdot \sim s \cdot c)$ does not. This then is another case for which subordinating order is needed to distinguish ambiguity, but only under a certain condition: the condition of the cluster *s* being negative. The conditions noted here, (a) mixed quantification and (b) negation of *s* are not the only conditions which block the operation of this rule of synonymy.[13]

4.3.4 *First rule of attribution*
In the present framework, we need a rule which will convert a down-graded attributive predication (*ie* a one-place predicate) into a compo-nential formula:

$$a' \, \langle \theta' \, b:m \rangle = abm$$

(Here again *abm* stands for the union of *a*, *b*, and *m*.) This equation ex-plains the synonymy of pairs such as 'a load which is heavy' and 'a heavy load'. The following is an exemplification in which use is made of the by now very familiar systems introduced in §2.2:

$+\text{HUM} +\text{MAT}' \langle \theta' \; +\text{HUM}: -\text{MALE} \rangle = +\text{HUM} +\text{MAT} -\text{MALE}$
'adult who is female' $\qquad\qquad =$ 'woman'

3*

In this illustration, no account is given of the factor of tense which distinguishes 'who is female' from 'who was female', etc. This factor, together with modal and adverbial meanings, is included in *m* in the formula. Whether they are all to be transferred from the left hand to the right hand of the equation is a difficult problem of detail. However, it is clear that many can be so transferred, and expressed by some form of premodification: *a former secretary* ('who was once/had once been secretary'); *a future Prime Minister* ('who is/was to be Prime Minister one day'); *a possible friend* ('who may be a friend'), etc. The modifiers exemplified here show their predicational origin in that they do not conform to the usual semantic pattern of adjectives: for example, whereas *A good secretary is a secretary* can always be given a tautologous interpretation, the same is not true of *A former secretary is a secretary*.

A question of theoretical interest may be raised here. The rule of attribution just given provides a means not only of converting a downgraded predication into a componential formula, but also of carrying out the reverse operation, *ie* converting a componential representation into a predicational one. Taking this process to its logical conclusion, we might re-express each componential formula as a set of downgraded predications. Thus the definition of man, +HUM +MALE +MAT, would be rewritten:

$$
\begin{array}{ll}
\varnothing' & \text{'(something)'} \\
\left\{
\begin{array}{l}
\theta': \text{+HUM} \\
\theta': \text{+MALE} \\
\theta': \text{+MAT}
\end{array}
\right.
&
\begin{array}{l}
\text{'that is human'} \\
\text{'that is male'} \\
\text{'that is mature'}
\end{array}
\end{array}
$$

If this method of statement were systematically preferred to the old one, the attribution rule above could be dispensed with entirely: there would no longer be any difference between the specifications of *a man, a mature male who is human, a mature human who is male*, etc, which would be distinguished only by rules of expression. However, for this saving of a single rule, we would have sacrificed a great deal in terms of the brevity of every componential specification. Which method of statement is therefore preferable?

One way to avoid this decision would be to treat componential formulae such as +HUM +MALE +MAT simply as notational abbreviations for the lengthier formulae expressed in terms of downgrading. The first attribution rule would then be not a rule of English semantics, but a rule simply belonging to the analyst's "spelling" system, which could be ignored in assessing the simplicity of alternative descriptions. However, one or two reasons can be tentatively put forward why the established concept of a componential formula should be retained on a theoretical footing. One is that the attempt to derive componential formulae from sets of downgraded predications is circular, since the concept of downgrading was defined (in §2.5.2) in terms of componential analysis, and indeed, there seems no other obvious way in which to define it. Thus to reduce componential analysis to predicational analysis in this way would be to define something by something more complicated than itself. A second argument is that the abolition of the above attribution rule would only be an apparent simplification of the description, as a compensatory increase in the complexity of the expression rules would then be necessary. If the meanings of both *a tired man* and *a man who is tired* are to be derived from the same semantic specification, which can be rendered '(something) which is human, which is male, which is mature, which is tired', then there has to be a rule which generates the formal representation for *a tired man* by assigning zero expression to θ in 'who is tired', and makes *tired* a modifier of *man*. This rule, or rather set of rules, would largely duplicate the work of the attribution rule of synonymy. A firm decision on this matter must, however, await a more detailed consideration of expression rules than has been possible here.

4.3.5 *Second rule of attribution*
This attribution rule, like the previous one, has the effect of converting a one-place predication with downgrading into a two-place predication, and vice-versa.

$$a:m'\langle \theta' \cdot r \cdot b\rangle = a \cdot r\, m \cdot b$$

Examples of the type of synonymy represented in this equation are:

'He's a philatelist' = 'He collects stamps'.
'He's a supporter of Jackson' = 'He supports Jackson'.
'He's a friend of ours' = 'He's friendly with/towards us'.
'He's Richard's teacher' = 'He teaches Richard'.

A troublesome ambiguity of many agent nouns may obscure the synonymy this equation is intended to express. Terms like *bookseller*, *baker*, and *singer* generally carry the additional meaning 'by trade' or 'by profession'. Hence in its most obvious sense, *He's a bookseller* is not quite synonymous with *He sells books*.

It may have been noticed that we have so far failed to deal adequately with converse relationships expressed by agent nouns and similar items. The mirror image convention on its own cannot show such sentences as 'That man is William's teacher' and 'William is that man's pupil' to be synonymous, since the converse relationship is here specified in a downgraded predication. However, with the help of the mirror image convention *and* the second rule of attribution, we are now able to account for these cases. Let $l =$ 'that lady, $\rightarrow t =$ teach, $w =$ William; then the following are definitions of *teacher* (*of*) and *pupil* (*of*) respectively:

$\varnothing'\langle\theta'\cdot{\to}t\cdot\varnothing\rangle$; $\varnothing'\langle\theta'\cdot{\leftarrow}t\cdot\varnothing\rangle$. The two assertions whose synonymy is to be demonstrated are:

$l\colon \varnothing'\langle\theta'\cdot{\to}t\cdot w\rangle$ 'That lady is William's teacher.'
$w\colon \varnothing'\langle\theta'\cdot{\leftarrow}t\cdot l\rangle$ 'William is that lady's pupil.'

The steps by which they are shown to be equivalent are:

$l\colon \varnothing'\langle\theta'\cdot{\to}t\cdot w\rangle = l\cdot{\to}t\cdot w$ (2nd attribution rule)
$\qquad\qquad\qquad = w\cdot{\leftarrow}t\cdot l$ (mirror-image convention)
$\qquad\qquad\qquad = w\cdot \varnothing'\langle\theta'\cdot{\leftarrow}t\cdot l\rangle$ (2nd attribution rule)

Similarly, we may show the analyticity of 'William is his teacher's pupil':

$w\colon \varnothing'\langle\theta'\cdot{\leftarrow}t\cdot \varnothing''\langle\theta''\cdot{\to}t\cdot w\rangle\rangle$ 'William is the pupil of William's teacher'

$= w\cdot{\leftarrow}t\cdot \varnothing'\langle\theta'\cdot{\to}t\cdot w\rangle$ 'William is taught by his teacher' (2nd attribution rule)

$= \varnothing'\langle\theta'\cdot{\to}t\cdot w\rangle\cdot{\to}t\cdot w$ 'William's teacher teaches William' (mirror-image convention)

This is a tautology in accordance with rule [G] of §2.8.4, since $\varnothing\cdot{\to}t\cdot w$ implies $\varnothing\cdot{\to}t\cdot w$ (every assertion implies itself). The second attribution rule can likewise be used to demonstrate that *The son of Pharaoh's daughter is the daughter of Pharaoh's son* expresses a tautology on one interpretation, and a contradiction on another; however, I leave the reader to work this out for his own satisfaction.

4.4 Substantive rules of synonymy

To illustrate the need for semantic equations which include mention of individual designative systems, we may consider the problem of describing the meaning of kinship terms in English. We could almost account for the semantic relations between such main terms as *father*, *daughter*, *grandson*, *nephew*, *aunt*, etc, simply by two systems:

$\begin{cases}+\text{MALE 'male'} \\ -\text{MALE 'female'}\end{cases}$ $\begin{cases}{\to}\text{PAR}\quad '(a)\text{ is parent of }(b)' \\ {\leftarrow}\text{PAR}\quad '(b)\text{ is parent of }(a)'\end{cases}$

The definitions of kinship terms contain downgrading, often to a depth of two or more, so for simplicity's sake designative components alone will be written in specifications, and will be abbreviated to a single initial. It will be understood that these are to be fitted, in the order given, into a definition of the following pattern:

$a'\langle\theta'\cdot r\cdot \varnothing''\langle\theta''\cdot s\cdot \varnothing'''\langle\theta'''\cdot t\cdot \ldots\rangle\rangle\rangle$

The full specification for 'great grandson', for instance is:

$+\text{MALE}'\langle\theta'\cdot{\leftarrow}\text{PAR}\cdot \varnothing''\langle\theta''\cdot{\leftarrow}\text{PAR}\cdot \varnothing'''\langle\theta'''\cdot{\leftarrow}\text{PAR}\cdot \varnothing\rangle\rangle\rangle$
('male child of child of child of')

whereas the abbreviated specification is +M; ←P; ←P; ←P. Other specimen formulae follow:[14]

+M; →P	'father' (='male parent of')
−M; ←P	'daughter' (='female child of')
−M; →P; →P	'grandmother' (='female parent of parent of')
+M; ←P; →P	'brother' (='male child of parent of')
+M; ←P; →P; →P	'uncle' (='male child of parent of parent of')

This method of analysis would distinguish various degrees of remoteness of generation and collaterality, and would also (by means of the second attribution rule of §4.3.5) account for the synonymy of converse sentences containing "reciprocal" kinship terms:[15]

William is Susan's father = Susan is William's daughter
William is Sam's uncle = Sam is William's nephew

and so on.

It would, however, have at least two critical defects.

Firstly, it would mark 'I am my own brother/sister' as a tautology, regarding it as equivalent to 'I am my parents' child', whereas in fact it is a species of contradiction. This error would be carried into all more distant collateral relationships: 'My father is my uncle' and 'I am my own cousin' would be marked as tautologies. To correct the error, we need to set up a reciprocal system ⇆S 'sibling', and define it by the following equation:

$$a; ←S →S; b \quad = a; ←P; →P; b$$
$$\text{[where } a \neq b\text{]}$$

'*a* is *b*'s sibling' = '*a* is *b*'s parent's child'
[where $a \neq b$]

The new system is assigned the logical properties of symmetricity and irreflexivity, so that 'I am my sibling's sibling' is marked as a tautology, and 'I am my own sibling' as a contradiction. The terms *brother* and *sister* are defined as +M; ←S →S and −M; ←S →S respectively. Other definitions follow from these:

+M; ←S →S; →P	'uncle'	−M; ←S →S; →P	'aunt'
+M; ←P; ←S →S	'nephew'	−M; ←P; ←S →S	'niece'

The equation above illustrates what is meant by a SUBSTANTIVE rule of synonymy. Systems whose meanings are defined by such equations (in this case ⇆S) may be termed DERIVED systems, as distinct from the BASIC systems in respect of which they are defined.

A second flaw of the original analysis is that it provides an unsatisfactory account of such terms as *ancestor, descendant, generation*. The first two can only be represented (if we adhere to the convention of the previous definitions) by formulae like:

$\rightarrow$P^1; $\rightarrow$P^2; $\rightarrow$P^3, . . . , $\rightarrow$P^i 'parent of parent of parent of . . .'
$\leftarrow$P^1; $\leftarrow$P^2; $\leftarrow$P^3, . . . , $\leftarrow$P^i 'child of child of child of . . .'

which we interpret: "Write $\rightarrow$P (or $\leftarrow$P) as many times as you like in succession." *Generation* must express a difference of one, in any given specification, between the number of P components with a left-hand arrow, and the number with a right-hand arrow (a minimum vertical difference on the family tree). Such definitions introduce a far more complex and oblique relation between form and meaning than has been entertained up to now. In fact they are not semantic specifications at all, in the sense in which we have been using that term, but rather arithmetical generalisations *about* semantic specifications. Presuming that we do not want to complicate rules of expression in this way, we have no choice but to introduce new systems to define these terms, showing their relationship to $\rightarrow$P by a special rule of synonymy:

$\rightarrow$P^1; $\rightarrow$P^2; $\rightarrow$P^3; . . . ; $\rightarrow$P^i = $\rightarrow$A iG
'parent's parent's parent's . . .'

= '1st, 2nd, 3rd, . . . generation ancestor'.

A relative system $\leftrightarrows$A ('ancestor'/'descendant') is here supplemented by a hierarchic system 1G, 2G, 3G, . . . , nG ('first generation'/'second generation'/'third generation'/. . . 'nth generation'), such that $\rightarrow$P; $\rightarrow$P is replaced by $\rightarrow$A 2G, $\leftarrow$P; $\leftarrow$P; $\leftarrow$P by $\leftarrow$A 3G; etc. As $\rightarrow$A 2G, $\rightarrow$A 3G, etc, are logically included in $\rightarrow$A, these alternative definitions of *grandparent*, *great grandparent*, etc, account for the analyticity of 'My grandparent is my ancestor'; 'My great grandchildren are descended from me'; etc.

To define more remote kinship relations, two further systems need to be introduced by another rule of synonymy. These are a reciprocal system 'cousin', and a hierarchic system of collaterality, 1L, 2L, . . . , nL measuring horizontal distance on the family tree, just as the system of generation measures vertical distance:

$\leftarrow$A iG; $\leftarrow$S $\rightarrow$S; $\rightarrow$A jG = $\leftarrow$C $\rightarrow$C min (i,j)L $|i-j|$G

The prescripts "min (i, j)" and "$|i-j|$" mean respectively "the smaller of i and j" and "the difference between i and j", where i and j are arbitrary positive integers. Examples of the application of this rule are:

$\leftarrow$A 2G; $\leftarrow$S $\rightarrow$S; $\rightarrow$A 2G = $\leftarrow$C $\rightarrow$C 2L 0G
('grandparent's sibling's grandchild' = 'second cousin')

$\leftarrow$A 1G; $\leftarrow$S $\rightarrow$S; $\rightarrow$A 2G = $\leftarrow$C $\rightarrow$C 1L 1G
('parent's sibling's grandchild' = 'first cousin once removed')

The prescripts of L and G coincide respectively with the use of numerical quantities in expressions such as *second cousin* and *cousin twice removed*. The zero prescript of OG indicates the absence of an expression "*x* times removed"; it may, in fact, be equated with the lack of any term from the system of generation.

Substantive rules of synonymy, as we have seen, lead in many cases to alternative definitions, which seem to represent overlapping frameworks of classification. For example, on the one hand uncles may be classified by reference to the inner family circle: +M; ←S →S; →P. On the other hand, they may be classified as the closest representatives of a "super-class" of all kin-types designated by an expression containing the item *uncle*; *ie* not only uncles, but great uncles, great great uncles, etc.[16] In the latter case the appropriate definition of the superclass is +M; ←S →S; →A, and of the subclass +M; ←S →S; →A 1G ('1st-generation uncles'). A similar ambivalence is felt in the meaning of *cousin* (= 'first cousin'), *aunt*, *nephew*, *niece*, and even of *father* and *children* (compare the biblical use of *fathers* for 'male ancestors' and *children* for 'descendants'). In general, the more concise definition seems to conform to habits of popular definition, and to be instinctively preferable.

Chapter 5

The limits of semantics

We are now in a better position than at the outset of this study to consider where to place the boundaries of semantics. The approach I have taken to be the only acceptable one is that voiced by Chomsky (1965: 159) with particular reference to the frontier between semantics and syntax: "In general, one should not expect to be able to delimit a large and complex domain before it has been thoroughly explored. A decision as to the boundary separating syntax and semantics (if there is one) is not a prerequisite for theoretical and descriptive study of syntactic and semantic rules." Notice that we do not ask where the boundaries of semantics lie, but rather where is the best place to put them. That is, we let the theory of semantics determine the extent of its subject-matter, rather than the other way round. The best decision is that which results in the most economical and general solutions to semantic questions, and (so far as they are known) those of related fields of study.

5.1 Semantics and grammar

We may start by considering how this principle affects the "demarcation" between semantics and grammar. According to the thesis of autonomy of levels (see §2.6) the vocabularies of grammatical and semantic description are separate, except for general theoretical terms such as "system" and "structure". Therefore the boundary between grammar and semantics has to be drawn somewhere – they cannot simply "shade into one another", or be regarded as inseparable.[1]

Whereas the role of semantics is to explain those concepts, such as meaningfulness and synonymy, discussed in §1.2, the primary purpose of grammar, crudely speaking, is to explain the formal distributional patterns of language: to separate items into classes and subclasses on the basis of their distribution, and to state the distributional properties of the classes in terms of constituent structure.

The domains of semantics and grammar overlap in two ways. Firstly, there is the question of well-formedness: an expression such as *foolish sage* might be rejected as "non-English" either on grounds of being ungrammatical or of being unsemantic (meaningless). In the given case, it is plain that the elimination can be made more economically by semantic means. If we show the oddness of this phrase in terms of an antonymy ±WISE ('wise'/'foolish'), we relate it to a general rule which will not only exclude this example, but also many other related absurdities: *a wise fool, a wise idiot, a foolish wise man, this wise man is a fool, this sage is foolish*, etc, etc. But in grammar, we could do little more than establish *ad hoc* classes of adjective and noun, consisting of *foolish* and *sage* respectively (together with any synonymous adjectives or nouns), and then make a rule which excludes their co-occurrence.

The question of ambiguity constitutes another area of overlap between the aims of semantics and grammar. If "ambiguity" is understood as "having more than one meaning", then the business of accounting for ambiguities belongs properly to semantics (see Ch. 2, n. 15). All the same, many ambiguities are dealt with in grammar, in the sense that the different meanings are separated through the assignment of different grammatical descriptions. One example is *I don't like worrying neighbours*, which may mean (a) 'I don't like causing worry to neighbours'; or (b) 'I don't like neighbours who cause worry'; (as well as (c) 'I don't like neighbours who worry about things', which we will leave out of account). The two interpretations (a) and (b) are distinguished in grammar by remarking that in case (a) *worrying neighbours* commutes with *worrying the neighbours, worrying new neighbours*, etc and is therefore *distributionally* like *buying furniture*, whereas in case (b) it commutes with *a worrying neighbour, the worrying neighbours*, etc, and is therefore distributionally like *giggling schoolgirls*. This is to say that the ambiguity is dealt with incidentally by rules which are in any case required for the statement of distributions. Nevertheless, numerous ambiguities lie outside the accepted realm of grammar: I am not aware, for example, that anyone has tried to separate grammatically the different interpretations of assertions under mixed quantification described in §3.5.

Where there is a potential overlap between grammar and semantics, three factors enter into the choice of how the facts are to be accounted for: the simplicity of semantic description, of grammatical description, and of the rules of expression which relate the one to the other. Halliday (1966) and Huddleston *et al* (1968) have recently introduced into the system-structure model the notions of "surface grammar" and "deep grammar" (inspired by the "surface structure" and "deep structure" of transformational grammar), of which the former is concerned with the distributions of items within constituent structures, and the latter with the underlying choices which determine these. It has been thought desirable that deep grammar should as far as reasonable reflect semantic relationships, perhaps, for example, in accounting even for ambiguities which are not reflected in distribution. In this modern view, therefore, grammar has extended its scope beyond the explanation of distributions to the relation of distributional facts to semantic facts. However, the goal of making deep grammar as semantically significant as possible should not be considered a duplication of the task of semantics, but rather as a means of bringing semantic and grammatical descriptions closer together, and thereby reducing the number of relationships which have to be covered by rules of expression.

Much work remains to be done on the independent description of grammar and semantics before the relative assessment of simplicity factors involved in the interrelation of the two can be seriously considered. The question to ask is: can the greater generalisation of given linguistic facts (*eg* of well-formedness) be achieved within grammatical or within semantic terms of reference? If the latter, then the semantic description in this particular case should be used to determine the relevant aspects of grammatical description. Two problems of linguistic description for which this is probably the best solution are briefly discussed below, simply as illustrations of the kind of assessment that has to be made.

[a] *Selection restrictions.* These are much more simply stated in semantics if, as we supposed in §4.1.2, all conditions of co-occurrence can be related to the choice of content in terminal elements, given the choice of a relative term in the medial cluster. In grammar, they would have to be stated with less generality, since there is a considerable variety of grammatical structures to which selection restrictions are relevant: Subject–Verb–Object; Subject–Verb–Prepositional Object; Head–Preposition–Prepositional Object; etc. Moreover, generalisations statable within the mirror-image convention of semantic notation could not be made on the grammatical level:

    (i) *Mrs Jones owns this carpet.*
    (ii) *This carpet belongs to Mrs Jones.*
    (iii) *This carpet owns Mrs Jones.*
    (iv) *Mrs Jones belongs to this carpet.*

A single contextual redundancy rule in semantics would account for the deviance of (iii) and (iv) compared with the well-formedness of (i) and (ii), whereas in grammar, so far as one can see, two separate statements, one for *belong* and the other for *own*, would be necessary.

[b] *Metalinguistic properties.* The notion of the "metalinguistic cluster" explained in §3.4 underlies certain features of grammatical description otherwise very troublesome. Provided it is in a context in which it can be given a metalinguistic interpretation, a nominal element of structure

can apparently be realised by any grammatical structure whatsoever: *Let's have no more "if only's"*; *The barometer needle is pointing at "cloudy to rain"*; etc. The choice is not even restricted to the set of possible English structures: *"I has very much hunger" said the foreigner* and *I'm reading Freud's "Abriss der Psychoanalyse"* are both perfectly reasonable English sentences, despite their inclusion of non-English elements. We have seen that semantics is able to explain the status within the utterance of the "metalinguistic" part (which in general is graphologically indicated by inverted commas). But in addition, semantics is best able to describe (through selection restrictions) the conditions under which a metalinguistic interpretation is possible: for example, why *"Yes" he said* is a well-formed utterance, whereas *"Yes" reads historical novels* is not.

5.2 Semantics and context

In the Firthian tradition of linguistic thought, as in some others, it has been customary to lump together semantics and what we may call "general stylistics"[2] (including the study of register) in one linguistic level ("context" or "context of situation") relating formal patterns to "non-linguistic events" (see Firth, 1957; Halliday, 1961; Dixon, 1964; Ellis, 1966). The separation of semantics from register is urged in the present study chiefly on the grounds that semantics, like grammar and phonology, is a systemic study, concerned with all-or-none choices, whereas register is primarily a probabilistic study, concerned with the likelihood of one choice rather than another in a given type of social situation. It is very rare for a particular form of language to be mandatory within a particular social context, and where this is so (as in a particular legal or religious formula spoken in a certain type of ceremony) we merely have a very special limiting case of maximum probability.[3]

Another reason for keeping semantics and general stylistics apart is that register statements have to be made about choices at all levels of systemic patterning, whereas semantic statements are only related to phonological and graphological statements through the intermediate level of form. Special intonation features are often observed in various styles of public speaking: in liturgical speech; in spoken advertising; in political oratory. Likewise, special punctuation conventions are employed in some types of written language, notably legal documents. If semantics and register are brought together within the same level, it is wrongly suggested that social context only influences phonological and graphological choice indirectly, through the intervening level of form.

Although stylistic variations have often been conflated with semantic variations, few people, strangely, have ever treated the dialectal

distribution of a form as constituting an aspect of its meaning. Dialect
surveys, on the contrary, rely heavily on a notion of synonymy in lexical
comparisons. Yet dialect and register are complementary studies of the
social aspect of language, the former dealing with language according to
user, and the latter with language according to use (see Halliday,
McIntosh, and Strevens, 1964: 77).

My view is that the separation of semantics from general stylistics is
desirable for an effective approach not only to dialect, but to register as
well. It is only when semantic analysis has isolated synonymic sets such
as *cast/throw/chuck* and *father/daddy/pop* that general stylistics can say
anything significant about the conditions under which one will be selected rather than another. Comparative formal statements of register, as
of dialect, require a constant factor of meaning in the things to be
compared.

I have suggested why there has to be a boundary *somewhere* between
the two studies, but have not stipulated how it is to be drawn. The study
of "general stylistics", as understood here, embraces not only factors of
register (social role, degree of familiarity, medium of communication,
etc) but also factors of thematic emphasis, of "given" and "new" in
discourse analysis, and of feeling, tone, and attitude.[4] It is in this last
area, that designated "emotive meaning" in a broad sense, that the
most obvious difficulties of delimitation occur. A case in point is the
personal noun *quack*, used in the sense 'an ignorant pretender to medical
skill'. It seems as if much of the derogatory import of this word follows
automatically from its meaning, as conveyed by above definition, whereas additional pejorative overtones have to be attributed to factors of
style: what kind of social situation would be implied by its use, etc.
Similar terms for which the unfavourable overtones are probably even
stronger are *tyrant, madman, dunce, idiot, thug*.

It would be premature to put forward hard and fast solutions to these
problems of indeterminacy without a great deal of thought and research;
however, at least some guiding principles can be suggested:

[a] Other things being equal, a semantic account of a particular set of
observations is preferable to a stylistic one, as a deterministic study
of meaning has greater explanatory power than a probabilistic study
of style.

[b] A distinction should be made between EVALUATIVE MEANING on
the one hand and FEELING-TONE on the other. By evaluative meaning, I mean a type of designative meaning in which overt reference is
made to values, whether aesthetic, moral, ethical, or otherwise: the type
of meaning found in the antonymies 'good'/'bad', 'right'/'wrong',
'nice'/'nasty', or with greater intensification in 'excellent', 'superb',
'dreadful', 'ghastly', etc. These meanings, it will be noticed, are

organised in terms of synonymy and antonymy, and can be handled by componential analysis. In contrast, a sentence such as *I'll knock your block off* conveys the hostility of its user in no uncertain terms, but this hostility cannot be pinned down to the meaning of any particular part of the utterance. In cases like this, it is difficult to see how semantic analysis as we have studied it could help us in a statement of attitudinal purport: this must be a matter of feeling-tone, entirely beyond the range of systemic description.

[c] Once we have drawn this distinction, we can, where appropriate, recognise a dependence of feeling-tone on certain elements of designative meaning. For example, we may say that any negatively evaluative terms, including such notions as 'injustice', 'crime', 'folly', 'ignorance', 'cruelty', carry implications of a pejorative feeling-tone. Perhaps in this way the denigratory character of the terms *tyrant*, *thug*, etc, mentioned above would be accounted for; and perhaps, also, this would provide a partial explanation of factors of taboo and euphemism in language.

5.3 Semantics and questions of fact or belief

We return now to a question touched on in §1.8: how do we decide, by standards internal to a semantic theory, whether a particular observation reflects the rules of language, or the natural law of the universe? Is 'This elephant has eighty legs' logically or factually absurd? Is 'The elephant is the largest land mammal' logically uncontradictable, or factually so? As I pointed out before, these questions really boil down to questions about meaning and reference. If 'four-legged', for example, is considered a necessary element in the definition of 'elephant', then 'This elephant has eighty legs' has to be considered a contradiction.

Briefly, I shall try to argue that if semantic analysis is carried beyond a certain point, the technique of semantics become ineffective. This point, therefore, is best treated as the limit of semantic analysis: the point where questions of meaning give way to questions of mere reference. In this, my argument will be similar in method and effect to that of Katz and Fodor (1963: 176–81), who show that a semantic theory, in explaining a person's interpretation of sentences, cannot take into account the "socio-physical" setting of the act of speech. I shall not, however, follow them in prescribing the sentence as a cut-off point for contextual factors relevant to interpretation. Indeed, I shall not discuss the question at all from Katz and Fodor's "interpretative" point of view, which I consider to be relevant to semantic performance rather than to semantic competence.[5]

We may express all designative definitions as statements about reference simply by interpreting each component as a property of all

referents of the term defined. For +HUM +MALE −MAT 'boy', for instance, we may say "If and only if x has the properties of being human
male, and immature, x is a referent of 'boy'". However, whereas all such
definitions can be converted into statements of referential conditions,
not all statements of reference can be turned into statements of meaning.
The properties of being featherless, two-footed, ten-toed, vulnerable,
mortal, incapable of breathing under water, under twenty-one years old,
etc, all belong to referents of 'boy', but surely do not all need to be
mentioned in a definition of 'boy'.[6]

The problem of distinguishing "accidental" conditions of reference
from the "essential" features to be represented in componential definitions is most crucial in the study of what are generally known as "folk-
taxonomies" – *ie* ways in which natural languages subclassify, by genus
and differentia, such phenomena as plants, living creatures, topographical features, and diseases (see Ch. 2, n. 24). In the present semantic
framework, folk-taxonomies are characterised by a hierarchical ordering of systems in delicacy, so that a large number of meanings are logically
included in the meanings of a few more general terms, such as *plant* and
flower. They thus constitute relatively closed fields of meaning, which
lend themselves to study in isolation. Folk-taxonomies may be broadly
distinguished from "technical" taxonomies, or subclassifications which
are established in a deliberate effort to schematise concepts and terminology for scientific or other sophisticated purposes. In technical taxonomies, the semantic relationships between the terms are usually far
more structured, through both hierarchical and simultaneous classification. Compare the everyday use of terms like *animal* (which may express
at least three meanings of different generality – non-human mammals,
mammals including man, and the whole animal kingdom, as distinct
from vegetable and mineral matter) with the six-tiered hierarchical system of zoological taxonomy: *species, genus, family, order, class, phylum*.
Of course, there is no clear-cut division between folk- and technical
taxonomies: the latter are register-restricted, but tend to invade everyday usages to various extents, at least among well-educated speakers,
co-existing there with the corresponding "folk" usage. Consider, for
instance, the fairly widespread use of words like *mammal* and *vertebrate*
in present-day English.

When a certain level of classification is reached in semantic fields such
as that of the animal kingdom, we are faced with a rather large number of
terms which have to be semantically distinguished, although it is not
clear how or to what extent they are to be distinguished: *rabbit, sheep,
horse, rhinoceros, elephant*, etc. The temptation here is to resort to a
technical classification which would not reflect everyday usage (and in
any case would not provide an account of terms for fabulous beasts,
such as unicorns and jabberwocks). If, on the other hand, we avoid this

pitfall, we find numerous, perhaps innumerable, properties, of which one or a small selection would serve to differentiate the given species. For example, for the elephant: 'living on land'; 'larger than other land mammals'; 'having a trunk'; 'non-extinct'; 'ivory-producing'; 'having a gestation period of approximately 640 days'. How could the meaning of the word *elephant* be specified in terms of such properties?[7]

For a start, let us rule out one solution to this problem – that of embodying all the characteristics of the species (physical, social, geographical, etc) in the definition. The result would be an encyclopaedia entry, rather than a definition. As a specification, it could never be considered complete, since science might at any time discover further unsuspected facts about elephants; and to have an infinitely or indefinitely long semantic specification would run counter to the whole notion of an explicitly formulated semantic description we have been considering. A second solution would be a selection of any group of properties sufficient to distinguish elephants from other species. This would also be unsatisfactory, as there appears to be no systematic basis on which one set of properties could be preferred to another. Brevity would be no criterion for preference, for there would never be any guarantee that the simplest characterisation had been found, or even that there could be such a thing as a unique "simplest characterisation". The selection of criterial properties would therefore be arbitrary, and this would mean that we were allowing for innumerable semantic descriptions of the word *elephant*, and hence for the English language as a whole, between which the toss of a coin was the only criterion of choice.

We may conclude that no denotative properties of the kind we have been discussing can reasonably be incorporated into definitions as "essential" properties. And yet, if *elephant* is to be semantically distinguished from *kangaroo* or *anteater* or other animal words, its definition must differ in at least one feature from the definitions of these terms. The only available solution, it seems, is to assign a single contrastive component to every species, *eg* 1SPE for 'dog', 2SPE for 'cat', 31SPE for 'elephant', etc (the allotment of particular numerical prescripts is of course immaterial). This amounts to setting up a multiple taxonomic system dependent in delicacy on the term −HUM of the system ±HUM ('human'/'brute'). Thus a more complete definition of *dog* would be −HUM 1SPE and of *elephant*, −HUM 31SPE. In this analysis we fail to represent any of the known zoological facts about elephants – we merely note that the elephant is a distinct species, separate from and contrasting with all other species. 'This elephant is a tiger' is classed as a logical contradiction, whereas 'This elephant has eighty legs' is treated as well-formed (though, of course, factually absurd).

This approach has a widespread application in semantics, and is not limited to terms referring to natural phenomena. Similar problems

arise, for instance, in distinguishing the meanings of terms for different
kinds of vessel: *vat, tub, pail, butt, bowl, mug, beaker, tumbler, cup, can,
kettle, glass, goblet, basin, jug, pitcher, ewer*, etc; or for different articles
of furniture for sitting or reclining on: *chair, bench, form, stool, sofa,
settee, stall, armchair, ottoman, chaise-longue, pew, settle*, etc. The problem in these cases is slightly different, because of the lack of the degree
of discontinuity found in the classifications of the biological world. Many
verbs also lend themselves to genus-differentia analysis in the same way:
walk, run, trot, saunter, lope, stride, slide, slither, roll, etc, refer to kinds of
locomotion; *snap, crack, thud, rumble, clatter, chime, buzz, whine, roar*,
etc, to types of noise. It is extremely difficult to devise criteria for distinguishing a 'snap' from a 'crack', and yet in general people are aware
that a different kind of sound is intended. It is the total "gestalt" of a
sound which is distinguished in a choice of terms, and this is what is
represented in a semantic analysis, if one contrastive component is
assigned to each different term within the semantic field.

In summary, we can say that an investigator has reached the limits of
semantics whenever he is faced with an indefinite number of criteria or
partial criteria for distinguishing the meanings of a set of terms within
the same semantic field. This is a pragmatic, rather than theoretical
criterion. None the less, some answer has been given, for the purpose of
linguistic semantics, to the claim of some philosophers that the line between meaning and reference can only be drawn in an arbitrary way.

A final comment on the connection between semantic definition and
lexicography may be appended here. It would be convenient if we could
say that a dictionary gloss, in contrast to an encyclopaedia entry, restricts
itself to the meaning of a term, and leaves merely referential information
aside. This is unfortunately not true, as we see from the encyclopaedic
(historical and other) information in the following gloss:

> VIOLONCELLO: *a large four-stringed musical instrument of the violin
> class, the quality of its tone even more sympathetic than that of the violin,
> held between the knees when playing – it superseded the viola da gamba
> in the early part of the eighteenth century.*
>
> (Chambers's Twentieth Century Dictionary, 1904)

It would be rash to criticise a popular dictionary for leavening its lump
of meaning with factual information in this way: dictionaries are, after
all, made to be of practical use to everyday speakers of the language. If
lexicographers restricted themselves to the ordinary meaning of words
like *elephant* and *bear*, they would (according to the principle laid down
in this section) say nothing about the specific properties of the animals
these terms refer to. Perhaps a picture, conveying a distinctive "image"
of each animal, rather than a verbal explanation, would come closest in
spirit to a semantic definition. A less justifiable course to which most

dictionaries resort in these cases is to give a technical definition, thus pandering to the popular myth that the "true" meaning of a word is provided by a scientific explanation of what it refers to,[8] and that in everyday language it is vaguely used or imperfectly understood. *The Concise Oxford Dictionary*, for example, defines *bear*[1] as "Heavy partly carnivorous thick-furred plantigrade quadruped ..." – a definition which is appropriate only for a scientific register of the language, and in which almost all the words are less familiar to an average reader than the word *bear* itself. Again, one would hesitate to condemn entirely the use of technical definitions in dictionaries of general usage: the abuse lies rather in the lexicographer's failure to distinguish systematically between different glossing techniques.[9]

5.4 Literal and transferred meaning

It has been said that a semantic theory which goes no further than to account for "humourless, prosaic, banal prose" (Weinreich, 1966: 399) is scarcely worth while: for a comprehensive theory of meaning, we have to explicate the creative or meaning-extending principle in the semantics of natural language; a principle which not only manifests itself in imaginative writing, but pervades ordinary language in a multitude of functions. Yet it may also be claimed that the study of the figurative or imaginative aspects of meaning cannot proceed without a clear idea of the literal usage underlying them. Moreover, it is relevant to ask how far the study of figurative usage falls within the study of semantic competence at all. This is my reason for treating figurative meaning as an afterthought to, rather than as a central theme of this study.

On many occasions, especially in literature, semantic rules appear to be violated, and yet the offending piece of language is not dismissed as a piece of nonsense. Everyone is familiar with the poetic or rhetorical use of paradox and oxymoron – for example, Orwell's *War is peace; freedom is slavery; ignorance is strength*. To explain how such expressions are understood, we may suppose (a) that regular (literal) interpretations are blocked by semantic violation (in this case contradiction); and (b) that because of this, a special interpretation is assigned by the invocation of an unorthodox (perhaps completely *ad hoc*) rule of expression. To make sense of *freedom is slavery*, we have to construe *freedom* and *slavery* in non-equivalent senses, for example 'freedom of body' and 'slavery of the mind'. This would be permissible only by virtue of a special expression rule allowing zero expression of 'of body' and 'of the mind'. In general, it seems that the blocked, regular senses are related to the irregular, transferred senses in systematic ways, so that it is possible to state RULES OF TRANSFERENCE which derive the irregular from the regular senses, thereby creating new cases of polysemy.[10] Two such rules, very roughly stated, are these:

1. If an expression E expresses a componential formula *a* containing the component 'place', then E may also express a formula of the form 'inhabitants (collectively) of *a*'.
2. If an expression E expresses a componential formula *a*, then E may also express a specification of the form '(someone/thing) (behaving) like/as if *a*'. (This seemingly rather cumbersome formula would, it is hoped, be much simpler if expressed in semantic notation.)

Rule (1) explains our interpretation of sentences like *The whole world loved him; Half the road have visited me in hospital; The U.S.A. is not without friends.* Because selection restrictions demand personal nouns, not nouns of place, as subjects of these sentences, the regular interpretation is blocked, and *the whole world* has to be construed as *the inhabitants of the whole world*, etc. Rule (2) is perhaps the most important of all rules of transference, and explains the semantic basis of metaphor. On the one hand, it applies to literary metaphors such as Shakespeare's *Life's but a walking shadow*, an assertion which is on the face of it absurd, but is universally assigned the sensible interpretation 'Life's . . . *like* a walking shadow'. On the other hand, it explains cases of established polysemy, such as many nouns and adjectives denoting types of human being or animal in mundane usage: *That man's a fox; He's an old woman; Be a man, my boy;* etc. These are scarcely felt to involve semantic violations, and in the case of the adjective *mature*, the transferred sense has almost superseded the literal (biological) sense in popular usage, so that *an immature woman* could scarcely be construed as expressing the oxymoron of the specification −MAT +HUM −MALE +MAT. It is interesting that *a human elephant*, literally an oxymoron, can be interpreted in two distinct ways, according to whether *human* or *elephant* is taken metaphorically; 'an elephant behaving like a human-being' or 'a human-being resembling (in certain respects – probably heaviness and clumsiness) an elephant'.

This analysis of metaphor by means of rules of transference begs a number of different questions. First of all, it may be felt that the distinction between literal and figurative meaning is a relative distinction only. To this I readily agree: all shades of unorthodoxy are possible in the application of these rules, from the strikingly original literary metaphor on the one hand to the banal "dead metaphor" on the other. The productivity of rules of transference is very much "item-bound", in the sense that one formal item may be readily given a transferred meaning, whereas another, even within the same semantic field, may not. In this, they are very much like rules of morphological derivation, such as that which adds -*y* to a noun X to form an adjective meaning 'like an

X'. *Mousy* (='like a mouse') is relatively acceptable in comparison with an adjective like *stoaty* and similarly, the noun *mouse* is much more easily taken in the sense 'one who acts like a mouse' than *stoat* may be taken in the sense 'someone who acts like a stoat'.

Secondly, the interpretability of an utterance by means of transference rules depends very much on circumstances of idiolect and register: who is addressing whom, and in what circumstances. Literary metaphors are totally unacceptable in some situations (*eg* in legal documents), and indeed are totally unacceptable to some literal-minded people in any situation. This suggests that figurative interpretation depends on individual performance, rather than on competence. As such, like the study of disambiguation as a whole, it is outside the normal range of linguistic study, and is only relevant to semantics in a marginal way – *eg* in relating meaningfulness to acceptability.[11] In this connection, we may return to the original example of the lack of correspondence between meaningfulness and acceptability in §1.6: *That girl is a boy*, a contradiction under its most obvious interpretation, can be made sensible by a transference rule which reads, in informal language, "If E expresses a componential formula *a* then it may express the meaning 'What is/has been/,etc called *a*'."[12] In other words, we may interpret the sentence as if it were written *That "girl" is a boy*.

There is another reason for considering figurative interpretation as a matter of performance rather than competence: a literal interpretation may be blocked by a factual, as well as by a logical absurdity. A convincing illustration of this is a famous saying from Bacon's essay "Of Studies":

> *Some books are to be tasted, others to be swallowed, and some few to be chewed and digested.*

This is clearly metaphorical, in that the verbs *tasted*, *swallowed*, etc, are meant to be understood in a mental sense, instead of in their customary physical sense. And yet the inevitably rejected literal interpretation is not logically absurd. Indeed, it scarcely qualifies as an absurdity at all, since eating books is merely an implausible, rather than an impossible physical activity.

What from the aesthetic point of view is the most important aspect of metaphor, the GROUND or warranty for the comparison, also appears to lie outside semantic competence. Consider, for instance, the paradoxical phrase *A father of the fatherless* (Psalm 68). The metaphor rule causes us to interpret *a father* as 'one like a father'; but it does not teach us *in what respects* God is like a father. This is a matter rather of recognising referential connections between the objects of comparison, and the obvious connection here is that God provides for the fatherless, just as a father does for his children. A quite different warranty for a metaphorical use of *father* is required in Dr Johnson's description of Dryden as *the father of English criticism*. The common property which provides the resemblance here is that of causing somebody or something to come into being. Plainly the means by which we arrive at the appropriate ground of a metaphor take us away from the study of meaning to a study of systems of belief, social institutions, and imponderable factors of individual psychology.

When a metaphorical sense has become fully institutionalised within a language, we may say that a semantic change has taken place whereby the meaning 'like X' has been replaced by a meaning incorporating the warranty of the comparison. One might argue, for example, that *fox*, as a term referring to human beings, has become a "dead metaphor" in this way: that it means 'a cunning person' rather than 'a person like a fox (in that he is cunning)'. The same could be said about other animal terms, such as *cat, beast, elephant*; and more positively about terms such as *low, mean, kind, gentle, noble*, which when applied to human-beings formerly referred to their social position, but now refer primarily to the moral character which has in the past been associated with social position.

We may conclude that it is possible to specify, in a semantic description, the rules of transference by which figurative meanings are brought into being, but not the multitude of particular circumstances which determine the choice, if any, of a figurative interpretation. Nor can we explain a large part of how a metaphor is understood, since the common ground of a metaphorical analogy is identified referentially, rather than semantically.

Rules of transference, viewed as devices for extending relations of multiple meaning, are an extremely powerful creative factor in language, although, as we have already noted, they are productive only relative to given items, given situations, and given interpreters. Their existence causes us to review the relationship between meaningfulness and acceptability discussed in §1.7. The distinction between meaningfulness and meaninglessness has been applied to semantic abstractions, not to formal abstractions such as sentences and lexical items. It has also been applied in an all-or-none way; that is, a reading is either meaningless or meaningful, well-formed or ill-formed, and no half-measures are permitted. Similarly, acceptability has been predicated of meanings not expressions, although various degrees of acceptability have been envisaged. The all-or-none approach to meaningfulness, which may have run counter to intuition at the time it was introduced, is now seen to be justified: for with the concept of a transference rule, we can allow that *expressions* may be graded with respect to the ease with which they can be assigned a *meaningful interpretation*. That is to say, we have at two extremes (a) an expression which has at least one regular meaningful interpretation and (b) (perhaps a hypothetical case) an expression for which no meaningful interpretation at all is possible; and between these two extremes, there are expressions for which all regular interpretations are blocked, but which may be assigned special interpretations, by means of rules of transference, at a certain "cost" to acceptability (see Ch. 5, n. 11). Even here, I have made an assumption that certain interpretations can be considered "regular" and others not. Perhaps this dichotomy, like those between competence and performance, or between synchronic and diachronic study, should be regarded as one of those convenient abstractions (or, if preferred, "fictions") which have to be accepted as a condition of further progress in linguistic analysis.

Part 2
On the semantics of English

Chapter 6

Preliminaries to semantic description

In this second part of the book, my aim is to apply the semantic theory outlined in Part 1 to the semantic description of English. Although various problems of meaning in English have been considered in earlier chapters, so far no attempt has been made to move in the direction of a comprehensive semantic account of the English language. Such an account is, indeed, far beyond practical consideration at this stage. Nevertheless, I propose to take at least one or two steps towards such an eventual goal by devoting the three following chapters to three prominent "semantic fields", those of time, place, and modality. As independent topics, each of these could fill many volumes (two of them, in fact, have done so already); therefore nothing but a rough descriptive sketch of each area can be attempted here. The object is not so much to extend factual knowledge of these areas of meaning (although it is hoped that this will be a by-product), as to systematise what knowledge is already available. If generalisations can be made to embrace such diverse semantic fields, and so to reveal the common principles of their organisation, an important step will have been taken towards the ideal of a comprehensive and unified semantic description of a language.

Needless to say, there is an extremely wide gap between this ideal and the practical achievement of this investigation. Many parts of the ensuing analysis are not only incomplete, but vague and uncertain on points treated. Many loose ends must be left. In apology, I cannot do better than urge, with Bendix (1966: 17), that "a rough road into the empirical semantic wilderness is preferable to a well-paved one timidly skirting the borders".

6.1 Semantic structure and clause structure

Before we turn to the individual fields of meaning, some attention must be given to general matters of description which have not emerged from the preceding theoretical chapters. One of these is the relation between elements of clause structure and elements of semantic structure. I have previously (in §3.5) given the name PRINCIPAL PREDICATION to a predication which is expressed by the subject, predicator, and complement part of a clause. A principle predication is normally a two-place predication ($a \cdot r \cdot b$) if the clause is extensive (*ie* is transitive or intransitive) and a one-place predicate ($a:m$) if the clause is intensive (*ie* has an equative verb). Clauses having indirect objects or object complements have semantic structures with embedding, as briefly explained in §4.2.2:

'He saw the train' $a \cdot \rightarrow r \cdot b$
'He gave me the cup' $a \cdot \rightarrow r \cdot (b \cdot \rightarrow s \cdot c)$
'He is tall' $a:m$
'He made me angry' $a \cdot \rightarrow r \cdot (b:m)$

Notice that in the first example 'He saw the train' there is a correspondence between

(a) subject and initial cluster
(b) predicator (verbal element) and medial cluster
(c) object and final cluster.

We shall assume that this is an expression rule of very general application, which it is worthwhile going to some trouble to uphold. It means that the definition of a noun has to be so framed as to fit into a terminal cluster a or b; and that the definition of a transitive verb must be so framed as to fit into a medial cluster $\rightarrow r$ such that the subject and object of the verb express initial and final clusters respectively. In the case of single-place predications, we note the further correspondence between

(d) adjective or noun complement and attributive cluster m.

This brings the additional requirement that adjective and noun definitions should in general be so framed as to fit into an attributive cluster m.

The structures of meaning corresponding to adverbial elements of grammar are not so straightforward as those corresponding to other clause elements. In §4.3.3 a reason was given for putting forward two alternative semantic structures for a clause containing an adverbial; in the two formulae below, $a \cdot r \cdot b$ represents the principal predication, and $c \cdot \leftarrow s \cdot (X)$ what we may call the ADVERBIAL PREDICATION (*ie* the predication expressed by an adverbial element in grammar):

(a) $c \cdot \leftarrow s \cdot (a \cdot r \cdot b)$ 'On Tuesday I saw John.'
(b) $(a \cdot r \langle \theta' \cdot \rightarrow s \cdot c \rangle \cdot b)'$ 'I saw John on Tuesday.'

The equivalence of (a) and (b) (except in those cases where r contains a negative formator) is guaranteed by the rule of subordination (§4.3.3). In terms of syntactic structure, (a) and (b) account for the ability of the adverbial element to occur not only in an initial, but also in a medial or final position. We assume here the existence, amongst the rules of expression, of an extraposition rule, which obligatorily or optionally moves the adverbial element from a position next to the verb to a position behind the object, so that '(I saw ⟨on Tuesday⟩ John)' becomes syntactically realised as *I saw John on Tuesday*. With this proviso, we can maintain the principle that semantic and syntactic structures have corresponding orderings, unless the regular syntactic ordering is upset by factors such as information focus or thematic emphasis.[1]

This coincidence of grammatical and semantic elements, which simplifies the rules of expression, provides a motive for preserving the match between grammatical and semantic structure in other ways. For example, distinctions of tense and modality are expressed by features of the predicator; hence we would like them, all other things considered, to be semantically part of the medial cluster. This is indeed the suitable place to put them in semantic description, tense and modality being largely capable of analysis in terms of downgraded predications in the position of $\langle \theta' \cdot \rightarrow s \cdot c \rangle$ in formula (b) above (see §§7.4 and 9.3–4 below). In this, a connection can be seen between verbal tenses and time adverbials, whose functions overlap within the same field of meaning.

6.2 The semantics of adverbials

Adverbials, as we have just seen in (a) above, may be represented by the formula $c \cdot \leftarrow s \cdot (a \cdot r \cdot b)$, simplified and generalised as $c \cdot \leftarrow s \cdot (X)$, where (X) stands for the rank-shifted predication. The second formula in turn may be replaced (according to the mirror-image convention) by $(X) \cdot \rightarrow s \cdot c$ as the archetypal notational form of a predication modified by an adverbial. This last notational variant will be preferred here because on the one hand it eliminates the complication of co-reference in downgrading, and on the other hand it imitates the dominant syntactic order, in which the rest of the clause precedes the adjunct. It is as well to bear in mind, however, that various alternative formulae are permitted by the mirror-image convention and the rule of subordination.

At s in the above formula occur a number of relative components corresponding in the main to the traditional categories of adverbial construction (time, place, manner, duration, etc). These relative components, indeed, generally constitute the entire inherent content of $\rightarrow s$, so that, for instance, adverbials of time or of place may be simply represented:

$(X) \cdot \rightarrow \text{TIM} \cdot c$ 'X at time c'
$(X) \cdot \rightarrow \text{PLA} \cdot c$ 'X at place c',

where a single relative term is substituted for $\rightarrow s$.[2] We set up, in other words, a number of "adverbial" systems ⇄TIM, ⇄PLA, ⇄MAN, etc, each having the contextual condition of being preceded by a rank-shifted predication. Another contextual condition of considerable generality is that what follows the adverbial term →TIM, ←PLA, etc must be a terminal cluster, not a rank-shifted predication. These two contextual conditions together have the effect of annulling the "reversibility" principle which was taken to be the distinguishing mark of relative systems on their first introduction (in §§2.2 and 2.3): in a specification such as $(X) \cdot \to \text{TIM} \cdot c$, the arrow can point only in the direction marked, for in the other direction it would violate contextual conditions. This neutralisation of directional contrast is a common enough effect of contextual rules of redundancy, and is by no means limited to adverbial predications.

Adverbial predications cannot be negated. The apparent negations 'nowhere' (='at no place') and 'never' (='at no time') etc, belong to quantificational predications rather than to the adverbial predications themselves (compare 'no cats', etc in §3.5). That a relative component of adverbial meaning (eg →TIM, →PLA) cannot be accompanied by the negative formator is merely a special application of the generalisation, just mentioned, that such components normally stand alone in the cluster.

To explain the semantics of clauses containing more than one adverbial, the factor of nesting or embedding is brought into play. A clause containing two adverbials can be readily analysed as follows, with one adverbial predication rank-shifted inside the other:

(i) $((a \cdot r \cdot b) \cdot \to s \cdot c) \cdot \to t \cdot d$
      '((I saw him) last Monday) at the match.'

The same embedding principle applies, whether or not the two adverbials are of the same class. Difference in the order of nesting potentially distinguishes two meanings, such as 'Usually he visits me on Wednesdays' and 'On Wednesdays he usually visits me'. In addition, some orders of embedding are impossible: contrast 'Last Monday I saw him at three o'clock' with 'At three o'clock I saw him last Monday', which can only occur with special initial information focus. In general, however, no difference of meaning is, apparently, entailed in the difference of ordering in subordination, and this equivalence (under specific conditions which cannot be examined here) must at some stage be explained by a rule of synonymy roughly of this form:

$$((X) \cdot \to s \cdot c) \cdot \to t \cdot d = ((X) \cdot \to t \cdot d) \cdot \to s \cdot c$$

By the rule of subordination (§4.3.3), formula (i) above is equivalent to

(ii) $(a \cdot r \langle \theta' \cdot \to s \cdot c \rangle \cdot b)' \cdot \to t \cdot d$

and this, by a second application of the same rule of subordination, is equivalent to

(iii) $(a \cdot r \langle \theta' \cdot \to s \cdot c \rangle \langle \theta' \cdot \to t \cdot d \rangle \cdot b)'$

When both adverbial predications are downgraded, as in (iii), the difference in ranking between them is apparently lost, since there is no ordering of features within the cluster. We may remember from §3.5, however, that the co-referential domain of θ' in downgraded predications such as that in (ii) is *the whole of the main predication with the omission of the downgraded predication itself.* Thus on the reapplication of the subordination rule for (iii), the co-reference of the second θ' is wider than that of the first, because it includes the already downgraded predication $\langle \theta' \rightarrow s \cdot c \rangle$. Some ranking is therefore implied in the fact that the co-referential domain of the second θ' includes that of the first, whereas the reverse is not true. This ordering principle, which arises whenever two predications are downgraded within the same cluster, can be indicated if necessary by numbered subscripts:

$$(a \cdot r \langle \theta' \cdot \rightarrow s \cdot c \rangle_1 \langle \theta' \cdot \rightarrow t \cdot d \rangle_2 \cdot b)'$$

A further notational innovation can be made at this point. It is convenient to have a way of representing a downgrading within the medial or attributive cluster of a predication without having to indicate any further details of that predication's structure or denotative content. For this purpose, we shall simply juxtapose the general predication symbol X and the downgraded predication formula, letting it be understood that the downgraded predication is within the medial or attributive cluster of X, not within one of its terminal clusters. Thus the following are abbreviated and more general versions of the equivalent formulae (i), (ii), and (iii) above:

(i) $((X) \cdot \rightarrow s \cdot c) \cdot \rightarrow t \cdot d$
(ii) $(X \langle \theta' \cdot \rightarrow s \cdot c \rangle) \cdot \rightarrow t \cdot d$
(iii) $X' \langle \theta' \cdot \rightarrow s \cdot c \rangle'' \langle \theta'' \cdot \rightarrow t \cdot d \rangle$

By this means, the convention of numbered subscripts just introduced can be dispensed with, as the different co-referential domains of the two definite formators can be indicated in (iii) more directly, by distinctive prime markings. The co-referential domain of θ'', in this formula, includes both X and $\langle \theta' \cdot s \cdot c \rangle$.

The quantification of the terminal element c of the adverbial predication provides definitions for a range of adverbs and adverbial phrases:

Universal quantification
$((X) \cdot \rightarrow s \cdot \varnothing') \cdot 1\alpha \leftarrow o \cdot \theta'$ 'always', 'everywhere', 'in every way', etc

Existential quantification
$((X) \cdot \rightarrow s \cdot \varnothing') \cdot 2\alpha \leftarrow o \cdot \theta'$ 'sometimes', 'somewhere', 'somehow', etc

In the following formula, which represents adverbials of definite meaning, the terminal cluster c contains the definite formator, and so is reanalysed as θd:

$$(X) \cdot \rightarrow s \cdot \theta \, d \quad \text{'then', 'there', 'thus', etc}$$

A further class of adverbials, the question adverbials, may be semantically specified as follows:

$$(X) \cdot s \cdot ? \quad \text{'when?' 'where?', 'how?', etc}$$

The question mark here symbolises a "question feature", the semantic function of which we need not examine at this juncture, apart from noting that in the underlying semantic structure of a *wh*- question, the question feature occurs in that terminal element about which information is desired (*eg* $? + \text{HUM} \cdot \rightarrow k \cdot g$ 'Who knows George?').

It appears to be a general well-formedness condition of question-and-answer sequences that the answer repeats the information of the question, giving additional information to replace the occurrence of the question formator. For example, appropriate answers to 'Who knows George?' are 'I know George', 'I know him', or 'I do' (in the latter two the "repetition" in the answer of the content of the question is shown indirectly by co-reference). Inappropriate answers would be 'I am hungry', 'Everyone likes George', etc, which do not fulfil the above condition. (There are, of course, acceptable responses which are not direct answers to the question, but ways of evading it, saying why it cannot be answered, etc.) The well-formedness condition can be represented, as it applies to the simplest case of a two-place predication, as follows:

Question: $a \cdot r \cdot ?$ Answer: $a \cdot r \cdot b$

As it applies to adverbial predications, the requirement is that a question beginning with 'when', 'where', etc, should be followed by a statement in which the cluster containing the question feature is replaced by a cluster containing new content:

Question: $(X) \cdot \rightarrow s \cdot ?$ Answer: $(X) \cdot \rightarrow s \cdot c$

eg 'Where did you see him?' '(I saw him) at the river.'

Apart from this substitution, the two specifications (subject to the rule of co-reference and the switching of first- and second-person reference) have to be identical. An example of an inappropriate response is:

Question: $(X) \cdot \rightarrow s \cdot ?$ Answer: $(X) \cdot \rightarrow t \cdot c$

eg 'Where did you see him?' '(I saw him) at half-past two.'

In this example the two medial clusters → *s* and → *t* are not identical; this, in syntactic terms, means that the two adverbials belong to different categories, and therefore do not match.

6.3 "General taxonomy"

Many features of semantic analysis are heavily restricted in occurrence, in that their choice presupposes a whole chain of precedent choices. An example of a feature in such a restricted "semantic field" is the feature representing 'barley', which presumably depends, by redundancy rules, on a feature for 'cereal', which in turn depends directly or indirectly on features for 'produce', 'vegetable', 'concrete', 'solid', etc. On the other hand, there are features such as 'mineral', 'concrete', 'mass', 'plural', etc, which presuppose few or no other features, and which moreover play a part in the semantic discrimination of a large number of lexical items or grammatical categories. Since these, in contrast to features like 'barley', can be considered a central part of the semantic framework of a language, it is convenient to deal with them in a preparatory section now, rather than in an incidental way in the course of the descriptive chapters which follow. The following two systems in particular have to be treated as of cardinal importance in what we may call the "general taxonomy" of the language.[3]

6.3.1 *System of 'concrete'/'abstract'*

$$\begin{cases} +\text{CONC} & \text{'concrete'} \\ -\text{CONC} & \text{'abstract'} \end{cases}$$

Class of system: binary taxonomic

This system frequently appears in contextual redundancy rules: for instance, 'see', 'hit', 'eat', etc, require concrete logical objects; sentences like *I ate the idea* or *He kicked Tuesday*, if not rejected as nonsense, call for some special transferred interpretation. Most nouns traditionally classed as abstract, however, do not have the feature −CONC in their definitions, but rather are semantically represented by rank-shifted predications with empty terminal clusters:

'kindness' = '(someone's) being kind'
'bribery' = '(someone's) bribing (someone else)', etc.

The feature +CONC stands at the head of a hierarchy of dependent systems representing what might be called "the material universe". As a first approximation, the less delicate stages of this hierarchy (stopping short of actual species of animals, plants, etc) are shown by the following diagram, in which the arrow indicates direction of dependence:

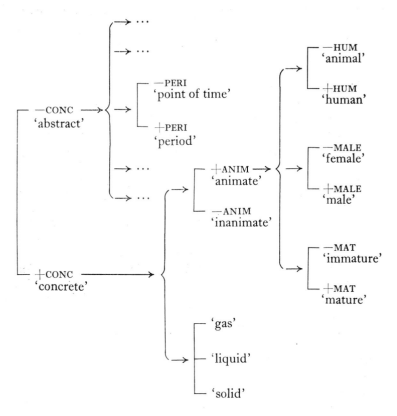

6.3.2 *System of countability*

$$\begin{cases} +\text{COU} & \text{`countable'} \\ -\text{COU} & \text{`mass'} \end{cases}$$

Class of system: binary taxonomic.

The system of countability is represented in the definitions of most, if not all nouns (exceptions may be words like *cake*, which we could regard as inherently unspecified for this system, since *some cake* and *some cakes* are equally possible). Many verbs (those classifiable as "event verbs") are also marked by definition as 'countable' (see §7.4.1). Dependent on the countability system are two interconnected systems, the hierarchic system of 'quantity' 1, 2, 3, . . . , nQUA and the binary system of 'plurality' ±PLUR, as shown in the diagram on the facing page.

The relationship between the systems of '*quantity*' and '*plurality*' is unusually complex: the terms 1QUA and −PLUR are interdependent, whilst iQUA (where $i > 1$) depends on +PLUR.

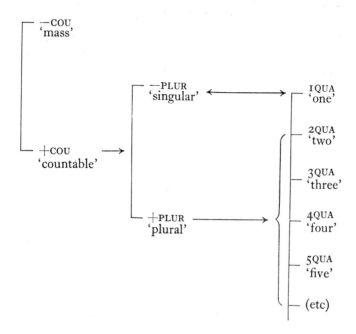

6.4 Presentation of descriptive analyses

Finally, in preparing the ground for the remaining chapters, something must be said about the method of presentation to be employed. I shall attempt to serve the interests of both precision and clarity of exposition by dividing the text clearly into three types of discourse: (1) formal statements of meaning (tabulated under system headings); (2) the informal introduction, explanation, and justification of the formal statements; (3) commentary (in smaller type-size) clarifying points of minor importance. The formal statements will always be made about a particular system (systems are numbered from the beginning of each chapter), and will give information on:

(a) The class to which a given system belongs (*eg* binary taxonomic, hierarchic, relative).
(b) In the case of relative systems, logical and contextual conditions (see §§4.1.1–2).
(c) Dependence rules (*ie* non-contextual redundancy rules) affecting co-occurrence of features within the same cluster.
(d) Substantive rules of synonymy, special rules of implication, etc.

*4

The informal discussion (2) will explain, as far as possible, the reasons for postulating each system, and for assigning it the stated properties. The sections labelled *"Commentary"* will handle less central matters, particularly apparent or real exceptions to generalisations made elsewhere, and technical matters of theory.

Chapter 7

Time

In this sketch of the semantics of time in English, I shall begin by studying the adverbials (adverbs, adverbial phrases, adverbial clauses), moving on later to the tenses and aspects of the verbal group. This syntactic division cuts across a semantic division into sections on "time when", "duration", and "frequency", the first of which will claim most of our attention. Not all problems of temporal meaning will be touched on; for instance, no consideration will be given to factors which determine choice from the various "future tenses" (*will come, will be coming, is about to come,* etc). Nor shall I attempt to deal with the inchoative, continuative, and conclusive aspects of verbal meaning (*begin to work, keep working, stop working,* etc).

7.1 "Time when"

Our starting point, naturally enough, is the system $\rightleftarrows$TIM, which, as explained in Chapter 6, has the contextual condition of being preceded by a rank-shifted predication. A further contextual condition is that $\rightleftarrows$TIM ascribes to the following clusters a member of the system 'period'/ 'moment', system 2 below. Notice, in the statement of contextual properties of system 1, the conventions for symbolising these two conditions:

SYSTEM 1 *'time when'*
$$\begin{cases} (x) \rightarrow \text{TIM} \ (y) & \text{`}(x) \text{ at time } (y)\text{'} \\ (x) \leftarrow \text{TIM} \ (y) & \text{`}(y) \text{ at time } (x)\text{'} \end{cases}$$
Class of system: relative
Contextual properties: $\{(X)\} \rightarrow \text{TIM} \ \{\text{PERI}\}$
Logical properties: asymmetric, irreflexive, intransitive, many–one

The first three logical conditions follow inevitably from the contextual conditions: if ⇌TIM were reflexive, symmetric, or transitive, to each of its termini would be simultaneously attributed rank-shifted status and the status of a componential formula. This would be a contradiction in terms. We notice that in effect, the ascription of mutually exclusive properties to the two termini nullifies the "reversibility" phenomenon associated with relative systems.

The force of assigning the logical property "many–one" to this system is to permit, within the language, the possibility of many events happening at the same time, whilst ruling out the possibility of one event (considered as an unrepeatable occurrence) happening at a number of different times. The point becomes important in §7.2.

The system 'period'/'moment' simply distinguishes time considered as a section of a continuum (as in 'last Friday') from time considered as a point on a continuum (as in 'at eight o'clock'); *ie* time with duration from time without duration:

SYSTEM 2 *'period'/'moment'*
$\left\{ \begin{array}{l} +\text{PERI} \\ -\text{PERI} \end{array} \right.$ 'period of time'
        'moment, point of time'
Class of system: binary taxonomic
Dependence rules: PERI depends on −CONC ('abstract') and on +COU ('countable') (see §6.3)

This system, amongst other things, represents semantically the difference between *in/on* and *at* as prepositions of time. *At* may be defined →TIM [−PERI] (ascribing subjective momentariness to the expression following), and *on* and *in* collectively as →TIM [+PERI], a more delicate discrimination between these two prepositions being that the former singles out a particular unit of periodic time, the day (see system 6 below). [+PERI] and [−PERI] in these definitions are (as the square brackets indicate) ascription features (see §4.1.2); this means that they do not belong to the following cluster, and so do not transgress the rule that definitions have to be restricted to a single non-embedded cluster. These definitions show the well-formedness of 'in April', 'in the morning', 'at six o'clock', etc, as opposed to 'at April', 'at Saturday', 'in the 25th June', 'on midnight', etc.

Commentary

a *On Monday morning* must be semantically construed 'on Monday in the morning', to account for the use of *on* rather than *in*. (Compare the carol's *On Christmas day in the morning* with the regular expression *On Christmas morning*.)

b Various preposition-dropping expression rules are needed to explain the occurrence of *I saw him yesterday evening* rather than *I saw him on yesterday evening*; of *I saw him last year* rather than *I saw him in last year*; etc.

c An irregular and idiomatic use of *at* occurs in such phrases as *at the week-end*, *at Christmas, at night.* These refer to periods rather than points of time, even if we take a liberal "psychological" intepretation of the contrast. They are exceptions, therefore, to the foregoing definition of *at* in its temporal sense.

d Other expressions which cause difficulty are *in that moment* and *at that period*, which occur alongside *at that moment* and *in that period*, and which appear to involve a clash of opposing terms of the ±PERI system. *At that period* is comparable with *at that time* in that it appears to co-occur with verbs referring to states (*eg: At that period he lived near London*) whereas *in that period* demands a verb referring to an event (*eg: in that period I visited him several times*). The use of *at* must be considered an idiomatic irregularity, like those of Comment *c* above. The explanation of *in that moment*, on the other hand, seems to be that the notion of momentariness is subjectively "stretched" into a state of affairs having duration: an effect which one would expect from the ascription feature [+PERI] in the definition of *in*. The solution here is to say that the noun *moment* is defined by some other means than by the feature −PERI, and is therefore inherently unmarked with respect to system 2.

SYSTEM 3 *'this'/'that'*

$\left\{\begin{array}{l} +\text{THIS} \quad \text{'this'} \\ -\text{THIS} \quad \text{'that'} \end{array}\right.$

Class of system: binary taxonomic
Dependence rule: THIS depends on θ

The system *'this'/'that'* is far from being confined to the domain of time, serving to distinguish the demonstratives *this* and *that* (defined as θ +THIS and θ −THIS respectively), also the locative adverbs *here* and *there* and the archaic directional adverbs *hither* and *thither*. Amongst temporal adverbs, *now* and *then*, paraphrasable respectively as *at this time* and *at that time*, manifest the same opposition, and are to be defined:

now: →TIM·θ +THIS 'at this time'
then: →TIM·θ −THIS 'at that time'

'Then' although it generally refers to past time, does not necessarily do so: 'I shall do it then' is a perfectly acceptable statement. Hence the definition simply characterises 'then' as "non-present".

In spite of the paraphrases 'at this time' and 'at that time' (see Comment *d* above), the definitions of *now* and *then* do not contain the ascription feature [−PERI] indicating momentariness. They are neutral, in fact, with respect to the 'period'/'moment' contrast, and a speaker has to avail himself of other adverbials, such as *nowadays, in those days, at that instant*, if he wishes to single out periodic or momentary time.

As the dependence rule indicates, +THIS and −THIS cannot occur except in the presence of the definite formator θ, in combination with which they have a referential DEICTIC or "pointing" function. They may "point" co-referentially to other parts of the discourse in which they are used, or may have extratextual reference to something near or remote in the speech situation. In conjunction with +THIS or −THIS, the reference of the definite formator θ is taken to be self-explanatory by appeal to context.

Commentary

e The above definitions of *now* and *then* seem to violate the condition (suggested in §2.7) that no lexical definition should exceed a cluster of a main predication in extent. We may make it a rule, however, that all adverbial definitions appear in a form resulting from the operation of the rule of subordination (§4.3.3) on the formula $(X) \cdot \rightarrow s \cdot c$. Recast in this way, the definitions of *now* and *then* would appear in the form of the downgraded predications $\langle \theta' \cdot \rightarrow \text{TIM} \cdot \theta +\text{THIS} \rangle$ and $\langle \theta' \cdot \rightarrow \text{TIM} \cdot \theta -\text{THIS} \rangle$. Bearing this in mind, we may continue to give definitions, as above, in their simpler non-downgraded form.

f *Now* can be used in reference to the past in narrative: *Now he spoke to them of his long struggle.* This use is stylistically restricted, and suggests the same kind of "narrator's licence" as the historic present (see §7.4.2).

7.1.1 *Precedence in time*

The notion of precedence in time is conveyed by a relative system, ystem 4:

SYSTEM 4 *'before'/'after'*

$$\begin{cases} (x) \rightarrow \text{BEF} (y) & \text{`}(x) \text{ comes before } (y)\text{'} \\ (x) \leftarrow \text{BEF} (y) & \text{`}(x) \text{ comes after } (y)\text{'} \end{cases}$$

Class of system: relative
Contextual properties: {PERI} $\rightarrow$ BEF {PERI}
Logical properties: asymmetric, irreflexive, transitive

Its logical properties place system 4 in the category of "ordering systems" as defined in §4.1.1. The unacceptability of the following statements confirms the first two logical properties:

'Tomorrow comes after the day after tomorrow.' (asymmetric)
'My birthday comes before itself.' (irreflexive)

The transitivity of the 'before'/'after' relation is demonstrated by the analyticity of the following statement:

'Yesterday (*ie* the day before today) comes before tomorrow (*ie* the day after today).'

The synonymy of *Friday comes before Saturday* and *Saturday comes after Friday* can be shown directly from the two specifications $a \cdot \rightarrow \text{BEF } b \cdot c$ and $c \cdot \leftarrow \text{BEF } b \cdot a$, which according to the mirror-image convention are equivalent.

The contextual conditions of system 4 restrict it to use as a link between clusters representing periods or moments of time, as in 'Sunday comes after Friday'. This limitation may appear to be too stringent, in view of the wide use of *before* and *after* as prepositions of time in sentences like *He came before midnight*. Should not the semantics of such sentences, following the pattern of adverbial structures so far introduced, be analysed as $(X) \cdot \rightarrow$BEF$\cdot c$, violating the contextual redundancy rule just given? If this solution were adopted, however, the rule of well-formedness of question-and-answer sequences (see §6.2) would be broken. A sentence like *He came before midnight* is capable of answering the question *When did he come?* This means that the two sentences must have semantically matching structures $(X) \cdot \rightarrow$TIM$\cdot$? and $(X) \cdot \rightarrow$TIM$\cdot c$. We therefore conclude that *before midnight* as an adverbial phrase should be more fully interpreted as 'at a time before midnight', so that the meaning of *He came before midnight* is to be specified:

$(X) \cdot \rightarrow$TIM$\cdot \varnothing'\langle\theta' \cdot \rightarrow$BEF$\cdot -$PERI $d\rangle$
'(He came) at a time $\langle$before midnight$\rangle$.'

Commentary

g Notice that although both $\rightarrow$TIM and $\rightarrow$BEF ascribe to a neighbouring cluster the system $\pm$PERI, neither member of this system need be chosen in a given specification (see §4.1.2); hence the null symbol $\varnothing$ occurs in this formula where $+$PERI or $-$PERI might have been expected.

Thus *before* and *after* in their most common prepositional function are defined:

before: $\rightarrow$TIM$\cdot \varnothing'\langle\theta' \cdot \rightarrow$BEF$\cdot \varnothing\rangle$ 'at a time which precedes'
after: $\rightarrow$TIM$\cdot \varnothing'\langle\theta' \cdot \leftarrow$BEF$\cdot \varnothing\rangle$ 'at a time which follows'.

The final $\varnothing$ in these formulae is to be "filled" by the semantic representation of the nominal phrase of time following the preposition.

Before and *after* as conjunctions are defined in a similar manner, except that an additional stage of downgrading is introduced, to preserve the contextual conditions of systems 1 and 4:

before: $\rightarrow$TIM$\cdot \varnothing'\langle\theta' \cdot \rightarrow$BEF$\cdot \theta''\langle\theta'' \cdot \leftarrow$TIM$\cdot \varnothing\rangle\rangle$
'at a time preceding the time at which'

after: $\rightarrow$TIM$\cdot \varnothing'\langle\theta' \cdot \leftarrow$BEF$\cdot \theta''\langle\theta'' \cdot \leftarrow$TIM$\cdot \varnothing\rangle\rangle$
'at a time following the time at which'.

These definitions are seen, for example, in:

1 $(X) \cdot \rightarrow$TIM$\cdot \varnothing'\langle\theta \cdot \rightarrow$BEF$\cdot \theta''\langle\theta'' \cdot \leftarrow$TIM$\cdot (Y)\rangle\rangle$
'I saw him before he saw me'

2 $(Y) \cdot \rightarrow$TIM$\cdot \varnothing'\langle\theta' \cdot \leftarrow$BEF$\cdot \theta''\langle\theta'' \cdot \leftarrow$TIM$\cdot (X)\rangle\rangle$
'He saw me after I saw him'

(where $X=$'I saw him' and $Y=$'he saw me').

It will be noted that the sentences *X before Y* and *Y after X* (where *X* and *Y* are declarative clauses) are cognitively synonymous, but that this relationship cannot be shown directly by means of the mirror-image convention, as was possible in the case of *Friday comes before Saturday* and *Saturday comes after Friday*. To demonstrate the equivalence, use must be made not only of the mirror-image convention, but also of the second attribution rule (§4.3.5). First of all, however, it should be pointed out that there is not absolute identity of meaning, since in *X before Y* the time at which *Y* happened is taken as given. This "givenness" is indicated by the definite formator θ'' in each of the specifications above: in the one case it "follows" →BEF (using "follows" with respect to the direction of the arrow) whereas in the other case it "precedes" it. If we abolish this minor difference, replacing θ'' by the zero $\varnothing$, we are able to show the equivalence of the two specifications as follows:

$$(X)\cdot\text{→TIM}\cdot\varnothing'\langle\theta'\cdot\text{→BEF}\cdot\varnothing''\langle\theta''\cdot\text{←TIM}\cdot(Y)\rangle\rangle$$
$$=\langle(X)\cdot\text{→TIM}\cdot\theta'''\rangle\varnothing''':\varnothing'\langle\theta'\cdot\text{→BEF}\cdot\varnothing''\langle\theta''\cdot\text{←TIM}\cdot(Y)\rangle\rangle$$
(2nd attribution rule)
$$=\langle(X)\cdot\text{→TIM}\cdot\theta'''\rangle\varnothing'''\cdot\text{→BEF}\cdot\varnothing''\langle\theta''\cdot\text{←TIM}\cdot(Y)\rangle$$
(2nd attribution rule)
$$=\langle(Y)\cdot\text{→TIM}\cdot\theta''\rangle\varnothing''\cdot\text{←BEF}\cdot\varnothing'''\langle\theta'''\cdot\text{←TIM}\cdot(X)\rangle \text{ (mirror-image)}$$
$$=\langle(Y)\cdot\text{→TIM}\cdot\theta''\rangle\varnothing'':\varnothing'\langle\theta'\cdot\text{←BEF}\cdot\varnothing'''\langle\theta'''\cdot\text{←TIM}\cdot(X)\rangle\rangle$$
(2nd attribution rule)
$$=(Y)\cdot\text{→TIM}\cdot\varnothing'\langle\theta'\cdot\text{←BEF}\cdot\varnothing'''\langle\theta'''\cdot\text{←TIM}\cdot(X)\rangle\rangle$$
(2nd attribution rule)

Allowing for the substitution of $\varnothing$ for θ'', the final line of this formula still does not quite correspond to specification (2) above, in that the prime markings are different. This is, however, a trivial notational discrepancy which makes no difference to the significance of the formula, any more than the substitution of *x*s for all *y*s and *y*s for all *x*s would alter the "meaning" of an algebraic expression.

The relationship we have discussed between the meanings of *before* and *after* as conjunctions is important elsewhere in time and place relations, and we may label it INDIRECT CONVERSENESS for convenience of later reference.

More immediately, it leads us to a similar semantic analysis of the subordinating conjunction *when*:

$$when: \text{→TIM}\cdot\theta'\langle\theta'\cdot\text{←TIM}\cdot\varnothing\rangle \quad \text{'at the time at which'}$$

This definition occurs in:

$$(X)\cdot\text{→TIM}\cdot\theta'\langle\theta'\cdot\text{←TIM}\cdot(Y)\rangle \quad \text{'I saw him when he saw me'}$$
$$(Y)\cdot\text{→TIM}\cdot\theta'\langle\theta'\cdot\text{←TIM}\cdot(X)\rangle \quad \text{'He saw me when I saw him'}$$

(where $X=$'I saw him' and $Y=$'He saw me'). The fact that these two sentences on one interpretation are synonymous (except for the "givenness" of the time of the second clause in each case) can be shown with the aid of the mirror-image convention and the second rule of attribution, by a process of deduction similar to that used with reference to *before* and *after*:

$$(X) \cdot \rightarrow \text{TIM} \cdot \varnothing' \langle \theta' \leftarrow \text{TIM} \cdot (Y) \rangle$$
$$= \langle (X) \cdot \rightarrow \text{TIM} \cdot \theta'' \rangle \varnothing'' : \varnothing' \langle \theta' \cdot \leftarrow \text{TIM} \cdot (Y) \rangle \text{ (2nd attribution rule)}$$
$$= \langle (Y) \cdot \rightarrow \text{TIM} \cdot \theta' \rangle \varnothing' : \varnothing'' \langle \theta'' \cdot \leftarrow \text{TIM} \cdot (X) \rangle \text{ (mirror-image)}$$
$$= (Y) \cdot \rightarrow \text{TIM} \cdot \varnothing'' \langle \theta'' \cdot \leftarrow \text{TIM} \cdot (X) \rangle \text{ (2nd attribution rule)}$$

We may call this relationship INDIRECT SYMMETRY.

Commentary

h There is a second sense of *when* (see §7.4.4 below) which denotes not simultaneity or overlapping of time reference, but temporal successivity (='immediately after'). If *when* is taken in this sense above, the two sentences are not, of course, synonymous.

i Another apparent violation of the contextual dependence rule of system 4 occurs in prepositional phrases like *before lunch, after the war, after Napoleon*, in which the nominal is not a time expression. These can, however, be considered metonymic condensations of 'before lunchtime', 'after the time of the war', 'after the time of Napoleon', which themselves must be regarded as condensed versions of something like 'before the time at which lunch is eaten', 'after the time at which Napoleon lived', etc. *Lunch, war*, and *Napoleon* in such expressions have to be treated as semantically derived from predications.

The definitions of *before* and *after* used as adverbs are much the same as their definitions as prepositions and conjunctions:

before (adv.): $\rightarrow \text{TIM} \cdot \varnothing' \langle \theta' \cdot \rightarrow \text{BEF} \cdot \theta \rangle$ 'at a time before it'
after (adv.): $\rightarrow \text{TIM} \cdot \varnothing' \langle \theta' \cdot \leftarrow \text{BEF} \cdot \theta \rangle$ 'at a time after it'

In this use, the final definite formator is generally co-referential, making *before* and *after* synonymous with *beforehand* and *afterwards*, or alternatively with the phrases *before that* and *after that* (which have, however, the additional feature −THIS). Elsewhere *before* can be used deictically to signify 'before now' or 'before this', as in *I've never been here before*.

7.1.2 *Units of calendar time*

Temporal nouns such as *hour, day, morning, April* all draw their meaning from the particular position they hold within that rather elaborate system of time reckoning employed within western society, the Gregorian Calendar. As a semantic taxonomy of a unique kind, the calendar cannot be omitted from even a cursory account of temporal meaning; at the same time, its analysis has no interest outside the temporal sphere, and must be disposed of here without too much attention to detail.

The first point to notice is that nouns like *hour* and *day* can designate either (a) units of time measurement, or (b) units which not only have a given length, but also begin and end at a given point. A 'year' in the first sense (*eg* in 'twelve years ago') is any period of twelve months; a 'year' in the second sense (as in 'this time last year') not only consists of twelve months, but begins on 1st January. This difference will be represented by system 5:

SYSTEM 5 '*calendar*'/'*non-calendar*'

$\begin{cases} +\text{CAL} & \text{'calendar'} \\ -\text{CAL} & \text{'non-calendar'} \end{cases}$

Class of system: binary taxonomic
Dependence rule: CAL depends on UNIT (system 6)

As the dependence rule indicates, there is a close association between system 5 and system 6:

SYSTEM 6 '*units of time*'

1UNIT	'second'
2UNIT	'minute'
3UNIT	'hour'
4UNIT	'morning/afternoon/evening'
5UNIT	'day/night'
6UNIT	'day'
7UNIT	'week'
8UNIT	'month'
9UNIT	'season of the year'
10UNIT	'year'

Class of system: hierarchic
Special class of tautologies:

$i+j$UNIT $a \cdot \rightarrow l \cdot i$UNIT b

(where $1 \leqslant i < i+j \leqslant 10$; $\rightarrow l =$ 'is/was longer than')

eg 7UNIT $\cdot \rightarrow l \cdot$ 6UNIT   'A week is longer than a day'

    4UNIT $b \cdot \leftarrow l \cdot$ 6UNIT a 'Yesterday morning was shorter than last Tuesday'

Dependence rules: UNIT depends on CAL, PERI (but see below).

The ordering of the features in system 6, as stated in the special class of tautologies, is with respect to length. A more precise relationship obtains between some of the units, in that, for example, one year *consists of* a given number of months; but this relationship does not apply between some other units, for example, between months and weeks.

   Of the many peculiar properties of system 6, we may notice certain restrictions on co-occurrence with the systems $\pm$CAL and $\pm$PERI. All time units, considered simply as units of measurement ($-$CAL), represent periods; but considered as markers of calendar orientation ($+$CAL), the three smallest units designate points, not periods of time: 'three o'clock', 'six minutes past three', etc. In other words, 1UNIT, 2UNIT, or 3UNIT, when combined with +CAL, must also combine with −PERI, where 4UNIT, etc, must combine with +PERI. The facts of the case are therefore more complicated than indicated by the rather vaguely formulated dependence rules for system 6, which state simply that any feature from system 6 presupposes a choice from the systems ±CAL and ± PERI. The statement of the special class of tautologies also has to be modified to exclude '6 o'clock is longer than 6 minutes past 5', and similar nonsensical assertions.

Further peculiarities of system 6 are (a) the lack of any general nouns expressing the meanings of 4UNIT and 5UNIT, which represent what we may call "unofficial" units of calendar time; and, connected with this, (b) the absence of expressions of time measurement (−CAL) using 4UNIT, 5UNIT, and 9UNIT. We do not speak, for example, of seeing a friend *three seasons ago*. It is difficult to decide whether such manners of speaking should be prohibited by semantic or by expression rules. If the former, we should have to expressly exclude, by dependence rules, the co-occurrence of 4UNIT, 5UNIT, and 9UNIT with −CAL. The status of these three members of the system is obviously different from that of the other members, and one might argue that they should be excluded, the meanings of *night*, *Spring*, etc, being explained in some other way.

Commentary

j Meanings expressed by three other nouns of time measurement, *fortnight*, *decade*, and *century* are not given separate status within the system, but are assumed to be derivable from other units: 'fortnight'='two weeks', etc. One might wonder whether units like 'minute' and 'hour' should be treated likewise, and defined as '60 seconds', '3600 seconds', etc. One objection to this is that whereas one feels that 'fortnight' and 'decade' are derivative from 'week' and 'year' respectively, it is by no means so clear that 'minute' and 'hour' are derivative from 'second': one might, indeed, argue for a derivation in the other direction, whereby 'minute' would be defined as 'one-sixtieth of an hour', etc. Another, more important, point is that if 'minute' is defined as '60 seconds', then the meaning of an expression like *five minutes* has to be specified as a multiplication sum: '5 × 60 seconds'. That is, the rule of expression interpreting this phrase and similar phrases would entail an arithmetical calculation, something quite foreign to rules of expression as so far considered. On the other hand, expressions of time measurement like *three fortnights* are unusual, if not unnatural, and do indeed seem to be interpreted by a process of mathematical reckoning. (One's reaction to the phrase *three fortnights*, if one came across it, would be to perform the sum '3 fortnights = 3 × 2 weeks = 6 weeks'.) About 'decade', 'century', and 'millenium' reactions are less sure, and a case can be made for accommodating them directly in the '*units of time*' system by adding three more terms, 11UNIT, 12UNIT and 13UNIT.

Dependent on individual terms of the '*units of time*' system are a number of systems which differentiate subcategories of each term. System 7 is representative of this group of systems:

SYSTEM 7 '*seasons of the year*'

$\begin{cases} 1\text{SEA} & \text{'spring'} \\ 2\text{SEA} & \text{'summer'} \\ 3\text{SEA} & \text{'autumn'} \\ 4\text{SEA} & \text{'winter'} \end{cases}$

Class of system: hierarchic, cyclic (see below)

Special class of tautologies:

$\left. \begin{array}{l} i\text{SEA} \cdot \rightarrow \text{BEF} \rightarrow \text{NEXT} \cdot i + 1\text{SEA} \\ 4\text{SEA} \cdot \rightarrow \text{BEF} \rightarrow \text{NEXT} \cdot 1\text{SEA} \end{array} \right\}$ where $1 \leqslant i < 4$

   eg 'Autumn comes before winter'

       'Winter comes before spring'

Dependence rule: SEA depends on 9UNIT, +CAL

Most of these systems, including system 7, belong to a particular class of hierarchic systems, which we may label CYCLIC. The relationship which orders the terms of a hierarchic system with respect to one another also obtains, in cyclic systems, between the last term and the first term of each system. This is what is indicated by the second part of the statement of tautologies above. Just as it is always true to say 'Sunday comes before Monday', 'Monday comes before Tuesday', etc, so is it true to say 'Saturday comes before Sunday'. All these are analytic statements. As 'comes before', in these assertions, is taken to mean 'comes directly before', the relationship between 'Tuesday' and 'Wednesday', etc, must be represented by the feature →BEF supplemented by a further relative feature →NEXT, introduced in system 8:

SYSTEM 8 '*contiguity*'

$\begin{cases} (x) \rightarrow \text{NEXT} \ (y) & \text{'}(x) \text{ is next to } (y)\text{'} \\ (x) \leftarrow \text{NEXT} \ (y) & \text{'}(y) \text{ is next to } (x)\text{'} \end{cases}$

Class of system: relative

Contextual properties: →NEXT {PERI *or* +CONC}

Logical properties: irreflexive, symmetric, intransitive (this system is therefore a reciprocal system – see §4.1.1.)

The special tautologies associated with cyclic systems of time can now all be specified by the following two formulae:

$\left. \begin{array}{l} i\text{S} \cdot \rightarrow \text{BEF} \rightarrow \text{NEXT} \cdot i + 1\text{S} \\ n\text{S} \cdot \rightarrow \text{BEF} \rightarrow \text{NEXT} \cdot 1\text{S} \end{array} \right\}$

where n is the number of terms in the system, and i is any positive integer less than n.

The system of '*contiguity*', which appears here in a temporal connection, is taken to be identical with that which finds expression in the spatial, concrete use of *next*, as in *His house is next to mine*. Hence under "contextual properties", {PERI} and {+CONC} are allowed as alternatives. The contextual redundancy rules operate in both directions, but need only be stated once, because of the reciprocality of system 8.

Commentary

k Since this is the first occasion on which medial clusters containing more than one relative component have been introduced, it is as well to point out that these have not been excluded from the theory. In §2.4 it was stated that medial clusters must contain one relative component; to this we add that it may also contain more than one. In a predication containing two relative components in its medial cluster, there is potentially a four-way directional contrast:

$$a \cdot \overrightarrow{\overrightarrow{\cdot}} r \cdot b, \; a \cdot \overrightarrow{\overleftarrow{\cdot}} r \cdot b, \; a \cdot \overleftarrow{\overrightarrow{\cdot}} r \cdot b, \; \text{and} \; a \cdot \overleftarrow{\overleftarrow{\cdot}} r \cdot b \cdot$$

Other hierarchic systems parallel to system 7 need only be briefly listed, it being understood that they could be described on a similar pattern.

SYSTEM 9 '*months of the year*'
$$\left\{ \begin{array}{ll} \text{1MON} & \text{'January'} \\ \text{2MON} & \text{'February'} \\ \vdots \\ \text{12MON} & \text{'December'} \end{array} \right.$$
(dependent on 8UNIT, +CAL)

SYSTEM 10 '*days of month*'
$$\left\{ \begin{array}{ll} \text{1DAYM} & \text{'first'} \\ \text{2DAYM} & \text{'second'} \\ \vdots \\ \text{31DAYM} & \text{'thirty-first'} \end{array} \right.$$
(dependent on 6UNIT, +CAL)

SYSTEM 11 '*days of the week*'
$$\left\{ \begin{array}{ll} \text{1DAYW} & \text{'Sunday'} \\ \text{2DAYW} & \text{'Monday'} \\ \vdots \\ \text{7DAYW} & \text{'Saturday'} \end{array} \right.$$
(dependent on 6UNIT, +CAL)

SYSTEM 12 '*day*'/'*night*'
$$\left\{ \begin{array}{ll} \text{1DAYN} & \text{'day(time)'} \\ \text{2DAYN} & \text{'night(time)'} \end{array} \right.$$
(dependent on 5UNIT, +CAL)

SYSTEM 13 *'morning'*/*'afternoon'*/*'evening'*

{
  1MAE   'morning'
  2MAE   'afternoon'
  3MAE   'evening'
}
  (dependent on 4UNIT, +CAL)

SYSTEM 14 *'years* (A.D.)*'*

{
  1YEAR   'A.D. 1'
  2YEAR   'A.D. 2'
  ⋮
  1968YEAR   'A.D. 1968'
}
  (dependent on 10UNIT, +CAL)

Commentary

l In a more extensive semantic description which included an account of ordinal number, system 10 would be redundant, as phrases like *1st January* could be semantically analysed as 'the first day of January', parallel to such expressions as *the first flight to the moon, my third child*, etc. However, because the semantics of ordinal number raises problems which cannot be dealt with here, the above must be accepted as a provisional solution. It is debatable whether other systems of the group could be satisfactorily eliminated in the same way. *January, February*, etc, for instance, might be defined 'the first month of the year', 'the second month of the year', etc; but there is no doubt that months are recognised by "gestalten" in the minds of language-users, and are referentially associated with typical weather conditions, stages in the cycle of husbandry, religious festivals, etc. Thus, if in some future calendar reform, March became the first month of the year and January and February became the last two, we would not be justified in saying that the word *March* now expressed what was formerly expressed by *January*. Another point in favour of systems 9 to 14 is that without them we should not be able to explain the ridiculousness of expressions like *the eighth day of the week, the twentieth month of 1965*. Admittedly, however, this is an area in which it is especially difficult to separate questions of fact and questions of semantics (see §5.3).

m Calendar time affords many illustrations of alternative systems giving "competing conceptualisations" of the same aspect of experience. Consider for instance, 'day'/'night' and 'a.m.'/'p.m.' as variant ways of dichotomising the twenty-four hour cycle. There is, in addition, the complication of cultural alternatives such as the Hebrew Calendar and the Moslem Calendar; these may be disregarded in this study, since only the Roman Calendar is implicated in time expressions of general use in English.

n System 14 deals only with years A.D. In a more comprehensive account, we could distinguish these from years B.C. by a separate system.

We shall dwell no longer on the structure of the calendar, except to observe that many minor problems of description have been left aside, and that some major questions, such as the specifications of "clock-time" ('6.30 p.m.', etc) have been omitted altogether.

7.1.3 Calendar "addresses"

Expressions locating a position in calendar time are not unlike postal addresses in that they have the structure of a hierarchy, working from small units towards large ones (although the order of the hierarchy is not always faithfully imitated by order on the page): compare *the evening of 25th February, 1968* with *Flat No. 2, Gordon Mansions, Maddox Street, Reading, Berks., England.* The semantic structure of such locutions is revealed more clearly in surface grammar if they are expanded through the insertion of prepositions: *the evening of the twenty-fifth day of January in the year 1968; the second flat of Gordon Mansions in Maddox Street in Reading in Berkshire in England.* The connecting link between the different units of time expressed here by *of* or *in* is the relation of 'inclusion':

SYSTEM 15 *'inclusion'*
$$\begin{cases} (x) \to\text{INC } (y) & \text{'}(x) \text{ includes } (y)\text{'} \\ (x) \leftarrow\text{INC } (y) & \text{'}(x) \text{ is (included) in } (y)\text{'} \end{cases}$$
Class of system: relative
Contextual properties: $\{+\text{PERI}\} \to\text{INC } \{\text{PERI}\}$
Special class of contradictions: (See below)
Logical properties: irreflexive, asymmetric, transitive.

The system of *'inclusion'* as detailed above applies exclusively to time. There is some concord between the terminal elements it links, in that both must contain a term from the $\pm\text{PERI}$ system; but there is also some lack of balance in the relationship, such that the inclusion of a point of time within a period is allowable, but not the inclusion of a period within a point of time. As is made clear above, a predication of the general form $a \cdot \leftarrow\text{INC } b \cdot -\text{PERI } c$ (*eg* 'Yesterday was (included) in 10 o'clock') constitutes a breach of contextual restrictions. In addition, the 'inclusion' relation can only link lower units to higher units on the scale represented by system 6: 'My birthday was in January' (day within month) makes sense, but not 'January was on my birthday' (month within day). This limitation may be expressed by a statement which excludes assertions of the following general form as contradictory:

Special class of contradictions:

$i\text{UNIT } a \cdot \to\text{INC } b \cdot j\text{UNIT } c$ (where $i \leqslant j$)
eg 'January includes a leap-year.'

The transitivity of system 15 is demonstrated by the analyticity of statements like 'The 25th January, 1965 was in 1965.' Simple examples of calendar addresses are:

(i) θ 3MAE'$\langle\theta' \cdot \leftarrow\text{INC} \cdot \theta$ 6DAYW$\rangle$ 'Friday evening'

(ii) θ 20DAYM$'\langle\theta'\cdot\leftarrow$INC$\cdot\theta$ 4MON$''\langle\theta''\cdot\leftarrow$INC$\cdot\theta$ 1960YEAR$\rangle\rangle$
'20th April, 1960'

(iii) θ 1MAE$'\langle\theta'\cdot\leftarrow$INC$\cdot$2DAYM$''\langle\theta''\cdot\leftarrow$INC$\cdot$2MON$'''\langle\theta'''\cdot\leftarrow$INC$\cdot\theta$
                                                                     1964YEAR$\rangle\rangle\rangle$
'The morning of the 2nd February, 1964.'

Each terminal cluster is given here in its skeletal form; more features (notably from the systems 1, 2, . . . , nUNIT and $\pm$PERI) are to be added by dependence rules. Such calendar addresses occupy the position of c in the general time-adverbial formula $(X)\cdot\rightarrow$TIM$\cdot c$.

7.1.4 Deictic definiteness of calendar meanings

The presence of the definite formator in every terminal cluster of the calendar addresses above demands elucidation. There is no necessary element of definiteness in the meaning of calendar terms (notice the indefiniteness of expressions like *one spring, a Sunday in April*); but a definite force is usually present, either because the calendar term is being used with deictic import, or because it has the inherent definiteness of a proper name. Both these factors require some discussion. To them may be added a third factor, and that is, that a one–one or one–many relation will produce "cataphoric definiteness" of one terminal cluster, given the definiteness of its other terminal cluster. 'A winter in 1967' or 'on a Friday last week' are nonsensical because we know there can only be one winter in the same year, or one Friday in the same week. This principle of cataphoric definiteness accounts for the definiteness of 'evening', '20th', 'April', etc in formulae (i) to (iii) above, if the definiteness of 'Friday', '1960', etc, is taken as given.

Let us turn first to deictic definiteness. It is clear that when we use such phrases as *on Tuesday, in January*, without making it clear *which* Tuesday or January is meant, the interpretation tends to be deictic; that is, we understand 'the Tuesday immediately after now' or 'the Tuesday immediately before now' according to context. (This assumption of deixis in the interpretation of definiteness is widespread within the language; compare 'the kitchen' = 'the kitchen in this house', 'the Queen', 'the town hall', etc.) If we wish to distinguish between the future and past interpretations, we can, of course, use the words *last* and *next*:

θ 3DAYW$'\langle\theta'\cdot\rightarrow$BEF $\rightarrow$NEXT$\cdot\theta$ +THIS$\rangle$ 'last Tuesday'
θ 3DAYW$'\langle\theta'\cdot\leftarrow$BEF $\leftarrow$NEXT$\cdot\theta$ +THIS$\rangle$ 'next Tuesday'

The deictic specification for *Tuesday* on its own is less explicit, for the feature $\rightarrow$BEF or $\leftarrow$BEF is omitted:

θ 3DAYW$'\langle\theta'\cdot\rightarrow$NEXT$\cdot\theta$ +THIS$\rangle$ 'Tuesday'

We now see that formula (i) in §7.1.3 above, is incomplete; if 'Friday' is understood deictically, it must be supplemented by the downgraded predication $\langle \theta'' \cdot \rightarrow$NEXT$\cdot \theta +$THIS$\rangle$ 'before/after now'.

Such expressions as *next Tuesday, next autumn, last Easter, last January*, are capable of a second interpretation 'the Tuesday of next week', 'the January of last year', etc. They are like *yesterday morning, tomorrow afternoon*, etc in that the period of time is related not directly to the present moment but through a period of time of which it is a part. So used, *next* and *last* are in contrast not only to one another, but to *this* in phrases such as *this Wednesday*. Notice that *this Wednesday, this afternoon*, etc, differ from *this week, this month*, etc, in that the period referred to need not include the present moment.

As a step towards explaining this group, let us define the adverbs *today, tomorrow*, and *yesterday* as follows:

today: $\qquad \theta$ +THIS 6UNIT 'this day'
tomorrow: θ 6UNIT$'\langle \theta' \cdot \leftarrow$BEF $\leftarrow$NEXT$\cdot \theta$ +THIS 6UNIT$\rangle$
$\qquad\qquad$ · 'the day immediately following this day'
yesterday: θ 6UNIT$'\langle \theta' \cdot \rightarrow$BEF $\rightarrow$NEXT$\cdot \theta$ +THIS 6UNIT$\rangle$

The meaning of *this afternoon* may now be represented:

θ 2MAE$'\langle \theta' \cdot \leftarrow$INC$\cdot \theta$ +THIS 6UNIT$\rangle$ 'the afternoon of today'

and *yesterday morning* as follows:

θ 1MAE$'\langle \theta' \cdot \leftarrow$INC$\cdot \theta$ 6UNIT$''\langle \theta'' \cdot \rightarrow$BEF $\rightarrow$NEXT$\cdot \theta$ +THIS 6UNIT$\rangle\rangle$

'the morning of the day immediately preceding today'

The meanings of *next Wednesday, last January, this Easter*, etc, can be specified in a similar fashion. From such an explication, it can be seen that the *this* of *this afternoon* applies semantically to the whole day of which the afternoon is a segment.

Temporal phrases like *last January* are thus ambiguous to the extent that they may mean 'the January before now' or 'the January of last year', etc. One might, for instance, distinguish between the coming August of this year and that of next year in such an utterance as this: *This August we'll be going to Crete, but next August we'll have to stay at home.* Here *next August* cannot be construed 'the August following now', but in other contexts there may well be confusion of alternative usages. *Last spring*, spoken in October 1968, could refer either to the immediately preceding spring (that of 1968), or to the spring of the preceding year (that of 1967).

Commentary

o Further confusion results from the tendency of some speakers to reserve *this Wednesday*, etc. for future reference. In my own usage, for example, a Wednesday of this week would tend to be designated *this Wednesday* if ahead of the time of speaking, otherwise simply (*on*) *Wednesday*: *I'll see him this Wednesday* is attestable, but rarely **I saw him this Wednesday*.

Last night, on the other hand, has to mean simply 'the night immediately preceding now', since the division between 'night(time)' and 'day (time)' straddles the division of 'days' as twenty-four-hour units. *Last winter* is a similar case: it cannot mean 'the winter of last year', because winter overlaps the boundary between years.

Expressions such as *that evening, that day,* etc incorporate the feature —THIS, and can, like *then,* convey either pastness or futurity. *I was on holiday that week* and *I shall be on holiday that week* are both semantically acceptable. 'That day' can therefore be straightforwardly symbolised θ —THIS 7UNIT, without any indication of 'after now' or 'before now'.

7.1.5 *Generic definiteness of calendar meanings*

The use of capital letters in the writing of days of the week, months of the year, etc, is a symptom of the quasi-proper-name function often associated with calendar terms. Yet only in the case of year names (*1960, 1965, 1970,* etc) is the condition of unique reference associated with proper names actually fulfilled. In other cases such as 'His birthday is in January' and 'Tuesday is always a busy day for me', the calendar term refers not to one single period of time, but to a regularly recurring period, or (to put it another way) a set of periods which share the same position in the taxonomy of the calendar.

This usage is an example of GENERIC DEFINITENESS, and can be compared with such expressions as *the tiger* in *The tiger is found in Africa, man* in *Man is mortal,* and *the Rolls Royce engine* in *The Rolls Royce engine is the best engine in the world.* What happens in each of these cases is that uniqueness is attributed to the set of animals, objects, etc, itself, and not to the individual members of the set. *The tiger is found in Africa* is therefore to be treated as a metonymic reduction of 'The race of tigers is a race the members of which are found in Africa'. To analyse such a statement, we need to bring in the relative system of '*set membership*', which plays a part in the definition of collective nouns such as *race, set, class, flock, crowd, species:*

SYSTEM 16 '*set membership*'
$$\begin{cases} (x) \to \text{SET} \ (y) & \text{`}(x) \text{ is/are member(s) of the set } (y)\text{'} \\ (x) \leftarrow \text{SET} \ (y) & \text{`}(y) \text{ is a set with the member(s) } (x)\text{'} \end{cases}$$
Class of system: relative
Contextual properties: $\{+\text{COU}\} \to \text{SET} \ \{+\text{COU}\}$ (see below)
Special rule of synonymy: (This rule is only roughly stated)
$\quad a{:}b = \theta$ —PLUR$'\langle \theta' \cdot \leftarrow \text{SET} \cdot a \rangle : \theta$ —PLUR$''\langle \theta'' \cdot \leftarrow \text{SET} \cdot b \rangle$
$\quad$ (where a is universally construed)
Logical properties: irreflexive, asymmetric, intransitive, one–many

This system, which is, of course, of wide application in the language, has an unusual contextual property: in any predication a —PLUR·←SET $b·c$, if c is universally construed, then a contains the definite formator θ. For instance, if 'tigers' in 'race of tigers' is universally construed as 'all tigers', then 'race' itself must be definite. It is sensible to talk of '*The* race of (all) tigers', but not of '*A* race of (all) tigers'. This means that if an expression is generic in meaning, an element of definiteness is necessarily involved.

We can now see how *the human race*, an example of a generic expression, may be defined

$$\theta +\text{COU} -\text{PLUR}'\langle\theta'·\leftarrow\text{SET}· +\text{COU} +\text{PLUR} +\text{HUM}\rangle$$
'the race of human-beings (in general)'

it being understood that the rightmost cluster is universally construed. We can see likewise, returning to the field of time, that *Tuesday* in *Tuesday is always a busy day for me* can be defined:

$$\theta +\text{COU} -\text{PLUR}'\langle\theta'·\leftarrow\text{SET}· +\text{COU} +\text{PLUR} \text{3DAYW}\rangle$$
'the set of Tuesdays (in general)'

Just as *The tiger is found in Africa* is synonymous with *Tigers are found in Africa*, so *Tuesday is always a busy day for me* is synonymous with *Tuesdays are always busy days for me*. Both these cases of synonymy fall within the scope of the substantive rule of synonymy stated above.

Commentary

p In defence of the preceding analysis, it may be noted that the "generic singular" of *Tuesday is always a busy day for me* is distinct from the "universal singular" of *A Tuesday is a busy day for me* or (with overt universal quantification) *Every Tuesday is a busy day for me*. In the case of the generic singular, as I have already said, definiteness and uniqueness are attributed to the class as a whole, whereas with universal 'a Tuesday' or 'every Tuesday', the members of the class are singled out individually, instead of being regarded *en masse*. Thus statements appropriate to the whole class, but not to its individual members, can be made in the generic singular: *The Volkswagen is the most successful car in the world; The wolf was once found over the whole of Europe.* Such statements become nonsensical, however, when the "universal singular" is substituted: **A/every Volkswagen is the most successful car in the world; *A/every wolf was once found over the whole of Europe.*

7.2 The pluralisation of time segments

7.2.1 *Number of times*

We now progress from "time" in the singular to "times" in the plural. The relation of the system $\pm\text{PLUR}$ ('singular'/'plural') to time has so far been almost ignored, but as all the time expressions considered so far have been singular in meaning, to make them more complete we must retrospectively mark their specifications with the feature −PLUR, in contrast to the +PLUR of such concepts as 'twice', 'four times', etc. Since −PLUR and 1QUA 'one' are mutually dependent features (see §6.3.2), the terminal cluster of →TIM· −PLUR 1QUA 'once', 'on one occasion', logically includes those of all the specifications given earlier, such as for 'on Tuesday', or 'last Spring'. That is, any statement of the form 'X on Tuesday', 'X last spring', and so on, inductively implies 'X once' or (more explicitly) 'X at least once'; for example, 'I saw him on Saturday' implies 'I once saw him'.

Here are some specifications of plural time:

$(X)·{\rightarrow}\text{TIM}· +\text{PLUR } 2\text{QUA}$	'twice'
$(X)·{\rightarrow}\text{TIM}· +\text{PLUR } 100\text{QUA}$	'a hundred times'
$((X)·{\rightarrow}\text{TIM}· +\text{PLUR}')·1\alpha \leftarrow o·\theta'$	'always, at all times'
$((X)·{\rightarrow}\text{TIM}· +\text{PLUR}')·2\alpha \leftarrow o·\theta'$	'sometimes'
$((X)·{\rightarrow}\text{TIM}· +\text{PLUR}')·2\alpha \leftarrow o +\text{MANY}·\theta'$	'many times, often'
$((X)·{\rightarrow}\text{TIM}· +\text{PLUR}')·2\alpha \leftarrow o -\text{MANY}·\theta'$	'a few times'
$((X)·{\rightarrow}\text{TIM}· +\text{PLUR}')·\sim2\alpha \leftarrow o +\text{MANY}·\theta'$	'not many times, not often, rarely, seldom'
$((X)·{\rightarrow}\text{TIM}· +\text{PLUR } 7\text{UNIT}')·2\alpha \leftarrow o·\theta'$	'some weeks'

All except the first two examples contain existential or universal quantification (see §3.5). The definition of *never*, we may assume, is simply $((X)·{\rightarrow}\text{TIM}· \varnothing')·\sim2\alpha \leftarrow o·\theta'$ 'at no time', without singular or plural specification, although grammatically *at no time* (compare *none* and *nobody*) is singular. This therefore lies strictly outside the province of time pluralisation. The same applies to expressions like *every day*, which gain their implications of plurality from the universal quantifier, but are probably best treated as semantically, as well as grammatically, singular, in the sense that their semantic specifications contain the feature −PLUR. (This view is borne out by the intuition that *every* somehow indicates the consideration of a group of things individually, or one by one.) At the same time, expressions with *every* as modifier are semantically bound up with the examples above, and may conveniently be classed with them for purposes of discussion.

Commentary

a The meanings of expressions containing cardinal numbers, such as *three men*, are not overtly quantified but are treated as existentially construed (see §2.8.2, §3.5). This accounts for the main difference between the first two specifications above and the remainder. One reason for this analysis is that phrases like *three men* cannot be negated in the same way as *many men, all men, a few men*, etc. A further point is that syntactic ordering in nominal phrases like *all three men, all the three men, all of the three men* favours the assignment of the feature 3QUA to the principal predication, not the quantificational predication.

7.2.2 *Pluralisation of events*

The many–one condition on $\rightleftarrows$TIM (system 1) requires that the element (X) of $(X)\cdot\rightarrow$TIM$\cdot c$ should be marked as plural if c is marked as plural. That is, if an event takes place on a number of separate occasions, the event itself must be regarded as pluralised. As (X), being a rank-shifted predication, can only be assigned features indirectly through one of its clusters, the feature +PLUR is actually attached to the medial cluster of X, and according to the notational convention introduced in §4.1.2, the predication may then be represented in an abbreviatory formula Y +PLUR (not "X +PLUR", since X with the addition of the feature +PLUR cannot be equal to X). In all the specifications listed in §7.2.1, X must be understood to contain the feature +PLUR in its medial cluster.

The necessity of regarding events, like objects, as pluralisable will come to the fore in the analysis of the habitual or iterative verbal aspect in §7.4.2.[1] At present, we may note, in support of this notion, that some-times two separate possibilities need to be recognised: (1) more than one event on the same occasion:

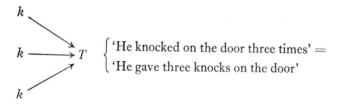

$$k \searrow$$
$$k \longrightarrow T \quad \left\{ \begin{array}{l} \text{'He knocked on the door three times'} = \\ \text{'He gave three knocks on the door'} \end{array} \right.$$
$$k \nearrow$$

and (2) more than one event on more than one occasion:

$$k \longrightarrow T$$
$$k \longrightarrow T \quad \left\{ \begin{array}{l} \text{'He knocked on the door three times'} = \\ \text{'He knocked on the door on three occasions'} \end{array} \right.$$
$$k \longrightarrow T$$

A reason for separating these is that only the former may occur in narra-tive sequences such as 'He leapt off his horse, knocked three times on the door, and demanded immediate admittance'. When such sequences are discussed in §7.4.4, it will be seen that the final cluster (corresponding to T in the above diagram) must be marked as singular. Thus 'three times' in this instance must be considered a pluralisation of the event, not of both the event and the occasion.

A third possibility, plurality of occasion combined with singularity of event, is the one we have already ruled out as logically impossible:

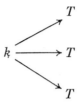

To some extent, however, plurality of times and plurality of events have to be treated independently.

7.2.3 *Frequency*

Often, sometimes, and similar expressions whose meanings involve the quantification of time are ambiguous, in that they may designate "number of times", as in §7.2.1, or frequency. There is a subtle difference between these two concepts, analogous to the difference between distance and speed: just as speed is a function of distance and time, so is frequency a function of length of period and number of times. To illustrate this ambiguity from an imaginary situation: John spent four weeks at the seaside and bathed ten times, whereas Jim spent one week at the seaside and bathed five times; John therefore bathed *more times* than Jim, but Jim bathed *more frequently* than John. In one sense, 'John bathed more often than Jim', but in another sense 'Jim bathed more often than John'.

These two meanings correlate (though it is difficult to determine precisely why) with tense and aspect distinctions. With the perfective, the interpretation is almost certainly "number of times":

'I have often visited France' $\begin{cases} = \text{'I have visited France many times.'} \\ \neq \text{'I have visited France with great} \\ \quad\text{frequency'.} \end{cases}$

But with the simple present, the meaning is inevitably frequency:

'I often visit France' $\begin{cases} \neq \text{'I visit France many times'.} \\ = \text{'I visit France with great frequency'.} \end{cases}$

The first step in a semantic analysis of frequency adverbials is to note the inappropriateness of sentences expressing frequency as answers to questions beginning *when*:

When do you collect the children from school?
*(I collect them) often.

This inappropriateness shows (following the principle laid down in §6.2) that frequency cannot be subsumed under the adverbial relation of time, but must be considered a separate relation. For which purpose, an adverbial system of '*frequency*' is required:

SYSTEM 17 *'frequency'*

$\begin{cases} (x) \rightarrow \text{FREQ}\ (y) & \text{`}(x)\text{ with frequency }(y)\text{'} \\ (x) \leftarrow \text{FREQ}\ (y) & \text{`}(y)\text{ with frequency }(x)\text{'} \end{cases}$

Class of system: relative

Contextual properties: $\{(X +\text{PLUR})\} \rightarrow \text{FREQ} \begin{cases} \{-\text{COU}')\ 2\alpha \leftarrow \text{o}\ c \cdot \theta'\} \\ \quad or \\ \{(\text{QUA}\ a \cdot \leftarrow \text{INC} \cdot +\text{PERI}\ b)\} \end{cases}$

Logical properties: asymmetric, irreflexive, intransitive.

The logical properties of this system are more or less the same as those of the adverbial system *'time when'* (system 1), and for the same reasons; no more need be said about them. The contextual properties, on the other hand, are peculiarly complex, and for clarity's sake may be verbally repeated as follows:

[a] →FREQ is always preceded by a rank-shifted predication containing, in its medial cluster, the feature +PLUR;

[b] →FREQ is always followed by *either* (i) an existentially quantified cluster containing −COU *or* (ii) a rank-shifted predication having the structure QUA $a \cdot \leftarrow$INC$\cdot$ +PERI b (where QUA indicates "any member of the system 1, 2, 3, ..., nQUA").

To explain these conditions further. Condition [a] formalises the fact that frequency can only be predicated of repeated happenings; *eg* 'My brother often visits me' makes good sense, but not 'My brother is often older than I'. Condition [b] states that frequency can be measured in two ways: (i) by a simple undifferentiated scale of existential quantification 'rarely'/'occasionally'/'often', etc; and (ii) by plotting happenings against periods of time ('once a week', 'three times a year', etc). Examples of the first type of frequency measure are:

$((X +\text{PLUR}) \cdot \rightarrow \text{FREQ} \cdot -\text{COU}') \cdot 2\alpha \leftarrow \text{o} \cdot \theta'$
'with some frequency, sometimes'
$((X +\text{PLUR}) \cdot \rightarrow \text{FREQ} \cdot -\text{COU}') \cdot 2\alpha \leftarrow \text{o} +\text{MANY} \cdot \theta'$
'with much frequency, frequently, often'
$((X +\text{PLUR}) \cdot \rightarrow \text{FREQ} \cdot -\text{COU}') \cdot 2\alpha \leftarrow \text{o} -\text{MANY} \cdot \theta'$
'with a little frequency, occasionally'
$((X +\text{PLUR}) \cdot \rightarrow \text{FREQ} \cdot -\text{COU}') \cdot \sim 2\alpha \leftarrow \text{o} +\text{MANY} \cdot \theta'$
'with not much frequency, not often, rarely, seldom'

(For the system ±MANY, see §3.5.) Examples of type (ii) are:

$(X +\text{PLUR}) \cdot \rightarrow \text{FREQ} \cdot (1\text{QUA} \cdot \leftarrow \text{INC} \cdot +\text{PERI}\ 1\text{QUA}\ 2\text{UNIT})$
'once a minute'
$(X +\text{PLUR}) \cdot \rightarrow \text{FREQ} \cdot (1\text{QUA} \cdot \leftarrow \text{INC} \cdot +\text{PERI}\ 3\text{QUA}\ 7\text{UNIT})$
'once in three weeks'
$(X +\text{PLUR}) \cdot \rightarrow \text{FREQ} \cdot (5\text{QUA} \cdot \leftarrow \text{INC} \cdot +\text{PERI}\ 1\text{QUA}\ 6\text{UNIT})$
'five times a day'

Commentary

b The formulae of this second set are simplified to some extent. In particular, the 'three weeks' in 'once in three weeks', etc, are understood to be consecutive weeks making up a single period; therefore the method of specification must follow the lines of durational formulae like 'for three weeks' (see §7.3.1 below).

The two methods of reckoning frequency are obviously connected, as we see from the tautological character of such assertions as 'Three times a week is more frequent than twice a week' and 'Once a week is as frequent as twice a fortnight'.

Expressions like *once every minute, twice every day*, and *five times every two weeks* are semantically equivalent to *once a minute, twice a day, five times in two weeks*, etc, merely making explicit the interpretation of the calendar expression as universally quantified. *Every minute, every day*, etc., must be assumed to express the semantic structure of 'once every minute', 'once every day', etc.

7.2.4 *Difficulties of interpretation*

One problem which arises is to decide which items the ambiguity of pluralisation/frequency applies to.

Occasionally and *frequently* are probably restricted to the sense of frequency: *I have seen him occasionally* does not, for example, seem to mean 'I have seen him a few times', but rather 'I have seen him at infrequent intervals'.

Always and *never* are two other items which need careful consideration. *Never* seems acceptable as a negation of *sometimes* (= 'with nil frequency'), but the notion of 'maximum frequency', attached to *always*, seems an unsatisfactory one, and for this reason I have restricted the frequency expressions of type (i) (in §7.2.3) to those expressing existential quantification.

If *always* is not definable in a 'frequency' sense, neither does it seem to make sense as 'maximum number of times', unless an additional factor of meaning is read in. Thus *I always have dinner in town* invites the interpretation 'I have dinner in town whenever I have dinner', or more explicitly, 'I have dinner in town on all occasions on which I have dinner'. It may be noticed that *He always collects the groceries on Tuesday* is ambiguous to the extent it may be paraphrased either 'He collects the groceries every Tuesday' or 'Whenever he collects the groceries, he collects them on Tuesday'. This second interpretation corresponds to that of *I always have dinner in town* in that it contains an implicit 'whenever'.

The best way to distinguish these two interpretations, it seems to me, is to attribute them respectively to the universal quantification of the cluster of time designation ('every Tuesday') and to the universal quantification of the event itself. We have assumed that rank-shifted predications may be pluralised, and it is only one further step to the supposition that they may be quantified. This involves the extension of the quantificational analysis of §3.5 to formulae such as the following:

$$\theta' \cdot \mathrm{I}\alpha \to \mathrm{o} \cdot ((X)' \cdot r \cdot b)$$
'for all events X, $(X) \cdot r \cdot b$'

The contrast between the two meanings of *He always collects the groceries on Tuesday* may be symbolised, with some simplification:

$$\theta' \cdot \mathrm{I}\alpha \leftarrow \mathrm{o} \cdot ((X) \cdot \to \text{TIM} \cdot 3\text{DAYW}')$$
'For all Tuesdays, he collects the groceries on Tuesday'

$$\theta' \cdot \mathrm{I}\alpha \leftarrow \mathrm{o} \cdot ((X)' \cdot \to \text{TIM} \cdot 3\text{DAYW})$$
'For all collecting-of-the-groceries, he collects the groceries on Tuesday'.

This difference is exactly parallel to that between 'all cats like fish' and 'cats like all fish' (see §3.5).

To summarise, *always* and *never* each have two distinct interpretations in the area of meaning covered by this section. *Never* can mean either 'at no time' or 'with nil frequency', and *always*, although it cannot apparently be used in the frequency sense, can represent a universal quantification either of events or of times.

Commentary

c There are, of course, further meanings of *always* and *never* not covered by this section. There is notably the durational sense of these items with the perfective, and an analogous use with the future: *I have always lived in England; I shall always live in England.* Here again a limitation on the absolute universality of *always* is implied: *I shall always live here* means approximately 'I shall live here for all the time I am alive' rather than 'I shall live here for ever' (='for all time').

7.3 Duration

7.3.1 *'For six weeks', etc*

Like frequency, duration has its own question form *How long?*, which cannot appropriately be replaced by the question form *When?*:

> *How long were you in France?*　*I was there for six weeks.*
> *When were you in France?*　　**I was there for six weeks.*

From this we may conclude, by the same argument employed in §7.2.3, that a separate adverbial system is involved:

5 + T.S.D.E.

SYSTEM 18 '*duration*'

$\begin{cases} (x) \rightarrow \text{DUR} \ (y) & \text{`}(x) \text{ lasts for } (y)\text{'} \\ (x) \leftarrow \text{DUR} \ (y) & \text{`}(y) \text{ lasts for } (x)\text{'} \end{cases}$

Class of system: relative
Contextual properties: $\{(X)\} \rightarrow \text{DUR} \ \{+\text{PERI}\}$
Logical properties: asymmetric, irreflexive, intransitive

For an explanation of the logical conditions of this system, see the discussion of the similar adverbial system, system 1.

In a principal predication, $\rightleftarrows$DUR may be expressed by the verb *take*, or by the verb *last* with or without the preposition *for*. More frequently, however, it has a purely prepositional syntactic realisation in *for*. These alternative realisations of $\rightleftarrows$DUR are exemplified in the virtual synonymy of the sentences:

> *Cutting the corn lasted (for) three days*
> = *They were cutting the corn for three days.*

In some circumstances *for* may be dropped from an adverbial phrase of duration:

> *I've lived here (for) ten years.*
> *He's kept me waiting (for) a whole day.*

Expressions such as *three weeks* referring to a period of time must be analysed semantically 'a period (consisting) of three weeks', otherwise there is nothing to indicate that the three weeks are consecutive. For this purpose we introduce the system '*consists of*' anticipated in the discussion of calendar time (§7.1.2), where it was noted that an exact account of the relation between units such as 'year', 'month', 'week', would require special analytic statements such as 'A year consists of twelve months'.

SYSTEM 19 '*consists of*'

$\begin{cases} (x) \rightarrow \text{CONS} \ (y) & \text{`}(x) \text{ consists of } (y)\text{'} \\ (x) \leftarrow \text{CONS} \ (y) & \text{`}(x) \text{ comprise(s)/make(s) up } (y)\text{'} \end{cases}$

Class of system: relative
Contextual conditions: $\{+\text{PERI}\} \rightarrow \text{CONS} \ \{+\text{PERI}\}$
Logical conditions: reflexive, antisymmetric, transitive

System 19 is described as "reflexive", because 'Water consists of water' is taken to be a tautology rather than a contradiction. The property "antisymmetric" is defined as "symmetric in the case $x=y$, otherwise asymmetric"; normally $x \cdot \rightarrow \text{CONS} \cdot y$ and $x \cdot \leftarrow \text{CONS} \cdot y$ are inconsistent assertions (*eg* 'This month consists of thirty days' is not compatible with 'Thirty days consist of this month', which indeed is nonsensical); but if x and y are identical, they are synonymous. The 'consists of' relation, as defined above, is a relation only between periods of time, although there may well be grounds for extending its application to other abstract or concrete fields of meaning: *eg* 'This book consists of ten chapters'. One condition which has not been incorporated in the contextual properties as stated is the condition that the period(s) designated x in the formula $x \cdot \rightarrow$CONS$\cdot y$ cannot be shorter than the period(s) designated by y.

The feature −CAL ('non-calendar') belongs to specifications of period time, since when we say 'for three weeks', we generally mean any period of twenty-one days, not necessarily a period beginning on Sunday and ending on Saturday.

With these various preliminary points in mind, we may turn to specimen durational formulae:

$\rightarrow$DUR$\cdot$ +PERI$'\langle\theta'\cdot\rightarrow$CONS$\cdot$ +PERI −CAL 5QUA 6UNIT$\rangle$
'for five days' (more fully, 'for a period consisting of five days')
$\rightarrow$DUR$\cdot$ +PERI$'\langle\theta'\cdot\rightarrow$CONS$\cdot$ +PERI −CAL −PLUR 1OUNIT$\rangle$ 'for a year'
$\rightarrow$DUR$\cdot$ +PERI +LONG 'for a long time'
$\rightarrow$DUR$\cdot$ +PERI −LONG 'for a short time'

+LONG and −LONG in these examples make up a polar system, the details of which need not be formally stated.

The system of '*duration*' is included in the definitions of *while*, *since*, *until*, and *during*, as I shall now proceed to show.

7.3.2 '*While*'

A sentence composed of two affirmative clauses linked by *while* (X *while* Y), if those clauses refer to states rather than events, is probably interpreted as 'X for the period for which Y', or in the notation:

[a] $(X)\cdot\rightarrow$DUR$\cdot$ +PERI$'\langle\theta'\cdot\leftarrow$DUR$\cdot(Y)\rangle$

The relationship represented by this formula is like that of a similar formula discussed in §7.1.1 as symbolising the meaning 'when', and like that formula, it can be shown to be nearly equivalent (by indirect symmetry) to the same formula with the positions of X and Y reversed. That is, understood in this way, the following two sentences are synonymous:

She did the shopping while I wrote the letter.
I wrote the letter while she did the shopping.

However, a more usual interpretation of *while*, especially if X expresses an event rather than a state, is 'X in the period for which Y', *ie*

[b] $(X)\cdot\rightarrow$TIM$\cdot$ +PERI$'\langle\theta'\cdot\leftarrow$DUR$\cdot(Y)\rangle$

Here $\rightarrow$TIM is substituted for $\rightarrow$DUR in the main predication, and the reciprocality of the relation is upset. A typical example of a sentence with this semantic structure is

John saw us while we were on holiday

which is not synonymous with the (meaningless) sentence
   We were on holiday while John saw us.

The difference between the two meanings of *while* can be shown visually as follows:

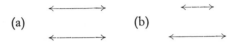

(a)   (b)

On interpretation (a), the two actions are temporally co-extensive, but on interpretation (b), the first action takes place within the time span of the second.

7.3.3 'Since' and 'until'
Since and *until* identify a period of time by marking its beginning and finishing points. Before we can specify their meanings, therefore, we need some means of describing the meanings 'end of' and 'beginning of'. These two relations have common contextual and logical properties, and I propose to mark their shared element of meaning by a single relative system ⇌EXT, distinguishing 'end' from 'beginning' more delicately by means of a binary taxonomic system ±END:

SYSTEM 20 *'extremity'*
$\begin{cases} (x) \to\text{EXT}\,(y) & \text{'}(x)\text{ is an extremity of }(y)\text{'} \\ (x) \leftarrow\text{EXT}\,(y) & \text{'}(y)\text{ is an extremity of }(x)\text{'} \end{cases}$
Class of system: relative
Contextual properties: {PERI} →EXT {+PERI}
Logical properties: irreflexive, asymmetric, intransitive

SYSTEM 21 *'beginning'/'end'*
$\begin{cases} +\text{END} & \text{'end'} \\ -\text{END} & \text{'beginning'} \end{cases}$
Class of system: binary taxonomic
Dependence rule: END depends on EXT

In phrases like *since 1900*, the beginning of the time period is mentioned, and the end-point is assumed to have a deictic interpretation as 'now' or 'then'. *Since 1900* can therefore be paraphrased by *between 1900 and now/then* or *from 1900 up to now/then*. The final point of time, since it is indiscriminately +THIS or −THIS, can simply be marked by the definite formator:

$$(X) \cdot \to\text{DUR} \cdot \theta \; +\text{PERI}' \langle \theta' \cdot \leftarrow\text{EXT} \; -\text{END} \cdot \theta \; 1900\text{YEAR} \rangle$$
$$\langle \theta' \cdot \leftarrow\text{EXT} \; +\text{END} \cdot \theta \rangle$$

   'since 1900'

This is the interpretation one expects with a predication referring to a state rather than an event. The end-point of the period does not necessarily mark, however, the termination of the state expressed by the accompanying verb. *I have lived there since 1900* marks off the period 1900-to-now as the period under discussion, but the aspect of the verb permits the understanding that the speaker lived there before 1900, and may continue to do so in the future. On the use of the perfective form of the verb in this case, see §7.6.1.

The two interpretations which exist for *while* also exist for *since*. If the principal predication refers to an event rather than to a state (see §7.4.1), the meaning of *since* is slightly different from that given above, in that →TIM replaces →DUR. Accordingly, *That house has been built since 1900* should be analysed 'That house . . . IN the period from 1900 to now' rather than 'That house . . . FOR THE DURATION OF the period from 1900 to now'.

This difference also applies to the conjunction *since*, the meaning of which is analysed on the same pattern as that of *before* as a conjunction (§7.1.1). To state the meaning of a clause such as *since he arrived here*, we take θ 1900YEAR from its position in the formula above, and substitute θ −PERI″$\langle\theta''\cdot$←TIM$\cdot(Y)\rangle$, Y standing for the rank-shifted assertion 'he arrived here'. A lengthier and more explicit paraphrase for *since he arrived here* is *between the time at which he arrived here and now*. The following is a relatively complete semantic specification of such a clause when following a "state predication":

$$\rightarrow\text{DUR}\cdot\theta+\text{PERI}'\langle\theta'\cdot\text{←EXT} -\text{END}\cdot\theta -\text{PERI}''\langle\theta''\cdot\text{←TIM}\cdot(Y)\rangle\rangle$$
$$\langle\theta'\cdot\text{←EXT} +\text{END}\cdot\theta\rangle$$

'for the duration of the period beginning at the time at which Y, and ending now/then'.

Until, like *since*, marks out a period of time by identifying its terminal points; but its meaning is the opposite of that of *since* in that the beginning-point of the period is taken as given (either 'now' or 'then'), and the end-point is overtly stated:

$$(X)\cdot\rightarrow\text{DUR}\cdot\theta +\text{PERI}'\langle\theta'\cdot\text{←EXT} -\text{END}\cdot\theta\rangle$$
$$\langle\theta'\cdot\text{←EXT} +\text{END}\cdot\theta \text{ 1971YEAR}\rangle$$

'I shall stay here until 1971'

$$(X)\cdot\rightarrow\text{DUR}\cdot\theta +\text{PERI}'\langle\theta'\cdot\text{←EXT} -\text{END}\cdot\theta\rangle \langle\theta'\cdot\text{←EXT} +\text{END}\cdot\theta -\text{PERI}''$$
$$\langle\theta''\cdot\text{←TIM}\cdot(Y)\rangle\rangle$$

'I shall stay here until you leave'.

Until is therefore paraphrasable *for the period from now to . . .* It does not match *since*, however, in all respects. It cannot be given the meaning of '*in* the period . . .' with "event predications", but is replaced by *before* in such contexts, except where the principal predication is negative:

> 'I shall sign the contract before next week'
> *'I shall sign the contract until next week'
> 'I shan't sign the contract until/before next week'.

Another difference is that *since* can stand on its own adverbially, in which case the cluster preceding ←EXT −END has zero expression (='since then'):

> *I haven't seen her since.*

This use is impossible with *until*:

> **I shan't see her until.*

In a positive sentence, *ever since* replaces *since* with "state predications": *I have loved him ever since*, not *I have loved him since*, which must refer to an event.

7.4 The meaning of the tenses

I define as TENSES, for the present purpose, those grammatical features of the verbal group which express relations of simultaneity or overlap of time (*ie* relations involving the system ⇄TIM), or else relations of 'before'/'after' (involving the system ⇄BEF). That the verbal group partially duplicates the semantic function of adverbials of time in this respect is shown by the special limitations of co-occurrence which make, for example, **I will see him yesterday* and **I have lived here until next week* meaningless sentences. However, it is my intention not to pursue this issue of "concord" between verbal and adverbial groups,[2] but to confine myself to the task of demonstrating that the same method of analysis as has been applied to adverbial expressions of "time when" (in §7.1) can also be applied to tenses. It will be shown, in fact, that no systems further to those introduced so far in this chapter need be called upon for this purpose.

7.4.1 *Event predications and state predications*
Already in §7.2.2 some reason has been given for applying the distinction '*singular*'/'*plural*' (±PLUR) to medial clusters as well as to terminal clusters. As the system ±PLUR depends on the feature +COU 'countable', we are led to suppose that features of the system ±COU may also appear in medial clusters. This means, in grammatical terms, that not only noun meanings but verb meanings can include the factor 'countability'. The contrast between 'countable' and 'mass', as applied to verbal meanings, is to be identified with the commonly drawn distinction between "event" verbs and "state" verbs (or rather senses of

verbs).[3] By relating this to the contrast between countable and mass nouns, we show how generalisation on a semantic level can bring together phenomena which are grammatically unconnected.

There are at least two reasons, however, why the "event"/"state" opposition, although quite widely recognised, has remained somewhat indeterminate in comparison with the parallel distinction located grammatically in noun groups and semantically in terminal clusters. The first reason is the obvious one that verbs are not *grammatically* marked for countability, as nouns are by their ability or lack of ability to be inflected for plural. The second is that neither are verbs necessarily *semantically* marked for countability, in the sense that a feature +COU or −COU appears in their definitions. There are certainly some verbal meanings (*eg* of *kick, open, start, fall*) that must contain the component 'countable' (="event"), but it is uncertain how far one should take the intrinsic marking of verbal definitions in this way.[4] To understand the grounds for making a decision on this question, we shall consider a number of criteria for classing a particular meaning as "event" or "state". Before doing this, however, let us replace the opposition of "event" and "state" verbs by the much more valuable concept of EVENT PREDICA-TIONS and STATE PREDICATIONS. We have noted in other connections that a feature belonging to the medial cluster of a predication (*eg* negation) can in many respects be deemed a property of the predication as a whole. There is, then, nothing odd about regarding the feature +COU or −COU in its medial cluster as marking the whole predication as an "event" or as a "state". In addition, the content of terminal clusters, as well as of medial clusters, can be important in determining this classification: in *I enjoy life*, it is the uncountability of the object of the sentence, corresponding to the final cluster, that identifies the meaning of the whole as referring to a continuing state. The plural object of *I enjoy films*, on the other hand, provides the major clue to its iterative interpretation, indicating a repetition of like events. Major criteria for identifying event predications are:

[a] Iterative interpretation with a perfect verbal group, *eg* 'I have always eaten a good breakfast' (see §7.6.2).

[b] The simple present interpreted in iterative or instantaneous senses, but not in the sense of a continuing state (see §7.4.2).

[c] Occurrence of adverbials within the semantic categories "number of times" or "frequency", *eg twice, sometimes, every Friday*. (According to the account of these categories in §§7.2.1 and 7.2.3, the feature +PLUR (and hence +COU) is automatically assigned to the principal predication by virtue of the contextual properties of the adverbial systems ⇌TIM and ⇌FREQ.)

[d] With transitive verbs, pre-modifying past participles referring to the

present result of a past event, not simply to a present continuing state: *a broken chair, a bent pin, a deserted house* instead of *a feared opponent, a much loved daughter, a known gambler, an occupied house.*[5]

> 'a broken chair' = 'a chair that has been broken'
> 'a feared opponent' = 'an opponent who is feared' ≠
>   'an opponent who has been feared'.

[e] In narrative using the simple past tense, verbs in a sequence semantically related by temporal successivity not by simultaneity (see §7.4.4):

> 'He saw me and ran away' (normally) ≠ 'He ran away and saw me'
> 'He loved his country and feared God'
>   = 'He feared God and loved his country'.

Commentary

a With the past tense, an "event" may span a far longer time-period than is possible with the present, on account of the psychological distancing effect of the feature —THIS. In 'He was born, lived, and died in Seville', for example, a man's whole life is seen, in historical retrospect, as a single event.

If a verb in a certain sense (*eg kick* in its usual physical sense) fulfils all of the five criteria above, it is right to mark the definition with the feature +COU.

The following are useful criteria for state predications:

[a] With a perfect verbal group, interpretation as a state extending from the past up to the present, not as a series of separate happenings; *eg* 'She has always loved opera'.

[b] With the simple present tense, interpretation as a continuing state of affairs, not as a series of happenings; *eg* 'Teak is harder than pine'.

To these may be added the negative counterparts of criteria [c], [d], and [e] above.

Verbal meanings are not intrinsically assigned the feature —COU, because there seems to be no verbal (or adjectival) meaning that cannot occur in the same clause with an adverbial of frequency or "number of times". 'He often knew that three times three was nine' is a bizarre statement on account of its implication that knowledge can be a repeatable event, yet it is possible to imagine a context (*eg* of a boy being continually subjected to mental arithmetic tests) in which it would be acceptable.

Adverbials of duration tend to occur with state predications, but this tendency must be treated as a factual likelihood rather than a semantic rule (see §5.3), since it is possible for adverbials of duration and adverbials of frequency to co-exist in sentences like *He often waited for ten minutes.* If the principal predication were assigned, by the contextual properties of $\rightleftarrows$DUR, the feature $-$COU, this would conflict, in such sentences, with the feature $+$COU assigned by $\rightleftarrows$FREQ.

Even in cases of patent absurdity such as 'He was a tall man several times', the conflict of "event" and "state" is of a kind that has to be explained by resort to factual knowledge – in the given instance, the fact that a person's stature, after a period of growth, keeps fairly constant, and does not ebb and flow like the tides. We can often see that a particular predication must refer to a state or to an event without being able to indicate this by means of semantic features. This is one reason why many potential ambiguities allowed by the semantic description of tense and aspect are in practice ruled out at the level of hearer performance. For instance, 'He has lived here all his life' is theoretically ambiguous in that it may indicate either a single continuing state, or a repetition of events, as in 'He has driven lorries all his life'; but in practice it has to denote a state.

This is perhaps the most appropriate place to introduce the concept of SEMANTIC CONCORD, which has an important, though rather obscure role in the elimination of ambiguity, particularly in the field of tense and aspect.

Semantic concord is analogous to syntactic concord in that it consists in the distribution of matching properties amongst different elements of a structure. Features from the systems of '*countability*' and '*singular*'/'*plural*' are amongst those which are frequently shared by more than one cluster within the same predication, and especially by the medial and final cluster, when these correspond to the verb and object of a clause. Consider the three sentences:

(a) *Jane writes* $j \cdot \!\!\rightarrow\!\! w \cdot \varnothing$ $(-\text{COU})$
(b) *Jane writes books* $j \cdot \!\!\rightarrow\!\! w \cdot b$ $(+\text{COU} +\text{PLUR})$
(c) *Jane writes a book* $j \cdot \!\!\rightarrow\!\! w \cdot b$ $(+\text{COU} -\text{PLUR})$

Whereas in (a) the verb *write* without any complement invites interpretation as an undivided state $(-\text{COU})$ ($=$ 'is a writer'), the plural countable complement *books* in (b) leads one to interpret the verb iteratively (*ie*, to extend to the medial cluster w the features $+\text{COU} +\text{PLUR}$). Equally, the singular *a book* of (c), if it permits one to interpret the sentence in any way whatever, permits only the interpretation of a single complete action in the present $(+\text{COU} -\text{PLUR})$, as, for example, in the "historic present" (see §7.4.2).

7.4.2 *The present tense*

As it enters into the interpretation of tenses, the distinction between event predications and state predications is more a psychological projection than an objective property of the real world. The sentence *Gordon works in a factory*, for example, may be thought of in two ways:

5*

it can either designate a series of events ('Whenever Gordon is at work, he works in a factory'), or it can designate a permanent state of employment ('Gordon is a factory-worker'). The difference between these two possibilities has nothing to do with what Gordon actually does with his life; it is merely a matter of whether the speaker *thinks* of the occupation as an intermittent or continuous affair. We therefore mark this difference not by means of inherent features, but by the ascription features [+COU] and [−COU] (see §4.1.2).

In addition, the medial cluster of the predication may independently contain the inherent feature +COU, either as a result of the application of contextual redundancy rules (*eg* with ⇄FREQ), or as part of the definition of the verb (*eg* of *kick*). In such a case, only the tense interpretation with [+COU] is available, since [−COU] in combination with +COU would constitute an oxymoron. In other words, there is no possibility of interpreting as a state predication a sentence which, by reason of its verbal or adverbial content, is already marked as an "event".

The three chief meanings of the present tense, leaving aside uses which refer to future time (present-in-future) or to past time (historic present), can be called the UNRESTRICTIVE PRESENT, the INSTANTANEOUS PRESENT, and the HABITUAL (ITERATIVE) PRESENT. The first of these three uses is restricted to state predications, and the latter two to event predications.

Since the unrestrictive present is the one sense associated with state predications, its definition must contain the ascription feature [−COU]. The unrestrictive present denotes a state of affairs of indefinite duration continuing through the present moment, and is "unrestrictive" in the sense that no initial or terminal point of the state is given, unless it is factually or contextually implied, or made explicit by an adverbial. General timeless truths therefore fall into this category: 'Enough is as good as a feast', 'Water contains hydrogen', etc. The unrestrictive present can be symbolised:

$(X) \cdot [-\text{COU}] \rightarrow \text{TIM} \cdot \theta + \text{THIS} - \text{PERI}$ 'I like roses', 'She is tall', etc.

In a word, the meaning conveyed by this formula is 'state-now'.

Commentary

b The feature −PERI appears in this and all other tense definitions because it is needed to explain certain discrepancies between the use of tenses and the use of adverbials of time, which are often marked +PERI. For instance, the instantaneous present, the meaning of which is no more than 'single-event-now', has to be applied to something apprehended as happening *at the present moment*, rather than *in a present period*; hence *I see him today* is not interpreted as instantaneous present. Furthermore, there is no contradiction involved in using the past tense ('before the present moment') with an adverbial which denotes a time-period including the present moment, as in *My car broke down today*.

In the preceding sections on time adverbials, I used the schema $(X) \cdot \rightarrow s \cdot c$ as the basis for symbolising temporal meaning, although I could have equally well used the equivalent schema with downgrading $X' \langle \theta' \cdot \rightarrow s \cdot c \rangle$. Now it must be supposed, since tense belongs grammatically to the verbal group, that rules of expression applying to tense always operate upon the variant formula containing downgrading instead of rank-shift. This revision in fact provides a more compact definition, constituting a single downgraded predication, to replace that just given:

Unrestrictive present: $\langle \theta \cdot [-\text{COU}] \rightarrow \text{TIM} \cdot \theta + \text{THIS} \rangle$

Commentary

c Note the extension here of the term "definition" to apply to grammatical features (*ie* terms of grammatical systems) as well as to lexical items. The same principles regarding polysemy and synonymy apply to grammatical as to lexical definitions: a term in a grammatical system may require several separate definitions. The match between grammar and semantics is aided, however, if a single feature in semantics corresponds to a single feature in grammar, as in this case, where the semantic feature is a downgraded predication.

The other two main meanings of the present tense apply to event predications, and so involve the ascription feature [+COU]. The simpler of the two definitions is that of the instantaneous present, which is identical to that of the unrestrictive present except for the substitution of [+COU −PLUR] for [−COU]:

Instantaneous present: $\langle \theta' \cdot [+\text{COU} -\text{PLUR}] \rightarrow \text{TIM} \cdot \theta + \text{THIS} -\text{PERI} \rangle$
                        'He scores a goal!'
                        'I name this ship *Victor*', etc.

The present tense interpreted in this way refers to an event psychologically perceived as taking place in its entirety at the moment of speech, or more briefly, 'single-event-now'.[6] The instantaneous present is restricted to certain contexts (occurring, for example, in sports commentaries, cooking demonstrations, and ceremonial utterances) because very rarely are happenings brief enough to be thought of as being started and finished in the very instant of utterance. Moreover, it is stylistically restricted, because for obvious reasons it has dramatic overtones which do not suit it to ordinary colloquial speech or discursive prose. Compare *I am opening the door* with *I open the door*. Where the former is an unremarkable description of a present happening, the latter is more dramatic, and seems to demand the accompaniment of an exclamation mark or some spectacular gesture. Again, it is a factual and psychological oddity – the oddity of such an event being perceived as a complete unit in the instant of speech – that prevents sentences like *He goes to bed* and *I write a letter* from bring fully acceptable out of context, although it is conceivable that they might occur in a narrative in the historical present.

Commentary

d The historical present, incidentally, requires no separate definition, but is taken to be a variant of the instantaneous present, whereby past events are understood to be described, as a kind of dramatic licence, as if they were happening at the present time. Many more utterances are acceptable in the historic present than are acceptable in the instantaneous present, because narrative "distancing" allows a past happening of considerable duration to be apprehended as an event in its entirety.

The habitual or iterative present is far more common than the instantaneous present as an interpretation of the present tense with event predications. 'He goes to bed at 10 o'clock', 'He digs his own garden' and 'He scores plenty of goals' are all most naturally apprehended as examples of the habitual present, which describes a general state of affairs continuing through the present moment and consisting of repeated events. This use thus combines, in a way, the meanings of both the instantaneous and unrestrictive presents. Yet from a notational point of view, it must not combine them in such a way as to bring about a clash between the features +COU and −COU, even as ascription features, within the same componential formula. A first stage in the analysis of this meaning, suggested by the preceding two definitions, is to construct a downgraded predication parallel to the previous definition (of the instantaneous present) except for the replacement of [−PLUR] 'single event' by [+PLUR] 'more than one event':

$$\langle \theta' \cdot [+\text{COU} +\text{PLUR}] \rightarrow \text{TIM} \cdot \theta +\text{THIS} -\text{PERI} \rangle$$

This is unsatisfactory, however, because it conveys the idea of a number of different events all happening simultaneously at the present moment. The defect remedied in a more complex definition below:

Habitual present:

$$\langle \theta' \cdot [+\text{COU} +\text{PLUR}] \rightarrow \text{TIM} \cdot +\text{PLUR} \rangle'' \langle \theta'' \cdot \rightarrow \text{TIM} \cdot \theta +\text{THIS} -\text{PERI} \rangle$$

This definition consists of two downgraded predications which are ordered with respect to the rule of subordination according to the principle explained in §6.2. The former predication, that is, is included within the co-referential scope of the definite formator in the latter. In informal language, the first part of the definition describes a set of events, and the second part identifies these events as constituting a state of affairs in existence at the present moment.

We thus have three senses of the present corresponding respectively to the classification of nouns expressing terminal clusters as uncountable (mass), countable singular, and countable plural. This correspondence, as we have seen, is important on a semantic level inasmuch as the medial cluster is often in concord with one or other of the terminal clusters with respect to the system ±COU and ±PLUR. For example, uncountable, plural, and singular objects (as in *He makes money*, *He makes toys*, and *He makes a toy*) will respectively tend to signal the unrestrictive, iterative, and instantaneous present.

Continuing this line of thought, we notice a significant connection between quantification and the systems ±COU and ±PLUR. It may be recalled from §7.2.4 that the quantification of a predication as a whole accounts for one interpretation of the adverbs *always*, *often*, etc. With terminal clusters, there is the possibility of both overt quantification ('all cats', 'some cats') and the implicit quantification which arises when a cluster such as 'cats' is "existentially construed" or "universally construed" (see §2.8.2 and §3.5). This possibility also applies to predications as a whole. *Men are unhappy* will tend to be understood as if the adverb *always* (in its quantificational sense of §7.2.4) has been inserted: 'Men are always/in general unhappy.' On the other hand, 'He scores goals', as an assessment of a footballer, will tend to be interpreted as 'He sometimes scores goals'. That is, in the first case the predication is universally construed, and in the second it is existentially construed. It is significant that these two interpretations correspond to the implicit interpretations of terminal clusters in the same predication: 'Men are unhappy' = 'All men/men as a whole are (always) unhappy'; 'He scores goals' = 'He (sometimes) scores some goals'. Thus there is some principle at work akin to the principle of semantic concord: when a predication is existentially or universally quantified (or construed as such), one of its terminal clusters will share the same property of being "existential" or "universal" as the case may be. This is evident in the synonymy (at least on one interpretation) of pairs like:

> { *All water contains hydrogen.*
> { *Water always contains hydrogen.*

> { *Cakes are sometimes expensive.*
> { *Some cakes are expensive.*

The principle operates equally well with state predications (corresponding to uncountable terminal clusters) and event predications (corresponding to countable terminal clusters). There is a restriction, however, in the case of the instantaneous present, which is invariably construed as if existentially quantified; hence 'Soldiers walk noisily down the street', envisaged as a present event (*eg* as a stage direction), must be understood 'Some soldiers...' rather than 'All soldiers...'. (*Sometimes* would be an inappropriate adverb to use here, because it designates a plurality of events, whereas the instantaneous present is −PLUR.) The instantaneous present is in this respect equivalent to the most prominent use of the continuous present: it is difficult, if not impossible, to interpret 'Soldiers are walking noisily down the street' otherwise than '*Some* soldiers are walking noisily down the street'.

Although the details of the relation between quantification and the trio of properties 'singular'/'plural'/'uncountable' are not precise, enough has been said to show why (as anyone who studies the examples in §2.8.2 will realise) the choice between existential and universal construal in terminal clusters is by no means random, but is influenced by a similar choice in medial clusters, as expressed through tense and aspect.

One possible misunderstanding must be averted, however, before we leave this subject. There is no necessary disassociation of singular number and universal quantification. Whereas it is true that *He scores a goal* on its own must denote a singular event (the instantaneous present), *He scores a goal every week*, by virtue of its adverbial element, must denote a set of events in the "universal singular". A semantic analysis of this sentence follows the pattern of the habitual present:

$$X'\langle(\theta'\cdot[+\text{COU}-\text{PLUR}]\rightarrow\text{TIM}\langle\theta'''\cdot\text{I}\alpha\leftarrow\text{o}\cdot\theta''''\rangle\cdot\text{7UNIT}'''')'''\rangle''$$
$$\langle\theta''\cdot\rightarrow\text{TIM}\cdot\theta+\text{THIS}-\text{PERI}\rangle$$

Commentary

e The function of the round brackets in this formula is simply to single out the first downgraded predication as the co-referent of θ'''.

The main predication of this specification is singular in concord with 'every week', which is both universally quantified and singular, and is comparable with 'every man', or with 'A man' in the statement 'A man has to live'.

7.4.3 *Past tense*

System 4 ($\rightleftarrows$BEF), which was earlier applied to the meanings of time adverbials, can be used now in the definitions of the past and future tenses. The most usual temporal meaning conveyed by the past tense inflexion is 'event before the present moment', and may be symbolised:

Simple past:

$$\langle\theta'\cdot[-\text{PLUR}]\rightarrow\text{TIM}\cdot\theta''\langle\theta''\cdot\rightarrow\text{BEF}\cdot\theta+\text{THIS}-\text{PERI}\rangle\rangle \quad \text{'I visited him', etc.}$$

The ascription feature [−PLUR] indicates a single event seen in its entirety, and of course depends on the feature [+COU], which is omitted here for the sake of brevity. This definition of the past tense corresponds to the instantaneous present, although its use is much wider. The connotation of 'complete event' is indeed general to the simple past, even with a verb like *live*, which is generally associated with states rather than events. *I lived here for ten years* carries the inference 'I no longer live here' (*ie* the residence is a complete chapter in my life), as opposed to *I have lived here for ten years*, which indicates continuation up to the present time.

To explain this notion of 'completeness' accompanying the use of the past tense, we must say that there is no use of the past corresponding to the unrestrictive present. That is, the definition of the past tense always contains the ascription feature [+COU]. There is, however, a contrast between 'singular' and 'plural' events: the habitual or iterative past, containing the feature [+PLUR], has a definition which follows the pattern of that of the habitual present:

Habitual past:

$$\langle \theta' \cdot [+\text{PLUR}] \rightarrow \text{TIM} \cdot +\text{PLUR}\rangle'' \langle \theta'' \cdot \rightarrow \text{TIM} \cdot \theta''' \langle \theta''' \cdot \rightarrow \text{BEF} \cdot \theta +\text{THIS}$$
$$-\text{PERI}\rangle\rangle$$

'I visited him (often)', etc.

The past tense in English carries the additional discrimination 'a *definite* time in the past',[7] and for this reason the definite formator θ is included to the right of the →TIM relation in the above two definitions. This definite formator generally co-refers to a time specification already made in a preceding part of the discourse, or to a time-adverbial having expression in the same sentence. Hence it is a customary requirement that the past tense should either accompany an adverbial expression of time (as in *I saw him last Friday*), or should occur in the middle of a discourse, within an already established framework of time reference (*eg: I've just been talking to your sister – I* SAW *her at the station*). The sentence *I saw your sister*, seen or heard in vacuo, begs the question *when?*[8]

Commentary

f It is true that colloquially examples of the past tense do occur without either of these contextual requirements: *Now where did I put my glasses?* etc. Cases of this kind can be explained as arising from "subjectively assumed definiteness"; they are parallel to the unspecified use of the definite article in phrases like *the milkman, the kitchen, the post-office*. The supposition 'I have put my glasses somewhere' is taken as given within the context (see Jespersen, 1931: 65). *I saw your brother at the station* assumes the information 'I have (just) been to the station'. Allowing for this difference, however, *I have seen your brother at the station* and *I saw your brother at the station* are effectively interchangeable within the same context.

g No element of definiteness is present when the past tense combines with *always* and *never* in such sentences as *I always said he was a crook, She never was a great artist*. This is an idiomatic exception to the above definitions.

h There is no incompatibility between the indefiniteness of *once* and the definiteness of *lied* in *Once he lied to me*, since the time indicated by *once* forms the co-referent of the definite formator in the specification of the past tense:

$$\theta' \cdot 2\alpha \rightarrow 0 \,(-\text{PLUR}' \cdot \leftarrow \text{TIM} \cdot (X'' \langle \theta'' \cdot \rightarrow \text{TIM} \cdot \theta' \langle \theta' \cdot \rightarrow \text{BEF} \cdot \theta +\text{THIS} -\text{PERI}\rangle\rangle))$$

Whether the tense specification can be linked by co-reference to the time-adverbial specification in this way seems to depend on whether the time-adverbial is non-downgraded, *ie* on whether it precedes the tense specification in order of subordination. There is therefore a contrast between the use of the past tense ('definite past time') in *Once he lied to me* and the perfect tense (indefinite past time) in *He has lied to me once*. It may be incidentally noted that the verbal construction with *used to* is generally synonymous with initial or medial *once* combined with the past tense: 'That's the man who used to be organist of St. Pauls' = 'That's the man who was once organist of St. Pauls'.

As preceding examples suggest, the definite past of *saw*, *lied*, etc is in contrast with the indefinite past which it is one of the functions of the perfect tense to express. The difference between 'I saw him' and 'I have seen him' is therefore parallel to that between *the man* and *a man*.[9] Just as at the beginning of a narrative, the definite article tends to be preceded by the indefinite article, which establishes the initial framework of reference, so that past tense tends to presuppose a framework of time reference already established by the perfect tense. Both tendencies can be observed in this utterance:

> *I have (just) spoken to a man and his wife. The man wanted to know whether there was any work hereabouts.*

The perfect, used in sentences like *I have been to the Scottish Highlands*, is indefinite both in the sense of indicating no particular time, and in the sense of indicating no specific number of occasions. It is 'countable', but is unmarked for number (although number may be indicated adverbially, as in *I've only once been to the Scottish Highlands*). The following specification for the 'indefinite past' may therefore be contrasted to that of the 'definite past' given earlier:

$$\langle \theta' \cdot [+\text{COU}] \rightarrow \text{TIM} \cdot \varnothing \text{''} \langle \theta'' \cdot \rightarrow \text{BEF} \cdot \theta +\text{THIS} -\text{PERI} \rangle \rangle$$
'I have been to the Scottish Highlands'

This is identical to the definition of the simple past, except for the omission of the definite formator and the ascription feature [−PLUR]. By this means we show that 'I went to the Scottish Highlands' inductively implies 'I have been to the Scottish Highlands'.

7.4.4 *Time sequence*
When two past tense verbs appear in succession, the temporal relation between them may be one of simultaneity or of successivity (see Diver, 1963: 167). In *He knew and loved the Classical poets*, the knowing and loving are assumed to be concurrent; but in *He opened the door and tripped over the mat*, the opening and tripping up are assumed to have happened in succession. Superficially, one would like to claim that concurrence is assumed in the case of "state predications", and succession in the case of "event predications". The situation seems to be a little

more complicated, however: the above statement is true of state predications, but in the case of "event predications", either interpretation (I feel) is possible.

After getting up, he shaved and listened to the news.

This sentence is ambiguous, in my judgement, according to whether the shaving and listening are taken to be simultaneous or in sequence. Taken in one sense, *he shaved and listened to the news* is synonymous with *he listened to the news and shaved.* Taken in another sense, it is not.[10]

The two interpretations of co-occurrence and sequence must have different semantic analyses, obviously. The simultaneity of two past events can be represented with little difficulty in this way:

$$X'\langle\theta'\cdot[-\text{PLUR}]\rightarrow\text{TIM}\cdot\theta'''\langle\theta''\cdot\rightarrow\text{BEF}\cdot\theta+\text{THIS}-\text{PERI}\rangle\rangle$$
'He shaved.'

$$Y''\langle\theta''\cdot[-\text{PLUR}]\rightarrow\text{TIM}\cdot\theta'''\langle\theta''\cdot\rightarrow\text{BEF}\cdot\theta+\text{THIS}-\text{PERI}\rangle\rangle$$
'He listened to the radio.'

The fact that he listened at the same time as he shaved is indicated, in the notation, simply by the co-referential marking θ''' which identifies the time referred to in the second assertion with that referred to in the first.

The representation of sequential events is slightly more complicated. It is necessary to introduce a further downgraded predication, specifying the time mentioned in the second assertion as directly following the time mentioned in the first. This relationship may be symbolised $\rightarrow$BEF $\rightarrow$NEXT, as in §7.1.2 above. The temporal connection between the two statements is again indicated by the co-reference of θ''' in the first assertion with θ''' in the second assertion:

$$X'\langle\theta'\cdot[-\text{PLUR}]\rightarrow\text{TIM}\cdot\theta'''\langle\theta''\cdot\rightarrow\text{BEF}\cdot\theta+\text{THIS}-\text{PERI}\rangle\rangle$$
'He shaved.'

$$Y''\langle\theta''\cdot[-\text{PLUR}]\rightarrow\text{TIM}\cdot\theta''''\langle\theta''''\cdot\rightarrow\text{BEF}\cdot\theta+\text{THIS}-\text{PERI}\rangle$$
$$\langle\theta''''\cdot\leftarrow\text{BEF}\cdot\leftarrow\text{NEXT}\cdot\theta'''\rangle\rangle$$

'He listened to the radio.'

The sense is now 'He shaved and *then* he listened to the radio'.

This brings us in passing to the observation that the ambiguity of concurrence and succession exists not only in the past tense but in the adverb *then* and the subordinating conjunction *when*. The meanings of these items considered in §7.1.1 were 'at that time' and 'at the time at which', but there is also the sequential interpretation of *then* as 'thereupon', or 'immediately after that':

then: $\rightarrow$TIM$\cdot\theta'\langle\theta'\cdot\leftarrow$BEF $\leftarrow$NEXT$\cdot\theta-$THIS$\rangle$

Equally *when* with event predications has the meaning 'at the time immediately following the time at which', or in formal notation:

$$X\cdot\rightarrow\text{TIM}\cdot\theta'\langle\theta'\cdot\leftarrow\text{BEF}\leftarrow\text{NEXT}\cdot\theta''\langle\theta''\cdot\rightarrow\text{TIM}\cdot(Y)\rangle\rangle \quad\text{'}X\text{ when }Y\text{'}$$
$$\text{or} \quad\text{'When }Y, X\text{'.}$$

This specification accords with the different sequence of events suggested by:

When I punched him on the nose, he swore at me

and

When he swore at me, I punched him on the nose.

In this sense, *when* is close in meaning to *after*:

When I reached home, I cooked some lunch.
After I reached home, I cooked some lunch.

It may also be noted that the sequential use of the past tense makes it close in meaning to the pluperfect; thus the pluperfect can replace the past tense in the two sentences above without any radical change of meaning:

When I had reached home, I cooked some lunch.
After I had reached home, I cooked some lunch.

The only semantic difference between all four of these sentences resides in the presence, with *when* and the simple past, of the feature ←NEXT, which signals that the succession of events is immediate.

7.4.5 *Other tense forms*

Only the briefest sketch of the meanings of other tense forms will be given.

A general formula for future tenses is:

Future: $\langle \theta' \cdot \rightarrow \text{TIM} \cdot \varnothing \, '' \langle \theta'' \cdot \leftarrow \text{BEF} \cdot \theta + \text{THIS} - \text{PERI} \rangle \rangle$

   'I will/shall see him', etc.

This formula, approximately rendered 'happening at a time after the present moment', represents what is common among the various ways of indicating future in the English verbal group: *will see, be going to see, be about to see*, etc. No attempt will be made to discriminate between the meanings of these various forms. In the future, there is no definite-indefinite distinction corresponding to the distinction between what is expressed by past and perfect.

The specifications of the pluperfect and future-perfect can be derived from those of the past and future respectively, all that is necessary being the insertion of a further downgraded predication $\langle \theta'' \cdot \rightarrow \text{BEF} \dots \rangle$.

Pluperfect: $\langle \theta' \cdot \rightarrow \text{TIM} \cdot \varnothing \, '' \langle \theta'' \cdot \rightarrow \text{BEF} \cdot \theta''' \langle \theta''' \cdot \rightarrow \text{BEF} \cdot \theta + \text{THIS} - \text{PERI} \rangle \rangle \rangle$

Future-perfect:

   $\langle \theta' \cdot \rightarrow \text{TIM} \cdot \varnothing \, '' \langle \theta'' \cdot \rightarrow \text{BEF} \cdot \theta''' \langle \theta''' \cdot \leftarrow \text{BEF} \cdot \theta + \text{THIS} - \text{PERI} \rangle \rangle \rangle$

These can be read 'happening at a time before the time before now' and 'happening at a time before the time after now'. Both the pluperfect and future-perfect have definite meaning, in the sense applying to the past tense; that is, they take a specific point of time in the past or in the future as given by context. Consequently, they cannot normally be used without some explicit time reference indicated adverbially or by a preceding part of the discourse. This is why the semantic glosses mention '*the* time before/after now' rather than '*a* time before/after now'.

The account of basic before-and-after relationships expressed by the English verbal group is now exhausted, except for the rarely occurring future-in-the-past, expressed by *was/were to* or *would* following by the infinitive:

> *Ten years later he would/was to prove a sculptor of genius*

This tense form can be defined on the pattern used for the future-perfect, except that the direction of the arrows of $\rightarrow$BEF and $\leftarrow$BEF is reversed:

Future-in-the-past:

$$\langle \theta' \cdot \rightarrow \text{TIM} \cdot \varnothing \, ''\langle \theta'' \cdot \leftarrow \text{BEF} \cdot \theta''' \langle \theta''' \cdot \rightarrow \text{BEF} \cdot \theta + \text{THIS} - \text{PERI} \rangle\rangle$$

'Happening at a time after the time before now'.

Commentary

h Was/were and *would* as indicators of future-in-the-past are confined to literary narrative style. They have other, more common, yet related uses which cannot be considered here. *Would* is used as a past equivalent of *will* in reported speech: *He said that he would let me know*. *Was/were to* is used as a past equivalent of *am/is/are to* in the sense 'was/were due to' (*eg: They were to leave England yesterday, but the flight was cancelled*). In these senses, *was/were to* and *would* do not guarantee that the actual state or event referred to came to pass, and therefore are not used in the true future-in-the-past sense, which is more or less equivalent to 'was/were destined to' in that it assumes the speaker's prescience of later events. *Be going to* and *be about to* in the past for the same reason do not truly express future-in-the-past: *He was going to attack me before you arrived* rather suggests, in fact, that the action mentioned did not take place. Similarly *will be going/about to* (Jespersen's "prospective future", 1931: 363) cannot be considered a "future-in-the-future" tense, as *He will be going/about to attack me before you arrive* does not predict that the attack will be actually carried out.

7.4.6. *Summary and conclusion*

The semantic relationships between tenses as indicated in this notation can easily be reconceived as a visual, diagrammatic account similar to those given by Jespersen (1931: 2), Bull (1960: 29–31), Close (1962: 70–8) and other writers. All definite formators occurring in tense specifications (apart from those arising inevitably in downgrading) signal what we may call temporal POINTS OF REFERENCE (to be visually symbolised by a black circle ●). The present moment, which enters into all tense specifications, may be regarded as the PRIMARY POINT OF REFERENCE (1PR), the starting point for all reckoning of time relationship.

Some tense definitions in addition contain a SECONDARY POINT OF REFERENCE (2PR); for example, the simple past makes reference to a definite, given moment or period of time prior to the present moment. Relations of 'before' and 'after' between one point and another can be shown by arrows: 'before' by ⟵ and 'after' by ⟶. We have thus a simple visual scheme as follows:

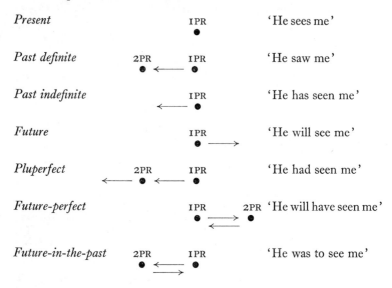

The exact length of time represented by each arrow is normally immaterial; it is thus possible for the event referred to in 'He will have seen me' to have happened before the present moment, despite what is suggested by the diagram. However, the future-in-the-past, 'He was to see me' (taking 'was to' in the relevant predictive sense) cannot describe a future event. Hence in *He was to see me next week, was to* must have the sense 'was due to'.

7.5 Continuous tense forms

The semantic opposition between simple tense forms of the verb (*eg: We* LIVE *here*) and the so-called "continuous" tense forms (*eg: We* ARE LIVING *here*) is notoriously problematic, and a major difficulty for foreign learners of English. I must leave aside here the use of the continuous forms in reference to future or intended happenings, and concentrate on their application to the present and past spheres of time. I pause only to note that a present/future ambiguity is detectable in such sentences as *I am going home*, which may be spoken either in anticipation of a homeward journey, or while the journey is actually in progress. The latter meaning is the one I shall be concerned with.

Because the various traditional labels for continuous tense forms ("progressive", "durative", "continuous" itself, and so on) are semantically unsatisfactory, the semantic feature which discriminates these forms from the simple tense forms will be called 'situation', a term which perhaps comes closer than any of the others to capturing their common distinctive meaning. This feature +SITU, together with its formally unmarked opposite −SITU, is introduced in system 22:

SYSTEM 22 *'situation'/'non-situation'*

$$\begin{cases} +\text{SITU} & \text{'situation'} \\ -\text{SITU} & \text{'non-situation'} \end{cases}$$

Class of system: binary taxonomic

No dependence rules are stated for this system, the features of which only occur as ascription features within the medial cluster of the rankshifted predication to the left of →TIM. The left-hand part of the contextual properties of system 1 (§7.1) should therefore be rewritten: $\{(X [\text{SITU}])\}$. Another omission which must now be corrected is the omission of the feature [−SITU] from the specifications of simple tenses in §§7.4.2–5. Thus the notational difference between "continuous" and "non-continuous" tenses in equivalent sentences appears in the following:

$X'\langle\theta'\cdot[-\text{PLUR} -\text{SITU}] \to\text{TIM}\cdot\theta +\text{THIS} -\text{PERI}\rangle$ 'He picks up a book'

$X'\langle\theta'\cdot[-\text{PLUR} +\text{SITU}] \to\text{TIM}\cdot\theta +\text{THIS} -\text{PERI}\rangle$ 'He is picking up a book'

Observe that because [+SITU] and [−SITU] are ascription features, the above assertions are not logically inconsistent. The difference between them is only a matter of the psychological light in which the action is regarded. They do not differ in truth value; hence the oddity of their negative conjunction in *'He picks up the book but is not picking up the book'.

To explain the meaning symbolised [+SITU], it is necessary to identify three "connotations" or properties which individually may or may not be contrastive in a given instance, but collectively distinguish it from [−SITU].[11]

1 *Duration.* The essential difference between 'He picks up the book' and 'He is picking up the book' is that in the former, the event is mentally conceived as an indivisible entity without extension in time, whereas in the latter, it is conceived as having duration. This connotation separates [+SITU] and [−SITU] in the case of event predications; in the case of state predications, which in any case signal duration, it has no distinctive value.

Commentary

a It has been noted that football and boxing commentaries often contain the instantaneous present ([−SITU]) (*Brown shoots for goal; He moves quickly in and gives Drake a couple of quick jabs to the body*) where commentators for such sports as rowing and cricket prefer the present continuous ([+SITU]) (*Oxford are moving over to the Surrey bank*). The inference is that in boxing and football events move so fast that it is possible to treat them as without duration; but this is less frequently the case with more leisurely sports.

2 *Limited time extension.*[12] [+SITU] signifies not just duration, but *limited* duration. In this it contrasts with the unrestrictive present: 'I live at Highgate' and 'I am living at Highgate' differ precisely in the suggestion that in the second case the residence is temporary. A similar distinction is felt between 'The engine works perfectly' and 'The engine is working perfectly'. In some cases the contrast does not apply: 'My leg hurts' and 'My leg is hurting' seem almost in free variation; likewise 'I feel ill' and 'I am feeling ill'.[13] This may be because verbs like *hurt, itch,* and *tingle* belong marginally to the class of verbs expressing "private predications" (*see, know,* etc) for which the distinction between [+SITU] and [−SITU] is not significant (see Joos, 1964: 115–20).

3 *Happening not necessarily complete.*[14] A happening or state described by the continuous aspect does not have to be complete. This is best illustrated by examples of the past continuous. In 'I played the piano from ten to eleven o'clock', we take it that the speaker began his performance at ten and finished it at eleven; but in 'I was playing the piano from ten to eleven o'clock', the actual times at which the pianist began and ended are unknown. In answer to a question, he might say: 'Yes, I was playing the piano between ten and eleven – in fact I played all morning'. With verbs having an inceptive or completive force, the difference is even more striking: 'He drowned' implies death, whereas 'He was drowning' does not.[15] It is quite possible to say 'He was drowning, but I rescued him', while *'He drowned, but I rescued him' is a contradiction in terms.

Commentary

b The possibility of incompleteness is also noticeable with the perfect continuous in such examples as 'I have been cleaning the car' and 'Who's been eating my dinner?' In contrast, 'I have cleaned the car' informs us that the job is finished, and 'Who has eaten my dinner?' makes it clear that the whole dinner has been eaten up.

4 *Continuousness.* The continuous is characteristically found with verbs denoting some kind of inexorable process:

The earth is turning on its axis.
Death is getting nearer every day.

The effect of [+SITU] here is to throw emphasis on the ceaseless persistence of the process. *Always*, in combination with the continuous, takes on the sense of *continually, for ever* (with which it may be replaced) in sentences like *He is always making fun of me*. The idea of 'persistence' here is strong enough to cancel out the second "connotation" above, that of "limited time extension". For this reason, it may be best to consider it a separate meaning of the continuous forms, not merely a separate connotation of the same meaning.

Commentary

c The distinction drawn here between senses and "connotations" corresponds to that drawn in §5.3 between meanings and referential properties. The need to regard referential properties as neutralised or non-distinctive in some contexts (as, for example, the connotation of "duration" is non-distinctive in state predications) is easily illustrated from more concrete domains of reference, such as that of sailing vessels: of the bundle of characteristics which identify the yawl from other kinds of vessel, the property "two-masted" is neutralised with respect to the brigantine, and the property "fore-and-aft rigged" is neutralised with respect to the schooner. It is the total "gestalt" formed by the bundle of "connotations" (1)–(4) that is represented by the feature [+SITU].

d A further effect of the continuous, it has been frequently suggested, is to give immediacy or dramatic vividness to the described happening. This may be explained as a "by-product" either of connotation (1) or of connotation (4). On account of connotation (4) "persistence", 'Death is getting nearer every day' confronts us with one of the facts of life more forcibly than 'Death gets nearer every day'. Connotation (1) comes to the fore in narrative contexts. It can provide dramatic immediacy by thrusting the reader in *medias res*, letting him see the episode from a momentary standpoint in the past: *Suddenly a voice was yelling at him through the gunfire*. It is appropriate to mention in this connection Jespersen's characterisation of the continuous (1931: 179) as providing a "frame" round one's temporal point of orientation. This framing effect arises when the continuous is synchronically related to a momentary event or point of time, since duration cannot be plotted against lack of duration without initial and final overlapping: *When I saw him, he was answering the phone*, etc. On the other hand, the "frame" is not a necessary concomitant of the continuous tense forms, and is absent from such sentences as *Yesterday afternoon I was playing tennis* (in which the action having duration is related to a period of time), and indeed from most cases of the perfect continuous.

Returning to the three uses of the simple present in §7.4.2, the unrestrictive, instantaneous, and habitual, we have noted that the continuous has the effect of psychologically shrinking the time-span of the unrestrictive present, and of stretching the time-span of the instantaneous present (see Twaddell, 1960: 7–8). The habitual or iterative present however, poses a problem in that it has two separate continuous counter-parts:

1 *On Sundays he is resting.*[16]
2 *I am buying my shirts at Harrods* (*ie* these days).

The function of the continuous form in these two examples is very different. In case (1), every individual member of a set of repeated events is construed as having duration. In case (2), the set of events itself is construed as a habitual state of affairs having *limited* duration. The two interpretations are accommodated, in the present analysis, by attaching the feature [+SITU] to the first and second downgraded predication respectively of the formula for the simple habitual:

1 $\langle \theta' \cdot [+\text{PLUR} +\text{SITU}] \rightarrow \text{TIM} \cdot +\text{PLUR} \rangle'' \langle \theta'' \cdot \rightarrow \text{TIM} \cdot \theta +\text{THIS} -\text{PERI} \rangle$
2 $\langle \theta' \cdot [+\text{PLUR}] \rightarrow \text{TIM} \cdot +\text{PLUR} \rangle'' \langle \theta'' \cdot [+\text{SITU}] \rightarrow \text{TIM} \cdot \theta +\text{THIS} -\text{PERI} \rangle$

(The features [+COU] and [−SITU] have been omitted from these formulae.) The former interpretation is associated with expressions of frequency (*eg: Every time I pass he is mowing the lawn*), and the latter with expressions of duration (*eg: She is having skiing lessons for a few months*).

7.6 Perfective tense forms

The foregoing semantic treatment of tenses has been founded on the assumption that grammatical features, like lexical items, can have more than one separate meaning. This conflicts to some degree with the traditional study of grammatical usage in terms of unitary meaning. It has been generally supposed, even by those who do not countenance a unitary approach to lexical meanings, that a grammatical category must have a "root meaning" to which all its various uses can be referred. In some instances, this approach works fairly well: all the meanings of the present tense, for example, reflect directly, or through transference, the root meaning "in existence at the present time". But the situation here need not be considered different from that of (say) the adjective *bad*, whose various senses ('inferior', 'unwell', 'putrid', etc) all contain a common element of unpleasantness, and are presumably of the same historical origin. Let it be said that in recognising the polysemy of grammatical constructions, we do not necessarily reject the validity of another (perhaps historical) kind of analysis, in which the common ground between different meanings is investigated.

The perfective is another grammatical category for which a unitary definition is generally attempted. Its use is often explained in such terms as these: "The perfective aspect refers to a past event or state which has current relevance."[17] The objection to this definition is not so much that it is inaccurate, but that it is too vague to explain the complex factors which determine the use and interpretation of the perfective in various contexts. In an attempt to elucidate these factors polysemantically, I shall distinguish four separate senses of the perfective.[18] The first applies to state predications, and the last three to event predications.

7.6.1 *Duration of state up to the present moment*
This use of the perfective is observed in examples such as:

> *They have lived here for ten years.*
> *The castle has been a ruin since the Civil War.*
> *I have loathed hypocrisy all my life.*

As state predications these are marked [−COU], but otherwise their definitions follow closely the specification of adverbials of duration in §7.3.3.

Perfective: definition 1

$$\langle \theta' \cdot [-\text{COU} \ -\text{SITU}] \rightarrow \text{DUR} \cdot +\text{PERI}'' \langle \theta'' \cdot \leftarrow\text{EXT} \ +\text{END} \cdot \theta \ +\text{THIS} \ -\text{PERI} \rangle \rangle$$

'State lasting through a period ending at the present moment.'

Such is the overlap between this and the specification of adverbials of duration that the phrase *since the Civil War* in the second example adds only one piece of information, concerning the starting point of the period in question. The ending point of the period, 'the present moment', does not, as already noted in §7.3.3, have to coincide with the end of the state of affairs denoted by the verb. 'I have lived here for ten years' permits the possibility of an addition '... and I shall continue to live here for years to come'.

In state predications, an adverbial of duration is virtually obligatory with the perfect tense.[19] Without it, the predication usually has to be construed as designating an event. *They have lived here* on its own is broadly synonymous with *They have lived here at least once*, and the residence is now an event viewed in its entirety, having a beginning and an end. Some predications ill-suited to interpretation with [+COU] ('event') are almost meaningless in the perfective unless an adverbial of duration is added:

> *Paris has stood on the Seine.*
> *Elephants have been the largest land-mammals.*

One has to think hard to find contexts in which these sentences would be acceptable, whereas there is no difficulty if some such phrase as *for ages* is added.

Commentary
a In some cases where the period of time is implicit, interpretation as a state predication is not inhibited by the absence of an adverbial of duration: *He has lived a good life; Have you had a nice time?* etc.

The perfective continuous often has the same interpretation as the simple perfective used as above, except for the substitution of [+SITU] for [−SITU] (the terms of ±COU need not be specified):

Perfective continuous:

$$\langle \theta' \cdot [+\text{SITU}] \rightarrow \text{DUR} \cdot +\text{PERI}''\langle \theta'' \cdot \leftarrow \text{EXT} +\text{END} \cdot \theta +\text{THIS} -\text{PERI}\rangle\rangle$$

No adverbial of duration is required here, but may be optionally added:

I have been reading.
I have been reading the whole evening.

The semantic difference between the simple and continuous perfective in the case of state predications is very slight, only the second criterion of "limited duration" being operative (see §7.5). *They have been living here . . .* suggests a smaller time-scale than *They have lived here . . .* and so *for a few days* would almost certainly go with the first, and *for thirty years* with the second. But as this is a difference of psychological extent only, it would be futile to try to state a length of period beyond which the continuous form would be unacceptable.

7.6.2 *Duration of habit up to the present moment*

If an event predication is expressed by the simple perfective in combination with an adverbial of duration, it is understood that reference is being made to a set of repeated events lasting collectively up to the present moment. This habitual perfective meaning is related to the preceding one exactly in the same way as the habitual or iterative present is related to the unrestrictive present. The formula below reflects this parallelism:

Perfective: definition 2

$$\langle \theta' \cdot [+\text{PLUR}] \rightarrow \text{TIM} \cdot +\text{PLUR}\rangle''\langle \theta'' \cdot \rightarrow \text{DUR} \cdot +\text{PERI}'''$$
$$\langle \theta''' \cdot \leftarrow \text{EXT} +\text{END} \cdot \theta +\text{THIS} -\text{PERI}\rangle\rangle$$

(The feature [−SITU] has been omitted from this definition.) The following sentences exemplify the iterative meaning of the perfective:

He has driven a taxi for several years.
She has made her own dresses since she was a girl.

The perfective continuous may also be interpreted in an equivalent way:

I have been finishing work early.
I have been walking to work since my car broke down.

The distinctness of definitions 1 and 2 can be seen in the ambiguity of this second sentence, which might refer to a daily repeated happening, or to a single period of activity, as in the previous section ('I have been walking to work . . . , but I haven't got there yet'). A similar ambiguity arises with *He has driven a taxi for several years*, except that the one interpretation ('He has been driving uninterruptedly for several years') is factually absurd. As with the non-habitual sense of §7.6.1, an adverbial of duration is again an optional accompaniment to the continuous form of the verb:

I have been finishing work early (for some time).

The formula for the habitual perfective continuous is the same as that for the habitual simple perfective, except for the substitution of [+SITU] for [−SITU].

7.6.3 *Indefinite past*

In §7.4.3 the perfective, used with event predications, was treated as the indefinite counterpart of the past tense (='at least once in the past'), and was given the following definition:

Perfective: definition 3a

$$\langle \theta' \cdot [+\text{COU}] \rightarrow \text{TIM} \cdot \varnothing ''\langle \theta'' \cdot \rightarrow \text{BEF} \cdot \theta + \text{THIS} - \text{PERI} \rangle\rangle$$

'Have you (ever) been to the Scottish Highlands?'
'She has met Mr Robinson once.'
'I *have* eaten lobster.'

This is the sense that occurs with adverbials such as *once, twice, many times*. There is no equivalent interpretation of the perfect continuous, unless, as in the following, the continuous expansion is given the sense of 'unfulfilled intention':

'I have been going to the Scottish Highlands several times.'

The above formulation for the definition of the 'indefinite past' use of the perfective has two advantages: first, it is fairly simple; and second, it correctly shows that the corresponding statement with the past tense logically implies the statement with the perfective: 'I went to Washington' implies 'I have been to Washington'. There is an alternative formulation, however, which accounts for some aspects of this usage not expressed in the above definition, and which moreover relates the 'indefinite past' more directly to the preceding two senses of the perfective:

Perfective: definition 3b

$$\langle \theta' \cdot [+\text{COU} - \text{SITU}] \rightarrow \text{TIM} \cdot + \text{PERI} - \text{PLUR}''$$
$$\langle \theta'' \cdot \leftarrow \text{EXT} + \text{END} \cdot \theta + \text{THIS} - \text{PERI} \rangle\rangle$$

This, which may be read 'happening at least once in a period leading up to the present', differs from definitions 1 and 2 above in only one or two details, such as the substitution of →TIM for →DUR.

There are two points to be made in favour of definition 3b.

In the first place, the perfective in the sense of 'indefinite past' frequently refers to the *recent* past: 'Have you seen my slippers anywhere?' would not be answered, except in joke, 'Yes, six months ago'. This extra restriction of temporal proximity can easily be read into definition 3b, if one allows that the period of time stretching up to the present moment can be measured, according to context, on a variable time-scale. In some cases (those quoted under definition 3a, for example) the period may be of indefinite length. In others it may be reduced, by subjective assumption of proximity, to a few minutes.

In the second place, as some writers have noted, the simple past and the perfective have different implications in such sentence pairs as:

1 *Did you see the Monet exhibition?*
2 *Have you seen the Monet exhibition?*

From (1) we infer than an exhibition has been held, but is now finished; from (2), on the other hand, we learn that the exhibition is still running. A rather similar contrast appears in:

3 *The Hittites produced few great sculptors.*
4 *The English have produced few great sculptors.*

To use the perfect tense in (3) would be to suggest, wrongly, that the Hittite nation is still in existence. Equally misleading, from a historical point of view, would be *The English produced few great sculptors*. What forces the difference between past and perfective in these examples is the requirement, in the case of the perfective, that a period leading right up to the present moment should be in question, even though the period may not be overtly mentioned in the context. In sentences (3) and (4), for example, some durational element of meaning such as 'during their history' is implicitly understood.

To reconcile the rival definitions 3a and 3b, we have to recognise that they do not really conflict, but rather render alternative accounts of the same thing. 3b 'happening in a period ending now' amounts to the same as 3a 'happening before now'; or, to be absolutely precise, the former implies the latter. As this relation of implication is not deducible by rule from the two definitional formulae, it has to be expressed in a special rule of implication:

$$(X) \cdot \rightarrow \text{TIM} \cdot +\text{PERI} \ -\text{PLUR}''\langle \theta'' \cdot \leftarrow \text{EXT} \ +\text{END} \cdot b\rangle \quad (\text{'}X \text{ in a period ending } b\text{'})$$

logically implies

$$(X) \cdot \rightarrow \text{TIM} \cdot \varnothing'\langle \theta' \cdot \rightarrow \text{BEF} \cdot b\rangle \quad (\text{'}X \text{ before } b\text{'})$$

(Here the non-downgraded versions of definitions 3a and 3b have been used.) For the cost of this special rule, the advantages of both definitions 3a and 3b are gained, since 3a can now be derived from 3b. The implication rule would, however, be in any case required, in a comprehensive description, to formalise the logical connection between the *'before'*/ *'after'* system and the *'beginning'*/*'end'* system. It would be needed, for instance, to explain why 'She got married when she was twenty' implies

'She got married before her twenty-first birthday', or why (assuming noon is the point dividing morning from afternoon) 'He spoke to me in the morning' implies 'He spoke to me before noon'.

7.6.4 *The resultative use of the perfective*
In many instances the perfective indicates that the result or outcome of an event is still in force. With the verb *to go*, this sense happens to be distinguished from the preceding one by the separate past participle form *gone* instead of *been*. While *He has been to the Scottish Highlands* refers to the indefinite past, *He has gone to the Scottish Highlands* is resultative, and implies that he is still there. To put the same point more generally, 'He has gone to x' implies 'He is at x'. Other examples of resultative implication are:

> 'He has broken the chair' implies 'The chair is (still) broken'.
> 'I've sold the car' implies 'The car is sold', 'The car is not mine (any longer)'.
> 'Tim has learnt to read' implies 'Tim knows how to read'.
> 'Fred has acquired some golf-clubs' implies 'Fred has some golf-clubs'.

These relationships of implication are confirmed by the fact that the negative conjunction of each of the pairs of statements is a logical contradiction; *eg* 'Tim has learnt to read, but he doesn't know how to read' is absurd, unless 'has learnt' is taken in the sense of 'indefinite past'.

The left-hand assertion of each pair above is an event predication, and has an obvious inceptive force. For the key to the analysis of resultative meaning, therefore, we return to the discussion of the inceptive formator system in §3.6. It was proposed there to show the relation between an inceptive assertion and an assertion denoting a resultant state (we use the last example above as our model) in the following manner:

Resultant state: $f \cdot \rightarrow h \cdot g$ 'Fred has some golf-clubs.'
Inceptive event: $f'' \cdot \rightarrow \iota \cdot (\theta'' \cdot \rightarrow h \cdot g)$ 'Fred acquires some golf-clubs' (or, in "Pidgin", 'Fred becomes he have golf-clubs').

The statement expressed with the resultative perfective, viz. 'Fred has acquired some golf-clubs', can be specified in the following way:

Resultative perfective: $(f'' \cdot \rightarrow h \langle \theta' \cdot \leftarrow \iota \cdot \theta'' \rangle \cdot g)'$

A rough translation of this specification is: 'Fred has some golf-clubs, which he came to have'. It is equivalent to the resultant state assertion 'Fred has some golf-clubs', except that it conveys the additional information that the inceptive event, viz the acquisition, has taken place. Therefore a possible reaction to the sentence *Fred has acquired some golf-clubs* is the reply *Oh? I thought he had had some all along*.

According to the rule of subordination (§4.3.3), the formula $f'' \cdot \rightarrow \iota \cdot$

$(\theta'' \cdot \rightarrow h \cdot g)$ 'Fred acquires some golf clubs' is equivalent to $(\theta'' \cdot \rightarrow h \langle \theta' \cdot \leftarrow \iota \cdot f'' \rangle \cdot g)'$, which in turn is equivalent, by a double application of the rule of co-reference (§4.3.1) to $(f'' \cdot \rightarrow h \cdot \langle \theta' \cdot \leftarrow \iota \cdot \theta'' \rangle \cdot g)'$ 'Fred has acquired some golf-clubs'. However, these two assertions, although closely related, are manifestly not synonymous; in particular, the acquisition in the one case is taken to be a present event, and in the other case a past event. This is because the formulae as they stand are incomplete: the factor of tense has to be added. Furthermore, the features −PLUR (entailing +COU) and [−COU], being completely predictable in this type of formula, also have to be added to the medial cluster of the inceptive predication and to the principal predication respectively.

It is now possible to supply a more complete definition of the resultative perfective with the factor of present tense included:

Perfective: definition 4

$$\langle \theta' \cdot \leftarrow \iota \; -\text{PLUR} \cdot \theta'' \rangle \langle \theta' \cdot [-\text{COU}] \rightarrow \text{TIM} \cdot \theta + \text{THIS} -\text{PERI} \rangle$$

(In this formula, θ' and θ'' co-refer respectively to the principal predication as a whole, and to one of its terminal clusters, as in the earlier formula for the resultative perfective.)

This account directly registers the relation of implication between 'Fred has acquired some golf-clubs' and the simple state predication 'Fred has some golf-clubs': the specification of the former is identical to that of the latter except for the addition of one feature (the downgraded inceptive predication), and therefore implies it according to rule [E] of §2.8.2. The formulation does not, however, make it clear that the inceptive event took place in the past – it merely says that a present state is the result of it. To convey this extra piece of knowledge, a special rule of implication, roughly as follows, must be added:

$$(a' \cdot r \langle \theta'' \cdot \leftarrow \iota \cdot \theta' \rangle \langle \theta'' \cdot [-\text{COU}] \rightarrow \text{TIM} \cdot \theta + \text{THIS} -\text{PERI} \rangle \cdot b)''$$

logically implies

$$(a' \cdot \rightarrow \iota \; -\text{PLUR} \langle \theta'' \cdot \rightarrow \text{TIM} \cdot \varnothing \,''' \langle \theta''' \cdot \rightarrow \text{BEF} \cdot \theta + \text{THIS} -\text{PERI} \rangle \rangle \cdot (\theta' \cdot r \cdot b))''$$

This rule, anticipated in §3.6, merely makes explicit what in common sense is taken for granted: that an event whose result is felt now must have taken place in the past. By it, the resultative perfective is shown to imply the 'indefinite past' perfective; that is, 'X has happened' according to definition 4 is shown to imply 'X has happened' according to definition 3a. It thus provides a link between the resultative sense and the other three senses of the perfective.

Chapter 8

Place

A convenient approach to the semantics of place in English is to begin with the simpler problem of static relations (those represented, for example, by the prepositions *at*, *on*, and *in*), before proceeding to dynamic relations, or relations involving movement (such as those expressed by *go* in combination with *to*, *into*, or *from*). §§8.1–5 of this chapter therefore concern the various ways provided by the language of determining static location – those respectively entitled here "position and 'dimensionality'", "relative position", "extremities and parts of locations", "compass points" and "orientation". As one cannot study dynamic relations of place without a prior notion of locomotion divorced from destination, one section of the chapter dealing with "movement" (§8.6) precedes the section (§8.7) dealing with movement with respect to location. Finally (in §8.8) notice is taken of two ways in which the static and dynamic aspects of locative meaning may be combined.

8.1 Position and "dimensionality"

Basic to all locative meaning is the system of '*place*', which is in many ways similar in status to the "adverbial" system of '*time when*' (§7.1):

SYSTEM 1 '*place*'
$$\begin{cases} (x) \rightarrow \text{PLA} \ (y) & \text{`}(x) \ \text{at/on/in place} \ (y)\text{'} \\ (x) \leftarrow \text{PLA} \ (y) & \text{`}(y) \ \text{at/on/in place} \ (x)\text{'} \end{cases}$$
Class of system: relative
Contextual properties: $\begin{cases} \{(X)\} \\ or \ \{+\text{CONC}\} \end{cases} \rightarrow \text{PLA} \ [\text{DIME}] \ \{+\text{CONC}\}$
Logical properties: asymmetric, irreflexive, transitive, many–one

There is, however, an important difference between this system and the system $\rightleftarrows$TIM, in that '*place*' is not neccessarily an "adverbial relationship" in the sense of §6.2. Its contextual properties allow for its function *either* as an adverbial relation involving a rank-shifted predication:

$(X) \cdot \rightarrow \text{PLA} \cdot c$ 'I saw her in the garden'

or as a straight-forward relation between terminal clusters containing the feature +CONC 'concrete':

$a \cdot \rightarrow \text{PLA} \cdot c$ 'She was in the garden'.

(In these and similar formulae, the possible occurrence of an ascription feature following →PLA is ignored.)

Equally, the two systems are similar, but not identical, with respect to their logical properties. The asymmetricity and irreflexivity of the '*place*' system are illustrated by the fact that one cannot say 'He is at/on/ in himself', and the fact that 'This case is in the box' is inconsistent with 'The box is in this case'. Transitivity, on the other hand, is shown by the inference of 'She is in Cambridge' from 'She is in the garden' and 'The garden is in Cambridge'.

In this chapter, I shall confine attention mainly to the non-adverbial type of place relation – *ie* that expressed in the formula $a \cdot \rightarrow \text{PLA} \cdot c$. This will, however, be a limitation of illustration only, not of descriptive coverage, for the same definitions apply whether the initial element of the main predication is a rank-shifted predication or a cluster.

Commentary

a The relation $a \cdot \rightarrow \text{PLA} \cdot c$ as a main predication corresponds, in grammar, to a clause of the structure Subject + *be* + Prepositional Phrase such as *She was in the garden*. In its downgraded form $\langle \theta' \cdot \rightarrow \text{PLA} \cdot c \rangle$, the relation is generally expressed by a prepositional phrase which is capable of expansion into a relative clause: *the house* IN THE WOOD (= *the house which is in the wood*). To simplify expression rules we may, indeed, postulate that grammar provides no means of expressing this relation *except* in its downgraded form; thus *She was in the garden* is assigned the semantic structure a: $\varnothing' \langle \theta' \cdot \text{PLA} \cdot c \rangle$, this being equivalent, by the second rule of attribution, to $a \cdot \rightarrow \text{PLA} \cdot c$. By this means we are able to preserve the relative isomorphism of grammatical and semantic structure, so that all clauses containing the verb *be* have the underlying semantic structure of a one-place predication a: m; we are also able to account for place relations entirely in terms of prepositional phrases with the semantic structure $\langle \theta' \cdot \rightarrow \text{PLA} \cdot c \rangle$, except in those few cases (*there, here, everywhere*, etc) where the relation is expressed by a single adverb. However, since the emphasis of the present discussion is semantic not grammatical, it will be simpler to use the non-downgraded variant formula $a \cdot \rightarrow \text{PLA} \cdot c$.

Calling the system of '*place*' asymmetric amounts to saying that in any relation $a \cdot \rightarrow \text{PLA} \cdot c$ the entities designated by a and c cannot be interchanged, despite their sharing of a common feature +CONC. It is thus necessary to make a clear mental distinction between the final cluster c

representing the LOCATION and the initial cluster representing the OBJECT to be related to the location. (The term "object" is here merely a terminological convenience, and by no means implies that the referential domain of *a* is limited to inanimate countables.) In most cases, if one endeavours to switch the direction of the relationship, the result is a nonsensical predication: 'John is at the house', but not *'The house is at John'.

There is a large number of instances which seem to contradict the asymmetry of place relations. For instance, *Jack is by* (=*next to*) *Jill* is synonymous with *Jill is by* (=*next to*) *Jack*, and likewise *Jack is with Jill* is synonymous with *Jill is with Jack*. These sentences do not, however, express a relation between "object" and "location", but rather a relation between two "objects". They are not strictly comparable to sentences of the type *Jill is at/on/in the cupboard*, and will be dealt with under the separate heading of RELATIVE POSITION in §8.2. In contrast, the relationship which is our present preoccupation, that expressed by *at*, *on*, or *in*, may be called one of SIMPLE POSITION.

8.1.1 'At', 'on', and 'in'

Associated with the system of '*place*', as we saw briefly in §4.1.2, is a system of ascription features, the system of '*dimensionality*', which distinguishes the locative meanings of *at*, *on*, and *in*:

SYSTEM 2 '*dimensionality*'

IDIME	'at – no dimension relevant'	✕	*or*	•✕
2DIME	'on – one/two dimensional'	—✕—	*or*	—✕—
3DIME	'in – two/three dimensional'	☒		

Class of system: multiple taxonomic

As ascription features, members of this system have only a subjective, psychological import: they do not directly reflect the actual physical character of the location. The difference between 'at the wall', 'on the wall' and 'in the wall' has nothing to do with the real dimensional properties of the wall, but only with those dimensional properties which are uppermost in the speaker's mind. For this reason, it is in many ways more satisfactory to try to elucidate the difference between them visually, as I have done, rather than verbally. In the diagrams above, ✕ represents the object, and the location is represented in turn by a black dot, by a line (which may be thought of as a single dimension, or as a two-dimensional object seen "side on"), and by a square representing an enclosed space (which may be interpreted two-dimensionally, as an area, or three-dimensionally, as a volume). These categories have obviously more to do with the human apparatus of visual perception than with the objective physical properties of objects as interpreted, for example, in Euclidian geometry.

At, on, and *in* as locative prepositions are defined:

> *at:* →PLA [1DIME]
> *on:* →PLA [2DIME]
> *in:* →PLA [3DIME]

At expresses simple contiguity or juxtaposition, where the dimensions of the location are not significant: *at the door, at the station, at the bus-stop,* etc. *On* represents contiguity or juxtaposition with a location seen as a "line" on the map (*on the road to London, on the River Nile, on the frontier, on the touch-line,* etc) or else seen as a surface (*on the wall, on the ceiling, on the page, on the window, on my shirt,* etc). *In* expresses the concept of 'enclosure' or 'containment' as applied either to two-dimensional or three-dimensional locations: *in the field, in Russia, in the park, in the garden* refer to areas, whereas *in the house, in the aeroplane, in the oven, in the air,* etc refer to volumes.

Commentary

b We must pass by at least two other spatial meanings of *on,* that found in *on the chair* (ie 'on top of the chair') and that found in *on the tree, on the hatstand* ('hanging from . . .'). There are in addition special idiomatic uses; in *Mr Bryant approached with Mrs Bryant on his arm,* for example, *on* can mean neither 'on the surface of', nor 'on top of', nor 'hanging from'. With *in,* too, there are idiomatic uses: *in the country,* for example, indicates neither an enclosed area nor a volume.

That the semantic contrast between *at, on,* and *in* cuts across absolute geometrical distinctions between one-, two-, and three-dimensional bodies reinforces the point that this system deals with subjective spatial "aspect", akin to the temporal "aspect" symbolised by ±SITU and discussed in §7.5. Furthermore, as concrete nouns are not semantically marked for dimensionality, it is quite possible for the same noun to be preceded by either *on* or *in,* depending on the "aspect" brought to the speaker's attention. While *in the island* is the general means of referring to an island as a location having area, *on the island* suggests something small enough to be perceivable as a single surface, like a lawn or a table; one cannot imagine the second phrase referring to a country-sized island such as Cuba or Ireland. The contrast of size works in the opposite direction with *in the boat* and *on the boat: in* points to a small open vessel like a rowing-boat, in which one may sit as within a circumscribed area; *on* suggests a vessel large enough to have a deck, and therefore a surface on which one may walk. *In the grass* suggests that the grass is long, *on the grass* that it is short. *At the corner, on the corner* and *in the corner* are variously applicable according to whether the corner is envisaged as a topographical point (*at the corner of the street*), as part of a surface (*on the corner of the ceiling*), or as part of an enclosed area or volume (*in the corner of the room*).

Here and *there* as adverbs of place are semantically marked [1DIME]:

here: →PLA [1DIME] · θ +THIS   'at this place'
there: →PLA [1DIME] · θ −THIS   'at that place'

Deictic meaning in conjunction with [2DIME] and [3DIME] is expressed by the appropriate preposition followed by *here* or *there*:

on here: →PLA [2DIME] · θ +THIS   'on this place'
in there: →PLA [3DIME] · θ −THIS   'in that place'.

A greater degree of semantic specification is obtained by substituting *this* for *here* and *that* for *there*, thereby adding the features +COU −PLUR to the final cluster:

on this: →PLA [2DIME] · θ +THIS +COU −PLUR   *ie* 'on this thing'.

The phrases **at here* and **at there* do not exist, their place in the paradigm being taken, as we have seen, by the simple adverbs *here* and *there*. In this respect 1DIME may be considered the unmarked member of the system: its presence is assumed when there is no formal specification to the contrary.

Commentary

c   *In here* and *in there*, however, have a narrower range of application than other *in* phrases. *In there* might be taken as a deictic substitute for *in the box* or *in the field*, but not for *in London: How long have you been staying in there?* would be an inappropriate response to *I am staying in London*. Although it is difficult to see any consistent principle underlying this discrepancy, one could account for it partially by postulating two definitions of *here* and *there*, one containing [1DIME] as above, and one having no feature of dimensionality, thus subsuming the meanings of *in here* and *on here*, *in there* and *on there*.

8.1.2 '*Away from*', '*off*', '*out of*'

The locative prepositions *away from*, *off*, and *out of* express the negative of the relations expressed by *at*, *on*, and *in* respectively:

'He is not at the match' = 'He is away from the match'
'He is not on the lawn' = 'He is off the lawn'
'She is not in the kitchen' = 'She is out of the kitchen'.

To define these prepositions one simply adds the negative formator to the previous definitions:

away from: $\sim$→PLA [1DIME]   'not at'
off: $\sim$→PLA [2DIME]   'not on'
out of: $\sim$→PLA [3DIME]   'not in'

On, in, away, off, and *out* are sometimes used colloquially as prepositional adverbs in a sense easily derivable from that already given, in that it arises from the combination of the prepositional meaning with zero expression of the definite formator:

My friend is away	$a \cdot \sim \rightarrow$PLA [1DIME]$\cdot \theta$	(*sc.* 'away from home', etc)
My friend is in	$a \cdot \sim \rightarrow$PLA [3DIME]$\cdot \theta$	(*sc.* 'in the office', etc)
My friend is out	$a \cdot \sim \rightarrow$PLA [3DIME]$\cdot \theta$	(*sc.* 'out of jail', etc)

There is no prepositional adverb corresponding to *at*, and thus no formal item having the definition $\sim \rightarrow$PLA [1DIME]$\cdot \theta$. This seems to be an accidental gap in the lexicon (on the "blocking" of the expression of well-formed predications, see §2.7). In practice, speakers may circumvent the difficulty by using *here* and *there* as appropriate, thereby adding an extra feature $+$THIS or $-$THIS to the final cluster.

8.2 Relative position

The definition of the question form *where?*, as indicated in §6.2, is simply the general place formula $\rightarrow$PLA$\cdot c$ with the substitution of the question formator for c:

where?: $\rightarrow$PLA$\cdot$?   'at/on/in what place?'

This definition, however, raises a problem of how to define prepositions of place such as *by* and *with*. The problem may best be presented in two stages, (a) and (b):

[a] Any locative expression answering the question *where?* must, according to the rule enunciated in §6.2, be specifiable by a formula of the general shape $\rightarrow$PLA$\cdot c$. Thus the question *Where is Jack?* ($a \cdot \rightarrow$PLA$\cdot$?) may have the answer *Jack is with Jill*, which must therefore express a statement of the form $a \cdot \rightarrow$PLA$\cdot c$. Likewise the question *Where is Jill?* may receive the answer *Jill is with Jack*, which must therefore express a statement of the form $c \cdot \rightarrow$PLA$\cdot a$. Further, the two statements *Jack is with Jill* and *Jill is with Jack* are synonymous. We have to accept, therefore, that the two formulae $a \cdot \rightarrow$PLA$\cdot c$ and $c \cdot \rightarrow$PLA$\cdot a$ represent the same meaning.[1]

[b] Yet $a \cdot \rightarrow$PLA$\cdot c$ and $c \cdot \rightarrow$PLA$\cdot a$ cannot be equivalent, because $\rightleftarrows$PLA has with good reason been characterised in §8.1 as an asymmetric system.

To see the way out of this dilemma, it is first of all necessary to see that *by* and *with* represent a relationship of a different order from *at, on,* etc. 'He is by the gate', for example, neither logically implies nor is logically inconsistent with 'He is at the gate'. In addition, it is possible to use *by* and *with* as connectives between nominals which could not be linked with *at*: one can assert 'John is with Jill' and 'My car is by your car', but not *'John is at Jill' and *'My car is at your car'. In a word, *by* and *with*, unlike *at*, *on*, etc express a relationship between comparables. The former two connect a pair of OBJECTS according to their RELATIVE POSITION: the latter connect an OBJECT to a LOCATION.

It was therefore a mistake, in [a] above, to identify 'Jack' with *a* and 'Jill' with *c* in the formulae $a \cdot \rightarrow \text{PLA} \cdot c$ and $c \cdot \rightarrow \text{PLA} \cdot a$, since this involved giving one the status of a location and the other the status of an object. Instead, a solution is suggested by the treatment of the conjunctions *before*, *after*, and *when* in §7.1.1. There, the logical and contextual properties of $\rightleftarrows$TIM compelled the establishment of a rule that "events are temporally related to one another not directly, but through the mediation of points and periods of time". In notational terms, this meant that downgraded structure had to be added, and that 'X happened before Y' had to be interpreted more explicitly as 'X happened at a time before the time at which Y happened'. In the same way, the asymmetricity of $\rightleftarrows$PLA necessitates a rule of the form: "two objects are spatially related to one another not directly but through the mediation of locations."

8.2.1 *'With'*

The solution suggested above is supported by the fact that *with* can be roughly paraphrased *at the place at which* or *at the same place as*:

'Where are my keys?'
$\begin{cases} \text{'They are with your wallet'}= \\ \text{'They are in/at the place in/at which your} \\ \quad \text{wallet is'}= \\ \text{'They are where your wallet is.'} \end{cases}$

Thus its definition follows very closely that of *when* (= 'at the time at which') in the temporal field (§7.1.1):

when: $\rightarrow$TIM$\cdot \theta' \langle \theta' \cdot \leftarrow$TIM$\cdot \varnothing \rangle$ 'at the time at which'
with: $\rightarrow$PLA$\cdot \theta' \langle \theta' \cdot \leftarrow$PLA$\cdot \varnothing \rangle$ 'at the place at which'.

As with *when*, it is possible to show by indirect symmetry (see §7.1.1) the virtual synonymy of two statements in which the relationship expressed by *with* is reversed: 'Jack is with Jill'='Jill is with Jack'. The only difference of meaning is that discussed in connection with *before* and *after* in §7.1.1: namely, that in the first statement it is Jill's location that is assumed to be known, whereas in the second it is Jack's.

Where expresses the same meaning as *with* in grammatical contexts where a conjunction rather than a preposition is required. Hence the synonymy of 'Your keys are with your wallet' and 'Your keys are where your wallet is'.

With, like other prepositions of the same kind, is neutral with respect to dimensionality, and no ascription feature is therefore included in its definition.

Away from, which was earlier defined as the negative of *at*, can also express a mutual relation between comparable objects, and can therefore act in opposition to *with* rather than *at*:

'My car is away from your car' = 'My car is not with your car'

A second definition must therefore be provided, to supplement that of §8.1.1:

away from: $\sim \rightarrow$PLA$\cdot \theta'\langle\theta' \cdot \leftarrow$PLA$\cdot \varnothing\rangle$ 'not with'

8.2.2 'By'

The locative definition of *by* may be derived, by the insertion of a further stage of downgrading, from that of *with*. In this, *by* is parallel to the time conjunctions *before* and *after*, whose definitions can be similarly derived from that of *when*. If the meaning of *with* is (roughly) 'at the place at which', that of *by* can be given as 'at a place proximate to the place at which', or notationally:

by: $\rightarrow$PLA$\cdot \varnothing'\langle\theta' \cdot \rightarrow$PROX$\cdot \theta''\langle\theta'' \cdot \leftarrow$PLA$\cdot \varnothing\rangle\rangle$.

In this definition use has been made of a new relative system, that of '*proximity*':

SYSTEM 3 '*proximity*'
$\begin{cases}(x)\rightarrow\text{PROX}(y) & \text{`}(x)\text{ is proximate to }(y)\text{'}\\(x)\leftarrow\text{PROX}(y) & \text{`}(y)\text{ is proximate to }(x)\text{'}\end{cases}$
Class of system: relative (reciprocal)
Contextual properties: [DIME] $\rightarrow$PROX [DIME]
Logical properties: symmetric, irreflexive.
Dependence rules: PROX depends on SID, $-$FAR (§8.2.3)

This definition of *by* is needed to account for facts observed in the introduction to §8.2. Through deductions parallel to those demonstrated in §7.1.1, two statements such as 'Jack is by Jill' and 'Jill is by Jack' can be shown to be "indirect converses", like '*X* before *Y*' and '*Y* before *X*'. In this case, however, converseness amounts to the same thing as symmetry, for $\rightleftarrows$PROX is a reciprocal system, not an ordering system. That is, we are able by this indirect means to establish the cognitive synonymy of *Jack is by Jill* and *Jill is by Jack*.

The concept of 'proximity', as we shall see in the next section, plays a part in the definition of a number of other prepositions.

Commentary
a The contextual properties of $\rightleftarrows$PROX simply ensure that a member of this system occurs only in a locative context. One might, however, wish to widen

the application of the system to include temporal and other abstract relations; for example, it could enter into the definition of words like *recent, just,* and *soon.*

b System 3 is classed as neither transitive nor intransitive: if '*a* is by *b*' and '*b* is by *c*' are true assertions, we have no basis for deciding the truth of either '*a* is by *c*' or '*a* is not by *c*'.

8.2.3 *Vertical and horizontal relations*

The prepositions and preposition-like locutions *over, under, in front of, behind, to the left of, to the right of* are like *with* and *by* to the extent that they refer to the relative position of two objects. Together, they constitute a three-dimensional framework of spatial orientation, consisting of one vertical axis ('over'/'under') and two horizontal axes. On the horizontal plane, there is a primary axis ('in front of'/'behind') and a secondary axis ('to the left of'/'to the right of').

What we understand by the "primary" axis depends on a number of factors. There is, first of all, the quasi-deictic interpretation of 'in front of' and 'behind' with reference to the observer's field of vision: as I look at a tree, anything between me and the tree is 'in front of' the tree, whereas anything concealed from my view by the tree is 'behind' it. In addition, 'in front of' and 'behind' (likewise 'front' and 'back') have two conventionalised uses. The 'front' of an object is sometimes 'that part of the object usually exposed to observation': this meaning applies to the 'front' of a building (that part facing the road), or to the 'front' of a piece of furniture (that part facing the middle of the room, as opposed to the 'back', which faces the wall). The other conventionalised use of 'in front of' and 'behind' applies to human beings, animals, and to mobile objects such as vehicles: here 'in front of' means 'in the direction in which the person or object normally moves or faces'.

The identification of the primary axis is like the question of "dimensionality" in that it seems to have much to do with the perceptual apparatus of the human body. The 'front' of a human-being is that region to which all his organs of perception are directed. Perhaps the assignment of a 'front' and a 'back' to vehicles has an anthropomorphic character, and is not too different from the animistic analogy whereby aeroplanes are endowed with a 'nose', 'wings', and a 'tail'.

The interpretation of the secondary horizontal axis depends on that of the primary one: the line going from 'side' to 'side' is at right angles to that going from 'back' to 'front'. There is, however, a curious discrepancy between the "field of vision" interpretation and the "mobile object" interpretation, in that the relation of 'left' and 'right' to the primary axis is reversed. The following diagrams (seen three-dimensionally) illustrate the difference:

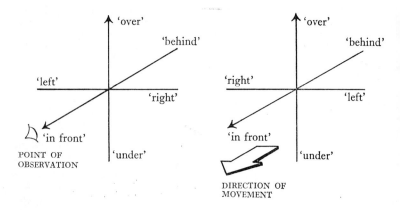

The reversal of 'left' and 'right' on these diagrams suggests that at least two separate definitions of *in front of* and *behind* in a locative sense should be given. Support for this view comes also from the observation of ambiguities: 'The church is behind the town-hall' can mean either 'The church is on the other side of the town-hall from where I am looking' or 'The church is on the other side of the town-hall from the road'. For the present purpose, however, I shall treat these different senses as variants covered by the same definition.

As the relations expressed by *over*, *under*, etc, are "relations between objects" in the sense applying to *with* and *by*, it simplifies analysis to recognise the common ground of meaning by the presence of a common relative feature. As before, however, it is necessary to relate objects through the mediation of locations: otherwise it will not be possible to explain the use of *over*, *under*, etc, in answer to the question *where?*:

Where is the ball? It's under the table.

We therefore set up a system which serves as a general connector of locations. Let us call it the '*side of*' system, and symbolise it ⇄SID. This system has the same contextual and logical properties as ⇄PROX: the close connection between the two systems can be formalised by making ⇄PROX dependent on ⇄SID; *ie* by ensuring that any cluster containing a feature of the former will also contain a feature of the latter.

SYSTEM 4 '*side of*'
$$\begin{cases} (x) \rightarrow \text{SID}\,(y) & \text{`}(x)\text{ is to the } \ldots \text{ side of }(y)\text{'} \\ (x) \leftarrow \text{SID}\,(y) & \text{`}(y)\text{ is to the } \ldots \text{ side of }(x)\text{'} \end{cases}$$
Class of system: relative (reciprocal)
Contextual properties: [DIME] →SID [DIME]
Logical properties: symmetric, irreflexive.

Dependence rule: SID depends on VER and/or FAR and/or PART (see systems 5, 7, and 9 below).

The dependence rule ensures that a term of system 4 never stands on its own, but is accompanied by a member of some other system. Thus ⇌SID is purely an abstraction from the relationships represented by 'over'/ 'under', 'in front of'/'behind', etc; it is an "archirelation", the postulation of which obviates the need to state the same contextual and logical properties many times over. An economy can also be made retrospectively by deleting the contextual properties of system 3: these need no longer be specified, since they follow from the dependence of system 3 on system 4.

The "archirelation" ⇌SID is present in all specifications of relative position except that of 'with'. The following is, therefore, a schema for a large number of formulae symbolising relative position:

[A] $a \cdot \rightarrow$PLA$\cdot b' \langle \theta' \cdot \rightarrow$SID $x \cdot \theta\ c'' \langle \theta'' \cdot \leftarrow$PLA$\cdot d \rangle \rangle$

In the remainder of this section we shall consider what features can occur at the position of x in this schema, filling out 'to the ... side of' as 'to the left side of', 'to the front side of', etc; b and c, on the other hand, are normally null.

Commentary

c In an alternative analysis, one could dispense with the dependence rule associated with system 4 by allowing x in the above schema to be null, but blocking by expression rules the occurrence of a medial cluster containing $\rightarrow$SID alone.

The value of the relation ⇌SID as a basic link between locations becomes more evident when we consider the logical ordering of vertical and horizontal axes by dependence rules. Such an ordering is revealed in three different interpretations of the phrase *at the side of*.

In a very general sense, *at the side of* has no reference to vertical or horizontal orientation: in an astronomical context, *Star x is at the side of star y* may mean no more than that the two stars are in spatial proximity. A less general sense of *at the side of* is found in *I placed my hat at the side of his*, which means '... close to his on a horizontal plane'; there is a sense, that is, in which '*x* is at the side of *y*' excludes the possibility of vertical proximity. A third and still more specific sense is observed in *His car was at the side of mine*, where *at the side of* is in contrast to *in front of* and *behind*, and therefore limits proximity to the secondary horizontal axis.

Commentary

d *by*, *beside*, and *by the side of* all seem to be full synonyms of *at the side of* in that they can replace it without change of meaning in the three contexts just given.

6*

By, for example, apart from having the general sense of proximity discussed in §8.2.2, can have its reference limited to horizontal proximity in *I placed my hat by his*, and to lateral proximity in *His car was by mine*. The phrase *next to* can also, it seems, be synonymous with *by* and *at the side of*, but also has a more specific meaning in connection with a row or array of objects: *He lives next to me* usually means that no house intervenes between his and mine.

This hierarchy of generality in the meaning of *at the side of* urges the postulation of two systems $\pm$VER ('*vertical*'/'*horizontal*') and $\pm$PRI ordered in dependence such that $\pm$PRI depends on $-$VER:[2]

SYSTEM 5 '*vertical*'/'*horizontal*'
$\begin{cases} +\text{VER} & \text{'vertical'} \\ -\text{VER} & \text{'horizontal'} \end{cases}$
Class of system: binary taxonomic
Dependence rule: VER depends on SID

SYSTEM 6 '*horizontal axes*'
$\begin{cases} +\text{PRI} & \text{'primary horizontal axis'} \\ -\text{PRI} & \text{'secondary horizontal axis'} \end{cases}$
Class of system: binary taxonomic
Dependence rule: PRI depends on $-$VER

The three senses of *at the side of* can now be represented by returning to the general schema [A], assuming *a*, *b*, *c*, and *d* to be null, and replacing *c* by the following features:

1 $\rightarrow$PROX
2 $\rightarrow$PROX $-$VER
3 $\rightarrow$PROX $-$VER $-$PRI

More fully specified, the definitions are:

1 $\rightarrow$PLA$\cdot$ $\varnothing'\langle\theta'\cdot\rightarrow$PROX$\cdot$ $\theta''\langle\theta''\cdot\leftarrow$PLA$\cdot$ $\varnothing\rangle\rangle$
2 $\rightarrow$PLA$\cdot$ $\varnothing'\langle\theta'\cdot\rightarrow$PROX $-$VER$\cdot$ $\theta''\langle\theta''\cdot\leftarrow$PLA$\cdot$ $\varnothing\rangle\rangle$
3 $\rightarrow$PLA$\cdot$ $\varnothing'\langle\theta'\cdot\rightarrow$PROX $-$VER $-$PRI$\cdot$ $\theta''\langle\theta''\cdot\leftarrow$PLA$\cdot$ $\varnothing\rangle\rangle$

The first definition is identical to that of *by* as given in §8.2.2; the second adds the feature $-$VER 'horizontal', and the last adds the feature $-$PRI 'secondary axis'. (The feature $\rightarrow$SID is omitted, although it would, of course, be added by dependence rules for every example.)

At the side of always entails proximity, so the feature $\rightarrow$PROX is added to the above specifications. On the other hand, *to the side of* (which cannot, it seems, be understood in sense (1)) says nothing about the distance between the objects; to give the meanings of this phrase, therefore, we simply omit the feature $\rightarrow$PROX from definitions (2) and (3) above.

By introducing an additional system $\pm$FAR at this stage, we can account for the meaning of the antonymous locative phrases *far from* and *near to*:

SYSTEM 7 *'distance'*

$\left\{\begin{array}{l} +\text{FAR} \quad \text{'far from'} \\ -\text{FAR} \quad \text{'near to'} \end{array}\right.$

Class of system: polar
Dependence rule: FAR depends on SID

For convenience of presentation, I shall follow the practice of omitting from subsequent definitions in this section all structural parts they have in common; this means that I shall give merely (as in the initial specifications of *at the side of* above) those features which occur at *x* in the general schema [A]. Hence to define *far from* and *near to*, a single feature alone is required:

far from: +FAR
near to: −FAR

The close connection between the systems of *'distance'* and *'proximity'* (system 3) is shown in the dependence rule of system 3, which adds −FAR to all feature formulae containing →PROX. This explains the relation of implication (or perhaps of synonymy) between 'The house is by the lake' and 'The house is near the lake'.

Systems 5 and 6 were introduced for the immediate purpose of distinguishing the senses of *at the side of*; but their value also lies in their use in the definition of other prepositions in this semantic field. Before we proceed to this task, however, an additional discrimination has to be made, since no account has so far been taken of the converse relationship between *over* and *under*, of that between *in front of* and *behind*, or of that between *to the left of* and *to the right of*. The contrast between each of these pairs falls into the category of an "ordering system" (see §4.1.1). This is shown, amongst other things, by the transitivity of each relation:

'The floor is under the carpet
       and   } implies 'The floor is under the rug'.
The carpet is under the rug'

'The house is behind the tree
       and   } implies 'The house is behind the wall'.
The tree is behind the wall'

In addition, the converse relation of 'over' to 'under', etc, is evident from such equivalences as:

'The lamp is over the door' = 'The door is under the lamp'.
'The cupboard is to the left of the fireplace' = 'The fireplace is to the right of the cupboard'.

Because these three relationships are comparable we can economise on the number of systems in the description by using a single ordering system to represent all three. This ordering system, because it is neutral with respect to the three axes, will be simply called '*plus*'/'*minus*':

SYSTEM 8 '*plus*'/'*minus*'

$\begin{cases} (x) \to \text{PLUS} (y) & \text{'}(x) \text{ is over/in front of/to the left of } (y)\text{'} \\ (x) \leftarrow \text{PLUS} (y) & \text{'}(x) \text{ is under/behind/to the right of } (y)\text{'} \end{cases}$

Class of system: relative (ordering)
Contextual properties: asymmetric, irreflexive, transitive
Dependence rules: PLUS depends on VER

The contextual properties of ⇄PLUS need not be separately stated, for this system depends of ±VER, which in turn depends on ⇄SID. As there is no neutral term between *over* and *under* or between *in front of* and *behind*, it might be suggested that selection from the system ⇄PLUS is compulsory in the presence of +VER or +PRI. Rather than build these requirements into the semantic analysis in the form of dependence rules, however, it seems better to treat it as an accident of expression that no single term meaning 'over or under' or 'in front of or behind' exists in the language. Such a neutral term does exist in the field of parts and extremities of objects (see §8.3), where the noun *end* can have the meaning 'front or back'. If, therefore, one declared +PRI to be dependent on ⇄PLUS, this rule could not be generalised to another, related field of meaning.

No further discussion need delay the following definitions, which are abbreviated (as explained above) to the extent of containing only those features which appear at *x* in schema [A]:

over:	+VER →PLUS
under:	+VER ←PLUS
in front of:	−VER +PRI →PLUS
behind:	−VER +PRI ←PLUS
to the left of:	−VER −PRI →PLUS
to the right of:	−VER −PRI ←PLUS

The redundant feature −VER is retained in the last four formulae for the sake of showing dependence relations.

Commentary

e It might be felt that there are no "positive" and "negative" poles of the opposition between 'left' and 'right', and therefore that the selection of →PLUS for 'left' and ←PLUS for 'right' is arbitrary in a sense that similar selections for 'over' and 'under', 'in front of' and 'behind' are not. This objection, however, would be based on a misunderstanding of the semantic notation. Except in cases where a general correlation between semantic directionality and syntactic structure has been set up (*eg* for transitive verbs and adverbials), nothing but a trivial notational difference is gained or lost by the substitution of →R for ←R and vice versa. Relative systems are in this respect no different from taxonomic systems: only an arbitrary decision determines whether one member of a binary opposition will be labelled $+x$ and the other $-x$. All these symbols indicate is that the concepts are in a certain kind of contrastive relationship. There may be undeniable expressional reasons for regarding one term as the positive member and another as the negative member of a binary opposition – for example, the choice of one adjective rather than another for the purposes of measure or comparison (*That tree is forty feet high*, not **That tree is forty feet low*; see Bierwisch, 1967: 9). But the distinction seems to have no logical consequences, and is therefore ignored in the present notation, which, being purely for semantic description, does not represent an expressional bias towards one form rather than another.

There is a slight difference in meaning, similar to that observed for *side*, between *to the left/right of* and *on the left/right of*. (These phrases may, indeed, be regarded as ellipses for longer phrases *to the left hand side of*, etc). The difference lies in the presence of the component →PROX for phrases beginning *on*. Hence 'His house is on the left of the road' implies that his house is by or near to the road. There is no analogous formal difference in the case of *over*, *under*, *in front of* and *behind*, but these prepositions are ambiguous to the extent that they need not carry the additional sense of 'proximity', but often do so; that is, →PROX is an optional component of their meanings. As usually interpreted, 'The clock is over the door' implies 'The clock is by (*ie* near to) the door'; and likewise 'the tree is in front of the cottage' implies 'The tree is by the cottage'. Yet in other contexts, no suggestion of propinquity is felt: 'The aeroplane was over our heads' does not lead us to infer that the plane was flying at a particularly low altitude.

Commentary

f Underneath and *beneath* as prepositions of place seem to be in all respects synonymous with *under*; but there are slight differences in meaning between *over* and *under* and the closely related pair of antonyms *above* and *below*. The first pair tends to indicate a direct vertical relationship approximating to the meaning of *right above* and *right below*; *above* and *below* on their own mean little more than 'higher than' and 'lower than'. In speaking of the design of a house, if we say that 'the kitchen is below the bathroom', we may mean simply that it is on a lower floor; but if we say that 'the kitchen is under(neath) the bathroom' we make it clear that it occupies approximately the equivalent position on a lower floor. Comment *b* of §8.4 discusses this kind of distinction as it applies to points of the compass.

8.3 Extremities and parts of locations

Although it is strictly outside the main theme of this chapter, a brief sketch of the semantic field of parts and extremities of locations will be given here, because of its role in supporting and extending the analysis of vertical and horizontal relations just given. The nouns with whose meanings we shall be chiefly concerned are *top*, *bottom*, *front*, *back*, and *side*.

It may be initially observed that these nouns are all ambiguous in the same way: they are capable of referring either to a part of a location or to its extremity. Therefore it is necessary to introduce two further systems, one standing for the relation between whole and part, and one standing for the relation between whole and extremity.

SYSTEM 9 '*partition*'

$\begin{cases} (x) \to \text{PART} (y) & \text{'}(x) \text{ is part of } (y)\text{'} \\ (x) \leftarrow \text{PART} (y) & \text{'}(y) \text{ is part of } (x)\text{'} \end{cases}$

Class of system: relative (ordering)
Contextual properties: [αDIME] →PART [αDIME]
Logical properties: asymmetric, irreflexive, transitive

The use of [αDIME] in the contextual conditions of this system indicates that the ascription features on both sides of the relation are the same.[3] For example, [3DIME] →PART [3DIME] is a well-formed formula, but not [2DIME] →PART [3DIME].

SYSTEM 10 '*extremity (spatial)*'

$\begin{cases} (x) \to \text{EXTS} (y) & \text{'}(x) \text{ is a spatial extremity of } (y)\text{'} \\ (x) \leftarrow \text{EXTS} (y) & \text{'}(y) \text{ is a spatial extremity of } (x)\text{'} \end{cases}$

Class of system: relative
Contextual properties: [iDIME] →EXTS [jDIME] $(i \leqslant j)$
Logical properties: asymmetric, irreflexive, transitive

This is the spatial counterpart of system 20 ($\rightleftarrows$EXT) of Chapter 7. The contextual redundancy rule associated with this system is unusual, like that of $\rightleftarrows$PART, but is unlike it in that it allows *lack of* match in dimensionality, so long as the feature ascribed to the initial cluster has a lower number than that ascribed to the final one. Thus [1DIME] →EXTS [2DIME] is well-formed, but not [2DIME] →EXTS [1DIME].

Commentary

a That the contextual properties of systems 9 and 10 are unusual, if not unique, is an indication that their terms belong marginally to the class of formators (see §3.1.4). This quasi-formator status is also seen in specific logical rules governing their use. Qualities attributed to an object as a whole, for instance, must generally be attributed to any part or extremity of the object. Hence the contradictory character of statements such as 'His property is in England, but part of it isn't'; 'This cup is hot, but the bottom of it isn't'. To make sense of such statements, a listener tends to assume that the speaker meant to say '*Most of* his property . . .', etc. It would be beyond my purpose here to enunciate the exact form of the rule that accounts for these and other similar facts.

Systems 9 and 10 between them account for the already-mentioned ambiguity of the nouns *side*, *top*, *bottom*, *front*, and *back*, which may refer either to parts or to extremities. In these two senses, their definitions conform respectively to the patterns $\varnothing'\langle\theta'\cdot\rightarrow\text{PART } x\cdot\varnothing\rangle$ and $\varnothing'\langle\theta'\cdot\rightarrow\text{EXTS } x\cdot\varnothing\rangle$. As before, I shall state the definitions in a curtailed form, leaving out everything except the medial cluster.

8.3.1 *Extremities: 'side', 'top', etc*
The definitions of *side*, *top*, etc, in the sense of 'extremity' are accordingly as follows:

side:	[2DIME] →EXTS [3DIME]
	(*eg* 'on the side of the dice')
top:	[2DIME] →EXTS +VER →PLUS [3DIME]
	(*eg* 'on top of the box')
bottom:	[2DIME] →EXTS +VER ←PLUS [3DIME]
	(*eg* 'on the bottom of the box')
side:	[2DIME] →EXTS −VER [3DIME]
	(*eg* 'on the side of the box')
front:	[2DIME] →EXTS −VER +PRI →PLUS [3DIME]
	(*eg* 'on the front of the car')
back:	[2DIME] →EXTS −VER +PRI ←PLUS [3DIME]
	(*eg* 'on the back of the car')
side:	[2DIME] →EXTS −VER −PRI [3DIME]
	(*eg* 'on the side of the car')

In the field of 'extremity', as in that of 'position', *side* has three meanings of diminishing generality. The completely unmarked use is to be found with an object like a dice, which has six 'sides' on an equal footing with one another, or with a spherical object such as a ball, the whole surface of which may be designated its 'side'. The second use of *side* may apply to a box which has no primary horizontal axis, or to an upright cylindrical object such as a telegraph pole, for which 'side' is in opposition to 'top' and 'bottom'. Thirdly *side* is used in contrast to 'front' and 'back' with reference to objects such as cars and houses.

All the words defined as above refer to surfaces. Because of the two features of dimensionality involved, the interpretation of such words largely depends on two factors of context: (a) the preceding preposition and (b) the kind of object denoted by the following noun. Every final noun in the above list of examples is readily interpretable as describing a three-dimensional location, and so accords with the [3DIME] in the same definition; however, the initial preposition is *on* in all cases, and so the noun immediately following it is construed in a 'surface' sense ([2DIME]). If *in* were substituted for *on* in the phrase *on the back of the car*, the noun *back* would immediately be taken to denote a part of the car, rather than a surface. Likewise with the other examples. On the other hand, *at*, ascribing the feature [1DIME] to the following noun, does not indicate the dimensional properties of 'front', 'back', etc, and thus is less specific than *on* and *in* in the same context. Compare *at the front/back of the bus* with *on/in the front/back of the bus*; *at the top/bottom of the tower* with *on/in the top/bottom of the tower*.

Other words whose definitions contain →EXTS are *edge* and *corner*:

edge: [2DIME] →EXTS [2DIME]
corner: [1DIME] →EXTS [2DIME]

These definitions are designed to account for the use of *edge* and *corner* with reference to surfaces, as in *on the edge of the field/table/handkerchief*, *at the corner of the field/table/handkerchief*. There are, of course, other meanings of these nouns, including partitive meanings, to be mentioned in the next section.

The preposition *on*, as noted earlier (in §8.1.1), can have the meaning of *on top of* (='on the top of'), and in this sense it may now be defined as follows:

on (top of): →PLA [2DIME] · $\theta' \langle \theta'$ · [2DIME] →EXTS +VER →PLUS
[3DIME] · ∅ $\rangle$

Similarly, *under/underneath* may be defined as 'on (or touching) the bottom of'. Hence it is possible to make a distinction between 'The coin is under(neath) my hand' and 'The coin is below my hand', the second of which does not allow the coin and the hand to be contiguous.

8.3.2 *Parts: 'side', 'top', etc*

It has already been pointed out that the relation 'extremity of' differs from that of 'part of' in that the two elements linked by the relation are not necessarily of the same dimensionality; otherwise the definitions to be given in this section resemble closely those already given in §8.3.1.

Before continuing, however, we must remark that *side*, *top*, etc used in the sense 'side part', 'top part', etc, refer to peripheral parts of an object, and as such are in contrast to the noun *middle*. Furthermore, they are often in contrast to the term *corner*, which represents the 'diagonal periphery' of an object. To make these discriminations, systems 11 and 12 are introduced:

SYSTEM 11 *'middle'/'periphery'*
$\left\{ \begin{array}{l} +\text{MID} \quad \text{'middle, centre'} \\ -\text{MID} \quad \text{'side, corner'} \end{array} \right.$
Class of system: binary taxonomic
Dependence rule: MID depends on PART

SYSTEM 12 '*diagonal*'

$\begin{cases} +\text{DIAG} & \text{'\textit{diagonal}'} \\ -\text{DIAG} & \text{'\textit{non-diagonal}'} \end{cases}$

Class of system: binary taxonomic

Dependence rule: DIAG depends on −MID

Definitions of *side*, etc, in the partitive sense may now be given:

side:	→PART −MID −DIAG
	(*eg* 'in the side of the sphere')
top:	→PART −MID −DIAG +VER →PLUS
	(*eg* 'in the top of the wardrobe')
bottom:	→PART −MID −DIAG +VER ←PLUS
	(*eg* 'in the bottom of the well')
side:	→PART −MID −DIAG −VER
	(*eg* 'in the side of the mountain')
front:	→PART −MID −DIAG −VER +PRI →PLUS
	(*eg* 'in the front of the bus')
back:	→PART −MID −DIAG −VER +PRI ←PLUS
	(*eg* 'in the back of the bus')
side:	→PART −MID −DIAG −VER −PRI
	(*eg* 'in the side of the hedge')

The examples above require matching ascription features [3DIME] . . . [3DIME] preceding and following the definition, since they refer to volumes. Parts of surfaces are also included in the definitions, but in this case the ascription features [2DIME] . . . [2DIME] must occur: *on the top of the window, on the front of the desk-lid, on the side of the picture,* etc. An interesting ambiguity arises in these examples: they may refer to either (a) a part of a surface, or (b) an extremity of a three-dimensional object, according to the definition given in §8.3.1. The ambiguity may be eluci-dated by these diagrams:

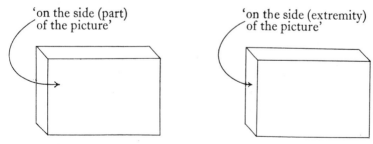

'on the side (part) of the picture'

'on the side (extremity) of the picture'

In contrast to the above definitions, which all contain the features −MID −DIAG, *middle* and *corner* may be defined:

    middle: →PART +MID

    corner: →PART −MID +DIAG

There is no combination +MID +DIAG, because of the dependence rule attached to system 12.

Again, different members of the *'dimensionality'* system may be ascribed to the 'middle' and 'corner' of a location, depending on the dimensionality of the location itself: 'corner' and 'middle' are partial surfaces ([2DIME]) in 'on the corner/middle of the carpet', but are partial volumes ([3DIME]) in 'in the corner/middle of the room'.

Commentary

b There is no incompatibility between the feature +DIAG and the systems ±VER and ±PRI: combinations such as →PART +DIAG +VER →PLUS may occur, but must be expressed by a phrase (*top corner, back corner*, etc), rather than by a single word.

c The analyses presented in §§8.3.1 and 8.3.2 are to be regarded as first approximations only, as they have one or two unsatisfactory features. Firstly, the systems ⇄EXTS and ⇄PART have so many properties in common, that it should be possible to economise by subsuming both relations under a single system; in that case, 'part of' would simply be the relation in the case of matching dimensionality, and 'extremity of' the relation in the event of unequal dimensionality. However, this is not quite possible in the present analysis, since the combination [2DIME] →EXTS *x* [2DIME], used to characterise a line which is the extremity of a surface (*eg* 'on the edge of the carpet') would then be indistinguishable from [2DIME] →PART *x* [2DIME], used to represent a surface which is part of a surface (*eg* 'on the corner of the carpet'). The alternative analysis would therefore require an alteration of the system of '*dimensionality*' so as to introduce a further contrast between 'line' and 'surface', at present both included under [2DIME] as different "aspects" of the same meaning. A further argument in favour of such a revision is that the system of '*extremity*' could then extend its reference (although 'extremity' would no longer be an appropriate label for it) to positions *within* a location, but of a different dimensionality to the location itself; namely, to the use of 'middle' and 'centre' in reference to a point within a line, surface, or volume, a line within a surface, etc. Such a use is observed in the phrase *the middle of the road*, applied to a line dividing one 'side' of the road from the other, *the middle/centre of the ring*, applied to a point rather than an area. The latter could be given the specification [1DIME] →R +MID [3DIME], where →R represents the feature signifying the meaning common to →PART and →EXTS. This revision of the analysis is attractive, but has far-reaching consequences which are difficult to evaluate: for example, it would mean giving up the unitary meaning of *on* (→PLA [2DIME]) as expressed by *on the border* (position on a line) and *on the carpet* (position on a surface), and therefore postulating a large number of dubious ambiguities, which it would be difficult, if not impossible, to justify.

8.4 Compass points

The compass points 'north', 'south', 'east', and 'west' can be accommodated in this description by the addition of two ordering systems:

SYSTEM 13 '*north*'/'*south*'

$\begin{cases} (x) \rightarrow \text{NOR} \ (y) & \text{'}(x) \text{ is (to the) north of } (y)\text{'} \\ (y) \leftarrow \text{NOR} \ (x) & \text{'}(x) \text{ is (to the) south of } (y)\text{'} \end{cases}$

SYSTEM 14 '*west*'/'*east*'

$\begin{cases} (x) \rightarrow \text{WEST} \ (y) & \text{'}(x) \text{ is (to the) west of } (y)\text{'} \\ (x) \leftarrow \text{WEST} \ (y) & \text{'}(x) \text{ is (to the) east of } (y)\text{'} \end{cases}$

The systems have identical properties:

Class of system: relative (ordering)
Contextual properties: (as for $\rightleftharpoons$SID, system 4)
Logical properties: asymmetric, irreflexive, transitive
Dependence rules: NOR, WEST depend on SID

Componential definitions are:

north of: $\rightarrow$SID $\rightarrow$NOR	*west of:* $\rightarrow$SID $\rightarrow$WEST
south of: $\rightarrow$SID $\leftarrow$NOR	*east of:* $\rightarrow$SID $\leftarrow$WEST

There is no requirement that these formulae should fit into a definition according with schema [A] in §8.2.3, because compass directions are used as links between locations, not between objects (in the senses of those words discussed in §8.2). In the normal way of conversation, we do not say *John is north of me* or *Your typewriter is west of mine* in the same way as we say *John is in front of me*, etc; the first two statements have a bizarre flavour, because their author seems to treat human-beings and material things as if they were locations on a map. As connectors of locations, *north of, east of*, etc, represent relations between comparables, but not in the sense applying to *by, with, in front of*, etc. As $\rightleftharpoons$SID is a reciprocal system, it is possible to show (by direct converseness) the equivalence of formulae for '*x* is north of *y*' and '*y* is south of *x*', and so account for the observation that these two statements are cognitively synonymous. The same is true of '*x* is west of *y*' and '*y* is east of *x*'.

Commentary

a The secondary cardinal points of the compass 'north-west', etc, can be defined by using a combination of features from systems 13 and 14:

> *north-west of:* $\rightarrow$SID $\rightarrow$NOR $\rightarrow$WEST
> *south-east of:* $\rightarrow$SID $\leftarrow$NOR $\leftarrow$WEST

etc. Because $\rightleftharpoons$NOR and $\rightleftharpoons$WEST are ordering systems, the combinations $\rightarrow$NOR $\leftarrow$NOR and $\rightarrow$WEST $\leftarrow$WEST are self-contradictory; hence the compounds *south-north* and *east-west* do not occur as indicators of compass direction.

b As in §§8.3.1–2, there is an unsatisfactory duplication in the above analysis: systems 13 and 14 share the same properties, and description would be more economical if these properties could be stated once only with reference to a common system of compass direction, or better still, if the ordering system $\rightleftharpoons$PLUS (system 8), with a slightly altered dependence rule, could be made to do service for both. One would then establish a binary taxonomic system $\pm$NOR to differentiate the north-south axis and the east-west axis, and would break $\rightarrow$NOR down into the components $+$NOR $\rightarrow$PLUS, $\leftarrow$WEST into $-$NOR $\leftarrow$PLUS, etc. The dicffiulty with this solution is that it renders impossible the definitions of secondary cardinal points as given in Comment *a* above; north-east, for example, becomes $\rightarrow$SID $+$NOR $\rightarrow$PLUS $-$NOR $\leftarrow$PLUS, which is doubly an oxymoron, because of the combination of contrasting features $+$NOR and $-$NOR $\rightarrow$PLUS and $\leftarrow$PLUS. The definitions of Comment *a* are based on the assumption that features of $\rightleftarrows$NOR and $\rightleftarrows$WEST can be combined; that is, 'north' is interpreted in a "field" sense rather than a "point" sense ('further north than' rather than 'due north of'). In such a sense, it is possible to expound the meaning of north-west as 'both north and west of'. However, the revised analysis involving the system $\pm$NOR only works with reference to "point" direction, where 'north' and 'west' are mutually exclusive categories. Within the original analysis of §8.4, it is possible to accommodate both "point" and "field" direction by introducing a binary system $\pm$POI, adding by an inconsistency rule the special restriction that if $+$POI ($=$'point direction') is present in a componential formula, that formula cannot contain features from both system 13 and system 14. The inconsistency rule would run as follows:

$$\begin{Bmatrix} x \cdot \rightarrow\text{NOR} \ +\text{POI} \ y \cdot z \\ x \cdot \leftarrow\text{NOR} \ +\text{POI} \ y \cdot z \end{Bmatrix} \text{ is inconsistent with } \begin{Bmatrix} x \cdot \rightarrow\text{WEST} \ +\text{POI} \ y \cdot z \\ x \cdot \leftarrow\text{WEST} \ +\text{POI} \ y \cdot z \end{Bmatrix}$$

The system $\pm$POI, although it is not formally included in this chapter's analysis of place relations, has applications in other areas of locative meaning: for example it distinguishes the meanings of *above* and *below* from those of the similar antonyms *over* and *under* (see Comment *f*, p. 173). This system is the locative equivalent of the temporal system $\pm$PERI (system 2 of Chapter 7). In summary, we may say that the description containing systems 13 and 14 proves, on more detailed consideration, to be adequate in a way in which the superficially more attractive solution in terms of $+$NOR and $\rightleftarrows$PLUS is not. But neither solution is entirely satisfactory.

8.5 Orientation

In the description of locative meaning so far, it has been necessary to refer to entities two kinds: objects and locations. Now a further factor is to be introduced, the POINT OF ORIENTATION. In statements such as 'The cloud is beyond that hill', the position of an object ('the cloud') is determined by reference not only to a location (in this instance 'that hill'), but to a point where in reality or imagination the speaker is standing. *Beyond* can be roughly paraphrased *on that side of* or *on the other/far side of*, and as such is in contrast to *on this side of*, which has no single prepositional equivalent in English.

8.5.1 *Point of orientation and point of observation*

The point of orientation introduces a subjective, deictic element of meaning, as is evident from the use of the words *this* and *that* in the phrases *on this side*, *on that side*. Previously in this thesis such an element of meaning has been represented by the definite formator θ, perhaps in combination with a term of the system ±THIS (system 3 of Chapter 7). In this respect the meaning of *beyond* resembles one of the uses of *behind* as discussed in §8.2.3, where it was noted that the primary horizontal axis can be interpreted as a line extending from the object to a point of observation. If we wish to distinguish this use of *in front of* and *behind* from others, we can add to the general definitions of those elements as given in §8.2.3 an extra downgraded predication to be read 'with respect to this or that point of observation':

in front of: +PRI →PLUS ⟨θ″·←OBS·θ⟩
behind: +PRI ←PLUS ⟨θ″·←OBS·θ⟩

These are, as before, abbreviated definitions, and must be expanded into complete definitions on the pattern of schema [A] in §8.2.3 (p. 169):

in front of: →PLA· ∅′⟨θ′· +PRI →PLUS ⟨θ″·←OBS·θ⟩·θ‴
                                    ⟨θ‴·←PLA· ∅⟩⟩″

behind: →PLA· ∅′⟨θ′· +PRI ←PLUS ⟨θ″·←OBS·θ⟩·θ‴
                                    ⟨θ‴·←PLA· ∅⟩⟩″

Two omissions from these specifications need to be explained: the feature −VER is omitted from the central cluster because it is redundant (±PRI depends on −VER); and no feature from the system ±THIS is included preceding ←OBS, because either +THIS or −THIS might be indicated in different contexts. (For instance, in *I can't see the boy – he's behind the hedge, behind* means 'on the far side seen from here'; but if *They* is substituted for *I* in this sentence, the meaning changes to 'on the far side seen from there'.)

I need not go into the details of the relative system ⇄OBS, nor into the other definitions of *in front of* and *behind*, since it is more central to my purpose to proceed to the similar but more important concept of a "point of orientation". Different prepositions involving a point of orientation are illustrated in the following statements:

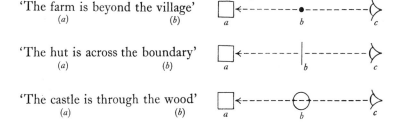

'The farm is beyond the village'
  (a)   (b)
  a   b   c

'The hut is across the boundary'
  (a)   (b)
  a   b   c

'The castle is through the wood'
  (a)   (b)
  a   b   c

In the diagram which accompanies each example, I have tried to set out schematically the spatial relationship between the three entities (object (*a*), location or second object (*b*), and point of orientation (*c*)). The arrow depicts what may be termed the "axis of orientation". All these examples contrast with:

'The house is on this side of the park'
   (*a*)   (*b*)

where the ordering is *b–a–c*, instead of *a–b–c*. The difference between *on this side of* on the one hand and *beyond/across/through* on the other corresponds to the difference between *in front of* and *behind*, where there is a similar contrast of orders (this time *c* represents the point of observation):

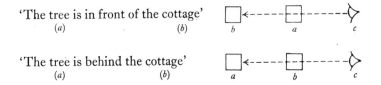

'The tree is in front of the cottage'
   (*a*)   (*b*)

'The tree is behind the cottage'
   (*a*)   (*b*)

This prompts us to suggest that the combinations +PRI →PLUS and +PRI ←PLUS, which signal the contrast between 'in front of' and 'behind', should also represent the contrast between 'on this side' and 'beyond', etc. Such an analysis, if accepted, accounts for the close synonymy of 'The tree is on this side of the cottage' and 'The cottage is beyond the tree', on the same grounds that apply to 'The tree is in front of the cottage' and 'The cottage is behind the tree'.

The pairs of assertions just mentioned are parallel, but not quite identical in meaning: where one pair relates position to a point of orientation, the other relates position to a point of observation. This is not merely a terminological difference. From 'The cottage is behind the tree' one makes the inference that the tree is visible, and that the cottage is hidden from view by it. (More precisely, the meaning is that, as the crow flies, the tree is directly on the way from here to the cottage.) In 'The cottage is beyond the tree', however there is no such inference, but rather the suggestion that in order to reach the cottage, one would have to pass by the tree. To make the first statement explicit, one could add parenthetically *seen from here*, a verbalisation of the downgraded predication $\langle \theta'' \cdot \leftarrow$OBS$\cdot \theta$ +THIS$\rangle$. It would be inappropriate to append *seen from here* to the second statement, but one could enlarge it merely by adding *from here*, roughly verbalising an analogous predication $\langle \theta'' \cdot \rightarrow$ORI$\cdot \theta$ +THIS$\rangle$, which we shall assume to be present in the meaning of *beyond*.

The system of '*orientation*', here introduced for the first time, is as follows:

SYSTEM 15 '*orientation*'

$\begin{cases} (x) \rightarrow \text{ORI}(y) & \text{`}(x)\text{ is the point of orientation for }(y)\text{'} \\ (x) \leftarrow \text{ORI}(y) & \text{`}(y)\text{ is the point of orientation for }(x)\text{'} \end{cases}$

Class of system: relative

Contextual properties: [DIME] $\rightarrow$ ORI $\{(X + \text{PRI})\}$

Logical properties: asymmetric, irreflexive, intransitive, one–many

---

Commentary

a The contextual redundancy rules for system 15 specify that the point of orientation (through the ascription of [DIME]) is a "place"; also, that the element following $\rightarrow$ ORI is a rank-shifted predication containing, in its medial cluster, the feature +PRI 'primary horizontal axis'. If the rule of subordination (see §4.3.3) is allowed for, this correctly defines the circumstances under which $\leftarrow$ ORI occurs in the definitions of *beyond*, etc.

The complete semantic specifications of *on this side of* and *beyond* ('on the other side of') are:

on this side of: $\rightarrow$ PLA $\cdot$ $\varnothing$ '$\langle \theta' \cdot +$PRI $\rightarrow$ PLUS $\langle \theta'' \cdot \leftarrow$ ORI $\cdot \theta \rangle \cdot \theta'''$
$$\langle \theta''' \cdot \leftarrow \text{PLA} \cdot \varnothing \rangle \rangle''$$

beyond: $\rightarrow$ PLA $\cdot$ $\varnothing$ '$\langle \theta' \cdot +$PRI $\leftarrow$ PLUS $\langle \theta'' \cdot \leftarrow$ ORI $\cdot \theta \rangle \cdot \theta'''$
$$\langle \theta''' \cdot \leftarrow \text{PLA} \cdot \varnothing \rangle \rangle''$$

These are identical with the definitions of *in front of* and *behind* except for the substitution of $\leftarrow$ ORI for $\leftarrow$ OBS.

8.5.2 '*Across*' and '*through*'

Returning to the diagrams in §8.5.1, we may now observe that the meanings of *across* and *through* in their static locative senses are closely parallel to that of *beyond*, and yet show an important difference. The difference is that *beyond* describes the relative position of two objects, and is in this respect like the prepositions discussed in §8.2; but *across* and *through* denote "simple position", *ie* the relation between an object and a location, and are thus like the prepositions of §8.1 rather than those of §8.2. (We leave the more common dynamic use of these prepositions to a later section, §8.7.3.)

In the diagram for *beyond*, *a* and *b* are both objects; while in the diagrams for *across* and *through*, *a* is an object and *b* a location. This explains why *beyond* is in a converse relationship to *on this side of*, just as *over* is the converse of *under*, etc. On the other hand, the *b* of '*a* is across/ through *b*' must be a location, because the preposition assigns it a certain dimensionality, [2DIME] in the case of *across* and [3DIME] in the case of *through*. The diagrams reflect this dimensionality, and also suggest the parallelism of:

	on	is to	*in*
as	*off*	is to	*out of*
as	*across*	is to	*through.*

The left-hand prepositions all have the ascription feature [2DIME], whereas those on the right have [3DIME].

Across and through may therefore receive the following definitions:

across: $\rightarrow$PLA$\cdot\; \varnothing'\langle\theta'\cdot+PRI\leftarrow$PLUS$\;\langle\theta''\cdot\leftarrow$ORI$\cdot\theta\rangle$ [2DIME]$\cdot\;\varnothing\rangle''$
through: $\rightarrow$PLA$\cdot\; \varnothing'\langle\theta'\cdot+PRI\leftarrow$PLUS$\;\langle\theta''\cdot\leftarrow$ORI$\cdot\theta\rangle$ [3DIME]$\cdot\;\varnothing\rangle''$

With *across*, like *on*, the ascription feature [2DIME] may apply to a location seen as a line on the map or to a location seen two-dimensionally as a surface. Similarly, *through* is like *in* in having the twofold interpretation of referring to an area or to a volume. The regularity of the correspondence will become clear after an examination of the following phrases as complements of a sentence beginning *He is . . .* or *It is . . .*:

		Position	*Orientation*
[2DIME]	LINE:	on the border	across the border
		on the river	across the river
	SURFACE:	on the page	across the page
		on the lawn	across the lawn
[3DIME]	AREA:	in the park	through the park
		in Europe	through Europe
	VOLUME:	in the kitchen	through the kitchen
		in the air	through the air

Notice, incidentally, that replacing *across* by *through* can have the same effect as replacing *on* by *in* in suggesting or stressing different characteristics of the thing identified as the location. This is more easily illustrated from the dynamic use of these prepositions (see §8.7.3) rather than the sense at present under consideration: 'He looked THROUGH the water' suggests under-water vision ('water' = 'volume'), whereas 'He looked ACROSS the water' suggests observation over the surface of the water ('water' = 'surface'). 'She walked ACROSS the grass' ('grass' = 'surface') similarly differs from 'She walked THROUGH the grass' ('grass' = 'volume') in suggesting that the grass is short.

In sentences such as 'The kitchen is through the living room', the

point of orientation remains implicit as 'here' or 'there', and is represented notationally by the definite formator, which has zero expression.
However, the point of orientation is sometimes separately indicated by a
from-phrase: *The hut is across the field from the railway line; The station
is through the tunnel from the signal box.*

Commentary

b A problem in this section is whether there is any preposition corresponding to
across and *through* and having the ascription feature [1DIME]. Possible candi-
dates are *through* and *past*, which have other, closely related meanings. Neither
of these prepositions gives clear evidence of ambiguity in this respect, although
each is used in contexts where the location appears to be treated as a point on
the map: *They live through/past the village.* (Note that *through* is used of a point
in geometry: *Line AB passes through point C.*) The only preposition which
unambiguously indicates [1DIME] in this area of meaning is *via*, which however
does not occur in static contexts: one can say *They went to Bristol via Tewkesbury,* but not **They live via Tewkesbury.*

c In the sense just discussed, *across* has the synonym *over*: 'He's over the river'
='He's across the river'; 'They live over the common'='They live across
the common'. This orientational meaning of *over* is clearly distinct from that
treated in §8.2.3: *They live over the common* does not mean that their home is
suspended directly above the common. It is also distinct from two further
meanings of *over* to be discussed in §8.5.3.

d In addition, *over* and *through*, retaining their implications of dimensionality,
can be used in a pervasive sense in combination with *all* or *whole*: *The weeds
are all over the garden; There is woodworm all through the house. Throughout*
can replace *all through* in this sense.

e *Across* is also subtly ambiguous: it can be used, without reference to dimensionality, in the more general sense which can be rendered 'on the other side
of'. Here *side* is understood, as in §8.3, as a part or extremity of the location:
He lives across London does not mean that he lives beyond London, but that he
lives in another part of the city, in a part remote from the point of orientation.
(It is to be noted that *across* in the sense which contains the ascription feature
[2DIME] could not be used with the noun *London*, any more than it would be
possible to make meaningful use of the sentence **He works on London.* A city
cannot be envisaged as a line or a surface.) Further, if *across* is paraphrased *on
the other side of, side* may be interpreted either in the sense containing the
feature −VER, or in the more precise meaning containing −PRI. In the latter
sense, *across* contrasts with *along,* which may be glossed 'at/towards the other
end of' when used statically, in such sentences as *His office is along the corri-
dor.* The choice between *across* and *along* in such cases is obviously connected
with the shape of the location, which determines the direction of the primary
horizontal axis. The alignment of the primary axis is automatic in the case of
one-dimensional locations: the contrast between 'across the border' and
'along the border' could not be clearer. But with two-dimensional and three-
dimensional locations, the contrast between 'across' and 'along' only arises
if the location is apprehended as having one "long dimension" and one "short
dimension". Otherwise, *across* is used as the neutral term: *across the circus-
ring* not **along the circus ring* (except as a metonymic substitute for *along the
edge of the circus-ring*).[4]

f 'Enclosure' is the common element of meaning that unites the 'area' and 'volume' aspects of [3DIME]; so it is not to be wondered at that *through*, the preposition which ascribes [3DIME] to the meaning of its complement, should be used with nouns referring to enclosures or apertures: *There was a beautiful view through the window; The station is through the tunnel.* The related idea of 'piercing' is present in *a pig with a ring through its nose.*

8.5.3 '*Past*', '*over*', and '*under*'

With verbs of motion, the prepositions *by* and *past* are synonymous: 'He went past the police-station'='He went by the police-station'. However, in a static sense, they are closely related in meaning, but not interchangeable: if we say *He lives past the post-office*, we mean that to reach his home, one would go *past* or *by* the post-office. More precisely, the axis of orientation passes through a place proximate to the post-office. The distinctiveness of the meaning of *past*, as of the meaning of *by*, depends on the presence of the feature →PROX:

$$past: \rightarrow\text{PLA}\cdot\varnothing'\langle\theta'\cdot+\text{PRI}\leftarrow\text{PLUS}\langle\theta''\cdot\leftarrow\text{ORI}\cdot\theta\rangle\cdot\varnothing'''\langle\theta'''\cdot\rightarrow\text{PROX}\cdot\varnothing\rangle\rangle''$$

A further point of resemblance to 'by' is that no particular feature of dimensionality is ascribed to the location in question.

Similar interpretations can be provided for *over* and *under*. *The station is under the bridge (from here)* means that the station is on the other side of the bridge, such that to reach it one would pass under the bridge ('under' implying proximity). To define this sense of *under*, one simply adds the features +VER ←PLUS to →PROX in the definition of *past* just given. It is difficult to find a matching example with *over* with static orientational meaning, because the force of gravity makes such an interpretation unlikely; however, a closely related interpretation of *over* is exemplified by *He lives over the hill, He was sitting over the table (from me)*, where *over* means 'over/across the top of', and suggests contact with, rather than proximity to, the location. This sense of *over*, which may be specified by the substitution of →EXTS +VER →PLUS for →PROX in the definition of *past*, invites comparison with the use of *on* in the sense 'on (the) top of' (see §8.1.2, §8.3.1).

The difference between these senses of *over* and *under* and those described in §8.2.3 can be observed in the ambiguity of sentences such as *The aeroplane is over the hill* (='above' or 'on the other side of'?) and *The ball is under the hedge* (='beneath' or 'on the far side of'?).

There is no analogous ambiguity of *in front of* and *behind, to the left of* and *to the right of*, as these can only be construed in the sense defined in §8.2.3, that of relative position.

8.5.4 '*Towards*'

Another preposition which is sometimes used to indicate static place relations is *towards*, although, like *past* and *through*, it is more often associated with movement. The static use of *towards* is paraphrasable by *in the direction of*, and is illustrated by sentences such as *The flower shop is towards the hospital (from here); He lives towards the centre of the town (from the factory)*. The possibility of adding *from here* or some other phrase of that kind is a clear signal of the relevance of *towards* to the place relations we have been considering: it specifies *position with respect to a point of orientation*, and like *beyond, across*, etc its meaning may be represented diagrammatically by a configuration of *a, b*, and *c*, where those symbols correspond to matching symbols in the formula '*a is towards b from c*':

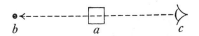

$$b \qquad\qquad a \qquad\qquad c$$

This ordering corresponds to that of 'on this side of', and one can see, indeed, that referentially, there is little or no difference between 'The flower shop is towards the hospital from here' and 'The flower shop is on this side of the hospital'. The difference seems to be that in the first example, the hospital is simply used as a location for the purpose of establishing the position of the flower shop; that is, whereas *a* and *b* in '*a is on this side of b*' are both objects, in '*a is towards b*', *a* is an object and *b* is a location. If this assumption is accepted, 'towards' falls neatly into the pattern of prepositions of orientation as already discussed. We already have two variables, the order of *a* and *b*, and the status of *a* and *b*:

beyond: order *a–b–c*; *a* and *b* both objects
on this side of: order *b–a–c*; *a* and *b* both objects
across/through: order *a–b–c*; *a* is an object, *b* a location

These three cases naturally lead us to expect a fourth, and the gap is filled by *towards*:

towards: order *b–a–c*; *a* is an object, *b* a location

Thus the definition *towards*, according to this diagnosis, follows those of *across* and *through*, apart from the reversal of the relation symbolised by ⇄PLUS:

towards: →PLA · ∅ '⟨θ' · +PRI →PLUS ⟨θ'' · ←ORI · θ⟩ · ∅ ⟩''

Towards does not assign any particular feature such as [2DIME] or [3DIME] to the location *b*, and therefore the positive evidence that *b* is a location, the attribution of dimensionality that one finds in the cases of *across* and *through*, is lacking here. But one may identify *b* as a location on the negative ground that since there is no converse of *towards*, as there is of *on this side of*, *a* and *b* cannot have the same status.

8.6 Movement

At this point we leave the subject of static place relations, and turn to the subject of dynamic relations with a very brief prefatory study of movement.

The difference between moving and remaining still is symbolised by the following system:

SYSTEM 16 *'movement'*
$\begin{cases} +\text{MOV} & \text{'mobile'} \\ -\text{MOV} & \text{'stationary'} \end{cases}$

Class of system: binary taxonomic, attributive (see below)
Contextual properties: [+CONC] MOV

An ATTRIBUTIVE system is one which bears a relation to an attributive cluster similar to that which a relative system bears to a medial cluster. A feature of such a system may freely occur in an attributive cluster, (as far as dependence rules permit), but can only occur in a terminal cluster if accompanied by other features, from the system ±CONC or ±COU. The clearest examples of attributive systems are polar oppositions such as 'rich'/'poor', 'high'/'low'. Attributive systems may be associated, like relative systems, with contextual redundancy rules; for example, the system +MOV, as we see above, requires that the adjacent terminal cluster should be marked 'concrete', so that 'His virtues are mobile' is marked as a deviant statement. By this means, it is possible to account for selection restrictions (see §4.1.2) in attributive predications.

The feature +MOV generally goes with event predications (see §7.4.1), and −MOV with state predications: in the simple present tense, *John moves* is interpreted as instantaneous or habitual, while *John is still* is interpreted as unrestrictive (see §7.4.2). However, this rule is not without exceptions, and is therefore not formalised as a rule of dependence.

Commentary

a The verb *move* has a very general meaning which embraces "partial movement" (*eg: She moved as I was taking her photograph*), as well as "full movement" or locomotion. In a more detailed description these would be distinguished; but we shall assume, for the limited purpose of this chapter, that 'movement' = 'locomotion'.

A large number of verbs in English can be designated "verbs of movement". In semantic terms, this means that the definitions of these verbs are logically included in the definition of *move* (which is, we assume, simply the feature +MOV); that is, they contain at least one other feature in addition to +MOV. Notice that a statement expressed by a sentence which contains such a verb of movement logically implies the same statement when *move* is substituted for the more specific verb of movement: 'John is running', etc implies 'John is moving'. This sort of relationship can be explained if we set up an open-ended multiple taxonomic system of *'types of locomotion'* dependent on +MOV:

SYSTEM 17 *'types of locomotion'*

⎧ 1LOCO 'walk'
⎪ 2LOCO 'run'
⎪ 3LOCO 'hop'
⎨ 4LOCO 'skip'
⎪ 5LOCO 'fly'
⎪ 6LOCO 'jump'
⎪ 7LOCO 'crawl'
⎩ 8LOCO 'fall'
  etc   etc

Class of system: multiple taxonomic, attributive
Contextual properties: (see below)
Dependence rule: LOCO depends on +MOV

This system, like ±MOV, is associated with contextual redundancy rules, which are, however, too varied and particular to go into here. The set of facts they have to cover includes the fact that 'walk' has to occur with an animate performer possessing legs ('The table walked', 'The herring walked', etc are nonsensical), and so on. The actions denoted by terms of this system can be grouped on the basis of shared properties: for example, 'fly' and 'jump' entail loss of contact with the ground, whereas 'slide' and 'roll' entail continuous contact. It is dubious, however, whether these matters are the concern of semantics: they are probably to be classed as referential criteria, rather than semantic properties (see §5.3).

Commentary

b Similarly, one might argue that most, if not all, of the properties (*eg* 'possessing legs') attributed by features of system 17 to the terminal cluster are referential rather than semantic properties, and therefore should not be formalised by contextual redundancy rules. In that case, 1, 2, . . . , *n*LOCO need no longer be classified as an attributive system.

There is a corresponding multiple taxonomic system describing modes of remaining stationary:

SYSTEM 18 *'posture'*

⎧ 1POS 'stand'
⎨ 2POS 'sit'
⎪ 3POS 'lie'
⎩ 4POS 'crouch'
  etc   etc

Class of system: multiple taxonomic, attributive
Contextual properties: (similar to those of system 17)
Dependence rule: POS depends on − MOV

The definitions of the intransitive verbs *run, sit, lie,* etc, are now self-evident: they consist of a single feature from system 17 or 18, with the feature +MOV or −MOV added, as appropriate, by dependence rule. The same verbs are mostly acceptable to some degree used transitively, in a causative sense:

'walk the dog' = 'cause the dog to walk'
'fly the plane' = 'cause the plane to fly'
'jump the horse' = 'cause the horse to jump'
'stand the vase on the shelf' = 'cause the vase to stand on the shelf'.

One exception is *lie,* which is provided with a special transitive verb *lay* (= 'cause to lie').

8.7 Movement and destination

The meanings of *come* and *go* resemble those of *walk, run,* etc, in implying movement; but they also have the additional force of *movement in respect of a goal or destination.* One way to appreciate this is to note *He was coming* or *He was going* are not semantically complete sentences in the sense that applies to *He was moving* or *He was walking*: there is an ellipsis (*ie* zero expression) of some such element of meaning as 'here' or 'there'. *He came* is in effect synonymous with *He came here/there*; *He went* with *He went away from here/there.*

It is also important to notice that *He came/went to the station* is in many respects synonymous with *He got/came to be at the station*; that is, it has the force of an inceptive statement containing the formator →ι (see §3.6). Thus

'He has gone/come to the station' implies 'He is at the station'.

Similarly, the following statements are tautologous:

'Having come/gone to the station, he was at the station.'
'Before coming/going to the station, he was away from the station.'

As a first attempt at the specifying the meaning of *He went to the station,* therefore, I suggest the following, which is a formula for inceptive sentences (see §3.6) with the factor of tense omitted:

$a' \cdot {\rightarrow}\iota \cdot (\theta' \cdot {\rightarrow} \text{PLA} \, [\text{1DIME}] \cdot b)$ 'He got/came to be at the station.'

Likewise for *He went there:*

$a' \cdot {\rightarrow}\iota \cdot (\theta' \cdot {\rightarrow} \text{PLA} \, [\text{1DIME}] \cdot \theta \, -\text{THIS})$ 'He got/came to be there.'

However, 'get' and 'come' here represent the non-motional, purely inceptive meaning of *become*. Consider, for example, the following exchanges:

> *How did that valley get (to be) there?*
> *It was gouged out by an ice-age glacier.*
> *How did the statue come to be in that enormous crate?*
> *They built the crate around it.*

No movement is suggested by these questions, which are clearly distinct in meaning from equivalent questions containing *come* or *go* in a motional sense. In fact, because valleys are by nature or definition immobile, the question *How did that valley go there?* has a ring of absurdity.

This factor of 'movement' can be built into the semantic specification by adding to the medial cluster of the main predication the feature +MOV:

$$a' \cdot \to\iota \; +\text{MOV} \cdot (\theta' \cdot \to\text{PLA} \, [\text{1DIME}] \cdot b) \quad \text{'He went to the station'}$$

The basic motional definition of *go* (*to*) can now be written $\to\iota$ +MOV. (For the purposes of this analysis the difference between *come* and *go* will be ignored.)[5] The formator $\to\iota$ adds to the concept of 'movement' the notion of 'destination', and as $\to\iota$ requires a following rank-shifted predication, this explains why *go* needs a prepositional phrase or equivalent expression as its "complement", except in the case of ellipsis noted above.

8.7.1 *'To', 'on to', and 'into'*
The prepositions *to*, *on to*, and *into* are respectively the dynamic equivalents of *at*, *on* and *in*, in that they ascribe [1DIME], [2DIME], and [3DIME] to the meaning of the following noun phrase:

$$a' \cdot \to\iota \; +\text{MOV} \cdot (\theta' \cdot \to\text{PLA} \, [\text{1DIME}] \cdot b) \quad \text{'He went to the station'}$$
$$a' \cdot \to\iota \; +\text{MOV} \cdot (\theta' \cdot \to\text{PLA} \, [\text{2DIME}] \cdot b) \quad \text{'He went on to the platform'}$$
$$a' \cdot \to\iota \; +\text{MOV} \cdot (\theta' \cdot \to\text{PLA} \, [\text{3DIME}] \cdot b) \quad \text{'He went into the restaurant'}$$

This relationship is borne out by the following cases of logical implication:

> 'He has gone to the station' implies 'He is at the station'
> 'He has gone on to the platform' implies 'He is on the platform'
> 'He has gone into the restaurant' implies 'He is in the restaurant'.

The specifications of *He ran/walked/drove/etc to the station* are the same as for *He went to the station*, except for the addition of the appropriate feature from the system of '*locomotion*'. This is as it should be, as 'He ran/walked/drove/etc to the station' implies 'He went to the station'. Another verb appearing in this type of context is *get* (*eg: He got to the station*), which so used must have the semantic feature +MOV in its definition. Hence the meaning of *He got to the station* differs, in the presence of the idea of motion, from that of *He got to be at the station*.

Although *at* and *to* are mutually exclusive in their semantic functions, *in* and *on* are frequently used in dynamic contexts, where they are stylistic variants of *into* and *on to*: there is no difference in meaning between *He got on the bus* and *He got on to the bus*. Consequently, there arises, with some verbs, an ambiguity depending on the choice between a static and dynamic interpretation of the preposition:

> *She jumped on the table:*
> (a:+MOV 6LOCO)·→PLA [2DIME]·b
> (*ie* 'She jumped while on the table')

> *She jumped on the table:*
> a'·→ι +MOV 6LOCO·(θ'·→PLA [2DIME]·b)
> (*ie* 'She jumped on to the table').

A similar choice exists for *She fell in the water, She walked on the grass.*

Prepositional phrases of destination, although generally classed as adverbial in grammatical description, do not fit into the semantic pattern which we have associated with adverbial elements: that is, their specifications do not conform to the schema $(X)·s·c$, where X is a downgraded predication and $s·c$ is expressed by an adverbial construction. This difference manifests itself syntactically in an impossibility of initial placement as an initial adjunct with intonational separation from the rest of the clause: **Into the water, she fell down* contrasts with *At the station, she fell down*. For this reason, the dynamic interpretation of *in* is virtually impossible in *In the water, she fell down*. (*Into the water she fell down* is possible as an inversion in a highly literary style, but in this case the adjunct does not coincide with a separate intonation group.)

Many causative verbs, such as *put, send, bring, take, lead*, have 'cause to go' as the basic part of their meaning, and therefore combine with prepositional phrases of destination. As in the case of *walk, run*, etc, there is often a choice here between *in* and *into*, *on* and *on to*:

> *I pushed my sister in the water* is synonymous with *I pushed my sister into the water.*

Here, also, the semantic function of the prepositional phrase inhibits initial syntactic placement: *I pushed my sister in the water while she wasn't looking* strongly recommends the dynamic interpretation of *in*, while on the contrary, *In the water, I pushed my sister while she wasn't looking* enforces the static interpretation 'While we were in the water . . .'.

Commentary

a It is difficult to prescribe, both with verbs of movement and causative verbs, the circumstances under which *on* may replace *on to* and *in* may replace *into*. There seems to be variation among lexical items without any semantic conditioning. Notice, for example, that *The children ran in the garden* and *The baby crawled on the furniture* are not ambiguous in the way just discussed. In other cases, the situation is reversed, and *into* and *on to* are rare or non-existent as alternatives to *in* and *on*: the insertion of *to* in *He placed the map on the table* is only marginally permissible.

b The inability of the destinational phrase to occur in initial position (except for rare literary inversions) in *He went to the station*, etc is an indication of its close syntactic and semantic relationship with the verb, and invites comparison with Verb + Preposition + Complement constructions of the kind (*They*) *looked at the picture*, (*I*) *wondered about your health*, where the verb forms an idiom with the following preposition. One point of similarity is that zero expression of the final element involves omission of the whole adverbial phrase, including the preposition: *He went* has the semantic structure of 'He went to this/that place', just as *He looked* has the semantic structure of 'He looked at this/that'. We are encouraged, therefore, to seek a definition not for *go* on its own, but for *go (to)* (or more fully, for *go (to . . . from . . .)* – see §8.7.2), allowing for the elimination of the prepositional phrase in certain semantically determined circumstances. In that case, with Gruber (1965: 85), we could regard *on to* and *into* as the outcome of expression rules which permute the semantic ordering of '(go) to on' and '(go) to in' respectively. (On the other hand, 'at', as the expressionally unmarked member of the trio, is not expressed at all in the environment of 'to'.) However, this course also leads us to treat *run to*, *walk to*, etc as idioms, and a less tortuous solution, within the present framework, may be to handle the colligation of *go* and *to*, etc, as a question of grammatical concord. That is, *go*, *run*, *walk*, etc, are classified syntactically as "motional verbs", and *to*, *on (to)*, *in (to)*, *from*, etc as "motional prepositions" (cf Gruber, 1965: 88), although they receive the same definitions as the "non-motional" prepositions *at*, *in*, *on*, etc. Then the rule which forbids the co-occurrence of **He stood to the door*, **He is crouching into the chair* is a purely syntactic rule which decrees that motional prepositions should be preceded by motional verbs. Either of these solutions is acceptable in that it enables us to adhere to the rule that lexical definitions do not exceed a cluster of a main predication in extent. In the former solution, *go* is defined $\rightarrow\iota$ +MOV and *at*, *on*, and *in* are defined as in their static use (§8.1.1); in the latter solution, *go* is defined as $\rightarrow\iota$ +MOV, and *to*, *on (to)*, and *in (to)* are assigned the same definitions as the non-motional prepositions *at*, *on*, and *in*. The part of the destinational formula which consists of the definite formator θ' within a rank-shifted predication does not enter into any definition, as it is supplied by the contextual properties of $\rightleftarrows\iota$.

c Some doubt may be felt about the equivalence of *at* and *to*, both of which have been assigned the ascription feature [IDIME], although *to* is sometimes used with nouns which can scarcely occur with *at*: *The gypsies came to England* is far more acceptable than *The gypsies were at England*, for instance. Certainly, *to* has a wider range of application than *at*; yet this can perhaps be attributed to the distancing effect of regarding a place as a destination rather than as a position. It is true that there is something to be said, semantically as well as syntactically, for Gruber's solution of regarding 'on to' as the summation of 'to' and 'on', and 'into' as the summation of 'to' and 'in'; that is, in semantic terms, of regarding 'to' as unmarked for the factor of dimensionality which distinguishes 'on to' from 'into'. On the other hand, more careful consideration leads one to conclude that the meaning of *to* does not logically include those of *on to* and *into*. 'He went into the house', for instance, need not imply

7 + T.S.D.E.

'He went to the house'. One can well imagine someone saying 'He didn't go TO the house – he was there all the time; but it wasn't until we arrived that he went INTO the house' (*ie* 'to' is a separate category, not a conflation of 'on to' and 'into').

d The discussion in this section is not meant to apply to the static use of *go, to,* etc with reference to paths, roads, etc, as in *This is the way to London; This road goes to Timbuktu.* However, it is possible (following the second solution of Comment *b*) to treat the verbs and prepositions in such sentences as *syntactically* motional, even though they are static in meaning. (One cannot say, for instance, *This road* IS *to Timbuktu.*) No difficulty, in any case, is encountered with phrases such as *the bus to London,* which can be interpreted in a sense involving movement as 'The bus which goes to London'.

8.7.2 '*From*', '*off*', *and* '*out of*'
(*Away*) *from, off,* and *out of* simply negate the destination indicated by *to, on to,* and *into* respectively. In this, they duplicate both the forms and semantic functions of *away from, off,* and *out of* used for static position, as discussed in §8.1.2:

$a' \cdot \rightarrow_\iota +\text{MOV} \cdot (\theta' \cdot \sim \rightarrow \text{PLA} \, [\text{1DIME}] \cdot b)$ 'He went (away) from the station' (*ie* 'He came, by motion, to be not at the station').
$a' \cdot \rightarrow_\iota +\text{MOV} \cdot (\theta' \cdot \sim \rightarrow \text{PLA} \, [\text{2DIME}] \cdot b)$ 'He went off the carpet.'
$a' \cdot \rightarrow_\iota +\text{MOV} \cdot (\theta' \cdot \sim \rightarrow \text{PLA} \, [\text{3DIME}] \cdot b)$ 'He went out of the room.'

There is only one trivial difference of expression: *from* can occur on its own in a dynamic context, but only in the combination *away from* in a static context: *He ran from the house* is acceptable, but not *He was from the house* (except in a resultative sense; see §8.8.1).

The double function of these prepositions as static and dynamic in meaning gives rise to the same type of ambiguity, with verbs of movement, as was noted in §8.7.1. *Aircraft were told to fly out of the danger zone* is an illustration: does it mean that aircraft inside the zone were told to leave it, or that those already outside the zone were warned to keep clear?

Every inceptive predication can be regarded in two lights: as a transition *into* a state, or as a transition *out of* an opposite state. Applied to verbs of movement, this means that every utterance containing *go* or a similar verb involves, in a way, a "positive destination" and a "negative destination"; or, in simpler words, every journey has both a point of departure and a point of arrival. A sentence beginning *He went . . .* requires, for complete explicitness, not only a preposition from the positive range *to, on to, into,* but one from the negative range *from, off, out of.* Syntactically, the relationship between the two prepositional phrases of *a went from b to c* is an unusual one, in that the two phrases in some respects behave as a single adjunct. This singularity can be traced to the underlying semantic structure, which is that of two co-ordinated rank-shifted predications:

$$a' \cdot \rightarrow\!\iota \; +\text{MOV} \cdot ((\theta' \cdot \sim\!\rightarrow\!\text{PLA}\,[\text{IDIME}]\cdot b) \; \& \; (\theta' \cdot \rightarrow\!\text{PLA}\,[\text{IDIME}]\cdot c))$$

John cycled from London to Edinburgh might be paraphrased awkwardly but with relevance to the semantic structure: *John by cycling came to be not at London, but at Edinburgh.*[6]

The conjunctive relationship (which is understood in a way similar to that of mathematical logic) can be represented, as above, by an ampersand, or else by a brace, as below:

$$a' \cdot \rightarrow\!\iota \; +\text{MOV} \cdot \begin{cases} (\theta' \cdot \sim\!\rightarrow\!\text{PLA}\,[\text{IDIME}]\cdot b) \\ (\theta' \cdot \rightarrow\!\text{PLA}\,[\text{IDIME}]\cdot c) \end{cases}$$

A parallel case outside the locative sphere is the statement 'John sold the book to Paul', from which we conclude that, after the transaction, the book belonged to Paul, and did not belong to John.

Yet often one or the other, the positive or the negative side of the event, is vague and unexpressed. 'The liquid turned red' does not tell us what colour the liquid was before the change, nor does 'Bill went to the station' tell us where Bill came *from*. For notational purposes, two courses are possible. The inexplicit half of the assertion can be omitted where possible from the specification; that is, one of the two conjoined predications can be regarded as optional. Otherwise, the inexplicit half can be specified in the most general terms as 'from somewhere-or-other' ($\theta' \cdot \sim\!\rightarrow\!\text{PLA} \cdot \varnothing$) or 'to somewhere or other' ($\theta' \cdot \rightarrow\!\text{PLA} \cdot \varnothing$) as the case may be. The empty cluster $\varnothing$ in each of these informationally vacuous predications has zero expression. The first of the two courses will be preferred here; that is, I shall specify the reverse side of a dynamic place relationship only when the explicit meaning of the sentence cannot be represented without it.

It is usual for the dimensionality of the two rank-shifted predications to match, where both are explicit: 'He hurried out of the kitchen into the hall', for example, has [3DIME] in both cases. This is not an invariable rule, however: there is nothing objectionable about mixing [IDIME] with [2DIME] in 'She went from the auditorium on to the stage'.[7]

8.7.3 *The dynamic use of other prepositions*
Once the foregoing analysis of the meanings of *to*, *on to*, *from*, etc is accepted, the description of the dynamic use of other prepositions follows without difficulty. No new systems need be introduced; since the specifications of all prepositional phrases of place (in the non-downgraded form) conform to the pattern $\rightarrow\!\text{PLA} \cdot c$, they merely have to be inserted in

the appropriate part of the formula for destinational meaning, which at its most general is:

$$a' \cdot \rightarrow \iota +\text{MOV } b \cdot \begin{cases} (\theta' \cdot \rightarrow \text{PLA} \cdot c) \\ (\theta' \cdot \sim \rightarrow \text{PLA} \cdot d) \end{cases}$$

The following are dynamic formulae corresponding to those of relative position in §8.2.3 (predictable features such as $\rightarrow$SID are omitted):

$$a' \cdot \rightarrow \iota +\text{MOV} \cdot (\theta' \cdot \rightarrow \text{PLA} \cdot \varnothing \ ''\langle \theta'' \cdot \rightarrow \text{PROX} \cdot \theta'''\langle \theta''' \cdot \leftarrow \text{PLA} \cdot b\rangle\rangle)$$

'a went by b'

$$a' \cdot \rightarrow \iota +\text{MOV} \cdot (\theta' \cdot \rightarrow \text{PLA} \cdot \varnothing \ ''\langle \theta'' \cdot \rightarrow \text{PROX} +\text{VER} \rightarrow \text{PLUS} \cdot \theta'''$$
$$\langle \theta''' \cdot \leftarrow \text{PLA} \cdot b\rangle\rangle)$$

'a went over b'

$$a' \cdot \rightarrow \iota +\text{MOV} \cdot (\theta' \cdot \rightarrow \text{PLA} \cdot \varnothing \ ''\langle \theta'' \cdot \rightarrow \text{PROX} +\text{VER} \leftarrow \text{PLUS} \cdot \theta'''$$
$$\langle \theta''' \cdot \leftarrow \text{PLA} \cdot b\rangle\rangle)$$

'a went under b'

$$a' \cdot \rightarrow \iota +\text{MOV} \cdot (\theta' \cdot \rightarrow \text{PLA} \cdot \varnothing \ ''\langle \theta'' \cdot \rightarrow \text{PROX} +\text{PRI} \rightarrow \text{PLUS} \cdot \theta'''$$
$$\langle \theta''' \cdot \leftarrow \text{PLA} \cdot b\rangle\rangle)$$

'a went in front of b'

$$a' \cdot \rightarrow \iota +\text{MOV} \cdot (\theta' \cdot \rightarrow \text{PLA} \cdot \varnothing \ ''\langle \theta'' \cdot \rightarrow \text{PROX} +\text{PRI} \leftarrow \text{PLUS} \cdot \theta'''$$
$$\langle \theta''' \cdot \leftarrow \text{PLA} \cdot b\rangle\rangle)$$

'a went behind b'

$$a' \cdot \rightarrow \iota +\text{MOV} \cdot (\theta' \cdot \rightarrow \text{PLA} \cdot \varnothing \ ''\langle \theta'' \cdot \rightarrow \text{PROX} -\text{PRI} \rightarrow \text{PLUS} \cdot \theta'''$$
$$\langle \theta''' \cdot \leftarrow \text{PLA} \cdot b\rangle\rangle)$$

'a went to the left of b'

$$a' \cdot \rightarrow \iota +\text{MOV} \cdot (\theta' \cdot \rightarrow \text{PLA} \cdot \varnothing \ ''\langle \theta'' \cdot \rightarrow \text{PROX} -\text{PRI} \leftarrow \text{PLUS} \cdot \theta'''$$
$$\langle \theta''' \cdot \leftarrow \text{PLA} \cdot b\rangle\rangle)$$

'a went to the right of b'

In these specifications, a place 'by b' or 'over b' or 'under b', etc is identified as the destination of a. The feature $\rightarrow$PROX (which depends on $\rightleftarrows$SID) is specified because the destinational use of *over*, *under*, etc, usually seems to include the notion of final proximity to b. For example *He crept behind me* ('and stayed there') or *He rushed in front of me* ('and stayed there') suggests '*close* behind' and '*close* in front'.

It is necessary to add '. . . and stayed there' to the above examples, in order to distinguish the meaning intended in those examples from a more common dynamic interpretation, where *He rushed in front of me* means that he passed in front of me, but did not stop there. This is the dynamic counterpart of the orientational meaning explained in §8.5.3, and it may be called TANGENTIAL meaning, because it implies that the course the moving object takes is firstly towards, then away from, the stationary object or location. The ambiguity of *under*, observed in *The station was under the bridge* (§8.5.3) is reproduced in a far more marked and general form in dynamic contexts. Here are some examples which lend themselves equally well to the tangential as to the destinational interpretation:

> *A mouse scuttled behind the lampstand.*
> *Someone ran to the left of the goal.*
> *The ball rolled under the hedge.*

In all three cases, we are left asking the question 'Did the moving object stay there, or did it continue its journey?'

Commentary

e In addition, of course, the ordinary static meaning of these prepositions can occur with verbs of movement, as we noted in §8.7.1. *A mouse scuttled behind the lampstand* permits the interpretation that the mouse remained behind the lampstand all the while that it was scuttling (see Gruber, 1965: 89). *They marched in front of the barracks* may thus be construed in three different ways: (a) they started elsewhere and ended up in front of the barracks (destinational); (b) they passed in front of the barracks on the way to some other destination (tangential); (c) they started and ended in front of the barracks (static).

For the tangential sense, the verb *pass* is diagnostic; if it is substituted for one of the verbs in the three examples above, the ambiguity is resolved.[8] The preposition *past*, too, is specialised to tangential meaning, just as it is specialised to an orientational meaning in static contexts. This means that *past* can replace *by* in one of its dynamic meanings, but not in the other.

To formalise the tangential meaning of prepositions, it is necessary to make one change to the analysis of orientational meaning in §§8.5.2–3. In the latter, the point of orientation is normally assumed to have the deictic interpretation of 'here'/'there'; but to *The boat went across the river* must be added for full explicitness '. . . from where it was before it started'. The information can be incorporated into the definition of *across* by co-reference, if we use the fully explicit dynamic formula (see §8.7.2), in which the "negative destination" (or point of departure) is specified as well as the "positive destination":

$$a' \cdot \rightarrow \iota \; + \text{MOV} \cdot \begin{cases} (\theta' \cdot \sim \rightarrow \text{PLA} \cdot \varnothing''''') \\ (\theta' \cdot \rightarrow \text{PLA} \cdot \varnothing''\langle\theta'' \cdot +\text{PRI} \leftarrow \text{PLUS} \langle\theta''' \cdot \leftarrow \text{ORI} \cdot \theta'''''\rangle \\ \qquad\qquad [\text{2DIME}] \cdot b\rangle''') \end{cases}$$

'The boat went across the river'

The identity of point of departure with point of orientation is symbolised by $\varnothing''''. . . \theta''''$. By substituting [3DIME] for [2DIME] in this formula, we arrive at the tangential specification for *through* in *He wandered through the fields*. Similar specifications can be provided for *towards* and *past*:

$$a' \cdot \to \iota +\text{MOV} \begin{cases} (\theta' \cdot \sim \to \text{PLA} \cdot \varnothing''') \\ (\theta' \cdot \to \text{PLA} \cdot \varnothing''\langle \theta'' \cdot +\text{PRI} \to \text{PLUS} \langle \theta''' \cdot \leftarrow \text{ORI} \cdot \theta'''' \rangle \cdot b \rangle''') \end{cases}$$

'The boat went towards the harbour'

$$a \cdot \to \iota +\text{MOV} \begin{cases} (\theta' \cdot \sim \to \text{PLA} \cdot \varnothing''') \\ (\theta' \cdot \to \text{PLA} \cdot \varnothing''\langle \theta'' \cdot +\text{PRI} \leftarrow \text{PLUS} \langle \theta''' \cdot \leftarrow \text{ORI} \cdot \theta'''' \rangle \cdot \varnothing'''' \\ \qquad\qquad\qquad \langle \theta'''' \cdot \to \text{PROX} \cdot b \rangle \rangle''') \end{cases}$$

'The boat went past the headland'

Except for the addition of co-reference, the static definition of these prepositions is inserted whole into the second rank-shifted predication. Definitions on the same principle can be given for *over*, *under*, *behind*, etc.

Commentary

f The ambiguity of destinational and tangential senses does not arise in all cases: *He jumped over the fence*, for instance, does not allow the interpretation that his destination was a position vertically above the fence – but this is rather a matter of natural law (*viz* the law of gravity, which does not allow people to stay suspended in mid-air after a jump) rather than a matter of language.

8.8 Static and dynamic meaning

To conclude this survey of place relations, I shall turn to two areas of meaning in which the static and dynamic uses of prepositions are both involved at once.

8.8.1 *Resultative position*

Firstly, prepositions of place can express, in combination with the verb *to be*, RESULTATIVE POSITION, that is, static position resulting from movement. As such, their interpretation is clearly related to the resultative interpretation of the perfective aspect, and in fact, rough paraphrase relationships can be set up as follows:

'The picture is off the wall' = 'The picture has come off the wall'.
'He's just out of prison' = 'He's just come out of prison'.
'"Jonah's Whale" is already over the last fence' = '"Jonah's Whale" has already gone over the last fence'.
'In a second he was beside me' = 'In a second he had come beside me'.

With some prepositions – those associated with negative position and with static orientation – the resultative interpretation is more common than the simple static interpretation; it is, indeed, almost their habitual interpretation with subjects referring to human beings, animals, or mobile objects. *He is across the fence* or *He is through the window* will naturally be construed as 'He has got across/through . . .'. These classes of prepositions are those which are more common in dynamic than in static contexts, and it might be argued that in some sense their meaning is basically dynamic, and only secondarily static. Such a feeling makes sense when we notice that resultative meaning, despite the presence of the verb *to be*, can be most easily expressed by those prepositions syntactically designated "motional". The three prepositions *on to*, *into*, and *from*, which are exclusively motional, can be used unambiguously in a resultative sense in sentences such as:

The speaker was on to the platform already.
The car is just into the garage.
He is from the house.

Because of the basically motional character of expressions of resultative position, adverbials of time such as *already*, *just*, and *yet* strongly suggest resultative meaning.

Commentary

a To is an exception: although a motional preposition, it cannot normally be used in a resultative sense: **He is to the station*. I am informed (by John Lyons), however, that locutions such as *He is away to the shops* are quite common in Scots English.

To specify resultative position, we take the general formula of resultative meaning given in §7.6.4, and adapt it to the field of place relations; that is, we embed within the ordinary static formula a downgraded inceptive predication:

The speaker is on the platform (static position):

$a \cdot {\rightarrow} \text{PLA} \, [\text{2DIME}] \cdot b$

The speaker is on to the platform (resultative position):

$(a'' \cdot {\rightarrow} \text{PLA} \, \langle \theta' \cdot {\leftarrow} \iota + \text{MOV} \cdot \theta'' \rangle \, [\text{DIME}] \cdot b)'$
ie (roughly) 'The speaker is on the platform, having got there'.

As shown by this analysis, a resultative statement logically implies an equivalent "static" statement: if it is true to say 'The speaker is on to the platform', it is also true to say 'The speaker is on the platform'.

With prepositions of orientational meaning, one sign of resultative meaning is the tendency to identify the point of orientation with the point of departure of a completed movement. *They are through the wood* interpreted in the orientational sense described in §8.5.2 means 'They are on the other side of the wood *from here*'; in a resultative sense, it means 'They are on the other side of the wood from where they started'. *We are through the wood* can scarcely be construed without resultative meaning, because with ordinary static orientation, *through* would have deictic implications ('from here') conflicting with those of *we*, which itself entails proximity.

Commentary

b The use of the non-perfective verb *to be* with expressions of resultative meaning is widespread within the English language. The examples in this section
may be compared with the resultative passive of *The house is sold*, and with
numerous prepositional usages of more abstract meaning: *The battle is over; At
last we are out of danger; Food prices are up;* etc.

8.8.2 *'Go' and 'stay'*

Gruber (1965: 80) points out that the relationship between 'stay' or
'remain' on the one hand and 'go' on the other is analogous to the relationship between 'all' and 'some'. In terms of this present description,
this means that the contrast between 'stay' and 'go' is characterised by
an inversion system like the system $1\alpha/2\alpha$ which distinguishes 'all'
from 'some' in §3.5. The characteristics of inversion systems (of which
we shall see more in Chapter 9) are as follows:

[a] They have only two terms.
[b] They occur in the medial cluster of a predication containing a rank-
shifted predication.
[c] There is a special logical relationship between the two terms ("inverses") of the system, such that the following rules of synonymy hold
($1K/2K$ symbolises any inversion system):

$$\begin{cases} a \cdot \sim r \, 1K \cdot (b \cdot s \cdot c) = a \cdot r \, 2K \cdot (b \cdot \sim s \cdot c) \\ a \cdot \sim r \, 2K \cdot (b \cdot s \cdot c) = a \cdot r \, 1K \cdot (b \cdot \sim s \cdot c) \end{cases}$$

In ordinary language, these rules declare that if one changes the position
of the negative and changes the term of the inversion system, the meaning
remains the same (*eg* 'Not all cats like fish' = 'Some cats do not like
fish'; 'He did not go into the room' = 'He stayed out of the room').

Further equivalences are explained with the aid of the rule of negated
negation (§4.3.2). Let us suppose that *s* in the above formula itself contains the negative formator, and may therefore be rewritten, in the first
equation above, as $\sim t$; then:

$$a \cdot \sim r \, 1K \cdot (b \cdot \sim t \cdot c) = a \cdot r \, 2K \cdot (b \cdot \sim \sim t \cdot c)$$
$$= a \cdot r \, 2K \cdot (b \cdot t \cdot c)$$

(by the rule of negated negation)

By this indirect means one shows the synonymy of, for example, *Not all
fathers neglect their children* and *Some fathers look after their children*
(taking *neglect* to be the negative of *look after*).

Returning to the problem of 'stay' and 'go', let us suppose that the
contrast between these two meanings is represented by an inversion
system $1\delta/2\delta$. We must further assume, in this light, that the analysis of
inceptive meaning up to this point has been too simple, and that the inceptive formator system $\rightleftarrows\iota$ has to be re-analysed in terms of two separate

systems, a relative system $\rightleftarrows\mu$ and the inversion system $1\delta/2\delta$, just as the meanings 'all' and 'some' were analysed into two mutually dependent components in §3.5. Thus the combination $\rightarrow\mu\ 2\delta$ henceforth replaces $\rightarrow\iota$. Now it is possible to state the following approximate equivalences:

1 $a'\cdot\rightarrow\mu\ 1\delta\cdot(\theta'\cdot\rightarrow\text{PLA}\ [\text{1DIME}]\cdot b)$ $=8$
  'James stayed at the bus-stop'
2 $a'\cdot\rightarrow\mu\ 2\delta\ +\text{MOV}\cdot(\theta'\cdot\rightarrow\text{PLA}\ [\text{1DIME}]\cdot b)$ $=7$
  'James went to the bus-stop'
3 $a'\cdot\rightarrow\mu\ 1\delta\cdot(\theta'\cdot\sim\rightarrow\text{PLA}\ [\text{1DIME}]\cdot b)$ $=6$
  'James stayed away from the bus-stop'
4 $a'\cdot\rightarrow\mu\ 2\delta\ +\text{MOV}\cdot(\theta'\cdot\sim\rightarrow\text{PLA}\ [\text{1DIME}]\cdot b)$ $=5$
  'James went away from the bus-stop'
5 $a'\cdot\sim\rightarrow\mu\ 1\delta\cdot(\theta'\cdot\rightarrow\text{PLA}\ [\text{1DIME}]\cdot b)$ $=4$
  'James did not stay at the bus-stop'
6 $a'\cdot\sim\rightarrow\mu\ 2\delta\ +\text{MOV}\cdot(\theta'\cdot\rightarrow\text{PLA}\ [\text{1DIME}]\cdot b)$ $=3$
  'James did not go to the bus-stop'
7 $a'\cdot\sim\rightarrow\mu\ 1\delta\cdot(\theta'\cdot\sim\rightarrow\text{PLA}\ [\text{1DIME}]\cdot b)$ $=2$
  'James did not stay away from the bus-stop'
8 $a'\cdot\sim\rightarrow\mu\ 2\delta\ +\text{MOV}\cdot(\theta'\cdot\sim\rightarrow\text{PLA}\ [\text{1DIME}]\cdot b)$ $=1$
  'James did not go away from the bus-stop'

In these formulae, *go* is defined $\rightarrow\mu\ 2\delta\ +\text{MOV}$ and *stay* (or the less collo-quial verb *remain*) as $\rightarrow\mu\ 1\delta$. The former definition involves movement, but having a more general sense, *stay* and *remain* are defined simply $\rightarrow\mu\ 1\delta$, in opposition to *become*: *He remained happy* means 'He didn't become unhappy'; *He stayed alive* means 'He didn't become dead ($=$ die)', etc. In the same way, *He stayed at the bus-stop* means, strictly speaking, 'He didn't get to be away from the bus-stop', as the factor of movement is not involved. There is thus a slight difference of meaning in the state-ments equated above, although in practice they seem to be logically identical.

Commentary
a There is a separate sense of *stay* which has no negative implications and in which *stay* is not a synonym of *remain*: *I stayed with my friends at the Red Lion for a week* (*ie* 'I boarded with them'). The above definition does not cover this use.

Chapter 9

Modality

The meaning of the modal auxiliaries has exercised the minds of many writers on English grammar and semantics, and because of some peculiar difficulties of the subject, it might be doubted whether it is susceptible to the semantic technique of analysis that has been developed in this book. One recent writer, Madeline Ehrman (1966),[1] has avoided a componential approach, preferring the more traditional method of looking for a basic meaning (*Grundbedeutung*) which may be coloured by various "overtones" in various contexts. My own view is that a structural and componential description can go a long way towards explaining the use of these auxiliaries, even though psychological and situational pressures (modesty, politeness, irony, etc) conspire to strengthen or weaken, to widen or narrow, their use in certain contexts. To study the "overtones" without taking note of the underlying logical relationships is rather like investigating the anatomy of the human body while overlooking the fact that it has a bone structure. One may well put matters round the other way, and say that it only becomes possible to discuss psychological overtones (what we might call the "pragmatics" of usage)[2] once the logical structures have been taken into account. It is to the "bone structure" of modal auxiliary usage that I shall address myself in this chapter; the psychological connotations will only be dealt with incidentally, in the commentary sections. I shall mainly confine myself to a discussion of some meanings of the six auxiliaries *can, may, have to, must, will,* and *shall*. (*Have to,* whether or not it is grammatically classed as an auxiliary verb, must be treated as equivalent to the other items in the list for semantic purposes.)

9.1 Some meanings of some modal auxiliaries

The first stage of this discussion is to set out, as in a dictionary, the meanings which will form a focus of attention. The tool of analysis to be used for demonstrating different meanings will be that of paraphrase: each example will be followed by a semantic gloss designed to bring out the distinctiveness of its meaning.

Commentary

a There are also formal criteria for distinguishing the various meanings. *May* in the sense of 'possibility', for example, differs from *may* in the sense of 'permission' through its (1) lack of a question form; (2) lack of a contracted negative form *mayn't*; (3) possession of perfective and continuous tenses *may have gone, may be going*, etc.

MAY

1 'PERMISSION'
You may smoke in here. ('I permit you to smoke . . .')
May I open the window? ('Will you permit me to open . . .?')
2 'POSSIBILITY' (not in questions)
It may be raining in Devon. ('It is possible that it is . . .')
He may recover. ('It is possible that he will recover')

CAN

1 'PERMISSION' (in colloquial English, familiar style)
You can smoke in here. ('You are permitted to smoke . . .')
Can I open the window? ('Am I permitted to open . . .?')
2 'POSSIBILITY' (especially in negatives and questions)
Electricity can kill. ('It is possible for electricity to kill')
Can I be dreaming? ('Is it possible that I am dreaming?')
3 'CAPABILITY, ABILITY'
Our team can easily beat your team.
('Our team is capable of easily beating your team')
He can speak six languages.
('He is capable of /knows how to . . .')

MUST

1 'OBLIGATION'
You must be back by ten. ('You are obliged to be back . . .')
I must go now. ('I am obliged to go now')
2 '(LOGICAL) NECESSITY'
I must be dreaming. 'It is necessarily the case that . . .',
    ie 'No other explanation is possible than that . . .')
There must be some mistake. ('It is necessarily the case . . .')

HAVE TO

1 'OBLIGATION'
You have to be back by ten. ('You are obliged to be back . . .')
She'll have to sleep in the kitchen. ('She'll be obliged to . . .')

2 '(LOGICAL) NECESSITY'
Even the best of us has to die. ('It is necessary that even the best of us
should die')
Someone had to be the loser. ('It was necessary for someone to be the
loser')

WILL
1 'WEAK VOLITION, WILLINGNESS'
Who will lend me a cigarette? ('Who is willing to . . .?')
He will do anything for money. ('He is willing to . . .')
2 'STRONG VOLITION, INSISTENCE' (not common; *will* is stressed)
He will go swimming in dangerous waters. ('He insists on . . .')
Why will you keep banging that door? ('Why do you insist . . .?')

SHALL
1 'SPEAKER'S WILLINGNESS' (not common)
He shall get a polite answer if he is patient. ('I am willing to give him . . .')
Be a good dog, and you shall have a bone. ('. . . I am willing to let you
have a bone')
2 'SPEAKER'S INSISTENCE' (not common)
You shall obey my orders. ('I insist that you obey . . .')
No one shall stop me. ('I insist that no one stop me')

Commentary
b We shall ignore, for the purpose of this discussion, the use of *will* to indicate
habitual or characteristic behaviour (*A lion will rarely attack a human being*) or
to announce a decision (*Tonight we'll celebrate!*); also, the use of *will* and *shall*
to refer to future happenings (see §7.4.5) without any implication of volition
(*This time next week I shall/will be in Chile*).

It is clear that the listed senses of these six auxiliaries are related to one
another in various ways, and the problem to which we now turn is that of
determining how they resemble and contrast with one another. The
following diagram summarises these relationships visually:

'Permission'	MAY (1) CAN (1)	MUST (1) HAVE TO (1)	'Obligation'
'Possibility'	MAY (2) CAN (2)	MUST (2) HAVE TO (2)	'(Logical) Necessity'
'Willingness'	WILL (1) SHALL (1)	WILL (2) SHALL (2)	'Insistence'

(The third sense of *can* will be ignored for the present.)

Items shown sharing the same box of this diagram have similar, but not absolutely identical meanings. Later, the more or less slight differences between them will be considered. For the present, however, let us turn to the more important question of the contrast between the left-hand boxes and the corresponding right-hand boxes of the diagram; that is, to the nature of the relationship between 'permission' and 'obligation', between 'possibility' and 'necessity', and between 'willingness' and 'insistence'. In each of these three instances, the contrast is of the kind which has been noted elsewhere in this study as a relation between "inverses": in the cases of 'all' and 'some' (§3.5) and of 'go' and 'stay' (§8.8.2), the principle of inversion systems, roughly worded, is: "if one term is substituted for the other and the position of the negative is changed, the utterance undergoes no change of meaning". This rule also applies to the three oppositions at present under scrutiny, as we see from the following equations:

These lines can't be by Shakespeare:

'It is not possible for these lines to be by Shakespeare' = 'It is necessary for them not to be by Shakespeare'.

Students may not earn money in the vacation:

'Students are not permitted to earn money in the vacation' = 'Students are obliged not to earn money in the vacation'.

I won't interfere:

'I am willing not to interfere' = 'I do not insist on interfering'.

We may therefore conclude that the contrasts in meaning between *can* and *have to*, *may* and *must*, etc, are to be formally represented by that type of system previously called an "inversion system". Let us now, however, give attention to each semantic contrast one by one, so as to assign a precise semantic description to the types of sentence just illustrated.

9.2 Agency and authority

The first topic to be considered is that of the opposition 'permission'/ 'obligation'; that is, the semantic dimension which may be designated 'AUTHORITY'. A discussion of 'authority', in turn, presupposes some mention of the related notion of 'agency', since a number of verbs (including *let*, *allow*, *permit*, and *make*) can be used to convey either the one or the other meaning. Agency I take to be a particular instance of the broad concept of causation: it is namely a limitation of that notion to human causes.[3] Authority is different from causation, since if one is permitted to perform a certain action, it does not necessarily follow that that action is performed. In other terms, in a situation where authority is exercised, the person under authority has a choice of action; but in a situation of causation, no choice is possible for the "causee".

This difference may be clarified by an example:

(a) *By turning the tap, he allows the water to escape from the tank.*
(b) *People are allowed to smoke in this room.*

From the first sentence, we infer that water actually does escape from the tank; but from the second, we do not know whether smoking takes place or not, because there is always a possibility that no one takes advantage of the permission.

Commentary

a The view that 'authority' leaves a choice of action appears to be challenged in some examples, particularly examples of event predications in the past: 'He allowed me to borrow his car' seems to compel the inference 'and moreover I did borrow it'. This phenomenon arises in other spheres of modality: for instance, *was able to* (as opposed to *is able to*) usually carries an implication of fulfilment: *Despite the delay, he was able to catch his train* is generally understood to mean 'He had the ability to catch it, and what is more did so'. However, the actual circumstances determining the possibility or otherwise of this interpretation are obscure, and may remain so for the purposes of this study.

Although the verbs *permit*, *oblige*, and *compel* seem to lend themselves to the 'authority' sense, and *let* and *make* to the causative sense, one cannot say that either interpretation is ruled out by these verbs. The negative items *prevent...from* (='not allow') and *forbid* (='not allow') are, on the other hand, restricted respectively to the senses of 'causation' and 'authority'. The modal auxiliaries *may*, *must*, *can*, and *have to* likewise occur in the 'authority' sense only.

Another difference between the 'causation' and 'authority' interpretation is evident from examples like these:

The damp weather caused rust to attack the metal parts.
The damp weather caused the metal parts to be attacked by rust.

The boys compelled Mike to kiss Joan.
The boys compelled Joan to be kissed by Mike.

Between the first pair there is no difference of cognitive meaning, and their meaning may therefore be represented by the same formula, which conforms to the general scheme $a \cdot \rightarrow$CAU $b \cdot (X)$. $\rightarrow$CAU here symbolises the relative feature of causation, and (X) symbolises the rank-shifted predication 'the metal parts were attacked by rust', which may be expressed indifferently by an active or passive infinitive construction. The second two sentences, however, are not synonymous, since the substitution of the active for the passive construction indicates that a different person is under duress: in the former sentence, it is Mike who is the "compellee", but in the second it is Joan. This difference of meaning is also evident in sentences which express compulsion or obligation by means of modal auxiliaries: *Mike had to kiss Joan* and *Joan had to be kissed by Mike* clearly differ in the same respect as the earlier sentences.

This problem is very like that encountered in §3.6, where it was observed that *John is getting to behave like his young sister* and *His young sister is getting to behave like John* are not synonymous sentences. The solution will be the same as that taken in the case of inceptive meaning: each statement of the form 'Mike had to kiss Joan' will be analysed into a main predication and a rank-shifted predication, and the observed choice of meaning will be provided for by a co-referential link between the terminal cluster of the main predication and one of the terminal clusters of the rank-shifted predication:

$$a' \cdot \rightarrow \text{AUT } c \cdot (\theta' \cdot \rightarrow r \cdot b) \quad \text{'Mike had to kiss Joan.'}$$
$$b' \cdot \rightarrow \text{AUT } c \cdot (\theta' \cdot \leftarrow r \cdot a) \quad \text{'Joan had to be kissed by Mike.'}$$

Here the feature →AUT merely symbolises the idea of 'having to' without specifying an agent of compulsion. To introduce the factor of agency conveyed by the verbs *compel*, *oblige*, etc we must add another stage of rank-shifting, as follows:

$$d \cdot \rightarrow \text{CAU } (a' \cdot \rightarrow \text{AUT } c \cdot (\theta' \cdot \rightarrow r \cdot b))$$
'The boys compelled Mike to kiss Joan'
$$d \cdot \rightarrow \text{CAU } (b' \cdot \rightarrow \text{AUT } c \cdot (\theta' \cdot \leftarrow r \cdot a))$$
'The boys compelled Joan to be kissed by Mike'.

By this method of analysis, the meaning of *compel* is broken down into two relationships →CAU and →AUT: it is equated with 'cause ... to have to'.

Commentary
b Compel, with similar items, therefore belongs to the class of verbs which have discontinuous definitions (see n. 20, p. 270). In this respect it is like other causative verbs: *give* ('let ... have'), *drop* ('let ... fall'), *lay* ('cause ... to lie'), etc.

9.2.1 *Causation*
The system of '*causation*' must now be formally described:

SYSTEM I '*causation*'
$$\begin{cases} (x) \rightarrow \text{CAU } (y) & \text{'}(x) \text{ causes } (y)\text{'} \\ (x) \leftarrow \text{CAU } (y) & \text{'}(x) \text{ is caused by } (y)\text{'} \end{cases}$$
Class of system: relative
Contextual properties: →CAU $(X + \psi)$ (see §9.2.2 below)
Logical properties: asymmetric, irreflexive, transitive

Under the heading of contextual properties, it is noted that →CAU must be followed by a rank-shifted predication.

Commentary

c When the verb *cause* is followed by a direct object, the noun head is abstract and expresses a predication: *eg: He caused difficulty* (= 'He caused things to be difficult') is meaningful, but not **He caused the table.*

The element preceding →CAU is completely unspecified: it may be a cluster specifying a human agency, or a non-human, even inanimate cause. It is also possible for the preceding element as well as the following to be a rank-shifted predication, in which case →CAU is generally expressed by *because* or some other causative conjunction.

The difference between "weak causation" (expressed by *let, allow*, etc) and "strong causation" (expressed by *make, compel*, etc) is represented by the inversion system $1\pi/2\pi$, which will be more fully discussed below. The causative definition of *let* and its synonyms is thus →CAU 1π, and that of *make* and its synonyms is →CAU 2π. It is evident that *allow* and *compel* are semantic "inverses" from the cognitive synonymy of sentence pairs such as *The high wall did not allow the prisoners to escape* and *The high wall compelled the prisoners not to escape.*

The system of '*causation*' is not necessarily accompanied by a feature of the inversion system $1\pi/2\pi$: there is a neutral idea of causation, perhaps expressed by the verb *cause* itself, and certainly expressed by such a verb as *give*, which may mean 'let ... have' or 'make ... have' according to context.

9.2.2 *Actuality*

The feature $+\psi$ specified in the contextual properties of ⇄CAU above is one member of a formator system of '*actuality*':

SYSTEM 2 '*actuality*'
$$\begin{cases} +\psi & \text{'actual, real'} \\ -\psi & \text{'non-actual, unreal, hypothetical'} \end{cases}$$
Class of system: binary taxonomic, formator
Special conditions:
   (a) Members of the 'actuality' system only occur in medial clusters.
   (b) The rule of implication [E] (§2.8.2) only operates in the event of both predications containing $+\psi$.

The formator $+\psi$ is introduced at this point to explain the already observed difference between the notion of 'causation' and the notion of 'authority'. 'Causation' guarantees the fulfilment of the happening caused, whereas 'authority' does not guarantee the fulfilment of the happening authorised. Put more formally:

$a \cdot \rightarrow$CAU $b \cdot (X)$ implies X
(*eg* 'He showed me the picture' implies 'I saw the picture')

$a \cdot \rightarrow$AUT $b \cdot (X)$ does not imply X
(*eg* 'You are allowed to buy the picture' does not imply 'You (will) buy the picture')

The implication relationship is signalled formally by a contextual redundancy rule which assigns the feature $+\psi$ ('actual') to the medial cluster of the rank-shifted predication in the case of $\rightleftarrows$CAU, but not in the case of $\rightleftarrows$AUT. This difference of interpretation is found in many verbal definitions in English: *see*, *know*, and *discover*, for example, are like *cause*:

'I saw him cross the street' implies 'He crossed the street'.
'I know he has gone' implies 'He has gone'.
'I discovered him working' implies 'He was working'.

We must suppose, therefore, that the definition of each of these verbs contains a relative feature $\rightarrow$R which assigns, by contextual redundancy rule, the feature $+\psi$ to the following predication; *want*, *believe*, and *ask*, on the other hand, are like *allow* in its authorisation sense:

'I wanted him to help me' does not imply 'He helped me'.
'I believe he has gone' does not imply 'He has gone'.
'I asked him to leave' does not imply 'He left'.

From what has so far been said, the formator $+\psi$ is to be associated with a special implication rule as follows:

$a \cdot r \cdot (b \cdot s + \psi \cdot c)$ implies $b \cdot s \cdot c$

It will be seen, however, that this implication relation may in any case be established with the help of the rule of subordination (§4.3.3):

$a \cdot \rightleftarrows r \cdot (b \cdot s + \psi \cdot c) = (b \cdot s + \psi \langle \theta' \cdot \rightleftarrows r \cdot a \rangle \cdot c)'$

The right-hand formula thus implies $b \cdot s \cdot c$ (by rule [E] of §2.8.2); therefore the left-hand formula also implies $b \cdot s \cdot c$.

Thus there is no need to state a new rule of implication applying to $+\psi$: all that need be supplied is a restriction on the rule of subordination as stated in §4.3.3. It would appear from the above discussion that this restriction should be in the form of a requirement that the rank-shifted predication $b \cdot s \cdot c$ should contain, in its medial cluster, the feature $+\psi$, so as to prevent the theory from hypothesising an implication relation between (for example) 'I asked him to leave' and 'He left'. In fact, however, it is better to ensure the same outcome by limiting not the rule of subordination, but the rule of implication, rule [E] of §2.8.2, in the manner stated under the heading of system 2. That is, rule [E] as amended should read: "one predication $a \cdot r \cdot b$ implies another predication $a \cdot s \cdot b$, only if (i) r is logically included in s, and (ii) r and s both contain $+\psi$".

The reason for applying the restriction to the rule of implication rather than to the rule of subordination is twofold. First, it is useful, for the purpose of expression rules, to allow the operation of the rule of subordination in circumstances where the truth of the rank-shifted predication is not guaranteed: *can* in the sense of possibility, for instance, may by this means be given a definition included within a medial cluster (see §9.4.2), corresponding conveniently to the verbal group in syntax, even though the assertion 'All expert drivers can make mistakes' does not imply 'All expert drivers make mistakes'. Second, the formator $+\psi$ is of wider application than has so far been suggested: it is necessary to have such a feature, apart from present considerations, to distinguish between main predications "in the indicative mood" (*ie* those that involve commitment in terms of truth or falsehood), and those, such as commands and wishes ('God bless you', 'Damn that broken window-catch!', etc), for which truth and falsehood are an irrelevance. In this light, it is not merely rule [E], but every implication rule, that has to be limited to pairs of assertions containing $+\psi$.

Commentary

d This does not mean, however, that $+\psi$ is the marker of predications which have the status of assertions. There are assertions which do not contain $+\psi$ (*eg* hypothetical assertions such as 'If that stone were removed, the whole building would collapse'): there are also predications which contain $+\psi$ but which are not assertions (*eg* "indicative" questions such as 'Will it collapse?', in contrast to "hypothetical" questions such as 'Would it collapse?').

In English, there are no general rules determining the syntactic expression of an 'actual' predication (one containing $+\psi$) or of a neutral predication (one containing neither $+\psi$ nor $-\psi$). For rank-shifted predications, expression rules are tied to classes of verbs, or even to individual verbal items. It seems (at least in my own usage) as if *like* followed by a gerund clause belongs to the 'actual' class, whereas *like* followed by an infinitival clause belongs to the class of neutral actuality. That is to say, 'I like him staying at home' implies 'He stays at home', whereas 'I like him to stay at home' does not. If this observation is generally valid, it helps to explain why the gerund construction cannot be used with a hypothetical main clause: *I'd like him to stay at home* makes sense as an English sentence, but not **I'd like him staying at home*. In other examples, such as that of the main clause *It's lucky . . .* , the presence of the meaning 'actual' is signalled by a *that*-clause: *It's lucky to see a black cat* contrasts with *It's lucky that I saw you*.

Discussion of the 'hypothetical' formator $-\psi$ will be postponed until §9.7.

9.2.3 *Constraint*

The ground has now been cleared sufficiently to enable us to look at the properties of the formator system $1\pi/2\pi$ which distinguishes 'permission' from 'obligation':

SYSTEM 3 *'constraint'*

$\begin{cases} 1\pi & \text{'weak constraint' } (eg \text{ 'permission')} \\ 2\pi & \text{'strong constraint' } (eg \text{ 'obligation')} \end{cases}$

Class of system: inversion, formator, attributive
Contextual properties: $+\psi\, 2\pi\, \{(X +\psi)\}$

This system is set up for the purpose of explaining the "inverse" relationships of meaning which give rise to the equations stated at the close of §9.1: *eg* 'Students are not permitted to earn money in the vacation' = 'Students are obliged not to earn money in the vacation'. If 'permission' is symbolised →AUT 1π and 'obligation' →AUT 2π, it can be shown, by the general rule applying to inversion systems (see §§3.5 and 8.8.2), that these two statements are equivalent:

$$a' \cdot \sim \to \text{AUT}\ 1\pi \cdot (\theta' \cdot r \cdot b) = a' \cdot \text{AUT}\ 2\pi \cdot (\theta' \cdot \sim r \cdot b)$$

The system of *'constraint'* will also distinguish 'possibility' from '(logical) necessity' and 'willingness' from 'insistence', and so can be used to demonstrate the parallel relationships between these concepts.

The contextual property of 2π (its attribution, when combined with $+\psi$, of 'actuality' to the rank-shifted predication) is needed to account for the following relationships:

'He is compelled to work for a small wage' implies 'He works for a small wage'
'I insist that he stay here' implies 'He stays here'
'It is necessarily the case that changes are being made' implies 'Changes are being made'.

That is to say that whoever asserts 'He is compelled to X', 'I insist on X', or 'It is necessarily the case that X' speaks with a full sense of certainty of X's occurrence. Hence the deviance of the following statements:

'He is compelled to work for a small wage, but he doesn't.'
'I insist on his staying here, but he doesn't.'
'It is necessarily the case that changes are being made, but they aren't.'

With event predications, the implication is often that the guaranteed happening will take place in the future.

Commentary

e The contextual redundancy rule of system 3 is theoretically permissible in so far as system 3 is an attributive system (see §8.6), but it is not of the kind generally allowed for, since the rule is conditioned not by a single feature, but by a combination of two features. This could simply be dismissed as an idiosyncrasy of 2π as a formator (since formators are allowed to have idiosyncrasies). In fact, however, it is not anomalous at all, but an instance of a general principle governing the actuality of rank-shifted predications. The principle may be stated as follows: "a rank-shifted predication cannot be actual unless the predication which contains it is also actual"; *ie* in notational terms, $a \cdot r \cdot (b \cdot s + \psi \cdot c)$ is not a possible formula unless r itself contains $+\psi$. The principle may be illustrated by reference to the system of 'causation' $\rightleftarrows$CAU. According to the analysis of this system in §9.2.2, the assignment of actuality to the following predication is unconditional; but further thought will show that this is wrong, and that the system of '*causation*', like the system of '*constraint*', only assigns actuality in cases where the main predication itself contains that feature. Let us consider the two sentences *She makes him work hard* and *It needs a bomb to make him work hard*. In the first, we make the inference 'He works hard', whereas in the second we do not. Assuming that the definition of *make* here contains the feature →CAU, we may attribute the difference between the two sentences to the presence of the feature $+\psi$ in the "indicative mood" of the finite verb *makes*, and its absence from the infinitive *to make*. The same point could be made about any other verb attributing actuality. The conclusion is that no contextual redundancy rule of the form →R $\{(X + \psi)\}$ functions unless the feature →R is itself accompanied by the actuality formator.

9.2.4 *Authority*

The properties of the system of '*authority*', formally stated, are as follows:

SYSTEM 4 '*authority*'

$$\begin{cases} (x) \rightarrow \text{AUT}(y) & \text{'}(x) \text{ has permission/is obliged to } (y)\text{'} \\ (x) \leftarrow \text{AUT}(y) & \text{'}(y) \text{ has permission/is obliged to } (x)\text{'} \end{cases}$$

Class of system: relative
Contextual properties: $\{+\text{PERS}\} \rightarrow \text{AUT} \{(\theta' \cdot r \cdot b)\}$
Logical properties: asymmetric, irreflexive, intransitive
Dependence rule: AUT depends on π

Certain differences between this system and the system of 'causation' (§9.2.1) have been anticipated already. $\rightleftarrows$AUT does not attribute actuality to the following predication; instead, it is a contextual property of this system that →AUT is followed by a rank-shifted predication tied by co-reference to the preceding element, which must be a cluster referring to a person (on ±PERS, see §9.5.1). Any formula containing →AUT therefore has to be of the general form $a' \cdot \rightarrow \text{AUT } b \cdot (\theta' \cdot r \cdot b)$ or of an equivalent form resulting from the rule of subordination.

Commentary

f Here, as in Part 1 of this study, it is notationally convenient to state rules in a form which applies to two-place predications, letting it be understood that similar formulae could be provided for one-place predications.

g The contextual redundancy rule above is of a kind mentioned under (d), p. 64, and is one that has to be allowed for in the theory, as it occurs elsewhere in connection with quantification (§3.5), where it applies to the system $\rightleftarrows o$, and in connection with inceptive meaning (see §§3.6, 8.8.2), where it applies to the system $\rightleftarrows \mu$. A further example of the same kind is the relative system expressed in the verbs *try* and *attempt*: it is possible to speak of 'attempting to win the election', but not (for example) of 'attempting for his friend to win the election'. That is, the subject of *try* and the implicit subject of the infinitive have to be referentially identified.

A further difference between the system of '*authority*' and the system of '*causation*' is that there is no neutral ground in the language between 'permission' and 'obligation', as there is between 'letting' and 'making' in the causative sense. This difference is conveyed by the dependence rule for system 4.

The auxiliaries *can* and *have to*, in so far as they express simple permission and obligation, may be defined:

can: $\rightarrow$ AUT $+\psi$ 1π 'have permission to'
have to: $\rightarrow$ AUT $+\psi$ 2π 'be obliged to'

On account of the special contextual redundancy rule associated with the combination $+\psi$ 2π, a sentence containing *can* in this sense is additionally distinguished in meaning from an equivalent sentence containing *have to* by the feature of 'actuality' in the rank-shifted predication:

$a' \cdot \rightarrow$ AUT $+\psi$ $1\pi \cdot (\theta' \cdot r \cdot b)$ 'You can leave your car here.'
$a' \cdot \rightarrow$ AUT $+\psi$ $2\pi \cdot (\theta' \cdot r \cdot +\psi \cdot b)$ 'You have to leave your car here.'

The presence of $+\psi$ in the rank-shifted predication of the latter formula indicates the speaker's feeling of conviction that the rule will be observed. 'You have to leave your car here' carries the supposition '. . . and I fully count on your doing so'. In this respect, the meaning of *have to* differs from the auxiliary complex *ought to*, which is also used in a sense of obligation:

'You ought to leave your car here' does not imply 'You (will) leave your car here'.

In other words, 'ought to' allows for the possibility that the constraining authority will be disobeyed. A definition taking account of this fact can be provided easily enough by omitting the actuality formator from the definition of *have to*:

ought to: $\rightarrow$ AUT 2π

As 2π is not now accompanied by $+\psi$, the contextual rule assigning $+\psi$ to the following predication no longer applies. *Should* may be used synonymously with *ought to* in this sense; both auxiliaries may, however, be additionally used in the sense of 'necessity' (see §9.4.1).

Commentary

h For 'possibility', there is no contrast of the kind that exists between 'ought to' and 'have to', since in any case there is no assignment of actuality to the following predication. The question of whether to add $+\psi$ to the definition of *can* is a vacuous one from the point of view of logical consequences. Nevertheless, the feature $+\psi$ is included in the meaning of *can*, because clearly 'can' is the inverse of 'have to' rather than of 'ought to'. In any case, $+\psi$ is associated with constructions containing finite verbs in the "indicative mood", and because *can* is paraphrasable by such a construction (*has/have permission to*) it must receive the same semantic specification.

May and *must*, as auxiliaries of permission and obligation, sometimes differ slightly in meaning from *can* and *have to* as defined above. This difference, however, will not be dealt with until §9.5.2.

Now definitions of the following causative verbs (in their 'authority' sense) may be given:

allow, let, permit: →CAU $+\psi\cdot($ . . . →AUT 1π
compel, make, oblige: →CAU $+\psi\cdot($ . . . →AUT 2π

These are discontinuous definitions of the kind mentioned in n. 20, p. 270; the gap indicated by . . . is to be filled by a terminal cluster referring to the person or persons "under authority".

Commentary

i It is well known that *can* in the sense of 'permission' has established itself in English usage against the entrenched resistance of generations of pedagogues. As a result its occurrence is limited mainly to colloquial, if not familiar discourse. An ironic extension of this meaning may, however, be detected in sentences such as *If you don't like it you can lump it; You can forget about your holiday.* Such utterances are disparaging in tone and have a stronger import than is expected with *can*: instead of merely permitting a course of action, they strongly recommend it. Perhaps, however, we may still treat these as instances of the 'permissive' meaning of *can*, by reading them as sarcastic offers of leave for the listener to do something that he knows he cannot avoid.

9.3 Volition

An account has so far been given of only one of the major contrasts on the box-diagram on p. 204, that between 'permission' and 'obligation'; but we may now proceed to the other oppositions with very little addition to the descriptive apparatus already provided. The contrast between 'willingness' (weak volition) and 'insistence' (strong volition) is the first to be considered.

We have noted earlier the application of the inversion system $1\pi/2\pi$ to the concepts of "weak" and "strong" volition. The definitions of the verbal expressions *be willing* and *insist* are in fact the same as those of *can* and *have to* above, except for the replacement of →AUT by a feature symbolising 'volition':

> *be willing:* →VOL 1π
> *insist:* →VOL 2π

These specifications reflect the clear analogy between this pair of terms and *can* and *have to*: 'willingness' denotes a yielding to someone else's will, and 'insistence' imposing of the will on someone else, just as submission of authority and imposition of authority are represented in the ideas of 'permission' and 'obligation'.

The characteristics of the system of '*volition*' are these:

SYSTEM 5 '*volition*'
$$\begin{cases} (x) \rightarrow \text{VOL } (y) & \text{`}(x) \text{ wishes } (y)\text{'} \\ (x) \leftarrow \text{VOL } (y) & \text{`}(x) \text{ is wished by } (y)\text{'} \end{cases}$$
Class of system: relative
Contextual properties: $\{+\text{ANIM}\} \rightarrow \text{VOL } \{(X)\}$
Logical properties: asymmetric, irreflexive, intransitive

There are three main points to notice about this system:

1 ⇄VOL allows for neutral ground between the concepts of 'willingness' and 'insistence': the feature →VOL on its own is expressed, in various syntactic contexts and various styles of English, by the verbs *want*, *wish* and *desire*.

Commentary
a The verb *want*, in apparent violation of the contextual properties of this system, can have a concrete object: *I want a new coat*, etc; but *want* so used must be interpreted 'want to have', and is therefore not definable by the feature →VOL on its own.

---

2 As with ⇄CAU, there is no necessary co-referential link between the initial cluster and the rank-shifted predication: it is possible to say 'I am willing FOR HIM to do it' and 'I insist ON HIM doing it', as well as 'I am willing to do it' and 'I insist on doing it'. This same choice is also evident in the two constructions 'I want him to do it' and 'I want to do it'.

3 Like ⇄AUT, system 5 does not attribute 'actuality' to the following rank-shifted predication (although actuality is entailed by the meaning

of 'insistence' – –→VOL 2π – through the contextual property of 2π). In syntax, this neutral actuality is signalled by the occurrence of a subjunctive verbal group in the *that*-clause following *be willing* and *insist*:

> *I am willing that he (should) be appointed.*
> *I insist that he (should) be appointed.*

But not:

> **I am willing that he is appointed.*

(*I insist that he is appointed* is, it is true, a possible English sentence, but only if *insist* is understood in a different way, as a verb of assertion.)

As the following are paraphrases of sentences containing the auxiliary *will*:

> *He is willing to help you* (= 'He will help you')
> *He insists on banging the door* (= 'He will bang the door')

the following must be definitions of *will* in the respective senses of 'be willing' and 'insist':

> *will:* →VOL $+\psi$ $1\pi\cdot(\theta'$ 'be willing'
> *will:* →VOL $+\psi$ $2\pi\cdot(\theta'$ 'insist'

(The actuality formator which occurs in these definitions arises from the "indicative" factor which is added to the neutral lexical definitions of *be willing* and *insist*.) These definitions occur in specifications of the following form:

> $a'\cdot$→VOL $+\psi$ $1\pi\cdot(\theta'\cdot r\cdot b)$ 'He will help you.'
> $a'\cdot$→VOL $+\psi$ $2\pi\cdot(\theta'\cdot r +\psi\cdot b)$ 'He will bang the door.'

As we see, *will* is only synonymous with *be willing* or *insist* if the initial clusters of the main and rank-shifted predications are indicated by co-reference; *ie* (in syntactic terms) if the subject of *will* and the implicit subject of the following non-finite verb are the same.

Commentary

b The above definitions of *will* violate the condition that definitions should fall within the scope of a cluster in a main predication. If we wish to preserve this principle, however, we may do so by substituting equivalent definitions consisting of downgraded predications: $\langle\theta''\cdot$ ←VOL $1\pi\cdot\theta'\rangle$ and $\langle\theta''\cdot$ ←VOL $2\pi\cdot\theta'\rangle$. To show the equivalence of these to the definitions already given, it is necessary to go through the following steps of deduction:

$$a'\cdot\text{→VOL } 1\pi\cdot(\theta'\cdot r\cdot b) = (\theta'\cdot r \langle\theta''\cdot\text{←VOL } 1\pi\cdot a'\rangle\cdot b)''$$
(rule of subordination, §4.3.3)
$$= (a\cdot r \langle\theta''\cdot\text{←VOL } 1\pi\cdot a\rangle\cdot b)''$$
(rule of co-reference, §4.3.1)
$$= (a'\cdot r \langle\theta''\cdot\text{←VOL } 1\pi\cdot\theta'\rangle\cdot b)''$$
(rule of co-reference)

c *Will* meaning 'insist' is always stressed, and cannot be contracted to '*ll*. The form '*ll* can therefore be used in only one volitional sense, that of 'willingness'.

d The strong volitional sense of *will* is not of common occurrence, and perhaps this may be explained by reference to the pungent emotive and attitudinal connotations of the concept of 'insistence'. In a sentence such as *I 'will marry her*, with a first-person subject, *will* carries strong overtones of obstinacy and petulance; whereas with a second-person or third-person subject (*eg: You 'will interfere; He 'will drive too fast*) *will* tends to underline the exasperation of the speaker in the face of somebody else's wilfulness. In no circumstance can a sentence containing strong volitional *will* be emotively neutral.

9.4 Possibility and (logical) necessity

The system of '*constraint*' $1\pi/2\pi$ may be applied equally well to the meanings of possibility and necessity, as to those of volition and authority. To see this, we note:

1 That 'possible' and 'necessary' are "inverses":

'It is not possible that he is here' =
'It is necessarily the case that he is not here'
'It is not necessarily the case that he is away' =
'It is possible that he is not away'.

2 That 'necessity' guarantees the truth of the rank-shifted assertion (and may therefore be represented by the feature 2π):

'It is necessarily the case that he is away' implies
'He is away'.

Commentary

a In the above, I have used *It is necessarily the case that* as an equivalent to *must*, rather than simply *It is necessary that*. The adjective *necessary* and the noun *necessity* cause some difficulty in paraphrase, because they are frequently used in senses which do not exactly correspond to the sense at present under consideration. The use of *must* and *have to* we are to have in mind in the present section are those which convey the certainty of logical inference. For example, the following rational process may be supposed to lie behind the remark *That must be my wife*, said by a man who has just heard the telephone ring: 'My wife said she would phone at this time – I have just heard the phone – therefore, my wife is phoning now'. *Must* and *have to* are not used of facts known by direct observation, but of those known by logical assumption. This factor of indirect knowledge has the effect of weakening the meaning of 'necessity', in certain conversational contexts, to what is effectively an expression of uncertainty: *You must be tired*. Notice, also, the ironic weakening of *must* in sentences like *If you must smoke, please use an ash-tray*. One might interpret this, reading the speaker's thoughts: 'If it is necessary for you to smoke (but of course smoking isn't a necessity, it is merely a vice which you could break if you wanted to). . . .' *Must* in such a context could easily be replaced by *will* in the sense of strong volition.

There is evidently an intimate relationship between the notion of 'authority' (§9.2.4) and the notion of 'contingency' (under which head we bracket together 'possibility' and 'necessity'). We may go so far as to claim, in fact, that 'possibility' and 'necessity' logically include 'permission' and 'obligation' – that 'permission' is a particular kind of 'possibility', and 'obligation' a particular kind of 'necessity'. So:

> 'I am permitted to open this letter' implies 'It is possible for me to open this letter'.
> 'I am obliged to open this letter' implies 'It is necessary for me to open this letter'.

The broad conception of 'possibility' adopted here is to be disassociated from any such narrower concept as 'physical possibility'. One could always force a finer distinction by reading in the qualification 'physically': 'I am permitted to open this letter, but it is not possible (*sc.* physically) for me to do so.' But this would be to add extra content to the bare notion of 'possibility' represented by 1π.[4]

'Possibility' and 'necessity' are thus to be specified by the formator system 1π/2π without the addition of any relative feature. It may be remembered that this system at its introduction was designated "attributive"; that is, one of its terms may stand alone in an attributive cluster (see §§4.2.1, 8.6). Thus in its simplest form, a predication of contingency consists of a terminal element, which is a rank-shifted predication, and an attributive element, consisting of 1π or 2π. We may add the feature +ψ to the attributive predication to make such a predication into an indicative assertion:

$$(X): 1\pi + \psi \quad \text{'}X \text{ is possible'}$$
$$(X): 2\pi + \psi \quad \text{'}X \text{ is necessary'}$$

In fact it may be better to reverse these formulae so as to make them conform to the order in which the elements are most commonly expressed: 'It is possible/necessary that X'. The attributive element will therefore be written in front of the terminal element: $1\pi + \psi:(X)$ and $2\pi + \psi:(X)$.

The close relation between these specifications and those for 'permission' and 'obligation' is reflected in the fact that *can, may, must* and *have to* can all be used with either meaning.

Commentary

b Some may feel that the notions of 'possibility' and 'necessity' are so intimately connected with those of 'permission' and 'obligation' that these two oppositions are inextricable. Certainly, it is sometimes difficult to distinguish one from the other, particularly in contexts of scientific or mathematical discussion (see Ehrman, 1966: 22). One may seemingly interpret the geometrician's sentence *The lines may meet without crossing* either as a statement of *what is permitted* by his axioms, or as a statement of *what is possible* within the ideal theoretical universe he has constructed. However, consideration of syntactic or semantic criteria will usually resolve this apparent indeterminacy. In many instances, the negative serves to distinguish them: the negative of possibility, *viz* impossibility, cannot be expressed by *may not*, which rather means 'It is possible that . . . not'; the negative of permission, on the other hand, can be expressed by *may not*. Now we may notice that it is possible to paraphrase the above sentence *The lines may meet but may not cross*. As the interpretation 'possible that . . . not' is clearly ruled out in this context, the meaning must be 'not permitted': that is, it must be the sense of 'permission' rather than 'possibility' that is used here, and presumably also in other similar contexts.

c The implication relation between statements of permission and statements of possibility is not shown directly by any of the rules of implication presented in this study; but it can be accounted for by a simple and natural extension of rule [E] of §2.8.2 to the condition: "a single-place predication $a:m$ logically implies a two-place predication $a \cdot r \cdot b$ if (a being the same in both formulae) m is logically included in r".

The rule associated with inverse systems has up to now been stated in a form which applies to two-place predications only. For the purpose of one-place main predications, and in particular for predications of contingency, it may be rewritten as follows:

$$\sim 1\pi + \psi : (a \cdot r \cdot b) = 2\pi + \psi : (a \cdot \sim r \cdot b)$$

'It is not possible that he will be dismissed' = 'It is necessarily the case that he will not be dismissed'

$$\sim 2\pi + \psi : (a \cdot r \cdot b) = 1\pi + \psi : (a \cdot \sim r \cdot b)$$

'It is not necessarily the case that he will be dismissed' = 'It is possible that he will not be dismissed'

Once again the rule is "if the position of the negative and the term of the inversion system are simultaneously altered, the meaning remains the same".

As a formator system, the system of '*constraint*' plays its part in the characterisation of special classes of tautologies, of which the following are specimen members:

'Your aunt must be female'
'Every philatelist must collect stamps'
'Your aunt can't be a man'
'A bachelor can't be married'

The rule which applies to the first two examples is: "If X is a tautology, then $2\pi + \psi : (X)$ is also a tautology"; or, in other words, if a statement X is true by definition, then a statement which asserts that X is necessarily true is also true by definition. The second pair of examples also falls within the scope of this rule, through the mediation of the rule which applies to inversion systems. 'A bachelor can't be married' may be transcribed $\sim 1\pi + \psi : (a \cdot r \cdot b)$ 'It is not possible that $a \cdot r \cdot b$', where $a \cdot r \cdot b$ is a contradiction. By the inversion rule, however, this is equivalent to

$2\pi +\psi:(a\cdot \sim r\cdot b)$, and in this formula $a\cdot \sim r\cdot b$, being the negation of a contradiction, must be a tautology. That is, the same rule which allows the construction of a tautology by the addition of 'must' to a tautology also allows the construction of a tautology by the addition of 'can't' to a contradiction.

It is time now to turn to the question of defining terms of possibility and necessity.

9.4.1 'Ought to'

The difference between the meanings of *ought to* and *have to/must* has already been discussed in the field of 'obligation'. The same difference exists also in the field of 'necessity'. We may contrast the following examples:

> { *That must be my wife.*
> { *That ought to be my wife.*
> { *They must have reached home by now.*
> { *They ought to have reached home by now.*

In the first sentence of each pair the speaker commits himself to the certainty of the proposition; but in the second sentence, he is not sure. Recalling that *must* here conveys the necessity of logical inference, we may say that *ought to* conveys the necessity, given the premises, of the conclusion, but doubt about the assumptions or logical steps upon which the conclusion is based. A latent 'if' is suggested: 'X is true, Y is true, and therefore (if my reasoning is correct) Z is true'.

The argument employed in §9.2.4 led to the omission of the actuality formator from the definition of *ought to*; similarly here, the definitions of *ought to* on the one hand and *must/have to* on the other differ in this one particular:

> *ought to:* 2π *must/have to:* $2\pi +\psi$

The downgraded equivalents of these definitions, $\langle \theta' : 2\pi \rangle$ and $\langle \theta' : 2\pi +\psi \rangle$, will be preferred for reasons to be given below. In the 'necessity' sense, as in the 'permission' sense, *should* is a synonym of *ought to*.[5]

9.4.2 'Can', 'may', 'have to', and 'must'

Grammarians have sometimes noted that *can* and *may* are not exactly interchangeable in the sense of possibility.[6]

The difference between them parallels a difference of grammatical construction following *It is possible*, as the following relations of synonymy show:

> *The Monsoon can be dangerous* is synonymous with *It is possible for the Monsoon to be dangerous.*
> *The Monsoon may be dangerous* is synonymous with *It is possible that the Monsoon is/will be dangerous.*

It is difficult to explain what difference of meaning is involved here. All that can be said is that in the first pair of sentences, the notion of possibility is general and theoretical; but in the second pair, it is a more particular and practical kind of possibility, often in the future. The second pair of sentences seems to have a slightly stronger meaning:

'The pound can be devalued.'

This is merely a statement which everyone knows to be true: that it is possible for currencies to be devalued, and that the pound is no exception. But:

'The pound may be devalued.'

This is a much more threatening statement, suggesting that the devaluation of the pound, as a practical course of action, is now under consideration.[7]

The same contrast exists between *must* and *have to* in the realm of necessity:

> *Someone has to be telling lies* is synonymous with *It is impossible for everyone to be telling the truth.*
> *Someone must be telling lies* is synonymous with *It is impossible that everyone is telling the truth.*

I have avoided paraphrases with the word *necessary*, because of a difficulty mentioned earlier. None the less, the periphrastic paraphrase with *impossible* makes the point effectively enough that the difference that exists between *have to* and *must* is the same as that which exists between *can* and *may*. The former indicates a theoretical and the latter a practical necessity – but in this case, the theoretical meaning seems to be the stronger. If, on being faced with conflicting evidence, a detective says *Someone* MUST *be telling lies*, he seems to voice no more than a suspicion; but *Someone* HAS TO *be telling lies* is a more weighty utterance which may amount to an accusation. *There* HAS TO *be a way out* adds a note of desperation or determination to *There* MUST *be a way out*: the speaker refuses even to contemplate any other possibility.

At first glance, one might suppose that the difference between "practical" and "theoretical" contingency is a matter of the presence or absence of the feature of 'actuality'. This cannot be so, however, since the meaning of *ought to*, which is of neutral actuality, already differs from that of *must* and *have to* in this respect; the definitions of *must* and *have to* therefore both contain $+\psi$. In any case, the contrast between *have to* and *must* or between *can* and *may* is not such as to make any great difference of truth value. If any logical differences do enter into the "theoretical"/"practical" opposition, it is that the "stronger" meaning implies the "weaker" in each case:

'The pound may be devalued' implies 'The pound can be devalued'.

'Someone has to be telling lies' implies 'Someone must be telling lies'.

However, the difference is subtle enough to make intuition uncertain, and only a tentative formulation will be suggested. If we wish to account for this apparent relationship of implication, we may represent the 'theoretical'/'practical' contrast by a formator system $\pm\tau$, and state implication rules as follows:

$$1\pi +\psi:(a\cdot r -\tau\cdot b) \text{ implies } 1\pi +\psi:(a\cdot r +\tau\cdot b)$$
$$2\pi +\psi:(a\cdot r +\tau\cdot b) \text{ implies } 2\pi +\psi:(a\cdot r -\tau\cdot b)$$

According to this analysis, each of the four auxiliaries under discussion will have a discontinuous definition on the following pattern:

can: $1\pi +\psi:(\ldots +\tau$

The discontinuity can be avoided, however, if the equivalent downgraded formula $(a\cdot r +\tau \langle\theta':+\psi \; 1\pi\rangle\cdot b)'$ is used; now the definition of each auxiliary is included within the medial cluster of the main predication, which is also an advantage for expression rules, because of the correspondence between medial clusters and verbal groups (see §6.1).

can: $+\tau\langle\theta':1\pi +\psi\rangle$ *have to:* $+\tau\langle\theta':2\pi +\psi\rangle$
may: $-\tau\langle\theta':1\pi +\psi\rangle$ *must:* $-\tau\langle\theta':2\pi +\psi\rangle$

The provisional solution given here is perforce *ad hoc*, since the distinction just examined has not been noted anywhere else in the language.

Commentary

d What appears to be a special development of the 'theoretical possibility' sense of *can* is its use in casual instructions like *You can pass me the hammer now, Tom.* This usage belongs chiefly to the context of familiar discourse between friends; it is more tactful than a direct imperative, and yet is impolite if used to strangers (one would scarcely say to a passer-by in the street *You can change this money for a phone call*). In an atmosphere of co-operation, it seems, suggesting even the theoretical possibility of a particular course of action has, by custom, become an effective means of ensuring its execution.

9.4.3 *'Can' in the sense of 'ability'*

Although attention has been given to *can* in the senses of 'permission' and 'possibility', there remains the third, and perhaps most common, sense of 'capability' or 'ability' to be considered. The division between 'capability' and 'possibility', like that between 'permission' and 'possibility', tends to become blurred in actual usage, so some justification for separating them must be given.

In the first place, *can* in the 'capability' sense can be replaced without change of meaning by *be able to*:

He can speak five languages is synonymous with *He is able to speak five languages.*

But:

Lions can be dangerous is not synonymous with the dubiously acceptable *Lions are able to be dangerous.*

Furthermore, there is synonymy of active and passive constructions when *can* is used with the force of 'possibility':

Waste can ruin a country's economy is synonymous with *A country's economy can be ruined by waste.*

But there is no such equivalence with *be able to*:

They were able to survive the siege is not synonymous with **The siege was able to be survived (by them).*

If we understand an active sentence in the sense of 'ability', the corresponding passive sentence has to be understood in the 'possibility' sense:

'He can (=is able to) beat the world champion' $\neq$ 'The world champion can be beaten by him'.

On the other hand, these differences should not disguise the very close connection of meaning, which is one of implication:

'He is able to speak five languages' implies 'It is possible for him to speak five languages'

'They were able to survive the siege' implies 'It was possible for them to survive the siege'.

'Ability' is in two respects like 'permission': (a) it implies 'possibility', and (b) it has the same kind of restriction of "reversibility" that we noted in the non-equivalence of 'Mike had to kiss Joan' and 'Joan had to be kissed by Mike' in §9.2. The first of these points may be incorporated into the analysis by making the definition of *be able to* include the feature 1π; the second point can be accommodated if a co-referential link between terminal clusters is established here, as it was in the case of 'permission'. We therefore introduce a system of '*ability*' similar in almost all respects to the system of '*authority*':

SYSTEM 6 '*ability*'

$$\begin{cases} (x) \rightarrow \text{ABLE} (y) & \text{'} (x) \text{ is able to } (y)\text{'} \\ (x) \leftarrow \text{ABLE} (y) & \text{'} (y) \text{ is able to } (x)\text{'} \end{cases}$$

Class of system: relative

Contextual properties: $\{+\text{ANIM}'\} \rightarrow \text{ABLE} \{(\theta' \cdot r \cdot y)\}$

Logical properties: asymmetric, irreflexive, intransitive

Dependence rule: ABLE depends on 1π

A predication of ability is therefore of the following form:

$a' \cdot \rightarrow$ABLE Iπ $+\psi \cdot (\theta' \cdot r \cdot b)$ 'They were able to survive the siege'

and the full definition of *can* in the 'ability' sense is

$\rightarrow$ABLE Iπ $+\psi$.

9.4.4 *'Possibly' and 'perhaps'*

The adverbs *possibly* and *perhaps* correspond to *may* in that they express practical, rather than theoretical possibility:

'Possibly he hasn't heard the news'
= 'Perhaps he hasn't heard the news'
= 'It is possible that he hasn't heard the news'
= 'He may not have heard the news'.

The definition of *possibly* and *perhaps* is accordingly

$-\tau \langle \theta' : I\pi +\psi \rangle$.

9.4.5 *Probability*

One may think of 'probability' as a scale extending from 'impossibility' (0% probability) at one end to 'necessity' (100% probability) at the other. In terms of this analysis, such a scale may be represented by a polar system dependent on Iπ:

SYSTEM 7 *'probability'*
$\begin{cases} +\text{PROB} & \text{'probable'} \\ -\text{PROB} & \text{'improbable'} \end{cases}$
Class of system: polar, attributive
Dependence rule: PROB depends on Iπ

The use of this system is illustrated in the following specifications:

Iπ $+\psi$ $+$PROB$:(X)$ 'It is probable that he will come.'
Iπ $+\psi$ $-$PROB$:(X)$ 'It is improbable that he will come.'

By this analysis, 'It is probable that he will come' is rightly shown to imply 'It is possible that he will come' (whereas, of course, 'It is improbable that he will come' does *not* imply 'It is impossible that he will come'). The following definitions may be given:

probable, likely: $+$PROB
improbable, unlikely: $-$PROB

One observation not accounted for in the above specifications is that *It is probable . . .* can only be followed by a *that*-clause, and is therefore related to "practical", but not "theoretical" possibility. This can be included as a contextual property of $\pm$PROB, whereby $-\tau$ is assigned to the medial cluster of the following rank-shifted predication.

The definition of the adverb *probably* is the same as that of *possibly* except for the addition of the feature +PROB:

$$-\tau \langle \theta' : \mathrm{I}\pi + \psi + \mathrm{PROB} \rangle.$$

9.5 Involvement of speaker and listener

Returning for a moment to the box-diagram on p. 204, let us note that the "inverse" relationships between the left-hand and right-hand boxes of the diagram have been examined, and that in addition, the slight differences of meaning within the 'possibility' and 'necessity' boxes have received attention. There remain, however, the differences between *can* and *may* in the 'permission' box and *must* and *have to* in the 'obligation' box; also, analogous differences between *shall* and *will*.

9.5.1 'Shall' and 'will'

We shall consider the question of *shall* and *will* first, as here the difference of meaning is more obvious, and easier to deal with.

The following volitional definitions were supplied for *will* in §9.3:

will: →VOL $\mathrm{I}\pi + \psi \cdot (\theta'$ 'be willing to'
will: →VOL $2\pi + \psi \cdot (\theta'$ 'insist on'

The difference between *will* in both these senses and the corresponding uses of *shall* is shown clearly in the following paraphrases:

'My chauffeur will help you' = 'My chauffeur is willing to help you'.
'My chauffeur shall help you' = 'I am willing for my chauffeur to help you'.
'I ǀwill marry her' = 'I insist on marrying her'.
'No one shall stop me' = 'I insist that no one stop me'.

With *will*, the subject of the auxiliary (*ie* the person who is willing or insists) is also the notional subject of the main verb; but with *shall*, it is the speaker who is the willing or insisting party.[8]

Commentary

a Both volitional meanings of *shall* are something of a rarity in present-day English, and no doubt the reason, as for strong-volitional *will*, is the unpalatable associations they have acquired. *Shall* in the weaker sense conveys the message 'I am conferring a favour on you', and is therefore reserved for addressing inferiors, particularly pets and children: *You shall have a bone if you're a good dog*, etc. The stronger meaning of *shall* is likewise associated with speech with one of lower status than oneself, but its connotation is one of imperiousness rather than condescension. Such forms do not find favour in the democratic social climate of today.

To specify the volitional meanings of *shall*, we first require a sketch of a semantic analysis of personal pronouns. (It will be unnecessary to specify systems and definitions in detail, however, as we are interested here only in the notion 'first-person'.) Initially a distinction has to be made between pronouns whose meanings contain the feature 'personal' (+PERS) and those which do not. *It* expresses the meaning −PERS ('non-personal'); *they* expresses neither personal nor non-personal meaning; and all other "personal" pronouns (in the grammatical sense) have the positive feature +PERS.

Commentary

b The feature +PERS should not be identified with +HUM, despite the overlap of their referential domains. The former applies not only to human beings, but to gods, angels, Martians, and (sometimes) to higher animals. Conversely, babies are often referred to as *it* (−PERS) when they are not felt to be old enough to qualify as "persons".

A system ±EGO discriminates between first-person reference (*viz* 'including the speaker(s)') and other persons ('not including the speaker(s)'). Then a further system ±YOU separates second-person reference ('including the addressee(s)') from third-person reference. Definitions are:

I/me:	+EGO −YOU −PLUR
you:	−EGO +YOU
he/him:	−EGO −YOU −PLUR +MALE +PERS
she/her:	−EGO −YOU −PLUR −MALE +PERS
it:	θ −PLUR −PERS
we/us:	+EGO +PLUR
they/them:	θ −EGO −YOU −PLUR

The features θ and +PERS are redundant in first-person and second-person definitions, because +EGO and +YOU both depend on the selections 'personal' and 'definite'. Similarly, since −PERS depends on the combination of −EGO and −YOU, these features are not included in the definition of *it*. In their assumption of definiteness, ±EGO and ±YOU show common ground with the deictic system ±THIS; indeed, they are in a sense deictic themselves, in that they derive their meaning from the immediate speech situation. However, it is doubtful whether this connection with ±THIS can be formalised by rules of dependence. A positive association of +EGO with +THIS and of +YOU with −THIS is encouraged by the oddity of *I am there and you are here* (except applied to some fictional speech context); but there is no necessary co-occurrence. *This cut on your knee here* and *That cut on my knee there* are not impossible expressions, even though they are less likely than the same expressions with the personal pronouns exchanged.[9]

The definition of *I/me* may be simplified by one feature to $+$EGO $-$PLUR if we recognise (by a dependence rule) that the combination of these two features is only possible if second-person reference is excluded. In this curtailed form, the meaning 'first-person singular' can now be entered in the specifications of predications containing *shall*:

$+$EGO $-$PLUR$\cdot\rightarrow$VOL 1π $+\psi\cdot(a\cdot r\cdot b)$ 'My chauffeur shall help you.'
$+$EGO $-$PLUR$\cdot\rightarrow$VOL 2π $+\psi\cdot(a\cdot r\cdot b)$ 'No one shall stop me.'

The two definitions of *shall* so stated exceed as they stand the normal extent of a definition, and should therefore be replaced by equivalent downgraded predications (by the rule of subordination, §4.3.3), as was previously suggested in Comment *b* of §9.3 for *will*.

With this improvement, the contrasting definitions of *will* and *shall* may be displayed as follows:

'*Willingness*'
 will: $\langle\theta''\cdot\leftarrow$VOL 1π $+\psi\cdot\theta'\rangle$ *shall:* $\langle\theta''\cdot\leftarrow$VOL 1π $+\psi\cdot$ $+$EGO $-$PLUR$\rangle$
'*Insistence*'
 will: $\langle\theta''\cdot\leftarrow$VOL 2π $+\psi\cdot\theta'\rangle$ *shall:* $\langle\theta''\cdot\leftarrow$VOL 2π $+\psi\cdot$ $+$EGO $-$PLUR$\rangle$

The definite formators θ'' and θ' co-refer respectively to the whole of the main predication and to the initial cluster of the main predication.

9.5.2 '*May*' and '*must*'

We return finally to distinctions in the meanings of auxiliary verbs expressing permission and obligation. In colloquial English, *may* and *must* in the 'authority' sense differ from *can* and *have to* in that they identify the speaker as the source of authority. The difference can be seen from a comparison of these examples:

$\begin{cases} \textit{You can smoke in here.} \\ \textit{You may smoke in here.} \end{cases}$

$\begin{cases} \textit{You have to be back in camp by ten.} \\ \textit{You must be back in camp by ten.} \end{cases}$

You can smoke . . . expresses the impersonal notion 'You have permission', without saying whether the permission emanates from the speaker or some other authority: it could thus be spoken in a neutral context such as the following:

A: *Can we smoke in here?*
B: *As far as I know you can smoke – there's no notice to the contrary.*

You may smoke . . . , on the other hand, makes it clear that the speaker is the person who grants permission.

Commentary

c In formal and polite usage, however, this difference between 'can' and 'may' does not exist, because *may* is preferred as the more "correct" form, even in contexts of impersonal permission. A guide-book might tell us: *For nine-pence, visitors may ascend the tower.*

The second pair of sentences above illustrates a parallel contrast: *Have to* indicates the general idea of obligation, but *must* more precisely identifies the speaker as the person who gives the orders. Thus, in a military context, *You must be back in camp . . .* would probably be spoken by an officer giving the orders, while *You have to be back in camp . . .* could well be spoken by an ordinary soldier informing his comrades of orders issued by someone else.

Must implicates the speaker as authority irrespective of the person of the subject of the clause.

> *He must be careful.*
> *You must be careful.*
> *I must be careful.*

All three of these sentences suggest that the speaker is the agent of coercion; and the last, quite consistently, indicates self-coercion (through a sense of duty, a sense of prudence, etc.) With first-person subjects, the difference between 'must' and 'have to' is therefore a difference between internal and external compulsion.

To specify this element of speaker-involvement, we may add to the definitions of *can* and *have to* given in §9.2.4 a downgraded predication $\langle \theta' \cdot \leftarrow \text{CAU} \cdot +\text{EGO} \rangle$ naming the speaker or speakers as the agent of authority:

can: $\rightarrow$AUT $+\psi$ Iπ 'has/have permission to'
have to: $\rightarrow$AUT $+\psi$ 2π 'is/are obliged to'
may: $\rightarrow$AUT $+\psi$ Iπ $\langle \theta' \cdot \leftarrow \text{CAU} \cdot +\text{EGO} \rangle$ 'is/are permitted by me/us to'
must: $\rightarrow$AUT $+\psi$ 2π $\langle \theta' \cdot \leftarrow \text{CAU} \cdot +\text{EGO} \rangle$ 'is/are obliged by me/us to'

Commentary

d The feature $-$PLUR is omitted from the specification of the agent here, because the agent is sometimes plural; for example, when the subject is "exclusive" *we*. *We must leave now, to catch the bus* can indicate a collective decision, as well as coercion of a group by one of its members.

e The contrast just outlined between *must* and *have to* is absent from the many grammatical contexts in which *must* cannot occur. For the two present tense forms *must* and *has/have to*, for instance, there is only the one past tense form *had to*. Similarly in the negative, *mustn't* and *don't have to* differ not so much with respect to speaker-involvement, as in the "scope" of the negation (see §9.6).

9.5.3 *Questions: involvement of the listener*
Instead of involving the speaker, questions containing *must* and *may* in the sense of obligation or permission appeal to the authority of the listener:

Must I press this button? (='Am I obliged [by you] to press this button?')

May we borrow your radio? (='Are we permitted [by you] to borrow your radio?')

Such questions anticipate the form that one would expect to find in the reply:

May we borrow your radio? Yes, you may.

The definitions of *may* and *must* in questions consequently differ, in one small particular, from their definitions in statements: the former contain the feature +YOU 'second person' in place of +EGO 'first person'.[10]

In the volitional sphere, a similar change occurs in the meaning of *shall* as discussed in §9.5.1. First-person questions with *shall* consult the will of the listener, instead of declaring the will of the speaker:

Shall I open a window? (='Is it your will that I should . . .')
Shall we go to the theatre this evening? (='Are you willing for us to go . . .')

This usage is to be associated with "weak" rather than "strong" volition; that is, the questioner appears to invite the addressee to express his willingness for, rather than insistence on, a certain course of action. Yet often the meaning of a question form does not seem to correspond exactly with either of the volitional meanings of the statement form. The lack of fit is particularly prominent with questions which are offers of help – *Shall I carry your bag for you?* – where the meaning is the neutral volitional 'Do you want me to . . .' rather than 'Are you willing for me to . . .'. There may be a case, therefore, for giving *shall* in questions a definition differing in two respects from those stated in §9.5.1: (1) +EGO is to be replaced by +YOU, and (2) the feature of 'constraint' 1π or 2π is to be omitted.

Commentary
f Volitional *shall* is very rarely found in questions with second-person or third-person subjects, but it seems at least a possibility in sentences like *Shall Virginia do your shopping for you?* (='Do you want . . .') in which (say) a mother offers her daughter's help to a third party.

9.6 Negative forms of modal auxiliaries

The complicated semantics of negative forms *may not, cannot*, etc is all too familiar as a problem for teachers and students of English as a foreign language, who have to face such apparent anomalies as the very different status of *must not* and *don't have to* as negations of *must* and *have to*.

Within the present framework, such meanings are readily described, since every formula of modality contains a main predication and a subordinate predication, each of which may be independently negated. The two possibilities are clearly demonstrated by paraphrase:

You don't have to drink all the wine.
  $a' \cdot \sim \rightarrow$AUT $+\psi\, 2\pi\, c\cdot(\theta' \cdot r \cdot b)$
  'You are NOT obliged to drink all the wine.'
You mustn't drink all the wine.
  $a' \cdot \rightarrow$AUT $+\psi\, 2\pi\, c\cdot(\theta' \cdot \sim r \cdot b)$
  'You are obliged NOT to drink all the wine.'

The predication containing 1π or 2π may be called the "modal predication", and the other may be called the "principal predication". In the above formulae, the principal predication is rank-shifted within the modal predication, although the rule of subordination (§4.3.3) also allows a second symbolisation, in which the modal predication is downgraded within the medial cluster of the principal predication. It will be simpler to present the negative specifications in the non-downgraded form already used above:

[A] 'PERMISSION' and 'OBLIGATION'
  You MAY NOT *go swimming* (= 'You are not allowed . . .')
  $(a\cdot \sim \rightarrow$AUT $+\psi\, 1\pi\, \langle\theta' \cdot \leftarrow$CAU$\cdot +EGO\rangle \cdot (X))'$
  You CAN'T *go swimming* (= 'You are not allowed . . .')
  $a\cdot \sim \rightarrow$AUT $+\psi\, 1\pi \cdot (X)$
  You MUSTN'T *go swimming* (= 'You are obliged not to . . .')
  $(a\cdot \rightarrow$AUT $+\psi\, 2\pi\, \langle\theta' \cdot \leftarrow$CAU$\cdot +EGO\rangle\cdot(\sim X))'$
  $\begin{cases} \textit{You} \text{ NEEDN'T } \textit{go swimming} \\ \textit{You} \text{ DON'T HAVE TO } \textit{go swimming} \ (= \text{'You are not obliged to . . .'}) \end{cases}$
  $a\cdot \sim \rightarrow$AUT $+\psi\, 2\pi \cdot (X)$

[B] 'POSSIBILITY' and '(LOGICAL) NECESSITY'
  They MAY NOT *be coming* (= 'It is possible that . . . not . . .')
  $1\pi +\psi:(\sim X -\tau)$
  They CAN'T *be coming* (= 'It is not possible . . .')
  $\sim 1\pi +\psi:(X)$
  $\begin{cases} \textit{They} \text{ DON'T HAVE TO } \textit{be coming} \ (= \text{'It isn't necessary . . .'}) \\ \textit{They} \text{ NEEDN'T } \textit{be coming} \end{cases}$
  $\sim 2\pi +\psi:(X)$
  (*Mustn't* is not used at all in the sense of 'necessity').

A contrast can be seen between those formulae in which there is negation of the main predication ("modal negation"), and those in which there is negation of the rank-shifted predication ("principal negation"). (The principal predication is represented simply by X, and the negation of the principal predication by $\sim X$.) *Can't*, *don't have to*, and *may not* in the 'permission' sense fall into the category of modal negation, while *mustn't* and *may not* in the sense of 'possibility' are examples of principal negation.

The factors distinguishing the meanings of *must* and *have to*, like those distinguishing *can* and *may*, tend to become blurred in the negative. Although *mustn't* and *may not* seem to retain the involvement of the speaker, the 'theoretical' side of the 'theoretical'/'practical' opposition is difficult to detect in *can't* and *don't have to*. *May not*, on the other hand, keeps its 'practical' sense, and its formula is accordingly marked with the feature $-\tau$. *Needn't* (in British English, at least) seems to be synonymous with *don't have to* in both senses.

Commentary

a   The two meanings of *may not* are largely differentiated by stress: *He 'may not go swimming* (with stress on *may*) strongly favours the 'possibility' sense, whereas *He may 'not go swimming* suggests the 'permission' sense.

b   In British English, *don't have to* competes with the variant forms *haven't got to* and *haven't to*, which are capable of interpretation, however, as examples of principal negation. They are particularly likely to receive this latter interpretation in indirect speech, where they sometimes have a function equivalent to *mustn't* in direct speech: *He says you haven't to make a noise while he's sleeping.*

c   *Oughtn't to* is similarly interpretable in terms of either modal or principal negation, according to context. In the sense of 'obligation' it is parallel to *mustn't*, and its meaning can be symbolised by the formula $a \cdot \rightarrow \text{AUT } 2\pi \cdot (\sim X)$; *eg: You oughtn't to be cruel to your little sister.* But in the sense of logical necessity it is parallel to *needn't*: *You oughtn't to have any difficulty getting a ticket.* This sentence is roughly understood: 'If my calculations are correct, you will necessarily not have difficulty . . .', and its meaning may be specified as $2\pi : (X)$. Both meanings of *oughtn't to* are also found with *shouldn't*.

Interestingly, *may not* and *mustn't*, despite the diametrical opposition of their positive meanings, are logical equivalents in negative sentences like:

> *You may not go swimming.*
> *You must not go swimming.*

These are both prohibitions, and the only difference in their import is the more urgent and positive tone of the latter. The reason for this curious equivalence is to be found in the inversion rule "change the place of the negative and the term of the inversion system, and the meaning remains the same". A glance at the semantic specifications of these sentences given above will show that they fulfil the conditions of the rule, and are therefore cognitively synonymous. The different categories of negation involved ("modal" in the case of *may not*, "principal" in the case of *must not*), cancel out the contrast between *may* and *must*. A further example of the same kind is the virtual equivalence of *may not* in the sense 'It is possible that . . . not . . .', and *needn't* in the sense 'It is not necessary that . . .':

> *You needn't have any difficulty getting a ticket.*
> *You may not have any difficulty getting a ticket.*

There is no difference between the cognitive meanings of these two, except for the presence of the feature $-\tau$ 'practical' in the second, and (possibly) the corresponding presence of $+\tau$ 'theoretical' in the former.

For this same reason, it is difficult to assign a precise analysis to *will* and *shall* as volitional auxiliaries. The two forms have a special status in that each of them is capable of expressing both sides of the same inverse relationship. We are therefore faced with the following choices of description:

> *She won't listen to what I say.*
> *I won't be treated like a slave.*

Are these to be assigned the reading:

$$a \cdot \sim \rightarrow \text{VOL} \ +\psi \ 1\pi \cdot (X) \begin{cases} \text{'She is unwilling . . .'} \\ \text{'I am not willing to . . .'} \end{cases}$$

or the logically equivalent reading:

$$a \cdot \rightarrow \text{VOL} \ +\psi \ 2\pi \cdot (\sim X) \quad \begin{array}{l} \text{'She insists on . . . not . . .'} \\ \text{'I insist on . . . not . . .'} \end{array}$$

A similar dilemma arises with the opposite meaning of *won't* in *Don't worry, I won't interfere.* Is this to be construed 'I shan't insist on interfering' or 'I am willing not to interfere'? Parallel examples with *shan't* are:

> *You shan't escape me.* (= 'I insist on your not escaping me' *or* 'I am not willing for you to escape me')
> *Don't worry, they shan't hurt you.* (= 'I insist on them not hurting you' *or* 'I am not willing for them to hurt you').

(There does not appear to be a "weaker" interpretation of *shan't* with the meaning 'I do not insist on . . .' or 'I am willing for . . . not . . .'.) The difficulty of assigning semantic specifications to these forms is due to an unusual coincidence of polysemy and synonymy.

9.7 The hypothetical use of modal auxiliaries

The auxiliary verb forms *could, might, would,* and *should,* to which we turn our attention in this final section, can be used either in reference to past time (both in direct and reported speech) or in a hypothetical sense. I shall say nothing further about them as past tense forms, for their meanings, so used, follow (with a few gaps) from the discussion of the corresponding non-past forms in this chapter, joined with the discussion of past tense in §7.4.3. Examples of past meanings are:

> *The prisoners* MIGHT *leave the camp when they wished.* (= 'The prisoners were permitted . . .')
> *He* WOULD *keep on interrupting me.* (= 'He insisted on keeping on interrupting me')
> *They* COULD *all speak English.* (= 'They were all able to . . .')

Before we examine the hypothetical meanings of these words, however, it will be necessary to consider the function of the hypothetical formator $(-\psi)$, which was introduced as a member of the system of '*actuality*' in §9.2.2.

9.7.1 *The hypothetical formator* $(-\psi)$

The role of the hypothetical formator is more restricted than that of the actuality feature $+\psi$, which occurs in most main predications and in many dependent predications as well. The hypothetical formator, in contrast, does not generally occur except through the operation of contextual conditions. It is for this reason that a hypothetical utterance such as *The weather would be cloudy*, standing on its own, strikes one as being semantically incomplete.

The following are miscellaneous examples of contexts in which a hypothetical formator may be introduced:

> 'I wish we were on holiday'.
> 'He acts as if he was a millionaire'.
> 'Just suppose we were being followed'.

By far the most important context, however, is that of conditional statements. The conditional formator system $\rightleftarrows\supset$ (§3.1.2) has to be both preceded and followed by rank-shifted predications, which match each other either (a) in being of neutral actuality or (b) in being non-actual (*ie* in containing the hypothetical formator). The following are therefore general formulae for conditional statements:

> $(X)\cdot\rightarrow\supset\ +\psi\cdot(Y)$ *eg* 'If John tells you that, he is lying.'
> $(X-\psi)\cdot\rightarrow\supset\ +\psi\cdot(X-\psi)$ *eg* 'If John told you that, he would be lying.'

Although the first of these is sometimes called a "real condition", "open condition" is a preferable term, since the whole statement is in fact neutral with respect to the actuality system; we do not know whether John is actually telling lies or not. If by "real" we understand "actual", there is no such thing as a "real condition"; no antecedent or

8*

consequent of a condition, that is, ever contains the actuality feature $+\psi$, for no conditional statement ever *implies* the truth of either of its component statements.

The following is a very rough statement of rules of expression applying to the hypothetical formator:

1 Within an independent clause and in reported speech, the hypothetical formator is expressed by *would/should*+Infinitive.

2 Within a dependent clause (except in reported speech), the hypothetical formator is expressed by the past tense (*eg: If John told you that*) or by the past subjunctive (*eg: If I were you*) or by *were to*+Infinitive (*eg: If I were to die*) or by *should*+Infinitive (*eg: If I should die*).

The modal auxiliaries, however, have no infinitive form, and therefore cannot conform to rule (1) in independent clauses. Instead, the past form of the auxiliary is simply used in both main and dependent clauses:

If you could drive a car, you could give me a lift.

In this sentence, the first *could* commutes with *were able to*, whereas the second commutes with *would be able to*.

In meaning, the hypothetical formator is the negative counterpart of the actuality formator; but it is slightly less uncompromising in its effect. The effect of the actuality formator within a predication $X +\psi$ (whether the predication is independent, rank-shifted, or downgraded) is to assert the truth of $X +\psi$ as an independent statement. To be exactly parallel to $+\psi$, $-\psi$ would have to have to function as an indicator of the falsehood of the corresponding statement, that is, a statement containing $X -\psi$ would have to imply $\sim X$. However, the semantic relationship between $X-\psi$ and $\sim X$ is the weaker one elsewhere called "presupposition".[11] This means that $-\psi$ has (at least in reference to present and future time) the meaning 'contrary to expectation'; only with past time reference does it tend to have the full force of 'contrary to fact' ("unfulfilled condition").

If your father caught you, he would be furious.

This sentence invites the presupposition 'but I don't suppose he will'; the equivalent past hypothetical sentence, on the other hand:

If your father had caught you, he would have been furious

calls for the more definite inference 'but he did not'. (Note that past meaning is expressed by the addition of *have*+Past Participle.)

9.7.2 *Hypothetical permission*

In the main clause of a conditional sentence, *could* and *might* are only dubiously acceptable as hypothetical equivalents of *can* and *may* in the sense of permission:

If you are over seventeen, you can/may drive a car.
?*If you were over seventeen, you could/might drive a car.

Instead, a locution such as *would be allowed to* is normally used:

If you were over seventeen, you would be allowed to drive a car.

However, *could* and *might* are both used for hypothetical permission in tentative requests such as the following:

Could I see your driving licence?
Might I ask you for your opinion?

So used, *could* and *might* are to be defined AUT 1π $-\psi$: that is, they have the same meaning as *can*, except for the substitution of $-\psi$ for $+\psi$.

Commentary

a It is difficult to detect any difference between the meanings of *could* and *might* here on grounds of listener involvement (see §9.5.3); but just as *may* is thought more polite than *can* (because of pedagogic prejudice against the latter), so *might* feels more polite (though less usual) than *could*.

In such questions the hypothetical forms obviously add an overtone of politeness to the meaning of the actual forms *can* and *may*. This is probably because the presupposition 'contrary to expectation' here means that the speaker does not expect the permission to be granted. The presupposition in the case of *Might I ask you for your opinion*, for example, may be verbalised as 'but I don't suppose I may'. Needless to say, this pose of modesty is often adopted, for the sake of politeness, by the people who in reality count upon compliance.

The use of hypothetical forms just mentioned is an irregularity in that the hypothetical formator occurs apparently *in vacuo*, and not in fulfilment of any of the contextual restrictions mentioned in §9.7.1. Such unconditional occurrences are not unusual in polite conversational exchanges, and many of them can be explained by means of an implicit *if*-clause. *I should love to go to the theatre*, for example, may be clarified by the proviso '. . . if someone invited me'. *Would you mind reading this letter* may be supplemented '. . . if you were asked'. Psychologically, the understood condition reflects the tentativeness, and therefore the politeness of the speaker: he is not bold enough to confront another person directly with his desires; instead, he hints that such desires *might* exist, hoping that his interlocutor will "take the hint" and act accordingly. Possibly, in the same way, as an alternative account of the "permissive" use of *could* and *might*, one may add an implicit "if I were to summon up courage and ask you", or some such evasive condition.

These usages, representing as they do the diplomacy of personal relations, share a fundamental characteristic with the language of international diplomacy: both of them avoid at all costs the appearance of a naked confrontation of forces. In both cases, too, the face-value meaning of an expression is all too often but a thin covering for harsher realities underneath.

There is little to be said about the expression of hypothetical obligation, except that *must* has no hypothetical equivalent, and that *would have to* is therefore the only expression available for this meaning. The same observation applies to hypothetical necessity.

9.7.3 *Hypothetical volition*

The use of *would* as an alternative to *will* in requests is a further instance of the hypothetical formator as an index of politeness:

Would you lend me sixpence?

is more tactful than

Will you lend me sixpence?

to the extent that the questioner does not seem to bank upon the generosity of the hearer. Again, one may postulate an unexpressed condition:

'*Would you be willing to lend me sixpence (if I were to ask you)?*'

(Care should be taken to distinguish the *would* used in such requests, *ie* the hypothetical form of *will* in the sense of 'willingness', from the *would* which is merely a marker of hypothetical meaning in main clauses.)

As the hypothetical reflex of *will* in the sense of "strong volition", *would* occasionally occurs without contextual conditioning, but only in rather stereotyped exclamations such as

Of course, he would put his foot in it.

(Actually, this sentence is ambiguous, as it might also be used with past time reference, meaning 'He insisted on putting his foot in it', as well as hypothetically, in the sense 'He would insist [*sc.* if ever he were given the opportunity] on putting his foot in it'.)

9.7.4 *Hypothetical possibility*

Could and *might* may occur (again unconditionally) in utterances with the meaning of 'hypothetical possibility':

It might rain tomorrow.
He could be waiting for you at the station.

The effect of the negative presupposition 'contrary to expectation' here is to make the predication less probable; the key connotation of the hypothetical form is consequently "tentativeness". *You might pass the exam* (= 'It is [barely] possible that you will pass . . .') expresses a less sanguine hope, for example, than *You may pass the exam.*

The opposition between 'theoretical' and 'practical' meaning seems less distinct in the hypothetical forms, and *could* and *might* are in many cases more or less interchangeable. The absence of this discrimination in the presence of the hypothetical formator is borne out by the non-occurrence of a *that*-clause following *It would be possible*: only the *for . . . to* + Infinitive construction, expressing $-\tau$, is allowable:

> *It would be possible for you to pass the exam.*
> **It would be possible that you will pass the exam.*

From this we may assume that the combination $1\pi -\psi$ in the modal predication bars the occurrence of $-\tau$ in the principal predication.

Commentary

b The use of *can* in familiar instructions (see Comment *d*, p. 222) is paralleled, with tentative overtones, by hypothetical *could* in remarks such as *You could put on the kettle for a cup of tea while you're there*, or *You could try asking for a key at the office*. As further evidence of the 'theoretical' meaning of both *could* and *might*, it may be observed that *might* can be substituted for *could* in these utterances, even though *can* cannot be replaced by *may* in the corresponding "actual" sentences.

There are circumstances, however, in which *could* and *might* are not synonymous: *might* is sometimes paraphrasable 'It is possible that . . . would . . .', representing a specification in which the hypothetical formator belongs to the principal predication, not to the modal predication. In this case, it cannot be replaced by *could*. A clear example of such a use is the *might* which occurs in tentative offers: *You might like to borrow this book* (= 'It is possible that you would like . . .').

The polysemy of *might* is particularly liable to cause confusion when it is combined with *have* + Past Participle, as the ensuing examples show:

1 *I might have enjoyed the trip more if it hadn't been so hot.*
2 *You might have warned me he was in a temper.*
3 *You might have left it at the station.*

Sentence (1) is taken to mean 'It is possible that I would have . . .' and is therefore the equivalent, with past time reference, of *You might like to borrow this book*. The second sentence, in which the speaker reproaches someone for not taking advantage of a past possibility, may be paraphrased 'It would have been possible for you to warn me that he was in a temper'. The final example carries the connotation of reduced probability and is interpreted 'It is (barely) possible that you have left it at the station'. The presupposition, with past time reference, of 'contrary to fact' is clearly felt in (1) and (2), more especially in (2), where the implicit 'but you didn't warn me!' contains the weight of the accusation. This presupposition, however, is absent from sentence (3), where the feature of hypothetical meaning belongs to the modal, not the principal predication. This sentence is simply a more tentative version of *You* MAY *have left it at the station.* I have assumed in discussing these examples that only one interpretation is available for each; but plainly ambiguities can be read into them, and are prominent in sentences like *He might have saved their lives,* which can mean either 'It is possible that he would have . . .', or 'It would have been possible for him to . . .', or 'It is (barely) possible that he has saved their lives'.

Chapter 10

Retrospect and prospect

As far as the subject itself goes, this concluding chapter can be no more than an "interim stocktaking", in which some assessment is made of what has been done and what has not been done in this book towards the eventual, though distant, goal of a semantic description of English.

Far from providing a comprehensive description, the preceding four chapters have furnished only a patchwork account of English semantics, with scarcely a word on such important topics as the meaning of comparative and superlative constructions, of co-ordination, and of adjectival modifications.

Yet the three semantics fields of which some detailed coverage has been given – those of time, place, and modality – have illustrated a wide range of descriptive problems, and it is not difficult to envisage the extension of the method of analysis to other fields.

It is my hope that in spite of their incompleteness, the theoretical and descriptive parts of this investigation have been seen as mutually supporting activities: that the theoretical apparatus has given explanatory weight to the description, and that the description has provided practical confirmation for the theory. I hope, too, that the individual topics of description have gained from being seen as part of a total pattern, instead of being treated as isolated problems.

If it is accepted that the last three chapters have represented a convergence, rather than a fragmentation of effort, then all that remains to me now is to bring together some of the loose ends, and to consider very briefly some issues left outstanding in the specialised analyses.

One outstanding question is the concept of "semantic fields". Although the phrase "semantic field" has been used freely in this inquiry, no attempt has so far been made to clarify its meaning. One clear interpretation that could be attached to it is "the set of all feature formulae containing a certain feature or combination of features"; thus the presence of the features +CONC +COU could delimit the field of "concrete objects". But this notion is of only limited application, and excludes all three "fields" dealt with in Part 2 of this study. Certainly, in each of the three there is what one may regard as a "focal system"; the relative systems ⇌TIM and ⇌PLA in Chapters 7 and 8, and the attributive system $1\pi/2\pi$ in Chapter 9. These are respectively connected, by contextual redundancy rules, with three other systems, ±PERI, 1, 2, 3DIME, and ±ψ, which provide a second point of departure for the investigation of topics (*eg* duration and frequency in the case of ±PERI) not directly involving the first three systems. Thus each of the three "fields" has not just one, but two points of focus:

'Time':   ⇌TIM ——— ±PERI
'Place':   ⇌PLA ——— 1, 2, 3DIME
'Modality': $1\pi/2\pi$ ——— ±ψ

This table comes somewhere near to displaying what we impressionistically single out as a coherent "semantic field".

Yet if this study has shown anything, it has surely shown that "semantic field" can be a vague and misleading concept. The whole point of Part 2 has been to demonstrate that it is unrealistic to try to treat individual areas of meaning separately, as if they were insulated from the rest of the language. The cardinal principle that has emerged is "semantic fields have no fences". Thus much has been made of the links between one part of the semantic description and another. Mention may be made here of the use of the system of '*countability*' in both noun and verb meanings (§§6.3.2, 7.4.1); of the use of the same basic analysis for the semantics of tenses and of time adverbials (§§7.1, 7.4); of the importance of inceptive meaning as a point of interaction between the fields of time and place; and of the application of the systems ±THIS, ±EGO and ±YOU to the explanation of deixis, as variously expressed through adverbs, demonstratives, pronouns, and auxiliary verbs.

A more detailed type of similarity exists between the two fields of time and place. It is well known that much of the vocabulary for describing spatial relations is duplicated in temporal relations: *at*, *on*, and *in*, for example, are prepositions both of time and place; likewise *first*, *next*, and *last* can refer equally to position in spatial and temporal sequence. Such formal correspondences reflect a certain degree of semantic isomorphism, which is borne out in the analyses. Parallels between the descriptions of time and place relations are: (1) the similar properties of the systems ⇌TIM and ⇌PLA; (2) the analogy between systems such as ⇌EXT ('*extremity (temporal)*', §7.3.3) and ⇌EXTS ('*extremity (spatial)*', §8.3); (3) the resemblance between the ordering systems ⇌BEF (§7.1.1) and ⇌PLUS (§8.2.3), particularly with respect to their function in characterising relations of indirect converseness. In addition, there are systems such as ⇄INC, ⇄PART, and ⇄NEXT, which might be applied not only to time and place, but to more abstract relationships as well.

It has not been resolved, in the present study, whether this partial isomorphism of the temporal and locative relations should be handled by using the same systems and the same definitions for both, or whether the relationship should be treated as one of polysemy by metaphorical extension. Should words like *beginning* and *end*, for example, be given separate definitions for their uses in temporal and spatial contexts? The question cannot be decided without a careful evaluation of the simplicity of the two solutions. It is obviously desirable, on the one hand, to econo-mise on systems and on dictionary entries, by using the same semantic features for both time and place; but such a course might on the other hand demand a prohibitive increase in the complexity of redundancy rules. This is also to some extent a matter of theoretical decision, be-cause the former solution would require the introduction of a new kind of contextual rule, imposing concord of systems between the two ter-minal elements of a predication. If, for example, the system ⇄EXT were to be applied to spatial partition (thus eliminating the need for system ⇄EXTS '*extremity (spatial)*'), there would have to be a match between the two sides of the relationship, so as to prevent the incongruity of a point of time being treated as the extremity of a place, or a location as the extremity of a period. Such redundancy rules have not been found necessary in the individual analyses so far, but it is possible that in the context of a total semantic description of the language, it would be advisable to make provision for them.

One of the major tasks left undone is the detailed formulation of rules of expression. It may be felt, indeed, that this is a task of far greater priority than has been accorded to it here. However, as most recent approaches to semantics have been made via syntax, it has seemed more valuable, in this particular endeavour, to concentrate on the justification of semantic analyses as far as possible on the purely semantic ground of "basic statements" of meaning (§1.5), rather than to widen the area of study to include the bridge between form and semantics. Ultimately, of course, semantics needs a secure anchorage on both sides: its descriptive statements need to be formulated so as to account precisely not just for the native speaker's semantic performance with respect to any given utterance, but for the correlation between this performance and the for-mal (lexical and grammatical) features of the utterance.

There remains, too, the labour of devising adequate informant tests, a subject on which I have written elsewhere (Leech, forthcoming).

Finally, another task which must be looked upon as a matter of future or hypothetical accomplishment is the extension of this method of analysis to other languages. Two issues are involved in this extension: those that Chomsky has distinguished under the headings of "formal" and "substantive" universals (1965: 27-30). The issue of formal universals is that of the general validity of the semantic theory; the question of substantive universals, on the other hand, is the question of how far the designative systems set up for the description of one language duplicate those set up for the purpose of describing another. Informal observation of the feasibility of translation, etc, leads one to suppose that a considerable amount of common semantic ground exists between languages, or at least between languages whose users share a similar cultural background.

Translation equivalence, on a cognitive level at least, may be treated as a relation of "interlinguistic synonymy", and therefore as an empirically basic concept along with those of intralinguistic synonymy, implication, etc. Hence if systems common to two or more languages are postulated, the procedure of verifying such a hypothesis is analogous to that involved in checking a hypothesis within a monolingual semantic desscription.

Whilst such avenues of semantic research open in all directions towards an apparently limitless horizon, the investigator of today must be content with more modest aims and more modest accomplishments. Returning to Weinreich's words quoted at the beginning of this book, I shall be satisfied if, while providing insight into three areas of meaning in English, I have progressed some way towards closing the "fatal abyss between semantic theory and semantic description".

Bibliography

ALLEN, R. L. (1966), *The Verb System of Present-day American English*. The Hague

ARIEL, S. (1967), "Semantic Tests", *Man*, 2, pp 535–50

AYER, A. J. (1946), *Language, Truth, and Logic* (2nd edition). London

BAZELL, C. E., CATFORD, J. C., HALLIDAY, M. A. K. and ROBINS, R. H. (ed) (1966), *In Memory of J. R. Firth*. London

BENDIX, E. H. (1966), *Componential Analysis of General Vocabulary*. Bloomington, Indiana

BENNETT, D. C. (1968), "English Prepositions: A Stratificational Approach", *Journal of Linguistics*, 4, pp 153–72

BIERWISCH, M. (1967), "Some Semantic Universals of German Adjectives", *Foundations of Language*, 3, pp 1–36

BROWN, R. (1958), *Words and Things*. New York

BLOOMFIELD, L. (1935), *Language*. London

BOYD, J. and THORNE, J. P. (1969), "The Semantics of Modal Verbs", *Journal of Linguistics*, 5, pp 57–74

BULL, W. E. (1960), *Time, Tense, and the Verb*. Berkeley and Los Angeles

CARNAP, R. (1955), "Meaning and Synonymy in Natural Language", *Philosophical Studies*, 6, pp 33–47

CARNAP, R. (1936–7), "Testability and Meaning", *Philosophy of Science*, 3, pp 420–71

CARNAP, R. (1956a), *Meaning and Necessity* (2nd edition). Chicago

CARNAP, R. (1956b), "The Methodological Character of Theoretical Concepts", in Feigl and Scriven (ed), pp 38–76

CATFORD, J. C. (1959), "English as a Foreign Language", in R. Quirk and A. H. Smith (ed), pp 164–89

CHOMSKY, N. (1957), *Syntactic Structures*. The Hague

CHOMSKY, N. (1964a), "Current Issues in Linguistic Theory", in Fodor and Katz (1964a), pp 50–118

CHOMSKY, N. (1964b), "Degrees of Grammaticalness", in Fodor and Katz (1964a), pp 384–9

CHOMSKY, N. (1965), *Aspects of the Theory of Syntax*. Cambridge, Massachusetts

CLOSE, R. A. (1962), *English as a Foreign Language*. London

CONKLIN, H. C. (1955), "Hanunóo Color Categories", *S.W. Journal of Anthropology*, 11, pp 339–44

CONKLIN, H. C. (1962), "Lexicographic Treatment of Folk Taxonomies", in Householder and Saporta (ed), pp 119–41

CRYSTAL, D. (1966), "Specification and English Tenses", *Journal of Linguistics*, 2, pp 1–34

DIVER, W. (1963), "The Chronological System of the English Verb", *Word*, 19, pp 141–81

DIVER, W. (1964), "The Modal System of the English Verb", *Word*, 20, pp 322–52

DIXON, R. M. W. (1964), "On Formal and Contextual Meaning", *Acta Linguistica*, 14, pp 23–45

EHRMAN, M. (1966), *The Meanings of the Modals in Present-Day American English*. The Hague

ELLIS, J. O. (1966), "On Contextual Meaning", in Bazell, Catford, Halliday, and Robins (ed), pp 79–95

ERADES, P. A. (1957), "Points of Modern English Syntax", *English Studies*, 38, p 283

FEIGL, H. (1956), "Some Major Issues and Developments in the Philosophy of Science of Logical Empiricism", in Feigl and Scriven (ed), pp 3–37

FEIGL, H. and SCRIVEN, M. (ed) (1956), *Minnesota Studies in the Philosophy of Science*, Vol I. Minneapolis

FILLMORE, C. J. (1966), "Deictic Categories in the Semantics of 'Come'", *Foundations of Language*, 2, pp 219–27

FIRTH, J. R. (1957), *Papers in Linguistics 1934–51*. London

FODOR, J. A. and KATZ, J. J. (1964a), *The Structure of Language*. Englewood Cliffs, New Jersey

FODOR, J. A. and KATZ, J. J. (1964b), "Introduction", in Fodor and Katz (1964a), pp 1–18

FRAKE, C. O. (1964), "The Diagnosis of Disease among the Subanun of Mindanao", in D. Hymes (ed), *Language in Culture and Society* (New York and London), pp 193–206

FRIES, C. C. (1952), *The Structure of English*. London

GARVIN, P. L., BREWER, J. and MATHIOT, M. (1967), *Predication Typing: A Pilot Study in Semantic Analysis. Language Monographs*, 27

GLEASON, H. A. Jr. (1961), *An Introduction to Descriptive Linguistics* (Revised edition). New York

GOODENOUGH, W. H. (1965), "Yankee Kinship Terminology: a Problem in Componential Analysis", in Hammel (ed), pp 259–87

GRUBER, J. S. (1965), *Studies in Lexical Relations*, unpublished Ph.D. Thesis, M.I.T.

HALLIDAY, M. A. K. (1961), "Categories of the Theory of Grammar", *Word*, 17, pp 241–92

HALLIDAY, M. A. K. (1963), "Intonation in English Grammar", *TPS*, pp 143–69

HALLIDAY, M. A. K. (1966), "Some Notes on 'Deep' Grammar", *Journal of Linguistics*, 2, pp 57–68

HALLIDAY, M. A. K. (1967, 1968), "Notes on Transitivity and Theme in English", Parts I, II and III, *Journal of Linguistics*, 3, pp 37–81, 199–244; 4, pp 179–216

HALLIDAY, M. A. K., MCINTOSH, A. and STREVENS, P. (1964), *The Linguistic Sciences and Language Teaching*. London

HAMMEL, E. A. (ed) (1965), *Formal Semantic Analysis*. Special Publication of *American Anthropologist*, 67

HAMP, E. P. (1957), *A Glossary of American Technical Linguistic Usage 1925–50*. Utrecht and Antwerp

HILL, A. A. (1958), *Introduction to Linguistic Structures*. New York

HJELMSLEV, L. and ULDALL, H. J. (1957), *An Outline of Glossematics*. Copenhagen

HOENIGSWALD, H. M. (1960), *Language Change and Linguistic Reconstruction*. Chicago

HOUSEHOLDER, F. W. and SAPORTA, E. (1962), *Problems of Lexicography*. Bloomington, Indiana

HUDDLESTON, R. D., HUDSON, R., WINTER, E. and HENRICI, A. (1968), *Sentence and Clause in Scientific English*. University College, London, Communication Research Centre

JESPERSEN, O. (1924), *Philosophy of Language*, London

JESPERSEN, O. (1931), *A Modern English Grammar on Historical Principles*, Part IV. London and Copenhagen

JOHNSON-LAIRD, P. N. (1967), "Katz on Analyticity", *Journal of Linguistics*, 3, p 82

JOOS, M. (1964), *The English Verb: Form and Meanings*. Madison and Milwaukee

KARLSEN, R. (1959), *Studies in the Connection of Clauses in Current English*. Bergen

KATZ, J. J. (1964a), "Semi-sentences", in Fodor and Katz (1964a), pp 400–16

KATZ, J. J. (1964b), "Analyticity and Contradiction in Natural Language", in Fodor and Katz (1964a), pp 519–43

KATZ, J. J. (1966), *The Philosophy of Language*. London and New York

KATZ, J. J. (1967), "Recent Issues in Semantic Theory", *Foundations of Language*, 3, pp 124–94

KATZ, J. J. (1968), "The Logic of Questions", in B. van Rooselaar and J. F. Staal (ed), *Logic, Methodology, and Philosophy of Science*. Amsterdam

KATZ, J. J. and FODOR, J. A. (1963), "The Structure of a Semantic Theory", *Language*, 39, pp 170–210

KATZ, J. J., and POSTAL, P. M. (1963), "Semantic Interpretation of Idioms and Sentences Containing them", M.I.T., Research Laboratory of Electronics, *Quarterly Progress Report* No. 70 (Cambridge, Massachusetts), pp 275–82

KATZ, J. J. and POSTAL, P. M. (1964), *An Integrated Theory of Linguistic Descriptions*. Cambridge, Massachusetts

KRUISINGA, E. (1931), *A Handbook of Present-Day English. Part II: English Accidence and Syntax*. Groningen

LAMB, S. M. (1964a), "On Alternation, Transformation, Realization, and Stratification", in *Report of the 15th Annual Round Table Meeting on Linguistic and Language Studies*, ed C. I. J. M. Stuart(Washington, D.C.), pp 105–122

LAMB, S. M. (1964b), "The Sememic Approach to Structural Semantics", *Amer. Anthrop.*, 66, 3, Part 2, pp 57–77

LAMB, S. M. (1965), "Kinship Terminology and Linguistic Structure", in Hammel (ed), pp 37–64

LEBRUN, Y. (1965), '*Can*' and '*May*' in Present-Day English. Brussels

LEECH, G. N. (1968), "Some Assumptions in the Metatheory of Linguistics", *Linguistics*, 39, pp 87–102

LEECH, G. N. (forthcoming), "On the Theory and Practice of Semantic Testing"

LEES, R. B. (1962), "Discussion", in *Report of the 11th Annual Round Table Meeting on Linguistics and Language Studies*, ed B. Choseed (Washington, D.C.), pp 52, 184–5

LINSKY, L. (ed) (1952), *Semantics and the Philosophy of Language*. Urbana

LOUNSBURY, F. G. (1964), "The Structural Analysis of Kinship Semantics", in *Proceedings of the IXth International Congress of Linguists*. (The Hague), pp 1073–90

LOUNSBURY, F. G. (1965), "Another View of Trobriand Kinship Categories", in Hammel (ed), *Formal Semantic Analysis*, pp 142–85

LYONS, J. (1963), *Structural Semantics*. Publications of the Philological Society XX. Oxford

LYONS, J. (1968), *Introduction to Theoretical Linguistics*. Cambridge, England

MATES, B. (1951), "Analytic Sentences", *Philosophical Review*, 60, pp 525–34

MARTIN, R. M. (1952), "On 'Analytic'", *Philosophical Studies*, 3, pp 42–7

MCCAWLEY, J. D. (1968), "The Role of Semantics in a Grammar", in *Universals in Linguistic Theory*, ed. E. Bach and R. T. Harms (New York), pp 125–69

NIDA, E. A. (1949), *Morphology*. Ann Arbor, Michigan

OGDEN, C. K. and RICHARDS, I. A. (1923), *The Meaning of Meaning*. London

OLSSON, Y. (1961), *On the Syntax of the English Verb*. Gothenburg Studies in English, 12

PAP, A. (1963), *An Introduction to the Philosophy of Science*. London

PALMER, F. R. (1965), *A Linguistic Study of the English Verb*. London

QUINE, W. V. (1951), "Two Dogmas of Empiricism", *Philosophical Review*, 60, pp 20–43 (also in Quine, 1953)

QUINE, W. V. (1953), *From a Logical Point of View*. Cambridge, Massachusetts

QUINE, W. V. (1960), *Word and Object*. Cambridge, Massachusetts

QUIRK, R. and SMITH, A. H. (ed) (1959), *The Teaching of English*. London

QUIRK, R. and SVARTVIK, J. (1966), *Investigating Linguistic Acceptability*. The Hague

REICHENBACH, H. (1947), *Elements of Symbolic Logic*. New York

RIES, J. (1894), *Was ist ein Satz?* Marburg

RUSSELL, B. (1920), *Introduction to Mathematical Philosophy*, 2nd edition. London. (Chapter on "descriptions" reprinted in Linsky, ed)

SCHEFFLER, I. (1964), *The Anatomy of Inquiry*. London

SCRIVEN, M. (1956), "A Study of Radical Behaviourism", in Feigl and Scriven (ed), pp 88–130

SOKAL, R. R. and SNEATH, P. H. A. (1963), *Principles of Numerical Taxonomy*. San Francisco and London

SØRENSEN, H. S. (1958), *Word Classes in English with Special Reference to Proper Names*. Copenhagen

STAAL, J. F. (1967), "Some Semantic Relations between Sentoids", *Foundations of Language*, 3, pp 66–88

STAAL, J. F. (1968), "'And'", *Journal of Linguistics*, 4, pp 79–82

STOLL, R. R. (1961), *Sets, Logic and Axiomatic Theories*. San Francisco and London

STRANG, B. M. H. (1962), *Modern English Structure*. London

SWEET, H. (1892), *A New English Grammar*, Part I. Oxford

THOMAS, O. (1965), *Transformational Grammar and the Teacher of English*. New York

TWADDELL, W. F. (1960), *The English Verbal Auxiliaries*. Providence, Rhode Island

WAISMANN, F. (1949–53), "Analytic-Synthetic", *Analysis*, 10, pp 25–40; 11, pp 25–38, pp 116–24; 13, pp 1–14, pp 74–89

WEINREICH, U. (1962), "Lexicographic Definition in Descriptive Semantics", in Householder and Saporta (ed), pp 25–43

WEINREICH, U. (1963), "On the Semantic Structure of Language", in *Universals of Language*, ed J. H. Greenberg (Cambridge, Massachusetts), pp 114–71

WEINREICH, U. (1964), "Webster's Third: a Critique of its Semantics" *IJAL*, 30, pp 405–9

WEINREICH, U. (1966), "Explorations in Semantic Theory", in *Current Trends in Linguistics*, Vol. III, ed T. A. Sebeok (The Hague), pp 394–477

WEINREICH, U. (1967), "On Arguing with Mr Katz: a Brief Rejoinder", *Foundations of Language*, 5, pp 284–7

WELLS, R. S. (1954), "Meaning and Use", *Word*, 10, pp 235–50

WHITE, M. G. (1950), "The Analytic and the Synthetic: an Untenable Dualism", in *John Dewey: Philosopher of Science and Freedom* (New York), pp 316–330. (Reprinted in Linsky, ed)

ZIMMER, K. E. (1964), *Affixal Negation in English and Other Languages*. Supplement to *Word*, 20, 2

Glossary of technical terms
of the semantic theory

This is an aid to the understanding of the preceding chapters, not an attempt to formalise their content. No apology is offered for inevitable circularity in the use of one term in the explanation of another. Relevant sections of the book are indicated within square brackets.

ACCEPTABLE (of any linguistic entity): recognised by native speakers as belonging to their language [§1.7]

AMBIGUOUS (of a formal item): having more than one meaning [§2.6]

ANALYTIC (of an assertion): tautological; true by virtue of meaning alone, without regard to factual content [§1.5, 1.8]

ASCRIPTION FEATURE: A feature which belongs to a medial cluster, and which does not form part of its componential content, but rather is matched against the content of an adjacent terminal cluster, such that co-occurrence with a systemically contrasting component is marked as a violation [§4.1.2]

ASSERTION: Statement, proposition; the type of predication to which properties of truth and falsehood are attributed

AUTONOMY OF LEVELS: The condition whereby levels of linguistic function (grammar, semantics, etc) are described without the use of terms employed in the description of other levels [§2.6]

BASIC STATEMENT: A descriptive statement which is held to be falsifiable by direct reference to observation [§1.5]

CLUSTER: A unit which is a constituent of a predication, and which consists of a set of semantic features [§2.4]

   ATTRIBUTIVE C: One of the two elements of a one-place predication, the other being either a terminal cluster or a rank-shifted predication. An attributive c. is parallel in function to the medial cluster of a two-place predication. It is often expressed by a form of the verb *to be* followed by an adjectival or nominal phrase [§4.2.1].

9+T.S.D.E.

EMPTY C: A c. (symbolised $\varnothing$) which contains no features, and which represents the maximum generalisation or undifferentiation of designative meaning. [§2.9].

MEDIAL C: A c. which occurs between the two terminal clusters of a predication, and which contains at least one relative component [§2.4]

METALINGUISTIC C: A c. denoting a linguistic entity, or a set of linguistic entities [§3.4]

TERMINAL C: A c. which occurs as initial or final element of a predication, and which contains no relative components [§2.4]

COMPETENCE (LINGUISTIC): A person's intrinsic knowledge or mastery of his language (as distinct from performance) [§1.6]

COMPONENT: A term in a semantic system [§2.4]

COMPONENTIAL ANALYSIS: Semantic analysis in terms of systemically contrasting features (components) and their combination [§2.2]

CONTEXTUAL REDUNDANCY RULE: A redundancy rule whereby the presence, in a medial cluster, of a feature of a relative system requires, for well-formedness, the assignment of a feature or some other property to a terminal element of the same predication [§4.1.2]

CONTRADICTION: An assertion which is invariably false by virtue of its meaning alone, without regard to questions of fact [§§1.8, 2.8.5]

CONVERSENESS, INDIRECT: A relationship between logical "converses" (*eg* 'in front of'/'behind') which is symbolised not directly, through the "mirror-image" convention, but indirectly, through the combined operation of the "mirror-image" convention and the second rule of attribution [§7.1.1]

CO-REFERENCE: A relationship of referential equivalence between a cluster and some other part of the same text, signalled by the presence of the definite formator θ in the cluster [§3.3]

DESIGNATIVE: A component or a downgraded predication [§2.5.2]

DEPENDENCE RULE: A redundancy rule whereby the presence of a feature of one system in a cluster requires, for well-formedness, the presence in the same cluster of a feature from some other system [§4.1]

DESIGNATOR: A component. A feature of designative meaning, as opposed to a formator, or feature of logical meaning [§3.0]

DOWNGRADED (of a predication): Occurring as a feature in a cluster, and hence (indirectly) as part of another predication [§2.5.2]

EVALUATIVE MEANING: A type of designative (componential) meaning involving aesthetic, ethical, moral, etc values [§5.2]

EXCLUSION, LOGICAL: A relation between two componential formulae containing systemically contrasting components, as in 'love'/'hate', 'boy'/'girl', 'dog'/'cat', etc [§§2.2, 2.8.1]

EXISTENTIALLY CONSTRUED: A cluster is e.c. when it is interpreted as if governed by the existential quantifier: *eg* 'People' in 'People were waiting', when interpreted as equivalent to 'Some people' [§2.8.2]

EXPRESSION, RULES OF: Rules relating meaning to linguistic form [§2.7]

FEATURE (SEMANTIC): A designator (component) or formator. Features, together with downgraded predications, make up the class of elements of which clusters are composed

FEELING-TONE: That which an utterance or text conveys about the feelings and attitudes of its originator [§5.2]

FORMATOR: A "logical" feature, whose function within semantic description is determined by special rules [§3.0]. The following specimen formators mentioned in the text are identified (a) by their notational symbols, and (b) by the words which most directly express them:

ATTRIBUTIVE F: $(\rightarrow\beta)$ *be* [§3.1]
CONDITIONAL F: $(\rightarrow\supset)$ *if* [§3.2.2]
DEFINITE F: (θ) *the* [§3.3]
NEGATIVE F: $(\sim)$ *not* [§3.2.1]

FORMULA, COMPONENTIAL: A set of designatives [§2.5.2]

FORMULA, EMPTY: The null set of designatives or components, symbolised $\varnothing$ [§2.9]

IMPLICATION: One assertion X implies another assertion Y if the truth of X guarantees the truth of Y. From §2.8.2 onwards, "implication" has been used as an abbreviation for "logical implication" (see below) [§§1.4, 1.7, 1.8]

DEDUCTIVE I: A type of implication in which the implying assertion differs from the implied assertion in being more general: *eg* 'Adults are sensible' d. implies 'Women are sensible' [§2.8.2]

FACTUAL I: Implication which rests upon knowledge o f the world, rather than upon meaning alone [§1.8]

INDUCTIVE I: A type of implication in which the implying assertion differs from the implied assertion in being more specific: *eg* 'Some women are sensible' i. implies 'Some adults are sensible' [§2.8.2]

LOGICAL I: Implication which rests purely upon meaning relations between two assertions [§1.8]

INCONSISTENCY (LOGICAL): A relation between two assertions which, by virtue of meaning, cannot both be true at once [§2.8.3]

INCLUSION, LOGICAL: One cluster x logically includes another y if all the designatives in x are also in y: *eg* 'fruit' logically includes 'apple' [§§2.2, 2.8.1]

INFORMATIVELY VACUOUS (of assertions): Conveying no information other than what is self-evident. Tautologies are i.v. [§1.8]

INVERSENESS: The relationship between the two terms of an inversion system [§3.5, 8.8.2, 9.1]

MEANINGFUL (LITERALLY): Having literal cognitive content. Contingent assertions (those that are neither necessarily false nor necessarily true) are classed as meaningful, whereas tautologies and contradictions are classed as meaningless [§1.7]

MEANINGLESS (LITERALLY): Not literally meaningful [§§1.4, 1.7]

"MIRROR-IMAGE" NOTATIONAL CONVENTION: The convention whereby two predicational formulae, differing only in the order of the elements and the mark of directionality (if such a mark is present), are said to represent the same predication; eg: $a \cdot \rightarrow r \cdot b = b \cdot \leftarrow r \cdot a$; $a{:}m = m{:}a$ [§2.3]

OXYMORON: A semantic violation resulting from the combination of forms whose meanings logically exclude one another, and consisting in the occurrence in one cluster of two different terms from the same system, as in 'male woman' [§2.2]

PARAPHRASE (of assertions, questions, etc): Equivalence with regard to truth and falsehood [§1.4]

PERFORMANCE (LINGUISTIC): The use a person makes of his intrinsic linguistic knowledge or COMPETENCE in interpreting or in composing utterances or texts [§1.6]

PLEONASM: An irregularity of expression resulting from the combination of one form with another whose meaning logically includes its own meaning, as in 'false lie', 'male boy' [§2.2]

POLYSEMY: Ambiguity (of single words or lexical items) [§2.6]

PREDICATION: A semantic unit having one, two, or three clusters or equivalent elements as its constituents. Assertion, question, and command are classes of predication [§2.3]

    ADVERBIAL P: A p. expressed by an adverbial element in syntax [§6.1]

    INDEPENDENT (OR MAIN) P: A p. which is not rank-shifted or downgraded; ie one which is not included, directly or indirectly, within another p.

    ONE-PLACE P: A p. having only one terminal element and corresponding to the one-place predicate of formal logic [§4.2.1]

    PRINCIPAL P: A p. expressed by the main elements of clause structure: subject, predicator, and (optionally) complement [§3.5, 6.1]

    TWO-PLACE P: A p. having two terminal elements, and corresponding to the two-place predicate of formal logic [§4.2.1]

QUANTIFICATION, MIXED: The occurrence of both the existential quantifier and the universal quantifier in the same predicational formula; such a formula is expressed, for example, in the sentence *All cats like some fish* [§3.5]

QUANTIFIER, EXISTENTIAL: The formator representing (roughly) the meaning of *some* [§3.5]

QUANTIFIER, UNIVERSAL: The formator representing (roughly) the meaning of *all, every, any* [§3.5]

RANK-SHIFTED (of a predication): Occurring as a constituent of another predication [§2.5.1]

REDUNDANCY RULE: A rule which attaches a certain condition of well-formedness to a system, by requiring the occurrence of a feature of that system to be accompanied by other features or properties, either in the same cluster, or in another element of the same predication [§4.1]

STRUCTURAL ANALYSIS: Semantic analysis in terms of predications and the clusters (or rank-shifted predications) which are their constituents [§§2.3, 2.4]

STYLISTICS (GENERAL): (The study of) linguistic variation relative to linguistic, social, and emotive context [§5.2]

SUBORDINATION (of predications): Rank-shift or downgrading.

SYMMETRY, INDIRECT: A symmetric relation (*eg* 'as tall as') symbolised not directly (as in the case of reciprocal systems) but indirectly, through the operation of the "mirror-image" convention and the second rule of attribution [§7.1.1]

SYNTHETIC (of assertions): True by virtue of fact, rather than meaning (as opposed to ANALYTIC) [§1.8]

SYNONYMY: The relation of two or more expressions having the same meaning [§2.6]. (This definition does not, however, include "factual" and "cognitive" synonymy below)

COGNITIVE S (of assertions): Equivalence of truth value [§1.4]

COMPONENTAL S: The equivalence of meaning of two or more expressions whose meaning is represented by the same componential formula [§2.2]

FACTUAL S: A paraphrase relationship which cannot be explained in terms of meaning alone [§1.8]

LOGICAL S: A paraphrase relationship which can be explained semantically [§1.8]

RULE OF S: A rule equating different semantic specifications [§§4.3, 4.4]

FORMAL R OF S: One which applies without respect to designative content [§4.3]

SUBSTANTIVE R OF S: One which applies to a given designative content [§4.4]

SYSTEM: A set of linguistic terms or features of which only one may be chosen for the purpose of characterising a given piece of language [§2.1]

ATTRIBUTIVE S: A s the features of which may occur freely (as far as dependence rules permit) in attributive clusters, and are associated with contextual redundancy rules [§8.6]

HIERARCHIC S: A system whose terms are systematically ordered with respect to one another: 'Sunday'/'Monday'/'Tuesday'/..., 'one'/'two'/'three'/ ... , etc [§2.2]

INVERSION S: A binary system (*eg* 'all'/'some') the terms of which are related by the following rule (roughly worded): "If one term of an inversion system is replaced by the other, whilst the position of the negative formator is changed from rank-shifted predication to main predication or vice versa, the meaning of the total predication remains unchanged" [§3.5]

ORDERING S: A relative system which is transitive, irreflexive, and asymmetric; *eg* 'above'/'below' [§4.1.1]

POLAR S: A system of two terms which are 'gradable', in the sense that they can be accompanied by a further component ('very', 'rather', etc) specifying degree of intensity; *eg* 'wise'/'foolish'; 'strong'/ 'weak' [§2.2]

RECIPROCAL S: A relative system which is symmetric; *eg* 'married to' [§4.1.1]

RELATIVE S: A system whose terms represent the directional contrast of logical converses: 'loves'/'is loved by'; 'owns'/'belongs to', etc [§2.2]

TAXONOMIC S: A system of two terms (BINARY) or of more than two terms (MULTIPLE) which is best defined negatively, as not having any of the attributes which distinguish other kinds of system mentioned above; *eg* 'male'/'female'; 'animal'/'vegetable'/'mineral' [§2.2]

TAUTOLOGY: A logically incontradictable assertion; *ie* one which is necessarily true, by virtue of its meaning alone [§§1.5, 1.8, 2.8.4]

TRANSFERENCE, RULE OF: A rule which derives irregular or transferred meanings from regular or literal meanings [§5.4]

UNIVERSALLY CONSTRUED (of clusters): Interpreted as if subject to universal quantification; *eg* 'Men' in 'Men are evil' is u.c. when interpreted as equivalent to 'All men' [§2.8.2]

Summary of notation

[Relevant sections of the book are indicated in square brackets]

[A] BASIC PRINCIPLES
1 If utterances are represented by the same notational formula, they have the same meaning [§2.3].
2 If utterances are represented by different semantic formulae, they have different meanings, unless they are shown to be equivalent by rules of synonymy [§§4.3–4].

[B] FEATURE SYMBOLS
1 +A, −A, 1B, 2C, etc represent non-relative components. Different terms of the same system are distinguished by different prefixes (usually + and − in the case of a binary system, otherwise 1, 2, etc). Terms of different systems are distinguished by different capital letters [§2.2].
2 More frequently it is convenient to use a sequence of capital letters to symbolise a system, so that the meaning of the symbol may be more easily remembered: +HUM 'human', −MALE 'female', etc [§2.2].
3 →R, ←L, →EMO, ←END, etc represent relative components. Systemic contrast (converseness) is indicated by the direction of the arrow: →EMO, ←EMO, etc [§§2.2–3].
4 Formators are represented by Greek letters or by general logical symbols, together with a prefix (+, −, 1, 2) or arrow if applicable: +ψ, π, θ, →⊃, etc [§3.0].
5 An ascription feature is symbolised thus: [+COU] [§4.1.2].
6 A full list of formator and system symbols is given separately below.

[C] FEATURE FORMULAE

1 A set of features is represented by an unordered combination of feature symbols: +A −B, θ +HUM −MAT, →EMO +LOV, etc [§§2.2–4].

2 A single feature symbol may represent a unit set consisting of one feature only: +HUM, →⊃, etc [§§2.2–4].

3 ∅ represents the empty set of features [§2.9].

4 x, y, z are variable symbols representing arbitrary feature formulae or rank-shifted predications.

5 a, b, c, d are variable symbols representing arbitrary feature formulae not containing any relative feature; they may function as "content variables" for terminal clusters [§§2.3–5].

6 r, s, t are variable symbols standing for arbitrary feature formulae containing at least one relative feature. →r, ←r are a pair of contrasting symbols which differ only in that →r contains some relative feature →R, where ←r contains some relative feature ←R. Likewise for ←s, etc, r, →s, ←t, etc may function as "content variables" for medial clusters [§§2.3–4].

7 m, n, p, q are symbols which may function as "content variables" for attributive clusters [§4.2.1].

8 a, b, c, . . . , z are sometimes used as constants representing a set of features, where for ease of comprehension the choice of letter corresponds with the initial letter of a word or phrase expressing the set, eg: l = 'likes' [§3.5].

9 A union of feature sets is represented simply by juxtaposition: eg the union of a and b is written ab. The union of a and ∅ is obviously a; the union of +HUM +MAT and b is +HUM +MAT b. Where both sets are expressed in terms of feature symbols, features which occur in both sets occur only once in the union formula: the union of +HUM +MALE and +HUM +MAT is +HUM +MALE +MAT.

10 In the case of reciprocal systems, the combination of systemically contrasting terms is written ←R →R, etc [§4.1.1].

[D] PREDICATION FORMULAE

1 A, B, . . . , X, Y, Z are variable symbols representing arbitrary predications [§§2.3–4].

2 However, predications are more commonly represented in terms of the feature formulae which make up their constituent clusters:
· $a \cdot r \cdot b$, etc in the case of two-place predications, $a:m$, etc in the case of one-place predications. Here, a, b, etc stand for terminal clusters, r, s, etc for medial clusters, and m, n, etc for attributive clusters. The directionality of r, s, etc may or may not be shown by an arrow. Clusters may be represented indifferently by variable symbols, by feature sets, or mixtures of both. Examples of predica-

tion formulae in which various options are used are: $\theta\, a\cdot r\cdot b$; $+$MAT $+$HUM$\cdot\to$PAR $b\cdot\, \varnothing$; a:$+$WISE [§§2.3–4, 4.2.1].

3 By the "mirror-image" convention, predications are equivalent if their formulae are alike except for the order of the elements and the direction of the arrow (if there is a medial cluster), *eg:* $a\cdot\to r\cdot b=b\cdot\leftarrow r\cdot a;\ a\cdot\leftarrow r\cdot b=b\cdot\to r\cdot a;\ a$:$m=m$:$a$ [§§2.3, 4.2.1].

4 The decimal point indicates a boundary between clusters in a two-place predication; the colon indicates a boundary between clusters in a one-place predication [§§2.3–4, 4.2.1].

5 Rank-shifted predications are indicated by enclosure in round brackets: $a\cdot r\cdot(b\cdot s\cdot c),\ a\cdot r\cdot(X)$ [§2.5.1].

6 Downgraded predications are signalled by angle brackets, *eg* $a'\langle\theta'\cdot r\cdot b\rangle\cdot s\cdot c$. All that applies to feature symbols in [c] above applies also to downgraded predications, which have the status of features [§2.5.2].

7 Features placed next to a predication variable are understood to be added to the medial or attributive cluster of the predication, not to a terminal cluster. For example, if $X=a\cdot r\cdot b$, then $X\,+$COU$=a\cdot r\,+$COU$\cdot b$ [§6.2].

[E] CO-REFERENCE

1 Co-reference between a definite formator and a neighbouring part of the text is indicated by matching prime markings: $a'\ldots\theta'$, $b''\ldots\theta''$, etc. The clusters a and b here are termed "co-referential domains" of θ [§3.3].

2 When θ co-refers to a rank-shifted predication, the prime marking is placed after the closing bracket: $a\cdot r\cdot(b\cdot s\cdot c)'\ldots\theta'$ [§3.5].

3 When the whole of a main predication is co-referred to, it is necessary to enclose it in brackets for the specific purpose of showing that the whole predication, not just its closing cluster, is the domain of co-reference: $(a\cdot r\cdot b)'\ldots\theta'$ is thereby distinct from $a\cdot r\cdot b'\ldots\theta$.

4 When a predication is downgraded within the medial cluster or attributive cluster of another predication, its semantic link with the main predication is provided by θ co-referring to the whole of main predication *with the exception of the downgraded predication itself.* For example, in $(a\cdot r\langle\theta'\cdot s\cdot c\rangle\cdot b)'$, the co-referential domain of θ' is $a\cdot r\cdot b$; in the equivalent formula $X'\langle\theta'\cdot s\cdot c\rangle$ (see [D]7) the co-referential domain of θ' is X [§§3.5, 6.2].

5 When two downgraded predications $\langle\theta\, a\cdot r\cdot b\rangle$ and $\langle\theta\, c\cdot s\cdot d\rangle$ occur in the same cluster, they may be ordered according to whether $\langle\theta\, a\cdot r\cdot b\rangle$ is included in the co-referential domain of θ in $\langle\theta\, c\cdot s\cdot d\rangle$ or vice versa. This difference is signalled by left-to-right sequence as follows: $x'\langle\theta'\, a\cdot r\cdot b\rangle''\ \langle\theta''\, c\cdot s\cdot d\rangle$. As it is a general rule that anything to the left of the prime-marking in the same cluster be-

longs to the co-referential domain, in this case $\langle \theta\; a \cdot r \cdot b\rangle$ is included in the co-referential domain of θ in $\langle \theta\; c \cdot s \cdot d\rangle$. The opposite is signalled by $x'\langle \theta'\; c \cdot s \cdot d\rangle''\; \langle \theta''\; a \cdot r \cdot b\rangle$. This is one case in which ordering within feature formulae may indicate a difference of meaning [§6.2].

6 A similar difference of ordering is possible in the case of downgraded predications within medial clusters (see item [E]4 above). $X'\langle \theta'\; a \cdot r \cdot b\rangle''\; \langle \theta''\; c \cdot s \cdot d\rangle$ indicates that whereas X alone is the co-referential domain of θ', the co-referential domain of θ'' is $X'\langle \theta'\; a \cdot r \cdot b\rangle$ [§6.2].

[F] ITALICS AND SINGLE QUOTATION MARKS

Items of language enclosed within single quotation marks are identified as semantic abstractions, *ie* as predications, clusters, etc, whereas italicised items are identified as formal abstractions such as words, lexical items, phrases, sentences. Thus 'My favourite film-star' = 'The film-star I like best' (because the two are synonymous), but *My favourite film-star* ≠ *The film-star I like best* (because formally, *viz* grammatically and lexically, they are different) [§2.6].

List of formator and system symbols

Systems are identified by the system symbol alone. The following are used as abbreviations for types of system: *bt* (binary taxonomic), *mt* (multiple taxonomic), *p* (polar), *h* (hierarchic), *r* (relative), *i* (inversion), *r–o* (relative–ordering), *r–r* (relative–reciprocal), *h–c* (hierarchic–cyclic). The section in which a system or formator is introduced is indicated in square brackets.

[A] FORMATORS AND FORMATOR SYSTEMS

α	(*i*)	'all'/'some' [§3.5]
β	(*r*)	'be' (attributive formator system) (this system is discarded in §4.2.1, with the introduction of one-place predications) [§3.2]
δ	(*i*)	'stay'/'become' [§8.8.2]
θ		'the' (definite formator) [§3.3]
ι	(*r*)	'become' (inceptive formator system) (this system is discarded in §8.8.2, with the introduction of $\rightleftarrows\mu$ and $1\delta/2\delta$) [§3.6]
μ	(*r*)	'become' [§8.8.2]
o	(*r*)	'of' (in quantificational predications, such as 'all OF the children were there') [§3.5]
π	(*i*)	'possible'/'necessary' (system of constraint) [§9.2.3]
τ	(*bt*)	'theoretical'/'practical' (of possibility and necessity) [§9.4.2]
ψ	(*bt*)	'actual'/'hypothetical' (system of actuality) [§9.2.2]
$\supset$	(*r*)	'if' (conditional formator system) [§3.1.2]
$\sim$		'not' (negative formator) [§3.1.1]
?		(question feature) [§6.2]

[B] DESIGNATIVE SYSTEMS

A	*(r–o)*	'ancestor'/'descendant' [§4.4]
ABLE	*(r)*	'is able to' [§9.4.3]
ANIM	*(bt)*	'animate'/'inanimate' [§2.8.1]
AUT	*(r)*	'has permission or is under obligation to' [§9.2.4]
BEF	*(r–o)*	'before'/'after' [§7.1.1]
C	*(r–r)*	'cousin' [§4.4]
CAL	*(bt)*	'calendar'/'non-calendar' (of time periods) [§7.1.2]
CAU	*(r)*	'causes' [§9.2.1]
CONC	*(bt)*	'concrete'/'abstract' [§6.3.1]
CONS	*(r)*	'consists of' [§7.3.1]
COU	*(bt)*	'countable'/'mass' [6.3.2]
DAYM	*(h–c)*	'first'/'second'/... (days of the month) [§7.1.2]
DAYN	*(h–c)*	'day'/'night' [§7.1.2]
DAYW	*(h–c)*	'Sunday'/'Monday'/... [§7.1.2]
DIAG	*(bt)*	'diagonal'/'non-diagonal' [§8.3.2]
DIME	*(mt)*	'at'/'on'/'in' [§8.1.1]
DUR	*(r)*	'lasts for' [§7.3.1]
EGO	*(bt)*	'includes speaker(s)'/'excludes speaker(s)' [§9.5.1]
EMO	*(r)*	'has an emotional disposition towards' [§2.4]
END	*(bt)*	'end'/'beginning' [§7.3.3]
EXT	*(r)*	'is a temporal extremity of' [§7.3.3]
EXTS	*(r)*	'is a spatial extremity of' [§8.3]
FAR	*(p)*	'far'/'near' [§8.2.3]
FREQ	*(r)*	'with frequency...' [§7.2.3]
G	*(h)*	'1st generation'/'2nd generation'/... [§4.4]
HUM	*(bt)*	'human'/'brute' ('animal') [§2.2]
INC	*(r–o)*	'is included in' [§7.1.3]
LOCO	*(mt)*	'walk'/'run'/... [§8.6]
LOV	*(p)*	'love'/'hate' [§2.4]
MAE	*(h)*	'morning'/'afternoon'/'evening' [§7.1.2]
MALE	*(bt)*	'male'/'female' [§2.2]
MAN	*(r)*	'in... manner' [§6.2]
MANY	*(p)*	'many'/'a few' [§3.5]
MAR	*(r–r)*	'is married to' [§4.1.2]
MAT	*(bt)*	'mature'/'immature' [§2.2]
MID	*(bt)*	'middle'/'peripheral' [§8.3.2]
MON	*(h–c)*	'January'/'February'/... [§7.1.2]
MOV	*(bt)*	'moving'/'stationary' [§8.6]
NEXT	*(r–r)*	'is next to' [§7.1.2]
NOR	*(r–o)*	'north'/'south' [§8.4]
OBS	*(r)*	'is the point of observation for' [§8.5.1]
ORI	*(r)*	'is the point of orientation for' [§8.5.1]

PAR   (*r*)   'is parent of' [§4.4]
PART   (*r–o*) 'is part of' [§8.3]
PERI   (*bt*)   'period'/'point of time' [§7.1]
PERS   (*bt*)   'personal'/'non-personal' [§9.5.1]
PLA   (*r*)   'is at/on/in ...' [§8.1]
PLUR   (*bt*)   'plural'/'singular' [§6.3.2]
PLUS   (*r–o*) 'over/in front of/to the left of'/'under/behind/ to the right of' [§8.2.3.]
POI   (*bt*)   'point direction'/'field direction' [§8.4]
POS   (*mt*)   'stand'/'sit'/... [§8.6]
PRI   (*bt*)   'front/back'/'side' [§8.2.3]
PROB   (*p*)   'probable'/'improbable' [§9.4.5]
PROX   (*r–r*) 'is proximate to' [§8.2.2]
QUA   (*h*)   'one'/'two'/'three'/... [§6.3.2]
S   (*r–r*) 'sibling' [§4.4]
SEA   (*h–c*) 'spring'/'summer'/... [§7.1.2]
SET   (*r*)   'is a member of the set ...' [§7.1.5]
SID   (*r–r*) 'is to the ... side of' [§8.2.3]
SITU   (*bt*)   'situation'/'non-situation' [§7.5]
SPE   (*mt*)   'dog'/'cat'/... [§5.3]
THIS   (*bt*)   'this'/'that' [§7.1]
TIM   (*r*)   'at time ...' [§7.1]
UNIT   (*h*)   'second'/'minute'/... [§7.1.2]
VER   (*bt*)   'vertical'/'horizontal' [§8.2.3]
VOL   (*r*)   'wishes' [§9.3]
WEST   (*r–o*) 'west'/'east' [§8.4]
WISE   (*p*)   'wise'/'foolish' [§5.1]
YEAR   (*h*)   'A.D. 1'/'A.D. 2'/.../'A.D. 1968'/... [§7.1.2]
YOU   (*bt*)   'including addressee'/'excluding addressee' [§9.5.1]

Notes to chapters

CHAPTER I

1 See Bibliography.
2 However, notable contributions have been made to descriptive semantics since 1963. See especially Bendix (1966) and Bierwisch (1967).
3 This aspect of the delimitation of semantics is considered in §5.2.
4 See Mates (1951); Waismann (1949, 1951, 1952, 1953); Martin (1951). In declaring his intention to confine his explication (of meaning postulates) to artificial "semantical language systems", Carnap (1956a: 222–3) notes "it shares this character with most of the explications of philosophically important concepts given in modern logic, *eg* Tarski's explication of truth. It seems to me that the problems of explicating concepts of this kind for natural languages are of an entirely different nature." However, one need only study Reichenbach's "Analysis of Conversational Language" (1947: 251–354) to realise that logicians can contribute important insights to linguistic semantics.
5 See especially §§2.8.3–5 on logical inconsistency, tautologies, and contradictions; §3.3 on definite meaning; §3.5 on quantification; §4.1.1 on logical conditions on relative systems; §§4.3–4 on rules of synonymy; and §4.2.2 on many-place predicates. The reader is also referred to Ch. 2, nn. 7, 9, 25, 28, 29; Ch. 3, n. 11; Ch. 4, nn. 4, 14; in which comparisons are drawn with other models of semantic description, including the transformational semantics of Katz and Fodor (1963), and of Weinreich (1966); and the stratificational semantics of Lamb (1964a, 1964b, 1965). I shall not attempt a full critique of these alternative approaches.
6 This point would be too obvious to be worth making, except that various linguists in the past have felt obliged to "define" basic terms as a preliminary to embarking on a field of study. For a sensible discussion of the word "language" from this point of view, see Barbara Strang (1962: 2–3). The discussion of the notions of "language" and "sentence" in Thomas (1965: 27–8) is also relevant to this point. Thomas quotes Lees (1962: 52, 181–2) as remarking that just as a biologist would not attempt to define the fundamental concept of the "cell", so a linguist should not attempt to define the fundamental concept "sentence", since if we "already knew how to define 'grammatical sentence of English', there would be no earthly reason for trying to formulate

a theory of English sentences, *ie* an English grammar." To define the sentence as a "minimum free form" or "expression of a complete thought", etc, would merely shift the problem of explanation to other terms such as "form" and "thought".

7 Ogden and Richards (1923: 186–7) set a bad example when they introduced into semantics the sport of hunting down as many meanings of "meaning" as possible, in order to show how vague and ambiguous the term is. Like most common English verbs, "mean" can of course be used in a number of different senses; but like any term crucial to a particular branch of knowledge, it has also been *given* numerous technical definitions by philosophers, psychologists, etc, who wish to fit it into predetermined conceptual systems. Such technical definitions merely show that their authors have, for their own purposes, wished to explain "meaning" in terms of other entities regarded as more primitive – *eg* stimuli and responses. The trouble with "meaning" is not that it is in ordinary usage an ill-used and ill-understood term, but rather that it is germane to a large number of different spheres of knowledge, with the result that many people have decided to use the term in a great variety of ways. Again, as in the previous note, a parallel example is the term "sentence", for which Ries (1894) (see Fries, 1952: 17) collected 140 definitions, but which is treated as an undefined primitive in transformational literature.

8 A recent attempt to draw such lines has been made by Bennett (1968: 165–7), who distinguishes five linguistically useful notions of "meaning".

9 See, for example, Nida (1949: 152); Hoenigswald (1960). It is revealing that the only entry under "synonym" in Hamp's *Glossary* (1957) reads: "Bloomfield 1933, p. 145: 'We suppose, in short, that there are no actual synonyms.'"

10 See §2.6 on "autonomy of levels", and Ch. 2, n. 15 on "ambiguity".

11 Well-known attacks on analyticity are White (1950) and Quine (1951). In Quine (1960: 61–7) the author also dismisses cognitive synonymy (*ie* synonymy in terms of truth value) by showing that its viability rests on that of analyticity.

12 For example, Carnap (1955; 1956a: 222–9). Feigl (1956: 5–8) argues that Quine's view on analyticity stems from a confusion between artificial and natural languages. Counter-arguments to Quine from a linguistic point of view are put forward by Chomsky (1964a: 80–1) and Katz (1964b). However, Katz (1966: 8), like Fodor and Katz (1964b), seems to make a fallacious assumption that philosophers and linguists are engaged in the same kind of activity, so that philosophers may turn to linguistics for explications of important logical concepts. This appears to be just as much a fallacy as the opposite assumption that linguistics must follow the methods of philosophical analysis. To see this, we need only observe that linguistics itself, like any rational enterprise of the mind, presupposes the rules of logic. We would, for example, reject a linguistic theory which was logically inconsistent. The claim that linguistics both presupposes and is presupposed by logic obviously involves circularity.

13 Quine, as a philosopher, is interested in deriving the concepts of logical and philosophical semantics (and hence of science as a whole), with the fewest possible *a priori* assumptions, from observed verbal behaviour. The linguist, on the other hand, like scientists in other areas, takes the logical foundations of knowledge for granted: it is no more his business to investigate it, than it is the business of the biologist or physicist. Quine rejects the analytic/synthetic distinction, together with the logical concept of synonymy, because it has no behavioural correlates. But it is instructive to notice that other important dichotomies in linguistics, such as grammatical/ungrammatical, langue/

parole, grammatical/phonological, etic/emic, diachronic/synchronic, also have no behavioural correlates. This does not lead the linguist to abandon them. They are retained so long as their usefulness in providing a basis for new insights and advances endures. The acceptance of the necessity for theoretical terms (of which these are examples) as well as observation terms, and of the oblique relation between them, is scarcely challenged in the modern philosophy of science: "Knowledge, both on the level of common sense and on that of science, is now being regarded as a network of concepts and propositions tied in only a few places to the data of immediate experience, and for the rest a matter of 'free construction'" (Feigl, 1956: 16); for variant accounts of the same basic point of view, see Carnap (1956b: 43–7); Scriven (1956: 88–130); Scheffler (1964: 127–222). A reluctance to accept theoretical terms seems to be at the root of some semanticists' difficulties in handling basic notions such as "meaning". Lyons (1963: 56–8), for example, cites Quine in support of his proposal to define meaning in terms of meaning relations (including "synonymy"), thereby avoiding the postulation of "meaning" as a basic theoretical term.

14 It must in fairness be stated that Katz and Fodor's article (1963) was intended only as a starting-point, and that their approach has since been modified in Katz's later work (1966, 1967).

15 See Katz and Fodor (1963: 176), and Weinreich's criticism (1966: 397) that in practice the subject of Katz and Fodor's article "turns out to be far less broad" than they claim, not dealing adequately with the "content" of readings, nor with any of the additional "properties" or "relations" mentioned. The scope of the theory is considerably extended in Katz (1964b), where in addition to attempting definitions of "analyticity" and "contradiction", the author introduces partial explanations of negation, entailment, etc. See Ch. 2, nn. 28, 29; Ch. 3, n. 3.

16 See Katz and Fodor (1963: 193–4). As Weinreich notes (1966: 397), paraphrase is given only cursory mention by Katz and Fodor (1963: 195), who concentrate on disambiguation and the marking of semantic anomalies. This is probably because paraphrase is characterised within the theory as a relationship between outputs, rather than as an output in itself.

17 This tendency to oversimplification has been current in transformational literature, where the metatheory put forward by Chomsky has been so framed as to put the primary onus of empirical justification on the linguist's "intuition" as his own informant (eg Chomsky, 1964a: 53–79; 1965: 10–57), and where the only alternative to this position generally considered is that of structural "taxonomic" linguistics, which (in theory at least) confines itself to explicating texts or corpuses. Disparagement of operational informant tests (Chomsky, 1965: 11, 19) as an ineffective, though theoretically possible, means of eliciting a person's tacit knowledge of his language leads to the conclusion that the linguist's introspections provide the last arbitrament on questions of empirical fact. I have tried to show elsewhere (Leech, 1968) that this admission of the basic subjectivity of linguistic data is unnecessary within a different set of metatheoretical assumptions.

18 From now on, "literal meaningfulness" and "literal meaninglessness" will be abbreviated to "meaningful" and "meaninglessness". The present use of "meaninglessness" in the sense "cognitively non-communicative" conflicts with other uses of the term by philosophers and others; eg the logical positivist's sense of "empirically unverifiable"; it must also be distinguished from "non-communicative" in the widest sense. From tests I have carried out on a group of a hundred informants (in association with the Survey of English

Usage, under the direction of R. Quirk and with the advice of S. Greenbaum), it has so far been impossible to determine whether it is easier to test (say) implication rather than paraphrase or meaninglessness (see Leech, forthcoming). A different set of semantic testing procedures has been developed by Bendix (1966, esp. Ch. 2). Judgements of acceptability have been used by Zimmer (1964: 95–107) as a means of investigating semantic structure. Further references to exploratory work in semantic testing are provided by Ariel (1967).

19 Lyons (1963: 88–9, also 1968: 445–6) treats "pragmatic implication" and "pragmatic equivalence" as fundamental, and discusses how they might be checked against informants' reactions. Garvin *et al* (1967: 3) assert that "there are two kinds of observable and operationally tractable manifestations of linguistic meaning – translation and paraphrase". They go on to report the outcome of experiments in paraphrase judgement. (Translation does not come within the scope of this study, which is concerned with one language only, but is no doubt a primary source of evidence in cross-linguistic investigations.)

20 This is apparently what Lyons means by "pragmatic implication" (1963: 87–8), except that he prefers to talk in terms of "assertion" and "denial", rather than truth and falsehood. He justly makes the point that the conditional connective of propositional logic is interpreted in a manner alien to the natural language concept of implication: "Logicians have found it expedient to adopt what is called the 'material' interpretation, according to which 'implication' and 'equivalence' denote truth values of propositions, such that any proposition whatsoever (true or false) implies every true proposition. This is so much at variance with the everyday sense of "implication" that writers of textbooks of logic feel obliged to draw the reader's attention to the fact. . . . It is, however, precisely the connexion in meaning that is important for our purpose."

21 One virtue of paraphrase is that it can be tested by an operational method (*eg* getting informants to "express the same idea in different words") rather than by appealing to the informant's conscious judgement. On the advantage of the former over the latter, see Quirk and Svartvik (1966: 13–17). It may be noted, however, that conscious judgements on questions of meaning do not suffer from the most severe drawback of grammatical judgements as a source of data: *viz* the informant's preconceptions instilled by education.

22 Katz (1964b: 530) keeps semantic anomalies such as 'The paint is silent' separate from tautologies and contradictions. This is justifiable from the point of view of abstract logic, but on a behavioural level, all may be treated as varieties of semantic deviation, and this is indeed what Fodor and Katz do elsewhere (1964b: 15). On distinguishing various types of nonsensical utterance, see §4.1.

23 Chomsky (1964a) and Katz (1964a) recognise that not all ungrammatical sentences are equally ungrammatical, and propose a method of grading. On such an approach to both grammaticality and meaningfulness (between which he makes no distinction) see Weinreich (1966: 413, 466, 470–1). I find it expedient to make a straightforward dichotomy between "meaningful" and "meaningless", showing at a later stage (§5.4) how our intuitive feeling of graded acceptability can be satisfied by other means.

24 See Ch. 1, n. 17, and Leech (1968). Even if one accepts the extreme transformational position regarding the primacy of introspective evidence, there is need for a clarification of what kind of intuited facts are to be allowed as data.

25 Cf Carnap (1936–7) on "observation statements", "observation predicates", and "observation language", as distinct from "theoretical statements", etc.

For modern critiques of approaches to this distinction, which has remained basic to the positivist approach to significance in science, see Pap (1963: 24–7) and Scheffler (1964: 162–7).

26 Katz and Fodor (1963: 170–1); cf Chomsky (1965: 3–9).

27 Some relevant factors are mentioned in Chomsky's discussion of a "theory of performance" (1965: 13).

28 Exploratory informant tests I have carried out suggest, however, that people react with more certainty and uniformity to sentences which one would like to regard as semantically, rather than factually odd (Leech, forthcoming).

29 The arguments of White (1949) and Quine (1951) are largely reducible to these two points. See Ch. 1, n. 11.

CHAPTER 2

1 See, for example, Conklin (1955), Lounsbury (1964). Lyons (1968: 470–80) gives an introductory account of componential analysis as a method of semantic description.

2 This simple example is adapted from Hjelmslev and Uldall (1957: 45–6).

3 Cf Lyons (1963: 57–98; 1968: 443–70) on meaning relations, especially on incompatibility, hyponymy, and synonymy.

4 Discussion of this phenomenon of 'reversibility' is found in a paper by F. C. Southworth, University of Pennsylvania, "Paraphrase and Transformation in Semantic Structure", read to the New York meeting of the Linguistic Society of America, December, 1964. The equivalence of (a), and possibly of (b) and (c), would be accounted for in syntax rather than in semantics by a transformational grammar. The other examples appear to be beyond the explanatory capacity of transformational grammar as developed by Chomsky (1965: 162–3), although suggestions for coping with them have been made by Gruber (1965) and by Staal (1967). See the discussion of "converseness" in Lyons (1968: 467–9).

5 In cases such as *in front of/behind* and *before/after*, this account is in fact only a stage on the way to explaining a more complicated semantic structure of "indirect converseness" (see §§7.1.1, 8.2.3).

6 Cf the remark by Bendix (1966: 4–5) that "a definition may consist of both relative and class products".

7 "Cluster" is Weinreich's term for "an unordered set of features" (1966: 418) as distinct from a "configuration", or ordered set. By introducing this distinction, Weinreich avoids some of the drawbacks of Katz and Fodor's transformational semantics, including its inability to deal with most of the sentence pairs cited in §2.3 above. This defect (see Ch. 2, n. 4 above) is virtually acknowledged by Chomsky (1965: 162–3) when he points out that to account for certain paraphrase relations between sentences an even more "abstract" notion of structure is required than that of deep syntactic structure. What Weinreich in fact does by introducing the distinction between clusters and configurations is to set up a semantic constituent structure independent of deep syntactic structure, thereby overthrowing the principle of current transformational theory that the deep structure of a sentence defines all structural relations necessary for the determination of meaning. Weinreich's configuration may be most clearly interpreted as a unit which dominates (*ie* has as its constituents) two or more clusters (see Weinreich, 1966: 419), and may therefore be represented by tree diagrams such as the following, according to the number of its constituents:

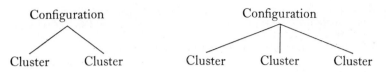

Configuration   Configuration

Cluster   Cluster   Cluster   Cluster   Cluster

(This is assuming that Weinreich's definition of "cluster" includes unitary sets consisting of one feature.) The arrow by which Weinreich indicates the relation between clusters in a configuration (as in $a{\to}b$) may be considered a means of representing the order of elements in a configuration independently of order in a syntactic phrase marker, paralleling the use of the arrow in my structural formula $a \cdot {\to} r \cdot b$. However, one may query Weinreich's use of the arrow as a property independent of the content of any cluster. For example, he has to represent the meaning of a transitive verb as a configuration in which features are divided, apparently arbitrarily, between two clusters, with a gap between them to be filled by the meaning of the object noun: (a, b, $K \to u$, v). In the present framework, the meanings of a large number of transitive verbs can be represented more straightforwardly as componential formulae containing one or more relative components.

8 The two terms, derived respectively from Halliday (1961: 251 and elsewhere) and from Hill (1958: 357–62), have been used in roughly equivalent senses in application to syntactic structure. In their present semantic application, there is a crucial difference between them, as explained on p. 26.

9 The possibility of structural (as opposed to componential) relations entering into the definitions of lexical items is not contemplated by Katz and Fodor (1963), who consequently have to leave the relative-clause-like parts of dictionary definitions unanalysed, within what they call "distinguishers" (*ie* the "idiosyncratic" or non-contrastive aspects of dictionary meaning (p. 185–7). Instances of distinguishers appearing in the dictionary entry for *bachelor* (p. 186) are [young knight serving under the standard of another knight], [who has the first or lowest academic degree], [young fur seal when without mate during the breeding time]. The fact that Katz and Fodor cannot cope with the relative-clause-like elements (corresponding to downgraded predications in the present theory) in contrastive semantic terms means that they cannot explain many facts of meaning, such as the analyticity (when the relevant sense of *bachelor* is in question) of 'The bachelor has never married'; 'This bachelor has the first or lowest academic degree', etc. Weinreich on the other hand correctly insists that "every relation that may hold between components of a sentence also occurs among the components of a dictionary entry" (1966: 446).

10 Cf the general syntactic condition on relativisation, in transformational grammar, that a matrix sentence and embedded sentence should contain "identical" noun phrases (see Chomsky, 1965: 137–8).

11 However, this might simply be treated as a "constructional ambiguity" (see Ch. 2, n. 15 below) calling for analysis in terms of different grammatical constituent structures rather than different semantic descriptions.

12 This specialised use of "formal" is that of Halliday, McIntosh and Strevens (1964: 18–21).

13 Cf the use of "interpretive" (*sic*) by Chomsky (1964a: 51–2): "The generative grammar of a language should, ideally, contain a central *syntactic component* and two *interpretive components*, a *phonological component* and a *semantic component*."

14 See, for example, Gleason (1961: 66).

15 The term "formal item" here designates an element or sequence of elements identified in *surface* grammar. Many ambiguities will manifest themselves in separate deep grammar representations for the same formal item. The question of what ambiguities should be distinguished in deep grammar is largely a question of the "economics" of the total language description, to be discussed in §2.7. All we assert by means of the above definition of ambiguity is that they *have* to be distinguished in semantics. It is worthwhile observing that in transformational grammar "ambiguity" has been treated as an unreduced concept – as something which is simply self-evident to the informant-analyst. But in practice, we separate ambiguities most readily by presenting paraphrases of the different senses (as in Chomsky, 1965: 21–2). An objection might be made to the present understanding of "ambiguity" on the grounds that it does not cover cases of purely "constructional ambiguity": *eg* the difference in constituent structure shown by bracketing in the following examples, which do not differ as to truth value (see Huddleston *et al*, 1968): (a) *(John and (Mary and Susan)) went home;* (b) *((John and Mary) and Susan) went home;* (c) *(John and Mary and Susan) went home.* How, it might be asked, can we know that these distinctions exist, except through our intuition of ambiguities of linguistic form? It is most likely correct to answer that even if we could find no empirical criteria for distinguishing these different analyses, we would nevertheless need, for simplicity of overall description, to postulate them. Amongst the factors to be considered in support of this view are (1) the possibility of distinguishing different constituent structures, as in this case, by placing intonation breaks in different places; (2) the difference of meaning between (a) and (b) if two different co-ordinators are used: *(John and (Mary or Susan))* . . . and *((John and Mary) or Susan.* Further motivations for separating the three types grammatically without invoking intuitive feelings of ambiguity as a distinct form of evidence are not difficult to find.

16 See Weinreich (1963: 130–47) on combinatorial semantics. Katz and Fodor's projection rules (1963: 193–207) might be described as the combinatorial part of their semantic theory.

17 If a sufficiently "deep" (*ie* semantically orientated) concept of grammar is entertained, many apparently discontinuous and overlapping idioms may well correspond to a single constituent at some level of grammatical analysis. This has yet to be shown, however. Suggestions on how to deal with idioms within an interpretative framework are made by Katz and Postal (1963), and Weinreich (1966: 46–7). Lamb's account of idioms (*eg* 1965: 46–7) in terms of neutralisation (*ie* as a function of the relation between strata) is closer to the present one.

18 A rather similar distinction in transformational grammar is that drawn by Katz and Postal (1964: 24–5) between sentences and sentoids, in order to remove a troublesome ambiguity in the former term. See also Ayer's distinction (1946: 8) between *sentences* and *statements.*

19 The idea that a language may contain well-formed semantic specifications which are incapable of being expressed within that language may smack of mysticism, but it is justifiable if it permits a simplification of rules of well-formedness. For example, if we treat *sibling* as a technical term of restricted usage, the notion 'sibling' cannot be expressed in everyday English except through the periphrasis *brother and/or sister* (see §4.4 for the analysis of kinship terms). It is simpler to represent this fact by not providing for the occurrence of 'sibling' on the right-hand of a dictionary entry than by showing (by an *ad hoc* rule) that the specification itself is ill-formed. (The periphrastic alternative can be explained by general rules showing the synonymy of

different specifications – see §4.3–4). Other, and perhaps clearer, examples involve the obligatory expression of number and sex in pronouns. In the sentence *Your friend is not – – –self this morning*, unlike the corresponding plural sentence, no pronoun form can be inserted in the gap without specifying the sex of the friend. This question is parallel to that of "accidental gaps" in phonology (see Chomsky, 1964a: 64).

20 There is one major exception to this rule. When expression rules collapse a rank-shifted predication and a main predication into a single clause, the definition of the verb is frequently discontinuous, and is composed of the medial clusters of both predications. Causative and inceptive verbs belong to this category: the meaning of *John gave William a book* may be transcribed $j \cdot \rightarrow c \cdot (w \cdot \rightarrow h \cdot b)$ (roughly, 'John caused William to have a book'), the meaning of *gave* being represented by $\rightarrow c \ldots \rightarrow h$, *ie* 'caused . . . to have'.

21 By "nominalisation" I mean (paralleling the use of that term in transformational literature) a noun phrase semantically equivalent to a whole clause. The equivalence in many instances can be demonstrated by paraphrase; for example, *Kindness to an enemy* could be replaced without change of meaning by *Being kind to an enemy* or perhaps by *To be kind to an enemy* in the sentence *Kindness to an enemy is one of the rarest of Christian virtues*.

22 Cf (within a transformational framework) Gruber (1965: 130).

23 The principle of "same meaning – same specification" (§2.3) has already catered for the fourth basic predicate of "logical synonymy" (see §§1.5, 1.8–9), which need not be further considered at this stage.

24 On "folk-taxonomies", see, for example, Conklin (1962) and Frake (1964).

25 Previous examinations of implication ("entailment") within natural languages have been made by Lyons (1963: 87–8) and Katz (1964b: 540–1). Katz attempts a formal characterisation of the relation, but deals for the most part only with implication between simple attributive assertions (see §3.2), and ignores the problem of quantification.

26 This illustration is based on that of Wells (1954: 247).

27 Katz defines inconsistency in terms of negation (1944b: 538).

28 For reasons stated in Ch. 2, n. 9, such cases cannot, it seems, be handled by the Katz and Fodor theory (except possibly by a separate definitional component, as tentatively sketched by Weinreich (1966: 446–50). Indeed, Katz (1964b) only deals successfully with tautologies of a simple attributive type, such as 'Women are female'; his account of other types is incorrect, as he puts forward a general definition (D10) which in fact applies only in cases of deductive implication. Hence he fails to recognise 'Boys who run fast to school run to school' as a tautology, and wrongly assigns analytic status to 'The man who came came by aeroplane'. He does not consider problems connected with quantification.

29 Compare Katz's definitions of contradiction (1964b: 533, 540), and notice that to arrive at these definitions, he has to go to great lengths to define a notion of "antonymous n-tuple", whereas the equivalent notion in this framework, that of "logical exclusion", is very simply described in terms of semantic systems (see §§2.2 and 2.8.1 above).

CHAPTER 3

1 Weinreich (1963: 120–30) gives a perceptive account of the relevance of the distinction between formators and designators (ultimately deriving from Charles Morris) to the semantic description of natural languages, and gives examples from many languages.

2 In propositional logic, if the antecedent of a conditional statement is false

and the consequent is true, the whole statement is regarded as true. The quoted assertion could not, under such an interpretation, be considered a contradiction, as its truth value would depend on that of the second constituent assertion. This merely demonstrates the divergence between the understanding of conditionals in logic and in ordinary usage, and adds force to Lyons' remark (see Ch. 1, n. 20) that "it is precisely the connexion in meaning that is important" for the semantics of natural language.

3 Cf Katz (1964b: 531). It is necessary to exclude, by condition (ii), p. 46, cases where *a* is existentially quantified or construed as if so quantified. 'Some unicorns are animals' is only true (if we follow the conventional interpretation of the existential quantifier) if unicorns exist.

4 This example is adapted from Carnap (1956b: 45).

5 On the logical properties of the definite formator, consult the classic account of "descriptions" by Russell (1920: 157–80), also Reichenbach (1947: 256–74). Here and elsewhere in our discussion of logical relations, the distinction between singular and plural is an irrelevance forced upon us by rules of expression in English (see Ch. 2, n. 19).

6 See Karlsen (1959) for a detailed exemplification of "zero connection" in English. It is necessary to impose strict controls on the circumstances in which zero expression is permitted, and it may well be desirable to restrict it to this case and the case of the empty cluster (§2.9). Such a restriction would closely resemble the principle of "recoverable deletion" (see Katz and Postal, 1964: 79–81) in effect.

7 Through the principle of recoverable deletion and the pronominalisation transformation, current versions of transformational grammar can account for the equivalence of the first and third sets of examples on the level of deep structure.

8 For a previous discussion of this much neglected topic in natural language description, see Sørensen (1958: 18–20), who draws his ideas on metalanguage largely from Tarski, Carnap, and other philosophers. I cannot see what relevance the distinction between "metalanguage" and "object language" has to natural languages.

9 Slightly adapted from Chomsky (1957: 100–1).

10 This point is made by Katz and Postal (1964: 72–3) in support of their thesis that syntactic transformations do not affect meaning.

11 Weinreich's account of quantification (1966: 426–8), which he admits is very tentative, does not seem to escape either of these inadequacies.

12 Cf Lyons (1963: 114–18) on the relation of "consequence".

CHAPTER 4

1 Cf the special restriction of the relativisation transformation in transformational grammar, and the elimination of violations through the "blocking" role of transformations (Chomsky, 1965: 137–8).

2 The most notable of recent grammatical accounts of co-occurrence restrictions is that of Chomsky (1965: 93ff). Katz and Fodor's "selection restrictions" (1963: 191) have a similar function within a semantic theory.

3 In criticism of Katz and Fodor's "selection restrictions" (Weinreich, 1966: 406–7). However, as Katz points out (1967: 162–3), a suggestion similar to Weinreich's, though more limited, had been put forward in Katz and Postal (1964).

4 Three degrees of "strength" can be recognised for co-occurrence restrictions: (a) that of Katz and Fodor's selection restrictions, which positively require

the presence of the specified features in the relevant context (hence "a pride of animals" is excluded, because of the absence of the feature [+LION]); (b) that of Weinreich's transfer features, to which the account I have just suggested is broadly equivalent; (c) a still weaker kind of restriction, which is considered later in this section. (See additional note, p. 277.)

5   See Catford (1959: 184-5). A more detailed treatment is given in §8.1.1 below.

6   This solution would resemble that of Weinreich in excluding systemically contrasting features from the relevant context, but would differ from it in carrying none of the other consequences of feature assignment (*eg* with regard to logical inconsistency).

7   The relation between a question and its "presupposition" might well be included amongst the empirically fundamental relations of semantics, with implication and synonymy. The term "presupposition" is used in this connection by Katz and Postal (1964: 116-17) and more extensively by Katz (1968). See §9.7.1, esp. Ch. 9, n. 11.

8   Notable attempts to deal with the semantics of natural languages by extending formalised predicate logic are Reichenbach (1947: 251-354) and Weinreich (1963: 130-142). Perhaps the gravest drawback of this approach within an integrated theory is the lack of systematic correspondences between the logical notation and the grammatical structure of the language – and hence the difficulty of formulating rules of expression.

9   The kind of sentence exemplified by *The poor shall inherit the earth* appears to be an exception; but in fact *The poor* is synonymous with *Poor people*, and therefore expresses the features 'countable', 'plural', 'concrete', and 'human', in addition to those constituting the meaning of the adjective *poor*.

10 Empirical justification by "exhibiting a model", the method employed here, is an apparent deviation from the system of confirmation through basic statements (§§1.4, 1.7-8). However, one might accommodate it in that system by presenting the test in the form of a statement of implication which an informant is invited to confirm or reject. The antecedent of the conditional would be a complex assertion formed by conjoining two sets of simple assertions: (a) the set of assertions describing the "state" of the model ('John committed larceny on Monday', etc) and (b) the set of assertions describing the model itself: 'There are only three crimes, larceny, burglary, and bigamy', etc. The consequent of the relation would be the quantificational assertion whose meaning was under investigation.

11 Cf Chomsky's formal and substantive universals (1965: 27-30). Semantic rules of synonymy are used by Bendix (1966: 5, 39).

12 This ambiguity has been noted from a phonological and grammatical point of view by Halliday (1963: 148) and Huddleston (1968). It is perhaps misleading to talk of an ambiguity here, as intonation or syntactic order nearly always distinguishes the two interpretations.

13 The above formulation as it stands is inadequate, because it is always possible, through the quantification rule or the rule of double negation, to give two equivalent specifications, one containing a negative formator where the other does not.

14 The ensuing sketch of some kinship relations in English is much simplified. In particular, it takes no cognisance of distinctions between half-kin, step-kin, and full-kin; nor does it deal with kin by marriage. Such details can, I believe, be added to this account without too much modification. Another rather obvious limitation is that terms are understood only in senses connected with kinship: no account is attempted of transferred senses such as 'uncle' = 'close male friend of parents' (for a child). For a detailed com-

ponential account of kinship terms in one variety of English, see Goodenough (1965).

15 *Father* and *daughter* may be taken as equivalent to *parent* and *child* in this context, where sex is in any case specified by the choice of proper names. The equivalent representation of reciprocal relations is also a feature of Lamb's sememic account of kinship terms (1965). The present analysis, although independently developed, shares a number of features with Lamb's, and claims the same virtues: (a) that of being constructed on principles which apply to the semantic description of the whole language, not just to kinship; (b) that of reducing the number of basic analytic terms, by abstracting out the factors of sex, parenthood, etc.; (c) that of focusing attention on kinship *relations* rather than kinship *types*, and by this means accounting economically for the converse or reciprocal character of such relations.

16 This relationship between the primary or closest member of a class of kinship types and rest of the class is most clearly revealed in the method of kinship analysis most recently developed by Lounsbury (*eg* 1964, 1965), in which "reduction rules" define the latter in terms of the former.

CHAPTER 5

1 This is in contrast to Weinreich's conclusion (1966: 367–70) that there is no real distinction between semantic and syntactic features. Weinreich argues for this conclusion within the "interpretative" framework of transformational semantics, of course, and his arguments do not have relevance to the "autonomy-of-levels" semantics assumed here.

2 The term general stylistics, suggested to me by R. G. Fowler, distinguishes the broader use of "stylistics" from its narrower use in application to the linguistic study of literature.

3 Lyons uses "having meaning" in a sense reminiscent of "information" in information theory when he says (1963: 26) that a form of language mandatory in a certain context "has no meaning". This quantitative use of "having meaning" bears no relation to the way in which I have used the term "meaning". Rather, meaning has been treated as a constant for the purposes of stylistic comparison.

4 For a classification and discussion of such factors, see Halliday, McIntosh and Strevens (1964: Ch. 4), and Ellis (1966).

5 Weinreich (1966: 398) suggests that "a scientific approach which distinguishes between competence . . . and performance . . . ought to regard disambiguation of potential ambiguities as a matter of hearer performance". The truth of this is evident when one considers that disambiguation may be brought about as easily through factual, as through logical absurdity. In *He's eating chips* the context effectively rules out 'chips' = 'gambling counters', although on such an interpretation the assertion would be highly improbable, rather than logically impossible.

6 See Brown (1958: 11–13) on actual and potential criteriality; also Weinreich (1962: 33–6).

7 An additional problem is that biological classification is not wholly a matter of discrete properties, but of "clines" or gradual transitions between one property and another. See Sokal and Sneath (1963).

8 This fallacy is a notable feature of Bloomfield's attitude to meaning: "We can define the names of minerals, for example, in terms of chemistry and mineralogy, as when we say that the ordinary meaning of the English word *salt* is sodium chloride (NaCl)" (1935: 139).

9 Cf Weinreich's critiques of lexicographic practice (in 1962, 1964).

10 Rules of transference correspond in essence to Weinreich's Construal Rule (1966: 461–6), which is best conceived of as a *set* of rules whereby non-contradictory interpretations are supplied for otherwise contradictory expressions.

11 See Ch. 5, n. 5. Weinreich makes an interesting formalisation of this aspect of linguistic performance in his "Semantic Evaluator" (1966: 466–7).

12 Cf Weinreich's "mentioning rule" (1966: 463).

CHAPTER 6

1 See Halliday (1967: 203–23) on "marked theme" and "marked information focus". A sentence such as *On* SAT*urday I didn't see her* would be cognitively equivalent to *I didn't see her on* SAT*urday* (with nuclear stress on SAT*urday* in each case), despite the different ordering.

2 An exception to this general rule must be allowed in the case of a quantificational predication downgraded within the medial cluster of an adverbial predication. For example, if the meaning of *always* is symbolised $((X) \cdot \rightarrow$TIM $\langle \theta' \cdot 1\alpha \leftarrow o \cdot \theta'' \rangle \cdot \varnothing'')'$, $\rightarrow$TIM is not the sole content of the medial cluster $\rightarrow s$. Ascription features are not counted as part of the "inherent content" of a medial cluster.

3 Compare Chomsky's "general taxonomy" (1965: 82–3) of syntactic features of nouns, which also includes such oppositions as $\pm$Countable and $\pm$Human. The fact that such features have to be recognised in syntactic analysis shows the overlap, in this aspect of classification, between semantics and grammar. However, their application is often wider in semantic analysis; for example, the opposition 'countable'/'uncountable' is relevant, semantically, to both verbs and nouns, whereas in syntax it applies to nouns only. (See §7.4.1 below.)

CHAPTER 7

1 Grammatical evidence for this view is furnished by Predicator + Object constructions of the following pattern: *He* TOOK A COUPLE OF SHOTS *at the target*; *You can* HAVE SIX TRIES *if you like. She keeps* GIVING *me* DIRTY LOOKS. These are evidently equivalent in meaning to the simple verbs, *shoot, try, look*, etc, except that they also express the factor of countability. The distinction between +COU +PLUR and +COU −PLUR as applied to verbal meaning is precisely conveyed in the contrast between *He was taking bites out of the apple* and *He was taking a bite out of the apple*. Textual examples of this type of construction are discussed in Olsson (1961: 209–11).

2 On the subject of semantic restrictions on the co-occurrence of verbal constructions and adverbials, see Crystal (1966).

3 The "event"/"state" distinction (under various terminological guises) has been made, for example, by Twaddell (1960: 7), Joos (1964: 113), and Allen (1966: 193). Allen points out the connection between this and the countable/mass contrast in nouns.

4 It is indicative of this indeterminacy that Twaddell (1960: 7) separates five classes of verb, including not only "durational" (="state") and "non-durational" categories, but a third category neutral as to duration.

5 This difference is pointed out and exemplified by Jespersen (1931: 92–3) with reference to what he calls "conclusive" and "non-conclusive" verbs.

6 Cf the discussion of the instantaneous present in Palmer (1965: 83).

7 The definiteness of the past tense has been noted by many grammarians, and is systematically discussed by Allen (1966: 152–8).

8 In at least some kinds of American usage, the past tense is used freely in con-

texts where there is no suggestion of definiteness: in combination, for example, with the adverbs *yet* and *already* in sentences like *Did you buy your ticket yet?* This difference between British and American usage is perhaps reflected in Diver's assignment (1963: 156–7) to the simple past tense of a neutral position on the definite/indefinite dimension.

9 The parallel between the application of definiteness and indefiniteness to verbal and nominal elements is convincingly developed by Allen (1966: 155–8).

10 The distinction between symmetric and nonsymmetric uses of *and* is the subject of a recent article by Johnson-Laird (1967) and a rejoinder by Staal (1968).

11 These properties are therefore criterial aspects of meaning, and are more essential than those which Bendix (1966: 23) calls "connotations", or what Twaddell (1960: 7) dismisses as "compatible byproducts".

12 For Joos (1964: 113), "limitation of duration" is the essential meaning of continuous verb forms.

13 Cf similar examples given by Allen (1966: 208); also by Palmer (1965: 96) and Joos (1964: 108).

14 Hill (1958: 209) regards incompleteness as the basic meaning of the past continuous. See also Palmer (1965: 79).

15 This example is given by Allen (1966: 204).

16 This type is illustrated by Jespersen (1931: 182).

17 One of the more satisfactory definitions of this kind is that of Sweet (1892: 98), who states that the perfective "expresses an occurrence which began in the past and is connected with the present, either by actual continuance up to the present time, . . . or in its results." A. A. Hill (1958: 212) notes, however, that this account does not cover the "indefinite past" use of the perfective, as in *I have been to Washington.*

18 Three of these senses are distinguished by Kruisinga (1931: 390–1) under the headings "resultative perfect", "continuative perfect", and "iterative perfect". Kruisinga does not recognise my third category of "indefinite past", unless it is identical with his "declaratory perfect" (1931: 392).

19 This point is confirmed by Crystal's study (1966: 27) of obligatory and optional adverbial modification in association with verbal meanings.

CHAPTER 8

1 It should be noted that although *Jack is with Jill* and *Jill is with Jack* are cognitively synonymous, they answer different questions: *Jack is with Jill* would be an inappropriate answer to *Where is Jill?*, just as *Jill is with Jack* would be an inappropriate answer to *Where is Jack?* A similar observation is made about other prepositions of place by Gruber (1965: 61), who notes that *Where is the dot?* can be answered *It is inside the circle*, but not *The circle is around it.* This discrepancy, in the present instance, follows naturally from the requirement that a question of the form $a \cdot \rightarrow \text{PLA} \cdot ?$ should be answered by $a \cdot \rightarrow \text{PLA} \cdot c$.

2 Bierwisch (1967: 13–21) postulates two similar oppositions ($\pm$ Ver, $\pm$ Second) in dealing with the semantics of the German adjectives *lang, hoch, breit*, and their antonyms.

3 Cf the use of α and β as variables to indicate matching or non-matching features in transformational phonology and syntax, eg in Chomsky (1965: 175–6).

4 The problems of meaning and co-occurrence of *across* and *along* are similar to those of the adjectives *long, wide, high*, and their antonyms. The German equivalents of these adjectives have been investigated in a valuable article by Bierwisch (1967: 13–21), who considers what inherent properties of dimension and shape are necessary to the objects to which the adjectives may apply.

5 The nature of the contrast between *come* and *go* (as between the similar causa-

tive verbs *bring* and *take*) is an interesting semantic problem in its own right. Without going into details, we may state that the definitions of *come* and *go* respectively incorporate the meanings 'towards here' and 'away from here', bearing in mind the following additional points: (a) 'here' may be understood either as the speaker's or as the listener's location; (b) the location need not be the *present* location of the speaker/listener; (c) the verb *go* is the "unmarked" verb, used when relative proximity to the speaker/listener is unimportant. Valuable discussion of the question is provided by Fillmore (1966).

6 Gruber (1965: 103) acutely observes that the *from . . . to . . .* construction fills a gap in the following paradigm:

The ball rolled out of the house and into the hole.

The insect crawled off (of) the table and on to my knee.

*The ball rolled and from the house and to the tree.

On purely syntactic grounds, that is, one might argue that a co-ordinating conjunction has been omitted from this construction.

7 I owe to John Lyons the observation that where there are no deictic implications, *come* generally marks a transition into a positive state, and *go* a transition into a negative one (*come right/go wrong; come into sight/go out of sight;* etc); also that many verbs "lexicalise" a positive transition (*get, learn, invent,* etc), but few a negative one (*die, lose, forget,* etc).

8 *Pass* as a transitive verb (=‘go past’) belongs to a class of verbs which "incorporate" the meanings of prepositions. Other examples are *cross* (=‘go across’) and *enter* (=‘go into’) The definitions of these verbs belong to that class of discontinuous definitions which break the normal restriction that definitions should not exceed the extent of a cluster in a main predication (see Ch. 2, n. 20). The "incorporation" of prepositions within verbs is discussed from a transformational point of view by Gruber (1965: 28–55). In the present context, "incorporation" means simply that the definition of the preposition is included in that of the verb.

CHAPTER 9

1 Despite the value of her close observation of data, the main drawback of Miss Ehrman's account is the general fault of unitary approaches to meaning (cf §7.6), *viz* the vagueness of the "basic meaning". For example, her definition of *will*, "the occurrence of the predication is guaranteed" (p. 34), fails in three respects: (a) it does not show in what ways *will* differs from *must, have to,* and other verbs whose presence (as we see in §9.2.2.) guarantees the occurrence of the predication; (b) it does not allow for some uses of *will* which do *not* guarantee the occurrence of the predication, *eg* that of 'willingness' (*My chauffeur will help you* is an offer of help of which the addressee may, or may not take advantage); (c) it does not account for the oddness of using *will* in some contexts where the occurrence of the predication is guaranteed: *eg: The sun rises every morning* is natural, but not *The sun will rise every morning* (see Palmer, 1965: 111).

2 This view is also taken by Diver, when he distinguishes "contextual" from "semantic" characteristics (1964: 322–3). We may use as an example the sentence *You may go*, which does not just permit, but strongly recommends, in a schoolmasterly Victorian way, the fulfilment of the action. Logically, the meaning of *may* in this sentence is 'permission'; but its pragmatic import is stronger: 'You are to leave my presence immediately'.

3 Lyons (1968: 352–3, 359–60) gives an excellent account of the semantic category of 'causation' in relation to grammatical functions.

4 Lebrun (1965) contrives a threefold distinction into "physical possibility" "moral possibility", and "logical possibility". This distinction does not seem

to be supported by evidence from within the language, and Lebrun's investigation as a whole suffers from reliance on *a priori* philosophical categories backed by a spurious appeal to corpus evidence. Lebrun's conclusion (that the difference of usage between *can* and *may* is mainly stylistic) bears little relation to what others have written on the subject.

5 Cf Ehrman (1966: 64): "As far as can be determined, *ought to* is a synonym for normative *should* in almost every respect."

6 For example, Erades (1957: 283) distinguishes *can* and *may* by the terms "subjective" and "objective" possibility.

7 Cf Diver (1964: 331): ". . . *can* admits only that the occurrence is a possibility. *May*, however, suggests that the speaker takes the possibility for granted and is willing, further, to speculate on its probability."

8 In his thorough account of *shall* in the sense of what he terms "volitional obligation", Jespersen (1931: 269-73) draws the distinction between "weak" and "strong" volition by pointing out that in the former case the obligation rests with the speaker, whereas in the latter it rests upon the hearer or some other person. An extension (to my mind, unwarranted) of the element of speaker-involvement to the definition of all modal auxiliaries is proposed by Boyd and Thorne (1969), using J. L. Austin's concept of "illocutionary force".

9 The foregoing account of personal pronouns is modelled (with some changes) on that of Fillmore (1966: 223, n. 11), and that of Lyons (1968: 257-8). It has the virtue of explaining why, in co-reference to coordinated constructions, the first-person pronoun prevails over the second-person pronoun; (*You and I like* OUR *brandy neat*); and why in similar circumstances the second-person prevails over the third-person pronoun (*I hope you and she are behaving* YOURSELVES). In the first sentence, 'you and I' includes reference to the speaker, and is therefore marked +EGO; and likewise 'you and she' includes reference to the addressee, and so is marked +YOU. It is debatable whether in the semantics of English "inclusive *we*" (involving reference to the addressee) needs to be distinguished from "exclusive *we*", as it is in some languages; in any case provision for this distinction is made in the possibility of two separate definitions +EGO +YOU +PLUR and +EGO −YOU +PLUR. (I am grateful to John Lyons for bringing some of these arguments to my notice.)

10 This switch from first-person to second-person is a common linguistic phenomenon, designated "shift of person" by Jesperson (1924: 219). See Fillmore (1966: 220-1).

11 See Ch. 4, n. 7. Implication and presupposition can be clearly separated by the fact that for any relation *X* implies *Y*, both *X* and *Y* are statements; whereas for any relation *X* presupposes *Y*, *X* may be some predication which has no truth value, such as a question, or a rank-shifted predication. Fillmore (1966: 222, n. 9) distinguishes further between presupposition and supposition, the former being restricted to the case where *X* is a question.

ADDITIONAL NOTE

In a well-argued essay I have read too late for proper acknowledgment, McCawley (1968) confirms my own position (§4.1.2) on the semantic character of selection restrictions. There are a number of other points of resemblance between McCawley's case and that expounded in this book.